INTERNATIONAL AGREEMENTS BETWEEN NON-STATE ACTORS AS A SOURCE OF INTERNATIONAL LAW

This book examines whether international agreements between non-state actors can be identified as a source of international law using objective criteria. It asks whether, beyond Article 38 of the Statute of the International Court of Justice, there is a system of rules, processes, beliefs or semantics by which these agreements can be objectively identified as a source of international law. Departing from the more usual state-centric analysis, it adopts postmodern legal positivism as its analytical tool. This allows for the reality that international law-making takes place in subjective social landscapes. To test the effectiveness of this approach, it is applied to agreements between petroleum agencies and corporations that allow two or more states to exploit disputed resources across boundaries, looking in particular at arrangements involving China, Vietnam and the Philippines. By so doing it illustrates an alternative way that states can manage disputes, without having to resort to conflict. This book will appeal to both scholars and practitioners of public international law, as well as civil servants.

Volume 88 in the series Studies in International Law

Studies in International Law

Recent titles in this series

The Role of Multilateral Environmental Agreements: A Reconciliatory Approach to Environmental Protection in Armed Conflict
Britta Sjostedt

Prosecutorial Discretion at the International Criminal Court
Anni Pues

Judicial Deference in International Adjudication: A Comparative Analysis
Johannes Hendrik Fahner

Human Rights Commitments of Islamic States: Sharia, Treaties and Consensus
Paul McDonough

Intervention in Civil Wars: Effectiveness, Legitimacy, and Human Rights
Chiara Redaelli

General Principles as a Source of International Law: Art 38(1)(c) of the Statute of the International Court of Justice
Imogen Saunders

The Law of Humanity Project: A Story of International Law Reform and State-making
Ukri Soirila

Extraterritoriality and Climate Change Jurisdiction: Exploring EU Climate Protection under International Law
Natalie L Dobson

International Law and the War with Islamic State: Challenges for Jus ad Bellum and Jus in Bello
Saeed Bagheri

Private Actors as Participants in International Law: A Critical Analysis of Membership under the Law of the Sea
Armando Rocha

Truth and Transitional Justice: Localising the International Legal Framework in Muslim Majority Legal Systems
Alice Panepinto

State Responsibility for Non-State Actors: Past, Present and Prospects for the Future
Richard Mackenzie-Gray Scott

International Agreements between Non-State Actors as a Source of International Law
Melissa Loja

For a complete list of titles in this series
see www.bloomsbury.com/uk/series/studies-in-international-law/

International Agreements between Non-State Actors as a Source of International Law

Melissa Loja

•HART•
OXFORD • LONDON • NEW YORK • NEW DELHI • SYDNEY

HART PUBLISHING

Bloomsbury Publishing Plc

Kemp House, Chawley Park, Cumnor Hill, Oxford, OX2 9PH, UK

1385 Broadway, New York, NY 10018, USA

29 Earlsfort Terrace, Dublin 2, Ireland

HART PUBLISHING, the Hart/Stag logo, BLOOMSBURY and the Diana logo are trademarks of Bloomsbury Publishing Plc

First published in Great Britain 2022

A catalogue record for this book is available from the British Library.

A catalogue record for this book is available from the Library of Congress.

Library of Congress Control Number: 2022938839

ISBN: HB: 978-1-50995-110-9
ePDF: 978-1-50995-112-3
ePub: 978-1-50995-111-6

Typeset by Compuscript Ltd, Shannon

Preface

CERTAIN INTERNATIONAL DISPUTES that were previously the reserved domain of diplomacy and warfare between sovereign states are presently managed through international agreements between government agencies and corporate entities. As these agreements fall below the radar of Article 38 of the Statute of the International Court of Justice, the question arises as to whether they are susceptible to identification as a source of international law using objective criteria.

To address the question, this book applies the postmodern legal positivist approach rather than the traditional state-centric positivist and sociological pluralist approaches to international law. The positivist approach is unable to account for the reality of international agreements between non-state actors, for it adheres to the stringent rules of Article 38, according to which only states have the inherent authority to give consent to the creation of international conventions and customs. The pluralist approaches are unreliable as they equate substantive validity, legitimacy and effectivity of the social practices of state and non-state actors with the legality of norms.

As opposed to the positivist and pluralist approaches, postmodern legal positivism unapologetically situates international law-making within subjective social processes in which state and non-state actors are involved. At the same time, it uncompromisingly delineates international law from other social norms according to objective rules. While the prevailing rules are found in Article 38, new rules can develop from the social conventions of law-applying authorities. Law-applying authorities are social actors that engage in the argumentative practice of invoking, adopting and applying formal criteria to identify international law.

Applying postmodern legal positivism, this book presents a case study of petroleum agencies and corporations that negotiate and conclude international agreements to manage disputes over ownership and control of petroleum resources that are exploitable by two or more states across maritime zones and boundaries (shared resources). Disputes over shared resources have an international character. Their object is a strategic resource that actually or potentially traverses maritime zones and boundaries of sovereign states. Their subject is inter-state competition for access and control over the resource. In the past, states resolved these disputes mainly through inter-state boundary agreements or joint development agreements. Failing this, they resorted to resource sterilisation and even warfare.

Empirical data from the case study show that these international agreements can be identified as a source of international law using objective and formal criteria. Authority to enter into the agreements is conferred upon petroleum agencies and corporations through treaties, laws, regulations, contracts, official statements and ceremonial acts. The legality of the norms defined in the agreements is established through verbal approval, such as a formal ratification; ceremonial approval, such as a joint attestation; or procedural approval consisting of the positive acts of prior consultation, concurrence and continuing monitoring by the participating governments or designated agencies thereof.

This book speaks to government agencies and corporations about their capability to generate legal norms that can minimise international conflicts. It speaks to domestic and international tribunals about the availability of objective rules by which norms generated by non-state actors can be identified and applied to resolve international disputes. It also speaks to international law scholars who might find the present approach and methodology useful in terms of engendering a better understanding of the sources of international law.

Acknowledgements

THIS IS A life's work which I owe to my supervisor Professor Simon Young and my examiners Professor Jean d'Aspremont, Professor Anselmo Reyes and Professor Shahla Ali; my mentors: Dr Manuel Espina, Dr Jovita Jadloc, Professor Ed Tadem, Professor Teresa Encarnacion, Professor Damian Chalmers and Justice Jose Sabio; those who trained me: Justice Godardo Jacinto, Justice Ma Alicia Austria-Martinez and Chief Justice Renato Corona; those who provided research, administrative and financial support: the University of Dundee Centre for Energy, Petroleum and Mineral Law and Policy, Coria Chan, Winnie Wong, Li Ka Shing Prize, Sohmen Foundation, Anna Wu Prize and the Dr Lo Kwee Seong Education Foundation; my landlady in Singapore, Madam Chia Lay Choo; my friends: Carol Ann, Cristina, Fe, Jane and Janet; my family: Shiela, Tadeo, Jerome, Cyrille, Farrah, Hazel, Froilan, Nobu, Cholpon, Monica, Charisse, Hailey, Alyssa, Sofia, Sakura and Kenji; my sons: Sol, Luc and Mel; and my parents: Nene and Dodong.

Contents

1

Introduction

CERTAIN INTERNATIONAL DISPUTES that were previously the reserved domain of diplomacy and warfare between sovereign states are presently being managed through international agreements between government agencies and corporations.[1] These agreements are comparable to agreements between states, in that their object is situated on international space[2] and their subject is matters of international relations.[3] They even require certain formalities, including ratification.[4]

[1] At the time when they had no diplomatic relations, China, represented by the China Fisheries Association, and Japan, represented by the Japan-China Fisheries Council, entered into a non-governmental Agreement on Fisheries of the Yellow Sea and East China Sea between the China Fisheries Association and the Japan-China Fisheries Council (1955, 1963 and 1965). The non-governmental agreement was renewed on an annual basis until an inter-governmental Agreement on Fisheries between the People's Republic of China and Japan was concluded in 1975 and revised in 1978, 1985 and 1997. Copies of the non-governmental agreements can be found in H Tian, C Ji and L Jiang (ed), *Collection of Documents on Sino-Japanese Post-war Relations: 1945–1970* (Beijing, China Social Science Publisher, 1996), 193. A copy of an unofficial English translation of the 1997 inter-governmental agreement can be found in SP Kim, *Maritime Delimitation and Interim Arrangements in Northeast Asia* (The Hague, Martinus Nijhoff, 2004) 338–47. The inter-governmental agreements confirmed the non-governmental agreements by maintaining six conservation zones and seven fishing closed zones. See D Tamada and K Zou, *Implementation of the United Nations Convention on the Law of the Sea: State Practice of China and Japan* (Basingstoke, Springer Nature, 2021) 6–7.

[2] See Federal Democratic Republic of Ethiopia, Model Petroleum Production Sharing Agreement, 2011, resourcecontracts.org/contract/ocds-591adf-9390285909/download/pdf. Article 9.1.4 provides that with respect to deposits of petroleum that 'extend to areas outside the boundaries of the State', the petroleum agency shall 'impose the special rules and conditions which may be necessary to comply with the general principles of international law and satisfy obligations under an agreement with an adjacent state'.

[3] See Hydrocarbons Law No 8/2006, 3 November 2006, droit-afrique.com/upload/doc/guinee-equatoriale/GE-Code-hydrocarbures-2006-EN.pdf. Article 56 provides: 'In the event that a Hydrocarbon reservoir lies across national boundaries into Areas that are part of the domain of neighboring countries, any agreements leading to the exploitation of such reservoir shall require the prior approval of the Government and ratification by the President of Equatorial Guinea'.

[4] See Total E&P Liban, Eni Lebanon, Novatek Lebanon, Production Agreement, Block 9, 2018, resourcecontracts.org/contract/ocds-591adf-1121032259/view#/pdf. Article 21.5 provides that:

> where a Reservoir straddles the delimitation line of the continental shelf or territorial waters subject to the jurisdiction of another country … any agreement … between the Right Holders and any other Entities in relation to the coordination of transboundary Petroleum Activities, or any decision to develop such Reservoir without any such agreement or arrangement, shall be subject to the prior approval of the Council of Ministers.

As government agencies[5] and corporate entities[6] are non-state actors that, strictly speaking, have no capacity to participate in international law-making,[7] whether through convention[8] or custom,[9] their agreements would fall below the radar of Article 38 of the Statute of the International Court of Justice (ICJ)[10] for the purposes of detection as a source of international law.[11]

Some would claim that it will take a Big Bang moment in 'our conception of the sources of law' in order for direct participation by these non-state actors to give rise to international law, and that presently there is no such new philosophy 'suggestive of the birth of a new source of international law, or a new, non-source-based theory of legal production'.[12] Others maintain that direct participation by non-state actors in international law-making is already a reality, and that substantive validity, legitimacy and effectivity clothe these non-state actors with legitimacy and the norms they generate with legality.[13]

Thus, this book asks the following questions: how can one tell whether international agreements between non-state actors are a source of international law? Are there objective identifying criteria? What are these criteria? How do they come about?

It addresses these questions through a case study. An observable phenomenon in the international petroleum industry is that petroleum agencies[14] and

[5] Committee of Legal Advisers on Public International Law (CAHDI), *Expression of Consent by States to be Bound by a Treaty: Analytical Report and Country Reports* (Strasbourg, Council of Europe, 2001), rm.coe.int/168004ad95, 13–15.

[6] P Malanczuk, 'Multinational Enterprises and Treaty-Making' in V Gowlland-Debbas, H Hadj-Sahraoui and N Hayashi (eds), *Multilateral Treaty-Making: The Current Status of Challenges to and Reforms Needed in the International Legislative Process* (Leiden, Brill, 2000) 58–62.

[7] 2016 Johannesburg Report of the International Law Association (ILA) Seventy-Seventh Conference, 608, 619–29. Under art 7 of the Vienna Convention on the Law of Treaties (VCLT), only the heads of state, heads of government, ministers for foreign affairs, heads of diplomatic missions and representatives accredited by states to an international conference are presumed to have authority to represent the state as parties to international agreements (1155 UNTS 231). Moreover, based on the practice of states in the European Union (EU), only heads of states and governments and foreign ministries are presumed to have legal capacity. See CAHDI (n 5).

[8] ibid.

[9] Commentary 8, Conclusion 4, International Law Commission (ILC) Draft Conclusions on Identification of Customary International Law, UN Doc A/73/10, para 65, (2018) 11 *Yearbook of the International Law Commission*, pt II.

[10] 33 UNTS 933.

[11] J Alvarez, *International Organizations as Law-Makers* (Oxford, Oxford University Press, 2006) 595–96.

[12] H Thirlway, *The Sources of International Law* (Oxford, Oxford University Press, 2014) 18–19.

[13] J Henckaerts and L Doswald-Beck, *Customary, International Humanitarian Law: Volume 1, Rules* (Cambridge, Cambridge University Press, 2005) 64–128.

[14] Under Danish law, the Danish Parliament shall 'authorize the Minister for Climate, Energy and Utilities … to enter into an agreement with the relevant country's authorities about the coordination of exploration and production [of] hydrocarbons [that] extends from Danish territory or waters … into another country's sovereign territory'. See art 11(2) and (3) of the Consolidated Act on the Use of the Danish Subsoil, as amended up to 1 May 2019, ens.dk/sites/ens.dk/files/OlieGas/consolidated_act_no._1190_of_21_september_2018_in_the_use_of_the_danish_subsoil.pdf.

corporations[15] may now directly negotiate and conclude cooperation agreements to manage disputes between their respective host states over petroleum resources that are exploitable by two or more states across maritime zones or boundaries (hereinafter referred to as 'shared resources').[16] Disputes over shared resources are triggered when one state engages in unilateral exploration or exploitation, or in what is generally known in both the domestic[17] and international contexts[18] as the rule of capture.

[15] Brunei's model production sharing contract authorises Brunei National Petroleum Company Sdn Bhd or PetroleumBRUNEI, in consultation with the contractor, to directly conclude international unitisation agreements with its foreign counterparts; see Article 11.4 (a) and 11.5 of the Production Sharing Agreement for Block L Brunei Darussalam between BNPC and Loon Brunei Limited and QAF Brunei Sendirian Berhad, 28 August 2006, resourcecontracts.org/contract/ocds-591adf-9845812582/view#/pdf.

The international agreements between petroleum agencies and corporations that are referred to in the case study are different from commercial agreements between national petroleum corporations. In the latter, the agreements involve shared resources; in the former, the agreement involves a resource which is not disputed. For instance, YPFB Petroandina SAM is a company formed between Bolivia's national petroleum corporation Yacimientos Petrolíferos Fiscales Bolivianos (YPFB), with 60%, and Venezuela's national petroleum corporation Petróleos de Venezuela, SA (PDVSA), with 40%. It is engaged in the exploration and production of hydrocarbons in 12 areas that undisputedly belong to Bolivia. See Memorandum de Compromiso entre la República de Bolivia y la Republica Boliviariana de Venezuela para la Exploración y Explotación de Hidrocarburos en el Norte de La Paz, signed by the presidents of the two governments on 9 August 2007, vendata.org/gacetas/2007/09/38760_03-09-2007.pdf?.

[16] The International Law Commission (ILC) Special Rapporteur Chusei Yamada uses the term 'shared natural resources' because 'as oil and natural gas are fluid, exploitation of such an oilfield by one party may affect other parties in another jurisdiction sharing the same oilfield'. See UN Doc A/CN4/580, 6 March 2007, 3.

Some laws define shared resources according to whether it is partly located on one side of a boundary and party on the other side, without regard to exploitability. See s 4-7 of Act No 72, 29 November 1996, as amended by Act No 65, 19 June 2015, npd.no/en/Regulations/Acts/Petroleum-activities-act.

[17] In some jurisdictions, a surface owner acquires title to oil that is brought up to the wellhead, even if it is proven that part of the oil might have migrated from the other side of a property line; the surface owner of the other side has no remedy except to compete for the remaining oil. See R Hardwicke, 'The Rule of Capture and its Implications as Applied to Oil and Gas' (1935) 13 *Texas Law Review* 393, citing *Wood County Petroleum Co v West Virginia Transportation Co* (1886) 28 W Va 10; *Westmoreland Natural Gas Company v DeWitt* [1889] 130 Pa 235; A Scott, *The Evolution of Resource Property Rights* (Oxford, Oxford University Press, 2008) 368–70.

Richard Posner criticized the court in *Westmoreland* for erroneously extending the rule of capture – which originally pertained to wild animals – to oil and gas, despite the lack of a suitable basis for analogy. Wild animals can be subjected to possession. Oil and gas, though fluid, are trapped in a structure and are released when the structure is perforated. See R Posner, 'Legal Formalism, Legal Realism, and the Interpretation of Statutes and the Constitution' (1986) 37 *Case Western Reserve Law Review* 183.

The UK avoided the rule of capture by providing in the 1918 Petroleum (Production) Bill that all mineral deposits found in the territory are reserved for the government (the Crown), which only gives out leases for exploration and development to qualified bidders (arts 1 and 2). See B McBeth, *British Oil Policy 1919–1939* (New York, Routledge, 1985) 17–18.

[18] See Explanatory Statement on the Proper Utilization and Development of Natural Resources of the Subsoil and Sea Bed of the Continental Shelf, Annex 2, Memorandum by the Assistant Chief of the Division of British Commonwealth Affairs (Parsons), 26 April 1945, in 'Formulation of United States Policy on the Resources of the Continental Shelf and on Coastal Fisheries' in United States Department of State (USDOS), *Foreign Relations of the United States (FRUS)*, 1945, vol II, 1502; UN Doc A/CN4/580 (n 16) 3–4.

Due to the strategic importance of petroleum resources, disputes over these are traditionally considered the reserved domain of states,[19] which will be dealt with through armed conflict[20] or maritime boundary agreement with a prescriptive cooperation clause[21] or an international unitization clause,[22] or a joint development agreement.[23] These agreements differ in their delineation of the cooperation area: international unitisation involves specific fields, whereas joint development applies to a defined area inside a zone where maritime claims overlap, but both recognise that the parties and their respective petroleum

[19] Paper on Oil and Gas of the ILC Special Rapporteur on Shared Natural Resources, UN Doc A/CN4/608 (18 February 2009), paras 4–5; Summary Record of the 23rd Meeting of the Sixth Committee, UN Doc A/C6/64/SR23, 18 December 2009, para 17; U Hammer, 'Models for State Ownership on the Norwegian Continental Shelf' in A McHarg and B Barton, et al (eds), *Property and the Law in Energy and Natural Resources* (Oxford, Oxford University Press, 2010) 159–60.

[20] A gunboat incident between Malta and Libya over Texaco's petroleum activity on a disputed continental shelf area is narrated in Memorial of Malta, *Continental Shelf (Libyan Arab Jamahiriya/Malta)*, Judgment [1985] ICJ Rep 422–28.

One factor that led to the 1991 Gulf War was Iraq's accusation that Kuwaiti installations were draining oil from Iraqi fields. See Letter dated 21 April 1991 from the Permanent Representative of Iraq to the United Nations addressed to the Secretary General, UN Doc S/22515, 22 April 1991; Provisional verbatim record of the 2977th Meeting (Part II) of the Security Council, UN Doc S/PV 2977, 23 February 1991, 7.

[21] A standard clause on shared resources can be found in Agreement between the Government of the United Kingdom of Great Britain and Northern Ireland and the Government of the Kingdom of Norway Relating to the Delimitation of the Continental Shelf between the Two Countries, 10 March 1965, 551 UNTS 213. Article 4 provides that the 'contracting parties shall, in consultation with the licensees … seek to reach agreement' on the effective exploitation of a shared resource and the equitable apportionment of the proceeds.

[22] In their agreement on shared resources in the Gulf of Mexico, the US and Mexico adopted a legal framework applicable to a defined area along their delimited boundary. A procedure for coordinated petroleum operations is activated when there is a discovery of a specific shared resource. See Agreement between the United States of America and the United Mexican States Concerning Transboundary Hydrocarbon Reservoirs in the Gulf of Mexico (2014 US-Mexico Transboundary Agreement) TIAS No 14-718, effective 18 July 2014.

[23] In their joint development agreement, Malaysia and Thailand defined an area within the undelimited part of their overlapping maritime zones and placed the same under a joint authority, regardless of whether there is a discovery of a specific shared resource. See Memorandum of Understanding between the Kingdom of Thailand and Malaysia on the Establishment of a Joint Authority for the Exploitation of the Resources of the Sea-Bed in a Defined Area of the Continental Shelf of the Two Countries in the Gulf of Thailand, 21 February 1979; C Lathrop (ed), *International Maritime Boundaries* (Leiden, Brill, 2011) 1105.

Citing the definition used in bilateral agreements and scholarly publications, R Lagoni et al defined joint development as a 'form of cooperation between states in the exploration for and exploitation of … identified deposits, fields or accumulations of non-living resources, which either extend across a boundary or lie in an area of overlapping claims', whereas unitisation is a mere 'contractual cooperation between contractors or concessionaires of a field which straddles the dividing line between concession areas'. Joint development is an international law concept, while unitisation is not. See International Law Association (ILA), Joint Development of Non-Living Resources in the Exclusive Economic Zone, 63 Int'l L Ass'n Rep CONF 1988, 511–12.

H Fox et al agreed with Lagoni et al, but the definition that they adopted applies to a defined area, regardless of whether there is an identified deposit. See H Fox (ed), *Joint Development of Oil and Gas: A Model Agreement for States for Joint Development with Explanatory Commentary vol 1* (London, British Institute of International and Comparative Law, 1989) 47.

agencies and corporations (whether as licensees, contractors, concessionaires or operators) have co-existing interests.[24] The agreements regulate resource exploration and exploitation according to a legal regime that is distinct from the respective national legal and contractual petroleum regimes of the competing states.[25] They resolve disputes that, in terms of their object (ie, potential or actual shared resources) and subject (ie, ownership and control of these resources) are of an international character.[26]

Yet, there are international agreements on shared resources that are negotiated and concluded directly between the petroleum agencies and corporations of the competing littoral states.[27] These agencies and corporations are not traditional agents of the state in treaty-making. Although subject to governmental control, performing governmental functions or conducting global operations, these entities have no authority to participate in the making of international conventions and customs.[28] Most authors relegate them to the role of developing transnational standards that are eventually incorporated into national law[29] or soft international law.[30]

[24] Memorandum on the Regime of the High Sea of the Secretariat of the International Law Commission, UN Doc A/CN4/32, 14 July 1950, 108–09.

[25] International law is identified as the source of norms of cooperation over shared resources. See art 6 of the Muscat Agreement on the Delimitation of the Maritime Boundary between the Sultanate of Oman and the Islamic Republic of Pakistan, 21 November 2000; Lathrop (n 23) 4022. Article 24 of Bolivia's Regulation of Unitization (Hydrocarbons Area) expressly states that international law standards shall apply. This Regulation is for onshore areas as Bolivia has no access to the Pacific Ocean. See Annex, Supreme Decree No 27124, 14 August 2003, gacetaoficialdebolivia.gob.bo/normas/buscar/27124.

[26] See, for example, Position of the Republic of Costa Rica on the Offering of Blocks for Oil Exploration by the Republic of Nicaragua, 2012, costarica-embassy.org/sites/default/files/Position%20of%20Costa%20Rica%20on%20the%20offering%20of%20blocks%20for%20oil%20explotation.pdf. Costa Rica characterised Nicaragua's licensing of blocks in disputed waters as a matter for international arbitration or adjudication.

[27] Danish Consolidated Act (n 14) art 11(3).

[28] S Tordo, *National Oil Companies and Value Creation*, vol 1 (Washington DC, World Bank, 2011) 15–19; CAHDI (n 5).

[29] S Trevisanut, 'The Role of Private Actors in Offshore Energy: Shifting Models of Participation' (2014) 29 *International Journal of Marine and Coastal Law* 651–57; T Hunter (ed), *Regulation of the Upstream Petroleum Sector: A Comparative Study of Licensing and Concession Systems* (Cheltenham, Edward Elgar, 2015) 14, 19–30; T Daintith, 'Against *Lex Petrolea*' (2017) 10 *Journal of World Energy Law & Business* 10–11. These authors doubt that instruments generated by agencies and corporations are a source of customary international energy law, for even international tribunals do not apply these instruments as evidence of custom. They cite *Government of the State of Kuwait v American Independent Oil Company* (1982) 21 ILM 976, paras 155–57. In this case, Kuwait urged the arbitration tribunal to decide on the basis of *lex petrolea* or a body of customary law arising from practices in the Persian/Arabian Gulf in which petroleum agencies and corporations invoke and apply certain principles on nationalization and compensation. The tribunal found no existing *lex petrolea*.

[30] See Daintith (n 29) 9–13; K Talus, S Looper and S Otillar, '*Lex Petrolea* and the Internationalization of Petroleum Agreements: Focus on Host Government Contracts' (2012) 5 *Journal of World Energy Law & Business* 3, 9–13.

To illustrate the plurality of the sources of norms governing shared resources, the provisions of the US Code on transboundary hydrocarbon speaks of four types of agreements. The first type are treaties entered into after 2013 'by the President and approved by Congress'.[31] The second are 'unitization agreements and related arrangements'[32] approved by the petroleum agency, pursuant to the US–Mexico Transboundary Agreement. The third are agreements pertaining to resources in the Eastern Gap in the Gulf of Mexico, in relation to which the petroleum agency is expressly denied authority to act as a party to any international unitisation agreement with Cuba.[33]

The fourth type are transboundary hydrocarbon agreements that '[do] not constitute a treaty in the judgment of the President',[34] but they shall, no later than 180 days from adoption by the parties, be submitted to the 'Speaker of the House of Representative; the Majority Leader of the Senate; Chair of the Committee on Natural Resources of the House of Representatives, and Chair of the Committee on Energy and Natural Resources of the Senate'.[35] Along with the agreement, the following documents relating to the legal effects of the agreement shall be submitted: (1) 'any amendments to the public lands law and other federal laws' that are necessary to implement the agreement; (2) an analysis of the economic impacts of the agreement or its amendments on 'domestic exploration, development and production of hydrocarbon resources on the Outer Continental Shelf'; and (3) a 'detailed description of any regulations expected' to be issued by the petroleum agency.[36]

In effect, though a non-treaty, the fourth type of agreements are a source of legal rules, as they govern activities relating to shared resources, and even bring about changes in national laws and regulations. The agreements are identifiable as a source of legal norms using criteria by which the authority of the parties and the legality of the norms created can be established. The authority of the parties is spelled out in the law itself. The legality of the norms defined in the agreement is signalled by the submission of the agreements and relevant documents to the legislature in order for them to have an effect on domestic laws and regulations.

A more focused case study of the practice of China of allowing China National Offshore Oil Corporation (CNOOC) to manage resource disputes in the South China Sea and East China Sea is examined in Chapter 5. A general case study of the petroleum instruments of 99 other countries is presented in

[31] Transboundary Hydrocarbon Agreements, 43 Code § 1356b, 26 December 2013, para a. The term 'petroleum agency' refers to the Secretary of the Interior or the Secretary of Energy/Federal Energy Regulatory Commission, 42 US Code § 7101.

[32] ibid para c (1).

[33] ibid para d.

[34] ibid para b.

[35] ibid para b (1).

[36] ibid para b (2).

Chapter 4. These case studies ascertain whether, on the basis of the petroleum instruments, there are objective criteria by which to identify: first, the authority of petroleum agencies and corporations to negotiate agreements to resolve disputes over shared resources; and, second, the legality of the norms of conduct that are defined in their agreements.

The data from the petroleum instruments are presented and analysed using postmodern legal positivism. Postmodern legal positivism provides the appropriate descriptive and predictive tools for understanding the role of non-state actors in international law. In contrast, as Chapter 3 will show, the mainstream positivist and pluralist approaches invariably stray into deformalisation by hovering between source ascertainment, functional analysis and governance review, and drawing from a mixed bag of formal consent, inherent validity and democratic legitimacy as criteria. Chapter 2 explains that the theoretical and conceptual tools of postmodern legal positivism are better able to account for the reality that, even in the international legal system, legal norms are generated outside of the state and more particularly through international agreements between non-state actors.

2

International Agreements between Non-state Actors

As spelled out in Chapter 1, this book examines the reality that non-state actors negotiate and conclude agreements to manage inter-state disputes. It asks whether these agreements can be identified as a source of legal norms. Thus, this volume takes part in the debate on whether pluralisation and informalisation in international law-making are supplanting[37] or co-existing[38] with traditional international law-making.

Pluralisation is characterised by overlapping legal and non-legal – that is, moral, religious, socio-economic and political – normative systems that govern the same subject matter.[39] Pluralisation raises such questions as: which rules from which system should prevail? How can these overlapping rules be demarcated? Should there be differentiation between legal and non-legal rules to begin with?[40] Informalisation is characterised by the involvement of sub-states[41] and entities other than states,[42] and the use of processes[43]

[37] R Higgins, *Problems and Process: International Law and How We Use it* (Oxford, Clarendon, 1994) 50; Report of the Panel of Eminent Persons on United Nations-Civil Society Relations (Cardozo Report), UN Doc A/58/817, 11 June 2004, 8–9, 12, 25–27.

[38] G Shaffer and M Pollack, 'Hard vs Soft Law: Alternatives, Complements, and Antagonists in International Governance' (2010) 94 *Minnesota Law Review* 712, 740.

[39] William Twining presents a study of legal, moral and political regimes simultaneously governing human rights: see W Twining, *General Jurisprudence: Understanding Law from a Global Perspective* (Cambridge, Cambridge University Press, 2009) 173–201; R Wolfrum, 'Legal Pluralism from the Perspective of International Law' in M Kötter, T Röder, G Folke Schuppert and R Wolfrum (eds), *Non-state Justice Institutions and the Law Decision-Making at the Interface of Tradition, Religion and the State* (London, Palgrave Macmillan, 2015) 216, 218–19.

[40] J d'Aspremont, 'From a Pluralization of International Norm-Making Processes to a Pluralization of the Concept of International Law' in J Pauwelyn, R Wessel and J Wouters (eds), *Informal International Lawmaking* (Oxford, Oxford University Press, 2012) 190–95; B Tamanaha, 'Understanding Legal Pluralism: Past to Present, Local to Global' (2008) 30 *Sydney Law Review* 390–94, citing S Moore, 'Law and Social Change: The Semi-autonomous Social Field as an Appropriate Subject of Study' (1973) 7 *Law & Society Review* 719.

[41] C Lipson, 'Why are Some International Agreements Informal?' (1991) 45 *International Organizations* 495–501.

[42] M Pollack and G Shaffer, 'The Interaction of Formal and Informal International Lawmaking' in Pauwelyn et al (n 37) 243–44; O Schachter, 'The Decline of the Nation-State and its Implications for International Law' (1997) 36 *Columbia Journal of Transnational Law* 12–15; M Noortmann, A Reinisch and C Ryngaert (eds), *Non-state Actors in International Law* (Oxford, Hart Publishing, 2015) 185–292.

[43] W Reisman, 'The Democratization of Contemporary International Law-Making Processes and the Differentiation of Their Application' in R Wolfrum and V Röben (eds), *Developments of International Law in Treaty Making* (New York, Springer, 2005) 17.

and forms,[44] other than consensual international conventions and customs, in the creation of international law.[45] Informalisation engenders questions about the accountability, authority and legitimacy of the involvement of non-state participants in international law-making.[46] Pluralisation and informalisation challenge the rules of recognition of international law, as these are currently expressed in Article 38 of the ICJ Statute.[47]

I. THEORIES ON THE LEGAL CAPACITY OF NON-STATE ACTORS

Most scholars are dismissive of norms generated by non-state actors, even by governmental agencies and corporations.[48] Non-state actors lack the legitimacy to participate in the creation of conventional and customary law,[49] and they generate norms that are not susceptible to formal criteria for identification as legally compellable rather than merely morally or socially desirable norms.[50]

For these scholars, states are the 'original, primary and universal subjects of international law',[51] for their sovereign will endow them with the objectivity to

[44] A Bianchi, 'Reflexive Butterfly Catching: Insights from a Situated Catcher' in Pauwelyn et al (n 37) 201–02; A Aust, 'The Theory and Practice of Informal International Instruments' (1986) 35 *International and Comparative Law Quarterly* 789–96.

[45] J Wouters and L Hamid, 'Custom and Informal International Lawmaking' in C Bradley (ed), *Custom's Future International Law in a Changing World* (Cambridge, Cambridge University Press, 2016) 334–37.

[46] J Ellis, 'Shades of Grey: Soft Law and the Validity of Public International Law' (2012) 25 *Leiden Journal of International Law*, 314; J Pauwelyn, 'Is it International Law or Not, and Does it Even Matter?' in Pauwelyn et al (n 37) 129–32.

[47] L Henkin, 'International Law: Politics, Values and Functions General Course on Public International Law' (1989) 216 *Collected Courses of The Hague Academy of International Law* 33–35, 183–85.

[48] P Weil, 'Towards Relative Normativity in International Law' (1983) 77 *American Journal of International Law* 414–17; P Weil, 'The Court Cannot Conclude Definitively … Non Liquet Revisited' (1998) 36 *Columbia Journal of Transnational Law* 112–14, 118–19; P Corbett, 'The Consent of States and the Sources of the Law of Nations' (1925) 6 *British Yearbook of International Law* 23–24, 30.

[49] J Beckett, 'Behind Relative Normativity: Rules and Process as Prerequisites of Law' (2001) 12 *European Journal of International Law* 643, 648–49. For Matthias Goldmann, it is doubtful that non-state soft law would meet the requirement of publicness, as it might conflict with democratically enacted municipal laws or undermine the established interpretation of these laws. See M Goldmann, 'Inside Relative Normativity: From Sources to Standard Instruments for the Exercise of International Public Authority' (2008) 9 *German Law Journal* 1866, 1869–70. With respect to corporations, Peter Muchlinski finds the divide between private and public international law sufficient reason for a positivist resistance to corporations as a subject of international law: see P Muchlinski, 'Multinational Enterprises as Actors in International Law: Creating "Soft Law" Obligations and "Hard Law" Rights' in M Noortmann and C Ryngaert (eds), *Non-state Actor Dynamics in International Law: From Law Taking to Law Making?* (Farnham, Ashgate, 2016) 10–11.

[50] Pauwelyn et al (n 37) 144–47.

[51] Malanczuk (n 6) 19.

consent to an agreement as a source of legal rules.[52] Being sovereign, states claim the legitimacy and authority to create rules that are of objective and general application as international law.[53] In contrast, regardless of whether non-state actors have legal personality,[54] they do not possess legal capacity as a subject of international law.[55] They have no inherent authority to create international conventional[56] or customary law;[57] they are incapable of public accountability, which is necessary in order to exercise the authority to create international law.[58]

In the view of the International Law Association (ILA), non-state actors merely indirectly participate in the treaty-making process between states.[59]

[52] Henkin (n 47) 46–47. For Henkin, even *jus cogens norms* 'must be recognized by States generally, by all the essential components of the international Community' (at 61). See also Memorandum from Monroe Leigh, Legal Adviser, Department of State, to all key Department personnel, 12 March 1976, US Department of State, *Digest of United States Practice in International Law* 263–67. State intent is the central requirement. Other requirements are that: (1) the agreement is of international significance; (2) the obligations undertaken are clearly specified and objectively enforceable; (3) the agreement has two or more parties; and (4) the agreement uses a customary form.

[53] C Fenwick, 'The Sources of International Law' (1918) 16 *Michigan Law Review* 394–95; C Parry, 'The Practice of States' (1958) 44 *Transactions of the Grotius Society* 145–86.

[54] A Lindblom, 'Non-governmental Organizations and Non-state Actors in International Law' in B Reinalda (ed), *The Ashgate Research Companion to Non-state Actors* (Farnham, Ashgate, 2011) 148–49. The question of the legal personality of non-state actors to enforce rights, obligations and responsibilities before an international tribunal is distinct from the question of whether they have the legal capacity to create conventional and customary international law. See Malanczuk (n 6) 56; R Baxter, 'International Law in 'Her Infinite Variety' (1980) 29 *International and Comparative Law Quarterly* 549–50, 555–56.

[55] J d'Aspremont, 'Non-state Actors from the Perspective of Legal Positivism: The Communitarian Semantics for the Secondary Rules of International Law' in J d'Aspremont (ed), *Participants in the International Legal System: Multiple Perspectives on Non-state Actors in International Law* (Abingdon, Routledge, 2011) 25–27; J Nye and R Keohane, 'Transnational Relations and World Politics: An Introduction' (1971) 25 *International Organization* 330, 342.

[56] For a detailed survey of administrative and executive agreements that are concluded by state organs and whether they are treaties, see J Klabbers, *The Concept of Treaty in International Law* (The Hague, Brill, 1996) 20–22, 97–106. Richard Baxter uses the term 'international agreements' to cover instruments concluded between governmental departments or agencies. He classifies them as soft law. See Baxter (n 54) 549–66.

Anne-Marie Slaughter argued that there is a different legal order where governmental actors/agencies participate in international law-making, not through treaties, but through soft law and other prescriptive instruments. See A-M Slaughter, 'International Law in a World of Liberal States' (1995) 6 *European Journal of International Law* 530–31; Reisman (n 43) 17, 21–28.

[57] As non-state actors generate only soft law, they are incapable of establishing the subjective element of custom. See ILC Draft Conclusions on Identification of Customary International Law (n 9) 131–32.

[58] See J Klabbers, *Introduction to Institutional International Law* (Cambridge, Cambridge University Press, 2002) 201–02; A Deshman, 'International Organizations and Horizontal Review: The World Health Organization, the Parliamentary Council of Europe, and the H1N1 Pandemic' in S Cassese et al (eds), *Global Administrative Law: The Casebook* (New York, Institute for International Law and Justice, 2012) 326–29.

[59] 2016 ILA Report (n 7) 608, 619–20. Florian Grisel found that, though a non-participant, the International Chamber of Commerce influenced the text of the Convention on the Recognition and Enforcement of Foreign Arbitral Awards: see F Grisel, 'Treaty-Making between Public Authority and Private Interests: The Genealogy of the Convention on the Recognition and Enforcement of Foreign Arbitral Awards' (2017) 28 *European Journal of International Law* 73–87. Cedric Ryngaert described how non-state actors play one-level games in international law-making by influencing

The Vienna Convention on the Law of Treaties (VCLT) acknowledges that there can be 'agreements concluded between other subjects of international law',[60] but the provision has been understood to mean agreements between a state and a non-state actor.[61] For the ILA, non-state actors are conferred authority through 'the international community's recognition of the contracting parties as international legal subjects that carry out work of value to it and are capable of making arrangements governed by international law'.[62] States are the 'gate-keepers' of the international legal system; they decide which and how other entities might qualify as formal parties in the making of international law, such as the Holy See and the Order of Malta, with whom states have had a long tradition of treaty-making.[63]

Certain armed opposition groups (AOG) are recognised as parties to special agreements with states to implement the provisions of the 1949 Geneva Conventions.[64] Some inter-governmental organisations have attained limited legal capacity through a process dictated by states.[65] As for new states, they are generally admitted through a bilateral and horizontal process, although admission to a multilateral arena constitutes the ultimate badge of 'statehood'.[66] Sub-state entities, such as autonomous, federal or indigenous territorial populations, qualify as subjects of international law when states 'enter into relations with them through agreements'.[67]

Unlike new states and sub-state entities, international corporations do not acquire status as subjects of international law by merely entering into agreements with sovereign states. Such 'state contracts [are] … unlikely to qualify

the actual behaviour of states during the negotiation of international agreements: see C Ryngaert, 'Non-state Actors: Carving out a Space in a State-Centred International Legal System' (2016) 63 *Netherlands International Law Review* 188–89.

[60] Article 7 VCLT.

[61] The participation of a non-state actor in an agreement involving states does not affect the legal force of the instrument. See P Okowa, 'Interpreting Constitutive Instruments of International Criminal Tribunals: Reflections on the Special Court for Sierra Leone' in M Fitzmaurice, O Elias and P Merkouris (eds), *Treaty Interpretation and the Vienna Convention on the Law of Treaties: 30 Years on* (The Hague, Martinus Nijhoff, 2010), 344–46, citing arts 2 and 3 VCLT.

[62] International Law Association, 'The Hague Conference on Non-state Actors' (2010) 74 *International Law Association – London Conference* 630, 641.

[63] 2016 ILA Report (n 7) 620, 628–29.

[64] International Law Association, 'Sofia Conference on Non-state Actors' (2012) 75 *International Law Association – London Conference* 658, 662–63, citing UN Doc A/44/971, S/21541, 26 July 1990, San Jose Agreement on Human Rights between the Salvadorian Government and Farabundo Martí National Liberation Front. The ILA describes the agreement as binding, for even if the AOG has no legal capacity, one party is a representative of the UN Secretary-General. Moreover, as the agreement is subjected to monitoring by a UN body, it is similar to a treaty. See also 2010 ILA Report (n 62) 642.

[65] See C Brölmann, *The Institutional Veil in Public International Law: The International Organisations and the Law of Treaties* (Oxford, Hart Publishing, 2007) 39–64.

[66] C Schreuer, 'The Waning of the Sovereign State: Towards a New Paradigm for International Law?' (1993) 4 *European Journal of International Law* 460.

[67] A Aust, *Modern Treaty Law and Practice* (Cambridge, Cambridge University Press, 2007) 71–74.

as treaties governed by international law, primarily because the parties may not intend such agreements to be fully governed by international (treaty) law'.[68] For Peter Malanczuk, no such formal treaty-making status is implicitly conferred on international corporations by the mere execution of an agreement with a state, for even international corporations that are wealthier than some states 'are still formally not subjects of international law' or 'parties to multilateral and bilateral treaties in the sense of international law'.[69] The idea that, by way of a commercial agreement such as a petroleum contract, a single state may grant formal status to an international corporation is fraught with mischief, for the corporation would then be elevated to the level of the state of its home country and entitled to diplomatic protection and sovereign immunities.[70] Moreover, international corporations primarily represent private commercial interests, and if they were allowed to create international law, they would not be expected to fulfil the broad demands of public accountability over and above the narrow interests of their private stakeholders.[71]

In the *Anglo-Iranian Oil Company Case*, the ICJ dismissed the concessionary contract between the Anglo-Iranian Oil Co (AIOC) and Iran as an international agreement as 'there is no privity of contract between the Government of Iran and the Government of the United Kingdom … [for] the Iranian Government cannot claim from the United Kingdom Government any rights which it may claim from the Company, nor can it be called upon to perform towards the United Kingdom Government any obligations which it is bound to perform towards the Company'.[72] Yet, the British government was heavily involved in the negotiations of the text of the concession contract in question, as with every other concession in the Persian/Arabian Gulf; it had a political agreement with AIOC and every British petroleum corporation regarding the latter's authority to operate in the region.[73]

[68] 2012 ILA Report (n 62) 663. Direct involvement of international corporations in international agreements is different from participation in the process that leads to the conclusion of such agreements between the states themselves. The ILA cites W Jenks, 'Multinational Entities in the Law of Nations' in W Friedmann, L Henkin and O Lissitzyn (eds), *Transnational Law in a Changing Society: Essays in Honor of Philip C Jessup* (New York, Columbia University Press, 1972) 73, 82–83. According to Jenks, corporations acquire status only if recognised by governments. Stephen Tully focused on the role of corporations in treaty negotiation and implementation, including gaining observer status: see S Tully, *Corporations and International Law-Making* (Leiden, Martinus Nijhoff, 2007) 48–65, 335–45.

[69] Malanczuk (n 6) 58–62, 71. Peter Malanczuk disagrees with Wolfgang Friedmann that a corporation is vested with formal status once its contract assigns to it certain state functions (at 59). See also W Friedmann, *The Changing Structure of International Law* (New York, Columbia University Press, 1964) 221–31.

[70] Malanczuk (n 6) 62, citing L Oppenheim, *International Law: A Treatise* (London, Longman, Green and Company, 1912) vol I, 62.

[71] Malanczuk (n 6) 58–62; G Teubner, 'Global Bukowina: Legal Pluralism in the World Society' in G Teubner (ed), *Global Law without a State* (Pennsylvania, Brookfield, 1997) 14–16.

[72] *Anglo-Iranian Oil Co Case (Jurisdiction)*, Judgment of 22 July 1952 [1952] ICJ Rep 93, 112.

[73] See File 82/34 II (F 94) APOC Concession [89r] (166/362), British Library: India Office Records and Private Papers, IOR/R/15/1/636, 53–209, in Qatar Digital Library, qdl.qa/archive/81055/vdc_100023415461.0x0000a7. The cancellation of the 1901 D'Arcy concession and renegotiation

Other scholars deny that states have a monopoly over objectivity and legitimacy in the creation of international law, for, in fact, state-made international law simply masks power.[74] In their view, social actors other than states are capable of generating norms of global governance,[75] as they exercise public authority[76] within a pluralised system of international law-making and enforcement.[77] The identification of international law is not based on any inherent capacity of the

of the Anglo-Persian Oil Agreement were raised by the British government before the League of Nations 'as a matter involving international law in which they take up … the case of the company, which is a British subject, and complain of the international wrong which has been perpetrated by the unilateral act of the Persian Government'. See E572/17/34, League of Nations, 31 January 1933, File 82/34 II (F 94) APOC Concession [47r] (112/362), 112–130, British Library: India Office Records and Private Papers, IOR/R/15/1/636, 53-2-209, in Qatar Digital Library, qdl.qa/en/archive/81055/vdc_100023415461.0x000071.

Regarding the involvement of the British government in the formulation of laws on the continental shelf in the Persian/Arabian Gulf, see File 39/23 I, Negotiations for Seabed Oil in Bahrain, Trucial Coast and Qatar, 20 Oct 1948–2 Jun 1949, British Library: India Office Records and Private Papers, IOR/R/15/2/889, in Qatar Digital Library 'File 39/23 I Negotiations for seabed oil in Bahrain, Trucial Coast and Qatar' [11r] (21/66), British, Library: India Office Records and Private Papers, IOR/R/15/2/889, in Qatar Digital Library qdl.qa/archive/81055/vdc_100025672086.0x000016.

Regarding the political agreements between the British government and British petroleum corporations operating in the Persian/Arabian Gulf, see Political Agreement of 5 June 1935 between His Majesty's Government in the United Kingdom and the Anglo-Persian Oil Company Limited, Qatar Oil Concession and connected documents, British Library: India Office Records and Private Papers, IOR/L/PS/18/B445, in Qatar Digital Library, qdl.qa/en/archive/81055/vdc_100023597596.0x000003. All communications between the host ruler and the British petroleum corporation are coursed through the British political agent. See 'File 10/14 III Bahrain unallotted area' [228r] (466/636), British Library: India Office Records and Private Papers, IOR/R/15/2/439, 466, Qatar Digital Library, qdl.qa/archive/81055/vdc_100024095818.0x000043.

[74] M Koskenniemi, 'Constitutionalism as Mindset: Reflections on Kantian Themes about International Law and Globalization' (2007) 8 *Theoretical Inquiries in Law* 14–15; A Carty, 'Critical International Law: Recent Trends in the Theory of International Law' (1991) 2 *European Journal of International Law* 4–22; J Klabbers and T Piiparinen, 'Normative Pluralism: An Exploration' in J Klabbers and T Piiparinen (eds), *Normative Pluralism: Exploring Global Governance* (Cambridge, Cambridge University Press, 2013) 13–15, citing the Kosovo intervention.

[75] Schachter (n 42); N Krisch and B Kingsbury, 'Introduction: Global Governance and Global Administrative Law in the International Legal Order' (2006) 17 *European Journal of International Law* 4–5.

[76] J Ruggie (2004), 'Reconstituting the Global Public Domain' 10 *European Journal of International Relations* 502–503; A Somek, 'Beyond Kelsen and Hart' in J Kammerhofer and J d'Aspremont (eds), *International Legal Positivism in a Postmodern World* (Cambridge, Cambridge University Press, 2014) 174, 177. According to Alexander Somek, the practices of non-state actors are relevant to the formation of customary international law. See also J Kammerhofer, 'Non-state Actors from the Perspective of the Pure Theory of Law' in d'Aspremont (ed) (n 55) 55–61.

[77] Slaughter (n 56) 522–28; Higgins, Problems and Process (n37); A D'Amato, 'Non-state Actors from the Perspective of the Policy-Oriented School: Power, Law, Actors and the View from New Haven' in d'Aspremont (ed) (n 55) 67. The liberal approach maintains the distinction between state and non-state actors, but sees certain non-state actors as necessary to the maintenance of global dialogue and peace; for this reason, it advocates for recognition of their legal status. See P Berman, 'Non-state Lawmaking through the Lens of Global Legal Pluralism' in M Helfand (ed), *Negotiating State and Non-state Law: The Challenge of Global and Local Legal Pluralism* (Cambridge, Cambridge University Press, 2015) 15–18; P Berman, *Global Legal Pluralism A Jurisprudence of Law beyond Borders* (Cambridge, Cambridge University Press, 2012) 166–71, 182. The global governance view is that domestic regulations are embedded in international regulations, and non-state actors play a prominent role in both. See Krisch and Kingsbury (n 75).

state to give command or consent, but on effectivity, substantive validity and the legitimacy of the process of law formulation, all of which are derived from social dynamics rather than state authority and will.[78]

The foregoing divergence of views regarding the legal capacity of non-state actors in international law extends to the legality of the norms they generate.

II. THEORIES ON THE LEGALITY OF NORMS GENERATED BY NON-STATE ACTORS

The prevailing view is that only the sovereign will of states is capable of manifestation or expression in positive, autonomous and voluntary consent[79] to either a treaty or custom,[80] although state consent to a treaty is the more tangible and material criterion for identifying international law.[81] International law is state-made law.[82] Non-state actors are incapable of exercising a will that is sovereign or separate from that of their individual members, or of expressing such will in the form of positive acts of consent to convention or custom.[83]

The opposing view is that the creation of international law depends not on the supposed essence of the state – as opposed to absence of that essence in non-state actors[84] – but on such criteria as the substantive validity of the rules that have been created,[85] the legitimacy of the processes, functions and institutions

[78] M Kamminga, 'The Evolving Status of NGOs under International Law, A Threat to the Inter-state System?' in G Kreijen, M Brus, J Duursma, E de Vos and J Dugard (eds), *State, Sovereignty, and International Governance* (Oxford, Oxford University Press, 2004) 392–99.

[79] C Parry, *The Sources and Evidences of International Law* (Manchester, Manchester University Press, 1965) 8–10, 24–27; G Tunkin, 'International Law in the International System' (1975) 147 *Collected Courses of The Hague Academy of International Law* 16–22, 124.

[80] C Hyde, *International Law Chiefly as Interpreted and Applied by the United States* (Boston, Little, Brown, and Company, 1922) 4–5; K Raustiala, 'Form and Substance in International Agreements' (2005) 99 *American Journal of International Law* 582, 586–87, 591–601; O Schachter, 'The Decline of the Nation-State and its Implications for International Law' (1997) 36 *Columbia Journal of Transnational Law* 7; Corbett (n 48) 20, 25, 30.

[81] Corbett (n 48) 30.

[82] B Simmons, 'International Law and International Relations' in K Whittington, D Kelemen and G Caldeira (eds), *The Oxford Handbook of Law and Politics* (Oxford, Oxford University Press, 2008) 187, 189–90.

[83] ILC Draft Conclusions on Identification of Customary International Law (n 9). Under Draft Conclusion No 4, the element of state practice can be generated only by states and some international organisations, whereas 'the conduct of other actors is not practice that contributes to the formation, or expression, of rules of customary international law'. Thus, the list of practices that the ILC treats as evidencing *opinio juris* are mostly instruments participated in by states, international organisations and judicial bodies.

[84] See generally M Koskenniemi, 'The Politics of International Law' (1990) 1 *European Journal of International Law* 8–14. See also T Kleinlein, 'Non-state Actors from an International Constitutionalist Perspective: Participation Matters!' in Kammerhofer and d'Aspremont (n 76) 41–43.

[85] See B Simma, 'NATO, the UN and the Use of Force: Legal Aspects' (1999) 10 *European Journal of International Law* 21–22; A Trindade, *International Law for Humankind: Towards a New Jus Gentium* (Leiden, Martinus Nijhoff, 2006) 164–72; H Lauterpacht, *The Function of Law in the Community* (Oxford, Clarendon Press, 1933) 437–38; B Kingsbury, 'The Concept of Law in Global

involved in the creation thereof,[86] and their effectiveness or beneficial outcome to society.[87] The new realities in the international legal system are that 'national government officials interact intensively with one another, adopt codes of best practices and agree on coordinated solutions to common problems'.[88] While having no legal force, this norm-making at the margins is as effective as treaty-making between states.[89] Officials and regulators come together as inter-governmental networks in international organisations that have been established by multilateral treaties, and in coordinating bodies that regularly convene to formulate the operational details of framework agreements.[90] Other networks spontaneously emerge, such as the Basel Committee.[91] These networks adopt normative instruments that take such forms as guidelines and memoranda of understanding,[92] compliance with which is manifested through periodic reports and information exchange.[93] Such instruments are soft law, in that they guide compliance rather than compel it.[94] Similar norm-making is observable among international organisations,[95] non-governmental organisations[96] and international armed groups.[97]

While there are scholars who acknowledge the normative output of inter-governmental networks, international organisations and other social actors,[98]

Administrative Law' (2009) 20 *European Journal of International Law* 31–33. For Kingsbury, the moral content of international law is the criterion of publicness – i.e, law is that 'wrought by the whole society, by the public, and … addresses matters of concern to the society as such' (at 31).

[86] See A Stone Sweet, 'Constitutionalism, Legal Pluralism and International Regimes' (2009) 16 *Indiana Journal of Global Legal Studies* 622, 630–33; Slaughter (n 56) 510–16; Klabbers and Piiparinen (n 74) 25–34. See A von Bogdandy, P Dann and M Goldmann, 'Developing the Publicness of Public International Law: Towards a Legal Framework for Global Governance Activities' in A Bogdandy, R Wolfrum, J Bernstorff, P Dann and M Goldmann (eds), *The Exercise of Public Authority by International Institutions: Advancing International Institutional Law* (New York, Springer, 2010) 11–27.

[87] A Peters, L Koechlin and T Förster, 'Towards Non-state Actors as Effective, Legitimate, and Accountable Standard Setters' in A Peters, L Koechlin and T Förster (eds), *Non-state Actors as Standard Setters* (Cambridge, Cambridge University Press, 2009) 500–02.

[88] AM Slaughter, *A New World Order* (Princeton, Princeton University Press, 2004) 163.

[89] ibid.

[90] ibid 45–47.

[91] ibid 48–49.

[92] ibid 178–80.

[93] ibid 188–94.

[94] ibid 174–93.

[95] Alvarez (n 11).

[96] Lindblom (n 54).

[97] A Roberts and S Sivakumaran, 'Lawmaking by Non-state Actors: Engaging Armed Groups in the Creation of International Humanitarian Law' (2012) 37 *Yale Journal of International Law* 107.

[98] A Peters, L Koechlin, T Förster and G Fenner Zinkernagel, 'Non-state Actors as Standard Setters: Framing the Issue in an Interdisciplinary Fashion' in Peters et al (eds) (n 87) 12–26; P Berman, 'A Pluralist Approach to International Law' (2007) 32 *Yale Journal of International Law* 315–17; Wolfrum (n 39) 218–26. Wolfrum discusses how indigenous/cultural groups and their norms shape interpretation of treaty instruments.

some of them regard this as soft law,[99] which is empty of meaning,[100] bereft of force[101] or gives only the bare outlines of custom.[102] Giving too much discretion to unaccountable non-state actors dilutes the normativity of international law.[103] Others view the normative output of non-state actors as enforceable law-like norms[104] that give rise to rights[105] and obligations[106] by reason of their substantive validity in relation to a universal norm,[107] their function of maintaining the international community[108] and their effectiveness in global governance.[109]

In sum, the foregoing approaches to the identification of international law regard authority and legality as essential qualities. They differ in terms of how these qualities are ascertained. For some, authority is inherent in the state by reason of its sovereignty and requires that legality be positively conferred by the state. Others equate authority to socially determined legitimacy, and legality to beneficial outcomes. Chapter 3 will demonstrate that both approaches relapse into deformalisation by dabbling in mere interpretation and even cost-benefit analysis in lieu of source-ascertainment, and fusing formal and non-formal criteria.

An alternative approach is offered by postmodern legal positivism. Its theoretical and conceptual tools are applied in this book.

[99] For most scholars, it is only through soft law that non-state actors participate in the making of international law. See Peters et al (n 87) 499–500. In general, soft law is defined as guidelines that are 'neither strictly binding norms of law, nor completely irrelevant political maxims'. See P Malanczuk, *Akehurst's Modern Introduction to International Law* (Abingdon, Routledge, 2002) 54–55.

[100] J Klabbers, 'The Redundancy of Soft Law' (1996) 65 *Nordisk Journal of International Law* 167–68.

[101] A Kiss and D Shelton, *Guide to International Environmental Law* (The Hague, Brill, 2007) 10–11.

[102] M Mbengue, 'Non-state Actors in International Environmental Law: A Rousseauist Perspective' in d'Aspremont (ed) (n 55) 385–86; J Dunoff, S Ratner and D Wippman, *International Law: Norms, Actors, Process* (New York, Kluwer, 2015) 95.

[103] Klabbers and Piiparinen (n 74). See also J Klabbers, 'The Undesirability of Soft Law (1998) 67 *Nordic Journal of International Law* 381, 383, 387–91.

[104] R Kolb, *Theory of International Law* (London, Bloomsbury, 2016) 153–55; C Redgwell, 'International Soft Law and Globalization' in B Barton, A Lucas, L Barrera-Hernández and A Rønne (eds), *Regulating Energy and Natural Resources* (Oxford, Oxford University Press, 2006) 98–99. Harold Koh refers to it as transnational norm with predictive value: see H Koh, 'Transnational Legal Process' (1996) 75 *Nebraska Law Review* 185–86, 206.

[105] J Nijman, 'Non-state Actors and the International Rule of Law: Revisiting the "Realist Theory" of International Legal Personality' in Noortmann and Ryngaert (n 49). Nijman argues that powerful non-state actors should be treated as object of obligations under international law (at 92–93, 109–10).

[106] J Tasioulas, 'In Defence of Relative Normativity: Communitarian Values and the *Nicaragua* Case' (1996) 16 *Oxford Journal of Legal Studies* 85, 93–104.

[107] M Goldmann, 'We Need to Cut off the Head of the King: Past, Present and Future Approaches to International Soft Law' (2012) 25 *Leiden Journal of International Law* 336–37.

[108] Tasioulas (n 105) 93–94; U Fasternath, 'Relative Normativity in International Law' (1993) 4 *European Journal of International Law* 323–24.

[109] A Boyle and C Chinkin, *The Making of International Law* (Oxford, Oxford University Press, 2007) 211–29.

III. NON-STATE ACTORS IN THE EYES OF POSTMODERN LEGAL POSITIVISM

Postmodern legal positivism unapologetically accepts the reality of pluralisation and informalisation in international law-making, and situates international law-making within subjective social processes in which states and non-state actors are involved (postmodernism).[110] At the same time, it uncompromisingly demands external, objective or formal criteria (legal positivism)[111] for delineating international legal norms from other social norms (the separation thesis).[112] These criteria certify the genealogy of a norm in the international legal order (the source thesis)[113] without regard to the inherent authority and functional legitimacy of the norm-maker or the validity of the substance and beneficial effect of the norm. Moreover, postmodern legal positivism seeks the secondary rules in Article 38 of the ICJ Statute as well as in the social conventions of law-applying authorities (the social thesis).[114]

The separation thesis, the source thesis and the social thesis characterise this approach as postmodern and legal positivist.

A. The Separation Thesis and the Source Thesis

The positivist-statist and pluralist approaches blur the distinction between law, power, morals and function,[115] in that they identify norms as law according to:

[110] D'Aspremont (n 40) 185–86.

[111] This tension between postmodernism and legal positivism is discussed in D Telman, 'International Legal Positivism and Legal Realism' in Kammerhofer and d'Aspremont (n 76) 241–63. John Salmond's classical legal positivism is evident in his emphasis on the primacy of the rules of recognition, without regard to the outcome of the norm:

> It has already been pointed out that a principle is a principle of law, not because it is true or has any rational foundation, but because it is recognized and acted on by the state. If the State, through its courts of law, does in fact recognize and act on the principle that it [State] possesses no legislative power, then that principle is a rule of law and legislative power of the State is legally non-existent. If, on the other hand, the courts of law recognize the rule that the will of the sovereign has the force of law, then the sovereign possesses in law unlimited power of legislation, although in fact he may have no power to enforce his legislation, and although his innovation may arouse rebellion (see J Salmond, *The First Principles of Jurisprudence* [Stevens & Haynes, 1893] 143).

In contrast, postmodern legal positivism finds the rules of recognition flexible for they have no essence or function. The rules are the outcome of social processes.

[112] J d'Aspremont, 'Non-state Actors and the Social Practice of International Law' in Noortmann et al (n 42) 16–17; J d'Aspremont, 'Subjects and Actors in International Lawmaking: The Paradigmatic Divide in the Cognition of International Norm-Generating Processes' in C Brolmann and Y Radi (eds), *Research Handbook on the Theory and Practice of International Law-Making* (Cheltenham, Edward Elgar, 2016) 53.

[113] J d'Aspremont, *Formalism and the Sources of International Law* (Oxford, Oxford University Press, 2011) chs 7–8. Chapter 7 is devoted to the source thesis and ch 8 to the social thesis.

[114] J d'Aspremont, 'International Law-Making by Non-state Actors: Changing the Model or Putting the Phenomenon into Perspective?' in Noortmann et al (n 42) 176–80.

[115] J d'Aspremont, 'Herbert Hart in Today's International Legal Scholarship' in Kammerhofer and d'Aspremont (n 76) 178–82; O Schacter, 'Towards a Theory of International Obligation'

(1) the intent and authority of the norm-maker;[116] (2) the essence of the norm that is discoverable by reason;[117] (3) the substantive validity of the norm;[118] (4) the effectivity of its outcome;[119] and (5) the legitimacy of the process of its formulation.[120]

In contrast, postmodern legal positivism separates the international legal order from other normative orders by positing that the parameters of the international legal order are delineated by secondary rules of recognition, while those of other normative orders are defined by abstract power, morals, reason and function.[121] The secondary rules certify the norms that are legal according to whether their source is the international legal order.[122]

Source-ascertainment differs from law-application, which is the invocation or assertion of a concrete rule in relation to a concrete case, although law-application also involves source-ascertainment, as the concrete rule to be applied

in M Koskenniemi (ed), *Sources of International Law* (Abingdon, Routledge, 2017) 116–21; J d'Aspremont, 'The Idea of "Rules" in the Sources of International Law' (2014) 84 *British Yearbook of International Law* 104–05.

[116] According to this paradigm, cognition of international law-making is based on the inherent qualities of the sovereign states. At one end of the spectrum, the state is the only subject of international law. This is rationalised by the concept of absolute sovereignty, the exercise of which supposedly enables the state to express consent through positive and independent acts (as opposed to other social actors that lack sovereignty and are incapable of autonomous consent). This view is attributed to German scholars who adhered to the Hegelian concept of the state; see Goldmann (n 106). At the other end of the spectrum, the state is regarded as the only subject of international law by reason of its democratic legitimacy, which gives the impression that international law is a liberal project. See Hyde (n 80) 7–8; Henkin (n 47) 64–66.

[117] See F Suarez, *Selections from Three Works: A Treatise on Laws and God the Lawgiver, A Defence of the Catholic and Apostolic Faith, A Work on the Three Theological Virtues: Faith, Hope, and Charity*, G Williams (trans) (Lancaster, Carnegie, 1944) 374–85.

[118] According to this paradigm, cognition of international law is by its pedigree or origin in a 'legal order whose validity is derived by the *Grundnorm* of that legal order'. The *Grundnorm* validates the secondary rule of recognition. See J Kammerhofer, 'Kelsen – Which Kelsen? A Reapplication of the Pure Theory to International Law' (2009) 22 *Leiden Journal of International Law* 242–44, citing H Kelsen, *The Law of the United Nations: A Critical Analysis of its Fundamental Problems* (Westport, CT, Praeger, 1954) 32. D'Aspremont's formalism differs from Kelsen's constitutionalism in that formalism does not rely on a fixed *Grundnorm* (be it *pacta sund servanda* or simply customary international law – that is, that 'states ought to behave as they have customarily behaved').

[119] According to this paradigm, international law-making is identified not by the authority that issued the law or by the inherent qualities of states as their maker or by a constitutive a priori rule, but by the entirety of the process of participation 'by competent persons making authoritative decision in response to claims which various parties are pressing upon them, in respect of various views and interests', with these claimants 'seeking to attain various objectives'. See R Higgins, 'Policy Considerations and the International Judicial Process' (1968) 17 *International & Comparative Law Quarterly* 59.

[120] According to this paradigm, global norms are identified by their publicness, in that they address concerns of society and are formulated through a legitimate process. See Kingsbury (n 85) 31–42. Samantha Besson and Jose Marti equate law-making authority or status to political legitimacy measured according to the 'ultimate, effective control of the people (or peoples) who is (or are) affected' by the law. See S Besson and J Martí, 'Legitimate Actors of International Law-Making: Towards a Theory of International Democratic Representation' (2018) 9 *Jurisprudence* 3–8.

[121] D'Aspremont, 'Non-state Actors' (n 112); d'Aspremont, 'Subjects and Actors' (n 112).

[122] D'Aspremont (n 115) 105.

must first be verified by its source in order to be a legal rather than a non-legal rule.[123] Source-ascertainment also differs from law-making, which, according to traditional notions, involves 'entering into treaties … making binding unilateral commitments … [and] providing practice and/or *opinio juris* for the purpose of identifying norms of customary international law'.[124] Source-ascertainment differs from interpretation, which is limited to deducing the exact meaning and content of what has already been deemed to belong to the category of law.[125] Source-ascertainment certainly differs from impact-assessment, which generally involves measuring how a law brings a desired result closer to reality. Thus, source-ascertainment relies on criteria that are found in the *instrumentum* rather than the *negotium*.[126]

The *negotium* is the content, substance or structure[127] of the norm or agreement, whereas the *instrumentum* is the container or vessel in which the *negotium* is reposed in order to separate and demarcate norms that are legal from norms that are non-legal.[128] Kal Rustiala and Laurence Helfer use the term 'form and substance', where form is decisive in source-ascertainment as it signals the adoption of legality or bindingness rather than the avoidance of legality by the law-makers.[129] In contrast, the choice of the *negotium* or content[130] has to

[123] D'Aspremont (n 113) 13; J d'Aspremont, 'Toward a New Theory of Sources in International Law' in A Orford and F Hoffmann (eds), *The Oxford Handbook of the Theory of International Law* (Oxford, Oxford University Press, 2016) 11.

[124] 2012 ILA Report (n 65) 658–59.

[125] I Venzke, 'Postmodern Perspectives on Orthodox Positivism' in Kammerhofer and d'Aspremont (n 76) 184–85.

[126] D'Aspremont (n 113) 12, 176.

[127] Raustiala (n 80) 582, 586–87. 'Substance' is that feature of the agreement that defines the substantive commitments of the parties. It answers the question of the extent to which the parties are required 'to depart from what they would have done', in the absence of the agreement. It 'refers to the deviation from the status quo that an agreement demands' (at 581, 584). 'Structure' of the agreement refers to the 'rules and procedures created to monitor parties' performance' (at 585). In contrast, form or legality reflects the parties 'choice between legally binding and non-legally binding accords' (at 581).

[128] D'Aspremont (n 113) 174–75. D'Aspremont cites James Brierly, who emphasised the difference between treaty as an instrument and treaty as an agreement. See Report on the Law of Treaties by Special Rapporteur James Brierly, UN Doc A/CN4/23, 14 April 1950, para 30.

[129] Raustiala (n 80); L Helfer, 'Flexibility in International Agreements' in J Dunoff and M Pollack (eds), *Interdisciplinary Perspectives on International Law and International Relations* (Cambridge, Cambridge University Press, 2013) 175–76. On the other hand, for Kenneth Abbot, the adoption of legality is evident from the precision of the instrument, such that it can be used as a basis for adjudication, and the delegation to a third party of the authority for its interpretation and implementation. See K Abbott, R Keohane, A Moravcsik, A Slaughter and D Snidal, 'The Concept of Legalization' (2000) 54 *International Organization* 401. For Christine Chinkin, forms of soft law are instruments that 'have been articulated in non-binding form according to traditional modes of law-making', 'contain vague and imprecise terms', 'emanate from bodies lacking international law-making authority', 'are directed at non-state actors whose practice cannot constitute customary international law', 'lack any corresponding theory of responsibility' and 'are based solely upon voluntary adherence; or rely upon non-juridical means of enforcement'. See C Chinkin, 'Normative Development in the International Legal System' in D Shelton (ed), *Commitment and Compliance: The Role of Non-binding Norms in the International System* (Oxford, Oxford University Press, 2000) 21, 30.

[130] Raustiala (n 80) 584–85.

do with the degree of precision in the definition of the rights, obligations and responsibilities of the law-makers or the robustness of the available monitoring and enforcement mechanisms.[131] These choices are dictated by domestic politics rather than considerations of legality.[132] Thus, the confidentiality of the text of an agreement or imprecision in its language will not impair its legality, for as long as the agreement is cast in the prescribed mould, such as an exchange of letter as *instrumentum*. Imprecision will affect only the interpretation of the extent of rights and obligations, without detracting from the legal nature of the provisions of the agreement.[133]

Postmodern legal positivism acknowledges that, in the prevailing international legal system, source-ascertainment depends on criteria spelled out in Article 38 of the ICJ Statute pertaining to (1) the appropriate authority that can create law, and (2) the appropriate form or process of adoption of legality.[134]

[131] ibid 587. In contrast, Christine Chinkin distinguishes hard law and soft law according to the precision in the language used. A treaty that employs general, hortatory words gives rise to mere soft law. Thus, 'if a treaty is to be regarded as "hard", it must be precisely worded and specify the exact obligations undertaken or the rights granted … [while] a treaty provides only for the gradual acquiring of standards or for general goals and programmed action it is itself soft'. See C Chinkin, 'The Challenge of Soft Law: Development and Change in International Law' (1989) 38 *International and Comparative Law Quarterly* 852–53.

[132] Helfer (n 129) Table 7.1.

[133] Raustiala (n 80) 583; D Costelloe and M Fitzmaurice, 'Lawmaking by Treaty: Conclusion of Treaties and Evolution of Treaty Regimes in Practice' in Brolmann and Raddi (n 13) 116–17. See d'Aspremont (n 113) 174–178, citing the practice of the ICJ in 1) *North Sea Continental Shelf Cases (Federal Republic of Germany v Denmark; Federal Republic of Germany v The Netherlands)* [1969] ICJ Rep 3, para 28 (hereinafter referred to as the *North Sea Cases*), with respect to the 1958 Convention on the Continental Shelf; (2) *Military and Paramilitary Activities in and against Nicaragua (Nicaragua v United States of America), Merits*, Judgment [1986] ICJ Rep 14, with respect to the Charter of the Organization of American States; and (3) *Oil Platforms (Islamic Republic of Iran v United States of America)*, Judgment [2003] ICJ Rep 61, with respect to the Treaty of Amity, Economic Relations and Consular Rights between Iran and the US. In the *North Sea Cases*, the ICJ emphasised that the agreed formal process of signifying consent is a criterion for law ascertainment (ibid paras 25–28).

US practice requires both *negotium* and *instrumentum*. The significance of the subject matter and the specificity of the statement of obligation for purposes of enforceability are important. Form as a criterion is also of much importance for 'the failure to follow a customary form to conclude an agreement may constitute evidence of an intent not to be legally bound', unless the content of the agreement and the context of its making clearly establish such intent. Form in this sense refers to expression of consent such as 'signature, exchange of instruments, ratification, acceptance, approval, accession or any other means if so agreed'. See Congressional Research Service, *Treaties and Other International Agreements: The Role of the United States Senate: A Study Prepared for the Committee on Foreign Relations* (Washington DC, US Senate, Library of Congress, 2001) 52–53; E McDowell, *Digest of US Practice in International Law* (Washington DC, Office of the Legal Adviser, 1977) 213, 262–67.

CAHDI refers to form as expression of consent such as 'signature, exchange of instruments, ratification, acceptance, approval, accession or any other means if so agreed'. See CAHDI (n 5) 16–18.

[134] D'Aspremont (n 113) 26. For Hans Kelsen, law is posited through a human act 'which has taken place at a certain time and a certain space', while natural law's existence is only 'presupposed in our mind'. See H Kelsen, *What is Justice? Justice, Law and Politics in the Mirror of Science: Collected Essays* (Berkeley, University of California Press, 1960), 359; O Schachter, 'International Law in Theory and Practice: General Course in Public International Law' (1982) 178 *Collected Courses of The Hague Academy of International Law* 60–62.

In particular, under Article 38, the state is the appropriate authority that can create international law,[135] while non-state actors have no inherent legal capacity to participate in international law-making, even if they possess international legal personality.[136] Moreover, the criteria that signal the adoption of legality are linguistic and material, specifically, a predefined written or unwritten language or a prescribed deliberative process, such as a specific form and period of ratification as required in treaties.[137] With respect to customary international law, the criteria lack formality, for even the International Law Commission (ILC) draft conclusions apply the same criteria to identify customary international law as the source of a rule and to delineate the content of said rule.[138]

Some authors argue that non-state actors can qualify if formal status is conferred upon them by the state as the central player in the international legal system. Hugh Thirlway doubts that new actors can step in without a revolution in philosophy about international law.[139] D'Aspremont notes that, apart from inter-governmental organisations,[140] no non-state actor has been conferred by the state with such authority.[141] Nonetheless, being embedded in social processes, the identifying criteria of authority and legality are dynamic and can change according to the social practices of law-applying authorities.[142] According to the social thesis, new rules can arise by which non-state actors can qualify as international law-makers,[143] and their agreements or practices as appropriate forms of international law-making.[144]

[135] D'Aspremont (n 55) 23–40; Peters et al (n 87) 496–98.

[136] B Simma and A Paulus, 'The International Community: Facing the Challenge of Globalization' (1998) 9 *European Journal of International Law* 273; d'Aspremont (n 55) 25–27; Nye and Keohane (n 55).

[137] See Appendices A, B, C, D and G in Aust (n 68). The terminologies used in treaties and memoranda of agreements were compared to show that the parties use a specific language to signal adoption of legality rather than avoidance of legality.

[138] D'Aspremont, 'Non-state Actors' (n 112).

[139] Thirlway (n 12).

[140] ibid 42, citing *Reparations for Injuries Suffered in the Service of the United Nations* [1949] ICJ Rep 174.

[141] D'Aspremont (n 55) 25–26; d'Aspremont, 'Subjects and Actors' (n 112) 44. Some authors urged the formal recognition of non-state actors as law-makers. See A Arend, *Legal Rules and International Society* (Oxford, Oxford University Press, 1999) 189–97; R Falk and A Strauss, 'On the Creation of a Global Peoples Assembly: Legitimacy and the Power of Popular Sovereignty' (2000) 36 *Stanford Journal of International Law* 191.

[142] J d'Aspremont, 'Softness in International Law: A Self-Serving Quest for New Legal Materials' (2008) 19 *European Journal of International Law* 1081–87; J Kammerhofer, 'Uncertainty in the Formal Sources of International Law: Customary International Law and Some of its Problems' (2004) 15 *European Journal of International Law* 538, 541–42. Other scholars agree that art 38 is only a starting point. See G Fitzmaurice, 'Some Problems Regarding the Formal Sources of International Law' in *Symbolae Verzjil* (Leiden, Nijhoff, 1958) 173–74. Goldmann notes that even the ICJ does not consider art 38 to be an exclusive list, as it added unilateral acts as a source of rules. See Goldmann (n 106) 348–49.

[143] See d'Aspremont, 'Subjects and Actors' (n 112) 48–51; d'Aspremont (n 114) 176–80; Tamanaha (n 40) 386–90; d'Aspremont (n 40).

[144] D'Aspremont (n 123) 560: 'In the pluralized contemporary international legal system, it would be entirely conceivable for law to emanate from non-state entities. The social theory of sources … is thus not averse to the theoretical possibility of international legal rules made by non-state entities.'

B. The Social Thesis

The social thesis can be traced back to the theories of jurisprudence of Thomas Holland and John Salmond. Holland[145] agrees with John Austin[146] that law is command accompanied by sanction,[147] without regard to the validity of its contents.[148] As this concept of law gives rise to a 'large development of uses',[149] it is 'the jurist [who] has to select that which he admits into his science'.[150] Holland does not identify the selection criteria, except for customary norms that judges recognise based on whether the norms 'come up to a certain standard of general reception and usefulness'.[151] He assigns the authority to select to judges as they are the delegate of the state.[152] There is no similar selection of norms of international law due to a lack of an international arbiter of disputes between sovereign states.[153]

For Salmond, law is identified based solely on rules of recognition, independent of considerations of substantive validity of the law or the inherent authority of the law-maker.[154] Rules of recognition are those that courts apply as a matter of fact.[155] The practices of judges determine the secondary rules because judges have 'the moral obligation … to observe their judicial oaths, and fulfil their appointed functions, by administering justice according to law'.[156] Like Holland, Salmond does not extend the social thesis to the international level, for there is no centralised judicial system.[157]

Hans Kelsen's international law identification presupposes an ultimate validating norm[158] that 'establishes custom – the reciprocal behaviour of the state as a law-creating material fact'.[159] Herbert Hart's rules of recognition, change

[145] T Holland, *The Elements of Jurisprudence* (Oxford, Clarendon Press, 1916) 16–26. Holland defines law as 'propositions commanding the doing, or abstaining from, certain classes of action; disobedience to which is followed, or is likely to be followed, by some sort of penalty or inconvenience' (at 20).

[146] J Austin, *The Province of Jurisprudence Determined* (London, John Murray, 1832) 5–7. For Austin, the identifying criteria are command and habitual obedience.

[147] ibid 8.

[148] ibid.

[149] Holland (n 145) 16.

[150] ibid.

[151] ibid 60. Holland defines this standard by reference to 'malus usus est abolendus' – ie, the customary norm must not be contrary to law.

[152] ibid.

[153] ibid 391–92.

[154] Salmond (n 111) 101.

[155] ibid 101.

[156] ibid 57.

[157] ibid 31–33. For Salmond, the 'law of nations is essentially a species of conventional law; that it has its source in international agreement; that it consists of the rules which sovereign states have agreed to observe in their dealings with each other' (at 32).

[158] H Kelsen, *General Theory of Law and State*, A Wedberg (trans) (Cambridge, MA, Harvard University Press, 1949) 399–404.

[159] ibid; H Kelsen, *Introduction to the Problems of Legal Theory*, B Paulson and S Paulson (trans) (Oxford, Oxford University Press, 1934) 107–09.

and adjudication are also 'legally ultimate in the sense that [they provide] a set of criteria by which, in the last resort, the validity of subordinate rules of the system is assessed'.[160] By reason of their function of adjudication, courts are the primary authorities that define these secondary rules.[161] They do so through judicial consensus on the 'general characteristics possessed by the primary rules'[162] and without regard to their motivations for adopting or adhering to the secondary rules. Hart does not detect a similar legal system (consisting of primary rules and secondary rules) at the international level due to a lack of a centralised legislature, court and enforcement body.[163]

Unlike Hart, Joseph Raz adopted the condition that law-applying institutions recognise normative statements (candidate laws) according to their effectivity in relation to the purpose for which they are intended.[164] This element of effectivity implies a hierarchical social practice.

Brian Tamanaha based the social thesis[165] on John Searle's theory of the social construction of reality:

> The secret of understanding the continued existence of institutional facts is simply that the individuals directly involved and a sufficient number of members of the relevant community ... continue to recognize the existence of such fact. Because the status is constituted by its collective acceptance, and because the function, in order to be performed, requires the status, it is essential to the functioning that there be continued acceptance of the status.[166]

For Tamanaha, a legal system exists when 'private citizens and legal officials conventionally act as if the products of certain persons – whom they treat as "legal officials" – are law'.[167] The emergence of secondary rules and the recognition of law-applying authorities that administer these rules are contemporaneous events.[168] Law as a social construct and law-applying authorities as social actors imply that law has no presupposed essence, function or institution; that is, there can be rules of recognition not only for state law but also for other manifestations of law in the social arena, regardless of their nature or function.[169] The role of scholars is to find out 'how groups of people talk about

[160] H Hart, *Essays in Jurisprudence and Philosophy* (Oxford, Clarendon, 1983) 359; H Hart, *The Concept of Law* (Oxford, Clarendon, 1961) Postscript, 258.

[161] Hart, *The Concept of Law* (n 160) 96–99; Hart, *Essays* (n 160) 362.

[162] Hart cites enactment by a specific body, long customary practice or judicial precedence as types of criteria that are defined by reference to the general characteristics of primary rules. See Hart, *The Concept of Law* (n 160) 95. Changes in primary rules are also governed by rules of recognition, such as the empowerment of a body or person to introduce revisions (ibid). See also Hart, *Essays* (n 160) 275–77, 362–63.

[163] Hart, *Essays* (n 160) 213–14.

[164] J Raz, *The Authority of Law: Essays on Law and Morality* (Oxford, Clarendon, 1979) 79–87.

[165] B Tamanaha, *A General Jurisprudence of Law and Society* (Oxford, Oxford University Press, 2001) 142.

[166] J Searle, *The Construction of Social Reality* (New York, Free Press, 1995) 117.

[167] Tamanaha (n 165).

[168] ibid.

[169] ibid 159–60.

law … and what people do with law … knowing that there may be more than one phenomenon that goes by the name of law'.[170]

Tamanaha describes the international legal system as a single yet uncertain system whereby norms of different forms and functions can be conventionally recognised as international law according to certain criteria of inclusion.[171] He cites the field of human rights, where there is a notable presence of non-state actors whose participation generates norms that may later on acquire the status of international law.[172]

William Twining adopted the social thesis and source thesis of law,[173] but looked beyond social phenomena within the confines of nation states and into 'all levels of relations and of ordering relations between these levels, and all important forms of law including supra-state (e.g. international, regional) and non-state law (e.g. religious law, transnational law, chtonic law i.e. tradition/custom) and various forms of soft law', especially traditions and practices in the non-Western world.[174] He criticised Tamanaha for emptying the rules of recognition of all essentialist and functionalist properties, and leaving their analytical value to the vagaries of local usage.[175] He proposed a modified social thesis that identifies 'law as a species of institutionalized social practice that is oriented to ordering relations between subjects at one or more levels of relations and of ordering', where ordering simply means patterning.[176] Given this redefinition, he considered all subjects, namely 'right- or duty-bearing units under the applicable norm', including corporations, as legal persons whose institutionalised social practices are relevant to source ascertainment.[177]

D'Aspremont referred to but did not rely on Ludwig Wittgenstein's view that the string of words that make up a law has no internal meaning that can regulate behaviour; rather, its meaning as either law (in the sense of regulating or ordering human activities) or non-law has a communitarian foundation,[178] in that the participants in the impacted human activities clarify the meaning and agree to it in their actions.[179] The level of communitarian semantics need not be an 'actual, total, and absolute agreement among law-applying authorities' or a concurrence of understanding of the criteria, for what are essential are 'a shared feeling of applying the same criteria'[180] and a confirmation that other law-applying

[170] ibid 156–57.
[171] B Tamanaha, *A Realist Theory of Law* (Cambridge, Cambridge University Press, 2017) 178–79.
[172] Tamanaha (n 165) 228–29.
[173] Twining (n 39) 92–95, 99–103.
[174] ibid 362.
[175] ibid 99–101.
[176] ibid 116–19.
[177] ibid 119.
[178] D'Aspremont (n 113) 199–200, citing L Wittgenstein, *Philosophical Investigations* (Hoboken, NJ, Blackwell, 2001) paras 201–02.
[179] ibid.
[180] ibid 201–03.

authorities share a perception of the criteria.[181] Agreeing with Tamanaha that law-application can take place among social actors, d'Aspremont acknowledged the possibility of divergence in their practices, especially at the level of international law,[182] but relied on the ICJ and other international arbitration tribunals, as primary law-applying authorities, to address such divergence.[183] Moreover, he agreed with Gerald Postema that the social convention of law-applying authorities can be characterised as a Humean convention which is based on mere reasonable expectation – rather than actual and consistent concurrence – among law-applying authorities that they will coordinate their decisions around a common set of criteria in order to maintain the unity of the legal system.[184] Unlike Twining, d'Aspremont does not condition social practice on the function of ordering.

Finally, Keith Culver and Michael Guidice examined the social thesis from the perspective of an ordinary person encountering clusters of norms administered by state and non-state institutions (such as the family, the school, the church, the state and regional organisations).[185] They disagreed with Tamanaha's view that law is what persons who are regarded as legal officials say it is, simply because 'there is doubt and worry among ordinary persons and theorists' over what agreement or practice amounts to law.[186] They addressed these doubts by presuming that the ordinary person intuitively knows that law and legality have settled cores.[187] Moreover, the interlocking normative systems in complex societies have hard, soft, overlapping and interacting borders.[188] These enable the ordinary person to navigate the 'daily operations' of the normative system without having to invoke a dispute-settling jurisdiction.[189]

[181] ibid.

[182] ibid 212–13.

[183] ibid. D'Aspremont acknowledges that this restores state-centrism and perpetuates the marginalisation of other actors, such as women, in the international law arena. The struggle to enhance the role of other actors would have to be waged elsewhere.

[184] D'Aspremont (n 115) 111–13, citing G Postema, *A Treatise of Legal Philosophy and General Jurisprudence*, vol II (New York, Springer, 2011) 493–97.

[185] K Culver and M Giudice, *Legality's Borders: An Essay in General Jurisprudence* (Oxford, Oxford University Press, 2010) 141.

[186] ibid 143–47.

[187] ibid 147.

[188] ibid 147–71. Culver and Giudice define four inter-institutional spheres: inter-state (such as between an indigenous group and the state); trans-state (autonomous private regimes that operate across borders, such as *lex mercatoria* or *lex digitalis*); supra-state (such as the EU); and super-state legality (such as an international body administering an obligation *erga omnes*).

In contrast, Jean Bonnici and Kees Mestdagh claim that non-state normative spheres encompass rather than merely intersect with state normative spheres. See J Bonnici and K Mestdagh, 'Balancing Norms in Cyberspace: State and Non-state Actor Normativity in Cyberspace' in I Dekker and W Werner, *Governance and International Legal Theory* (New York, Springer, 2004). Bonnici and Mestdagh examined four distinct but inter-dependent spheres of normativity, including the sphere occupied by non-state actors (particularly Internet Service Providers) and how this sphere expands (vis-a-vis other spheres of normativity, such as that of state legislation) to govern more cyberspace activities (at 356–59, 363–70).

[189] Culver and Giudice (n 85) 147.

To illustrate their inter-institutional theory of normativity, Culver and Guidice referred to the Greenland Conservation Agreement, which was signed by three international non-governmental organisations and a scientific council, and was administered by the devolved government of Greenland,[190] to impose a moratorium on commercial salmon fisheries in Greenland's territorial waters.[191] There are two possible objections to the legality of this agreement: first, it 'lacks official recognition by state authorities whose practices create the core and borders of legal systems';[192] and, second, 'it neither includes nor identifies law-applying institutions with dispute settling jurisdiction'.[193] To the first objection, the authors responded that the agreement is 'non-optional' because 'several institutions have deliberately created and now enforce a content-independent peremptory norm … shared amongst and exercised by several institutions which mutually refer to each to such a degree that they have effectively eliminated all licenses to commercial salmon fishing in Greenland's territorial waters'.[194] The parties as norm-subjects effectively 'act in ways which amount to the setting of law', even if it is 'conceptually and practically possible [that they were] acting under the guise of morality, even sincere belief that they are engaging in nothing more than moral agreement and practice'.[195] For the authors, the trans-state legality of the agreement depends on its effectivity.

Responding to the second objection, the authors contended that, though members of the fishing industry, the parties have 'multifaceted roles', including the settlement of disputes about the agreement's application.[196] Besides, a law-application clause is not necessary for the legality of the agreement; its omission will simply increase interaction between the agreement, the law-states and other normative orders.[197] In this sense, the parties are also law-applying authorities whose role is not to demarcate hard borders, but to engage at points of interaction with other normative orders. It is not necessary for law-applying authorities to exercise dispute-settlement functions.

To summarise, the social thesis situates in social conventions within the state and beyond, the development of rules, beliefs and languages for the delineation of legal norms vis-à-vis non-legal social norms. The authors discussed above diverged in their views on whether the relevant social practices have inherent essentialist or functionalist elements, or whether they are based purely on convention. The next subsection considers the institutions, authorities, officials and actors whose social conventions are relevant. These actors are referred to as

[190] ibid.
[191] ibid 155–57.
[192] ibid 156.
[193] ibid 158.
[194] ibid 156–57.
[195] ibid 157.
[196] ibid 158.
[197] ibid 158–59.

law-applying authorities or institutions, in that they engage in the social practice of invoking and applying formal criteria to ascertain whether a norm can be traced to the international legal order as its source.

C. Law-Applying Authorities

In their social thesis, Holland, Salmond, Kelsen and Hart refer to courts as law-applying authorities for different reasons. Holland cites the role of courts as agents of states, while Salmond cites their role and ethos as autonomous institutions. Kelsen sees in the courts a role in the promotion of a global constitutional order, while Hart relies on their function in the adjudication of disputes.

Tamanaha expanded law-application to include social actors outside the state that have been recognised and treated as legal officials by their relevant communities.[198] This expanded rank of law-applying authorities is warranted by the concept of law as 'the product of a complex of social practices' such that its identification necessarily involves legal authorities beyond the state.[199] Earlier, Twining streamlined the definition of social actors by preferring those who are invested in ordering/patterning behaviour, particularly subjects whose rights and duties are affected by the norm.[200] While Culver and Guidice claim that law-creating institutions perform multi-faceted roles that include law-application, in the end they do not offer a clear definition of law-applying authorities, consistent with their inter-institutional thesis that state and non-state normative institutions may actually have interactive borders rather than solid ones.[201]

D'Aspremont relied on Tamanaha's definition of law-applying authorities whose social practices include sharing claims, assertions and invocations about what is law in the abstract (source-ascertainment) and what the law is, given a concrete set of facts and issues at a given time (rule-determination).[202] Law-applying authorities are necessarily engaged in the argumentative process of publicly and purposively making assertions as to international law on a subject matter within their competence, and adopting criteria to point to its sources.[203] They challenge 'each other by invoking [international] legal rules and principles on which they have projected meaning that support their preferences

[198] Tamanaha (n 165) 142.

[199] ibid 159. Tamanaha found Hart's focus on state law to be restrictive because it leaves out other normative systems that govern large populations living outside Western state systems. Even pluralist views that strive to define the essence of law risk excluding other norms. See generally Tamanaha (n 40) 375–411; Tamanaha (n 165) 192–205.

[200] Twining (n 39) 119.

[201] Culver and Giudice (n 204) 169.

[202] Tamanaha (n 40) 396–97; d'Aspremont, 'Non-state Actors' (n 112).

[203] D'Aspremont, 'Non-state Actors' (n 112) 14–15.

and counteract those of their opponents'.[204] In the process, they apply standards, criteria, indicators and signals by which they point to the source of these norms.[205] Standardisation is the convergence of their practices or communitarian semantics.[206] Earlier, it was pointed out that standardisation or convergence approximates a Humean convention that is based on a reasonable expectation of coordinated decisions according to a common set of criteria.[207]

D'Aspremont acknowledged that the 'international legal order is not endowed with wide-ranging institutional and vertical structures which would systematically put an authority in a position to make a pronouncement on where the limit between law and non-law lies'.[208] States engage in both international law-making and source-ascertainment, although this 'is no longer so central, for international law nowadays has grown beyond its original strictly inter-state configuration'.[209] International and domestic judicial authorities engage in law-ascertainment, but, given their limited number and modest caseload, 'their practice has remained too scarce to generate communitarian semantics'.[210] However, in the *South West Africa Cases*, the ICJ knowingly examined the origin of the rules sought to be applied. It disregarded humanitarian considerations and the sacred trust of civilisation as mere material sources that do not create legal rights and obligations.[211] Rather, even if mere principles and interests, when these are 'given juridical expression and … clothed in legal form', such as the substantive provisions of the United Nations Charter, then they may generate legal rights and obligations.[212]

International organisations can engage in both norm-creation and norm-application, such as the International Committee of the Red Cross (ICRC), which attempted to formulate a new rule on the identification of customary international law and international humanitarian law.[213] D'Aspremont agreed with Tamanaha that law-application is no longer 'the monopoly of international tribunals or formal law-makers'.[214] Non-state actors, other than the

[204] ibid 12–13, citing M Koskenniemi, 'International Law and Hegemony: A Reconfiguration' (2004) 17 *Cambridge Review of International Affairs* 199.

[205] D'Aspremont, 'Non-state Actors' (n 112) 14–15. See Hart, *Essays* (n 160) 359; Hart, *The Concept of Law* (n 160) 258.

[206] D'Aspremont (n 113) 212–13. D'Aspremont identifies training, affiliation, dissemination and footnoting as factors that can influence social validation and, consequently, attainment of social consciousness. See J d'Aspremont, *Epistemic Forces in International Law: Foundational Doctrines and Techniques of International Legal Argumentation* (Cheltenham, Edward Elgar, 2015) 22–27.

[207] D'Aspremont (n 115).

[208] D'Aspremont (n 113) 141.

[209] D'Aspremont, 'Non-state Actors' (n 112) 24–25.

[210] ibid.

[211] *South West Africa, Second Phase*, Judgment [1966] ICJ Rep 6, paras 49–52.

[212] ibid para 51.

[213] See d'Aspremont, 'Subjects and Actors' (n 112) 38. D'Aspremont excluded the ILC as it does not distinguish between the work of codification and the work of the progressive development of international law. See d'Aspremont, 'Non-state Actors' (n 112) 25.

[214] D'Aspremont, 'Non-state Actors' (n 112) 20–26.

ICJ and the ICRC, can qualify for the role,[215] provided they contribute to the production of a vocabulary for the delineation of international law from non-legal social norms.[216] He did not identify these other non-state actors, but rather issued a negative list of those that do not qualify as law-applying authorities. In the negative list are the International Law Commission (ILC), which codifies the substantive content of international law, and scholars who interpret this content.

IV. CHAPTER SUMMARY

This chapter has examined a number of theoretical and conceptual tools that can be useful in addressing the question raised in Chapter 1: whether international agreements between non-state actors are susceptible to objective identification as a source of international law. The tools of postmodern legal positivism are preferred for this task. Postmodern legal positivism acknowledges the reality that norms can develop outside of the state, but maintains that the designation of those norms that are legal require objective criteria. This is applied in Chapter 4 to describe and analyse data from the case study on international agreements between petroleum agencies and corporations. It enables the identification of law-applying authorities, and the indicators or signals that the latter develop in their social practices for the purpose of denoting which agreement qualifies as a source of legal norms.

With positivism and pluralism, non-state actors do not quite know where they stand. Non-state actors and their agreements are invisible to state-centric positivism. It is only through state consent, rendered through certain formalities, that an agreement would qualify as a source of legal norms. While the role of non-state actors in the international legal system is recognisable to pluralism, the norms generated by non-state actors are loosely identified using such criteria as inherent value or social function. State-centric positivism and pluralism are the mainstream approaches to international law, but they are unable to account for the existence of international agreements between non-state actors. These inherent limitations are detailed in Chapter 3, which examines efforts since 1950 to identify international law governing disputes over shared resources. Employing the state-centric positivist and pluralist approaches, those efforts regressed into deformalisation by shifting between source-ascertainment and interpretation or even cost-benefit analysis, and fusing objective with subjective identifying criteria.

[215] D'Aspremont (n 113) 203–04; d'Aspremont (n 55) 27–32.

[216] D'Aspremont (n 55) 27. D'Aspremont has been criticised for abstraction by characterising social convention as a 'shared feeling'. See S Singh, 'Narrative and Theory: Formalism's Recurrent Return' (2004) 84 *British Yearbook of International Law* 331–39.

3

Deformalisation in the Identification of International Law

A Critique

DEFORMALISATION IN THE identification of international law is denoted in many ways. For Martti Koskenniemi, an 'increasing management of the world's affairs by flexible and informal, non-territorial networks within which decisions can be made rapidly and effectively' leads to a 'governance mindset [that] looks beyond formal law into the purpose of that law'.[217] Purpose as the defining feature of international law is shaped by a network of private interests and actors that are accountable only to 'an amorphous aggregate of stakeholders'.[218] This definition of deformalisation has been equated to increased norm-making by non-state actors.[219]

For d'Aspremont, Koskenniemi is only partly correct in equating deformalisation to the proliferation of soft law or non-law and the increased ubiquity of 'norm-making by informal non-territorial networks'.[220] Deformalisation is any resort to non-formal law-ascertainment criteria[221] as well as the substitution of source-ascertainment with 'effect – (or impact-)based or process-based' approaches to the identification of international law.[222] It is opposed to formalism, which distinguishes a norm as law rather than non-law by objective criteria, without regard to the substance or impact of the norm or any inherent qualities of the norm-maker.[223] Among the non-formal criteria that d'Aspremont surveyed are: (1) the substantive validity of the provisions of the

[217] M Koskenniemi, 'Global Governance and Public International Law' (2004) 37 *Kritische Justiz* 243, 252. For Koskenniemi, historically, deformalisation was more of a counterpoint to universal international law centred on European values rather than a negation of positive international law centred on the sovereign will of independent states (241–43).

[218] ibid 243.

[219] A Mulligan, 'Framing Deformalisation in Public International Law' (2015) 6 *Transnational Legal Theory* 636.

[220] D'Aspremont (n 113) 18.

[221] ibid.

[222] ibid 29.

[223] ibid 25.

norm, as measured against a priori principles of humanity;[224] (2) the actual or potential outcome of the norm, as measured by its acceptance by the end-users or stakeholders;[225] or (3) the purpose or function of the norm.[226] Recourse to these non-formal criteria is often justified by the complexity of international relations and the convenience of having readily available soft law to govern them.[227] Nonetheless, non-formal source-ascertainment leads to uncertainty, which in turn diminishes the normativity, authority and accountability of international law.[228] The problem of deformalisation that beset the traditional positivist-statist and pluralist approaches to the identification of international warrants resort to the postmodern legal positivism in this book.

As mentioned in Chapter 1, this book integrates the reality that non-state actors conclude international agreements to manage disputes between their host states. At the same time, it examines whether there are formal criteria by which to identify these agreements as a source of international law. Chapter 2 laid out the positivist, pluralist and postmodern positivist approaches that can be useful for the purpose of source-ascertainment. Later in Chapter 4, the post-modern legal positivist approach shall be applied in a case study of international agreements that are negotiated and concluded between petroleum agencies and corporations to address inter-state disputes over shared resources. Meanwhile, in this chapter, the application of the positivist and pluralist approaches in existing literature is reviewed. The review focuses on literature identifying international law on the sovereign rights of states over resources in the continental shelf and exclusive economic zone, including shared resources. The purpose of the review is to demonstrate that these efforts, including by the International Law Commission (ILC), regress into deformalisation.

Section I summarises the three main conceptualisations of the legal regimes of the continental shelf and the exclusive economic zone. These notions influence the methodology and criteria of source-ascertainment that are applied in a number of studies on international law governing disputes over shared resources. These studies are reviewed in section II. The discussion reveals that these efforts relapse into deformalisation by hovering between source-ascertainment,

224 ibid 119–22.

225 ibid 123–27.

226 ibid 128.

227 ibid 128–30.

228 See P Allott, 'Language, Method and the Nature of International Law' (1971) 45 *British Yearbook of International Law* 79; J Petman, 'De-formalization of International Organizations Law' in J Klabbers and A Wallendahl (eds), *Research Handbook on the Law of International Organizations* (Cheltenham, Edward Elgar, 2011) 398–401. See also D Bodansky, 'Customary (and Not So Customary) International Environmental Law' (1995) 3 *Indiana Journal of Global Legal Studies* 114–15. Bodansky noted that legal argumentation about environmental customary law has been reduced to the citation of verbal materials (ie, the views of tribunal and experts) rather than legal materials of actual state practice.

functional analysis and governance review, or by switching back and forth between formal identifying criteria and non-formal validating criteria.

I. CONCEPTUALISATIONS OF THE REGIME OF THE CONTINENTAL SHELF AND THE EXCLUSIVE ECONOMIC ZONE

The literature on the regime of the continental shelf and the exclusive economic zone is dominated by three conceptualisations. The voluntarist view is that rights and obligations in the continental shelf and the exclusive economic zone are brought to life by the sovereign will of states, as expressed through positive acts of consent to conventions and customs. The institutionalist view is that these rights and obligations are predetermined by the will of the international community whose transcendental values dictate the substantive contents of norms relating to the continental shelf and the exclusive economic zone. The functionalist view looks back and validates claims to rights and obligations based on their effectivity in advancing the purpose of the regime of the continental shelf and the exclusive economic zone, which is to ensure resource development and conservation.

A. The Voluntarist-Positivist View

In general, the voluntarist worldview is that there is no international law unless sovereign states will it into existence.[229] The sovereign will of the state is ascertainable from treaty instruments and 'usages generally accepted as expressing principles of law and established in order to regulate the relations between these co-existing independent communities or with a view to the achievement of common aims'.[230] This was the perspective adopted by the US when it formulated the continental shelf and the exclusive economic zone regime[231] under the Truman Proclamation.[232]

In the Truman Proclamation, the US declared that the continental shelf and fisheries zone as well as the resources therein are an extension of the land territory, such that the coastal state having full and absolute sovereignty over said land territory is presumed to have original, natural and exclusive rights to the extension under the sea and its resources.[233] Being sovereign, coastal

[229] See, generally, *SS Lotus Case (France v Turkey)*, 1927 PCIJ (Ser A) No 10, 18.
[230] ibid.
[231] Explanatory Statement on the Proper Utilization and Development of Natural Resources of the Subsoil and Sea Bed of the Continental Shelf (n 18).
[232] Proclamation No 2667, Policy of the United States with Respect to the Natural Resources of the Subsoil and Sea Bed of the Continental Shelf, 28 September 1945, 10 *Federal Register* 193, 12303-04.
[233] Annex 2, Proposed Decision with Respect to Natural Resources of the Subsoil and Sea Bed of the Continental Shelf, Memorandum by the Acting Secretary of State and the Secretary of the

states brook no limitation to their inherent rights, except those to which they may have given consent, through either bilateral agreement or acquiescence to a unilateral act.[234] Thus, the US immediately claimed jurisdiction over the continental shelf and fisheries zone even as it was in the middle of negotiations with neighbouring states and other maritime powers for recognition of said jurisdiction, or for an agreement to a delimitation if an overlap should be found.[235]

When applied to shared resources, the voluntarist point of view considers disputes over them as the reserved domain of states to be addressed solely through bilateral negotiation and agreement. In 2009, the US opposed the plan of the ILC to codify international law on shared oil and gas resources.[236] It found a lack of evidence of the crystallisation of custom for purposes of codification, and maintained that the matter should be reserved for the bilateral relations of states.[237]

The US shifted to a dual institutional-functional perspective in the *Gulf of Maine Case*, where its memorial invoked the welfare of humankind to argue that the identified fish stock on Georges Bank must be preserved as a single unit, which no boundary line should dissect, and that the fish stock as a unit should be managed by a single state (that is, the US as the main user-state) for the benefit of humankind.[238] The invocation of a priori principle of humanity is characteristic of the institutionalist approach.

B. The Institutionalist View

To frame its response to the claim of the US to jurisdiction over the resources of the continental shelf and fisheries zone, the UK initially adopted an institutionalist worldview, which presupposes that the continental shelf, the exclusive economic zone and the resources therein are part of the high seas. These areas

Interior (Ickes) to President Roosevelt, 22 January 1945, in Formulation of United States Policy on the Resources of the Continental Shelf (n 18), 1490–92. The decision was approved by President Franklin Roosevelt on 31 March 1945 (ibid).

[234] Annex 2, Explanatory Statement on the Proper Utilization and Development of Natural Resources of the Subsoil and Sea Bed of the Continental Shelf, Memorandum by the Assistant Chief of the Division of British Commonwealth Affairs (Parsons), 26 April 1945, in Formulation of United States Policy on the Resources of the Continental Shelf (n 18).

[235] Annex 2, Possible Procedures for Gaining International Understanding with Respect to This Jurisdiction, Memorandum by the Office of Economic Affairs, 23 September 1944, Formulation of United States Policy on the Resources of the Continental Shelf (n 18) 1495–503.

[236] See A/CN4/607 and Add 1, International Law Commission, Shared Natural Resources: Comments and Observations received from Governments, 29 January and 17 June 2009, YBILC, 2009, vol II, 125–26.

[237] ibid.

[238] *Delimitation of the Maritime Boundary in the Gulf of Maine Area, Judgment* [1984] ICJ Rep 246, 316–19.

are by nature common to humankind and not susceptible to appropriation by any state,[239] although modern technology may have already enabled the extraction of some resources.[240] Coastal states may claim only those rights to the continental shelf and the exclusive economic zone that have been conceded to them by the international community through agreement.[241] Unlike the US position of unilateral assumption of jurisdiction pending agreement, the UK position favoured a common regime unless there could be an agreement granting coastal states exclusive jurisdiction over drillable areas beyond and adjacent the territorial sea.[242]

In the Persian/Arabian Gulf, where British petroleum corporations held long-term concessions over entire land territories and territorial seas,[243] the seabed beyond the territorial sea has been deemed exploitable as *res nullius*, although a coastal state may claim licensing authority based on an agreement with the other coastal states.[244] In disputed areas, exploration may be undertaken only after giving other states prior notice to drill.[245] Permission to drill is deemed to be granted unless other claimant states expressly object to this.[246] Outside a defined international buffer or neutral zone, production activities shall proceed

[239] The UK did not comment on the Truman Proclamation, but declared that its silence should not be construed as acquiescence. See the Second Secretary of the British Embassy (Cecil) to Mr William Bishop, Assistant to the Legal Adviser (Hackworth), 31 August 1945, Formulation of United States Policy on the Resources of the Continental Shelf (n 18) 1527. The UK eventually issued its own continental shelf and exclusive economic zone proclamations. See Continental Shelf Act, 12 April 1964, legislation.gov.uk/ukpga/1964/29/pdfs/ukpga_19640029_en.pdf; and Petroleum Production Act 1934, legislation.gov.uk/ukpga/1934/36/pdfs/ukpga_19340036_en.pdf.

[240] See the practice of the UK in relation to international fisheries in Miscellaneous No 5 (1943), Final Act of the International Fisheries Conference, 1943–44, Command Papers, Cmd 6496, vol VIII, 791.

[241] British Embassy to the Department of State, 3 August 1945, Formulation of United States Policy on the Resources of the Continental Shelf (n 18) 1524.

[242] As early as 1939, Kuwait Oil sought to obtain from the Ruler of Kuwait a concession covering an area beyond the territorial sea. The response of the UK was that the high seas are international waters, while the seabed is *res nullius*, though subject to acquisition by acts of sovereignty with the consent of other states. See D.158. 86/1 – xi KUWAIT OIL', British Library: India Office Records and Private Papers, IOR/R/15/1/647, 210–23, qdl.qa/archive/81055/vdc_100000000193.0x00026d.

[243] See, for example, Oil Concession Granted by Shaikh of Qatar to the Anglo-Persian Oil Co Ltd, 17 May 1935, British Library: India Office Records and Private Papers, qdl.qa/en/archive/81055/vdc_100023599463.0x00000b. Article 1 provides that Anglo-Persian Oil Co has the sole right to explore and exploit petroleum resources throughout the entire territory of Qatar, defined as 'the whole area over which the Shaikh rules, and which is marked on the north of the line drawn on the map attached' to the contract (art 2).

[244] See, generally, Coll 30/186 'Oil: Koweit Territorial Waters. Jurisdiction over the sub-soil beneath the sea. Off-Shore Oil in the Persian Gulf' [31r] (61/737), 11–61, British Library: India Office Records and Private Papers, IOR/L/PS/12/3924, qdl.qa/archive/81055/vdc_100080590824.0x000040.

[245] India Office Whitehall to Ministry of Fuel and Power, 2 January 1947, 11/5 Negotiations with Ibn Saud Regarding Boundaries of Saudi Arabia', 89–90, qdl.qa/en/archive/81055/vdc_100028545187.0x00005a.

[246] Telegram 181 from the Political Resident, Bushire, to the Secretary of State for India, London, 18 October 1941, File 10/14 III (n 73) 460–66.

under a special agreement among the competing host governments and their concessionaires.[247]

In the Persian/Arabian Gulf, unilateral claims to continental shelf and exclusive economic zone[248] led to the award of competing concessions within areas of overlapping claims,[249] thereby causing tensions[250] and resource underdevelopment.[251] Thus, at least during the period of conceptualisation of the continental shelf and the exclusive economic zone regime, the UK held the view that access to resources on the continental shelf and the exclusive economic zone is not an unrestrained prerogative of sovereign states, but rather a grant from if not a tolerance of the international community.[252] As the source of rights is the will of the international community, coastal states shall enjoy only those rights over the continental shelf and the exclusive economic zone that have been granted to them by the international community as a pre-existing institution.[253] Absent such a grant, the continental shelf and the exclusive economic zone, being part of the high seas, remains accessible to all, subject to limitations inherent in

[247] Article 4, Agreement between His Excellency Shaikhk Ahmad Bin Rashid, Ruler of Umm-al-Qaiwain Arabia and Petroleum Concessions Limited, 20 March 1945, in Confdl. 86/47 Umm-al-Qawain Oil' [6r] (11/44), 14–15, British Library: India Office Records and Private Papers, IOR/R/15/1/701, qdl.qa/archive/81055/vdc_100025702415.0x0000.

[248] FO 462/1, Correspondence respecting the United States of America: part 1, Jan–Dec 1947, UK National Archives, 39–41; Minutes of meeting on jurisdiction over the sub-soil beneath the Sea, immediately adjacent to territorial waters, 16 January 1946, 186/1 XII (D 175) Kuwait Oil [202r] (401/454), 397–403, qdl.qa/archive/81055/vdc_100023614900.0x000002.

[249] See Telegram No 881, 15 August 1951, US Embassy, London to the Department of State, in *US Records on Saudi Affairs, 1945–1959*, vol II (Cambridge, Cambridge Archives Edition, 1997) 226.

[250] Memorandum of conversations by the First Secretary of the Embassy in the United Kingdom (Palmer), 16 April 1953, Subject: Boundaries between Saudi Arabia and Persian Gulf Sheikhdoms, USDOS, *FRUS* (1952–54), the Near and Middle East, vol IX, part 2, 2536. See, for example, Foreign Office S.W.I, E.151/160/25, 22 March 1947, in '11/5 Negotiations with Ibn Saud regarding Boundaries of Saudi Arabia' [5r], 121–22, qdl.qa/en/archive/81055/vdc_100028545187.0x00007a.

[251] See Memorandum on the Southern Eastern Frontiers of Saudi Arabia, Persian Gulf Residency, Bahrain, 1 August 1947, 11/5 Negotiations with Ibn Saud regarding Boundaries of Saudi Arabia [73r] (145/430), qdl.qa/archive/81055/vdc_100028545187.0x000092. With regard to disputed areas between Bahrain and Saudi Arabia, in 1950 Bahrain Petroleum Company (BAPCO) and American Arabian Oil Company (ARAMCO) adopted a 'policy of mutual restraint', the effect of which was to 'restrict BAPCO from operating in the area of the *Fasht bu Safah* shoal where they had done exploratory work prior to 1950 and which they consider[ed] … a promising reservoir of oil'. See EA1083/2, Eastern Department (Arabia), in P Tuson, E Quick and A Burdett, *Records of Bahrain Primary Documents (1820–1960)*, vol VII (Slough, Archive Edition, 1993) 515.

[252] Thus, the UK's annexation of the seabed of the Gulf of Paria was preceded by a delimitation treaty with Venezuela. See Treaty between His Majesty in Respect of the United Kingdom and the President of the United States of Venezuela relating to the Submarine Areas of the Gulf of Paria; *Treaty Series* No 10 (1942); Order in Council annexing the submarine areas of the Gulf of Paria and attaching them to Trinidad and Tobago for administration purposes, London, 6 August 1942, 144 *British & Foreign State Papers* 970, 1940–42.

[253] The UK eventually relented and allowed unilateral continental shelf claims. It circulated draft proclamations that the various rulers in the Persian/Arabian Gulf eventually adopted. See File 39/23 I (n73); File 06/29, Correspondence regarding the land beneath the sea outside territorial waters, 3–31, British Library: India Office Records and Private Papers, 2–3, 21, 27–35, 63, qdl.qa/en/archive/81055/vdc_100000000831.0x000393.

its nature or defined by international agreement.[254] The literature which adheres to this institutionalist view identifies norms of international law according to whether their substance can be validated by the pre-existing principles of fairness and equity.

C. The Functionalist View

In its preparatory work for the First Law of the Sea Conference, the ILC Secretariat took the view that the rationale of the continental shelf and the exclusive economic zone as a juridical concept is to allow economic activities that have been made possible through modern technology and, at the same time, to regulate these activities through resource conservation measures in order to protect the common interest of humankind.[255] This rationale dictates the nature and scope of rights and obligations relating to the continental shelf and the exclusive economic zone and its resources.

Noting that a mere agreement between states would not be able to prevent petroleum resources from traversing their boundary, the Secretariat proposed a provision in the draft continental shelf convention adopting a 'principle … of the essential unity of the deposit'.[256] The Secretariat acknowledged that the proposed provision is not based on any existing custom or convention, except analogous practices 'regarding fluvial rights', but its adoption is necessary to ensure the rational exploitation of the sea for the common good.[257]

This proposal was made in the context of the debate on the role of the ILC as an institution in the development of international law.[258] The ILC Secretariat at that time was headed by Yuen-li Liang,[259] an imminent jurist who had

[254] See the compromise sought by the UK in the British Embassy to the Department of State (n 25) 1524. In contrast, by declaring the continental shelf an extension of the land territory and subjecting it to sovereign control, the US had sought to prevent European powers drilling in the Gulf of Mexico. See Memorandum by President Roosevelt to the Secretary of State, 9 June 1943, Formulation of United States Policy on the Resources of the Continental Shelf (n 18) 1482.

[255] A/CN4/32 (n 24).

[256] Some authors erroneously attributed the idea of international unitisation or joint development to Gidel and Mouton. See Separate Opinion of Judge Jessup, *North Sea Cases* (n 133) 68; W Onorato, 'Apportionment of an International Common Petroleum Deposit' (1968) 17 *International & Comparative Law Quarterly* 1, 86; D Ong, 'Joint Development of Common Offshore Oil and Gas Deposits: Mere State Practice or Customary International Law' (1999) 93 *American Journal of International Law* 778–80; Fox (n 23) 33; D Roughton, 'Rights (and Wrongs) of Capture: International Law and the Implications of the *Guyana v Suriname* Arbitration' (2008) 26 *Journal of Energy & Natural Resources Law* 388.

[257] A/CN4/32 (n 24) i–ii.

[258] See, generally, United Nations, Report of the Committee on the Progressive Development of International Law and its Codification on the Methods for Encouraging the Progressive Development of International Law and its Eventual Codification' (1947) 41 *American Journal of International Law Supplement* 18; Y Liang, 'The General Assembly and the Progressive Development and Codification of International Law' (1948) 42 *American Journal of International Law* 66.

[259] Report of the International Law Commission covering its second session, 5 June–29 July 1950, *YBILC*, 1950, vol II, 365.

participated in The Hague Conference for the Codification of International Law of 1930 and published extensively on the subject of progressive development and codification of international law, and the role of the ILC in this process.[260] Liang had advocated for the ILC a role of codification *juridique* in the development of international law; that is, the ILC should not merely restate/codify existing laws, but should also prescribe forward-looking laws.[261] For Liang, this authority of the ILC to engage in the progressive development of international law is based on its own Statute and underlying responsibility to promote 'the interest of international society'.[262] Its forward-looking law can be formulated in a scientific way[263] and published in order to influence state behaviour.[264] The scientific method involves assessing opposing interests against a standard of value that advances the ends of international society.[265] Soft law formulated in this manner may not be binding, but it will, by its inherent merit, impress itself upon statesmen and judges, and in the process influence state practice and the progressive development of international law.[266]

Liang's views on the role of the ILC in the progressive development of international law explains the Secretariat's position that, notwithstanding the lack of custom or convention, a provision on a protective perimeter and unity of deposit can be codified. The provision would advance the purpose of the continental shelf and the exclusive economic zone regimes, which is to allow both optimum production and resource conservation for the common good.

The foregoing perceptions about the international legal regimes of the continental shelf and the exclusive economic zone are prominent in a number of studies on the norms of international law that are applicable to shared resources. The methodology and identifying criteria that are used in those studies are discussed in the next section.

II. THE IDENTIFICATION OF INTERNATIONAL LAW ON SHARED RESOURCES

This section critiques the existing literature on the norms of international law that are applicable to disputes over shared resources. A retreat to deformalisation is noticeable in the literature. It takes place through the substitution of

[260] Y Liang, 'The Progressive Development of International Law and its Codification under the United Nations' (1947) 41 *American Society of International Law Proceedings* 24.

[261] Y Liang, 'The Preparatory Work for the International Law Commission' (1950–51) 13 *Heidelberg Journal of International Law* 262–63.

[262] Liang (n 260) 38–39.

[263] Y Liang, 'Roscoe Pound and the Science of International Law' (1947–48) 22 *Tulane Law Review* 381.

[264] Y Liang, 'Methods for the Encouragement of the Progressive Development of International Law and its Codification' (1948) 2 *Yearbook of World Affairs* 270–71.

[265] Liang (n 263) 374–79.

[266] Liang (n 260).

source-ascertainment with such devices as textual interpretation, analogy, mechanical reference to expert opinion and cost-benefit analysis, and an almost unconscious conflation of formal and non-formal criteria.

For the purpose of organisation, the first set of materials to be discussed consists of the work of institutions, such as the ILC Committee on Shared Natural Resources. The second set consists of the work of individual scholars. Meanwhile, in order to provide the proper context to the critique of the existing literature on international law governing disputes over shared resources, it is necessary to briefly mention the scope and nature of these disputes.

A. Disputes Over Shared Resources

Disputes over shared resources have been marked by armed conflict[267] and resource sterilisation.[268] Tensions and skirmishes arose in the South China Sea over Vietnam's award to Mobil of Block 5-1b, which is adjacent to WAB-21 that China had awarded to Crestone,[269] and over China's deployment of the oil rig Haiyang Shiyou 981 proximate to Block 118 and Block 119 that Vietnam had awarded to ExxonMobil;[270] in the East China Sea, between China and Japan, over Chinese exploration activities on the Chunxiao and other oil and gas fields that are adjacent to the two countries' disputed waters;[271] in the Atlantic Ocean, between Guyana and Suriname, over exploration activities within the area of their overlapping maritime claims;[272] and, recently, between Venezuela and

[267] In the Caspian Sea, Iran, Azerbaijan and Turkmenistan have shared resources in their overlapping maritime zones. In 2001, an Iranian gunboat and aircraft forced British Petroleum to halt exploration of an area licensed from Azerbaijan. See H Zimnitskaya and J von Geldern, 'Is the Caspian Sea a Sea; and Why Does it Matter?' (2011) 2 *Journal of Eurasian Studies* 12. In 2008, it was Azerbaijan's turn to send a gunboat to disrupt the survey work of Turkmenistan's Canadian contractor Buried Hill Energy in the Caspian Sea. See N Grison, 'NATO's Energy Security Policy Put to the Caspian Test' (2003) 12 *Connections: The Quarterly Journal* 85–86. See also E Brunet-Jailly (ed), *Border Disputes: A Global Encyclopedia, Vol 1, Territorial Disputes* (Santa Barbara, ABC-CLIO, 2015) 113, 252 on disputes over petroleum resources between Colombia and Venezuela over Coquivacoa, and Malaysia and Indonesia over Ambalat.

[268] Memorandum on the Southern Eastern Frontiers of Saudi Arabia (n 251).

[269] J Barrett and N Burke, *Report on the Obligations of States under Articles 74(3) and 83(3) of UNCLOS in Respect of Undelimited Maritime Areas* (London, British Institute of International and Comparative Law, 2016) 97–98.

[270] Resolution No 47/NQ–CP, 8 July 2014, Socialist Republic of Vietnam, vbqppl.mpi.gov.vn/en-us/Pages/default.aspx?itemId=b375d174-4347-46f0-a731-604f8eee8203&list=documentDetail.

[271] See Ministry of Foreign Affairs of Japan, Press Conference, 22 June 2004 (answers to Question No 3), mofa.go.jp/announce/press/2004/6/0622.html#3. See also T Schoenbaum, *Peace in Northeast Asia: Resolving Japan's Territorial and Maritime Disputes with China, Korea and the Russian Federation* (Cheltenham, Edward Elgar, 2008) 15–18.

[272] *Award in the Arbitration Regarding the Delimitation of the Maritime Boundary between Guyana and Suriname*, 17 September 2007, Reports of International Arbitral Awards (RIAA), vol 30, 1–144, paras 150–52.

Guyana/Exxon Mobil over the Liza oil field situated offshore of the disputed territory Essequibo.[273]

States have adopted four types of bilateral agreements to deal with disputes over shared resources: first, a resource clause in maritime boundary agreements where they agree to notify each other and negotiate if a shared resource is found traversing the boundary;[274] second, a joint development agreement where the parties define a zone in an area within their overlapping maritime claims and adopt measures of cooperation;[275] third, an international unitisation agreement relating to an identified petroleum field that is situated across a maritime boundary or within overlapping maritime zones;[276] and, finally, a framework unitisation agreement where the parties stipulate on the mode of cooperation, which is carried out only after the delineation of a shared resource.[277] Most of the literature that will be discussed below focuses on these bilateral instruments.

A different type of agreement involves non-state actors, such as the agreement on the delineation, evaluation, development and utilisation of the shared resources of Mauritania and Senegal in the Grand Tortue Ahmeyim, which was entered into by their national petroleum corporations, Société des Pétroles du Sénégal (Petrosen) and Société Mauritanienne des Hydrocarbures et de Patrimoine Minier (SMHPM), and contractors Kosmos Energy Senegal and British Petroleum.[278] The susceptibility of such agreements to formal identification as a source of international law is examined in Chapter 4.

[273] Statement of His Excellency, Brigadier David Granger, President of the Cooperative Republic of Guyana to the 70th Session of the United Nations General Assembly, 29 September 2015, 3–4, un.int/guyana/sites/www.un.int/files/Guyana/unga_70_general_debate_statement_president_david_granger.pdf.

[274] Delimitation Treaty between the Kingdom of the Netherlands and the Republic of Venezuela, 15 December 1978, Lathrop (n 23) 631. Under arts 6 and 7, the parties shall notify each other prior to undertaking any petroleum activity that entails drilling within one nautical mile of their boundary. Moreover, if a shared resource is detected, the parties shall hold technical consultation and 'make an effort to reach an agreement regarding the most effective way of exploiting said structure or field, and on the way in which the costs and benefits related to said activities shall be shared'.

[275] Agreement between Japan and the Republic of Korea concerning Joint Development of the Southern Part of the Continental Shelf Adjacent to the Two Countries, 22 June 1978, 1225 UNTS (1981) 1114.

[276] Agreement relating to the exploitation of the Frigg Field Reservoir and the transmission of gas therefrom to the United Kingdom (with annexes), 1098 UNTS (1978) 2.

[277] Framework Agreement between the Republic of Cyprus and the Arab Republic of Egypt Concerning the Development of Cross-Median Line Hydrocarbons Resources, 16 September 2014, Registration No 56113.

[278] See Accord de Coopération Inter-Etats portant sur le développement et l'exploitation des réservoirs du champ Grand Tortue/Ahmeyim entre République Islamique de Mauritanie et la République du Sénégal, Journal Officiel du Sénégal (2018) No 7119, 14 January 2016, itie.sn/wp-content/uploads/2019/01/Accord-de-coopération-sur-le-GTA.pdf.

B. Efforts within Institutions to Identify International Law on Shared Resources

This discussion covers: (1) the work of the ILC and the First and Third Law of the Sea Conferences (LOSC) that produced the 1958 Convention on the Continental Shelf[279] and the 1982 United Nations Convention on the Law of the Sea (UNCLOS),[280] respectively; (2) judgments of the ICJ and other international arbitration tribunals; and (3) the studies of the International Law Association (ILA).

i. The ILC and the Law of the Sea Conferences

To recall, in its preparatory work for the First LOSC, the ILC Secretariat proposed the adoption of a principle of unity of deposit, notwithstanding that there was no existing custom or convention governing disputes over shared resources.[281] It derived this rule from both the values which the ILC as an institution is tasked to promote and the purpose of the regime of the continental shelf.

Among the individual experts consulted by the ILC, only JL de Azcarraga supported the adoption of the 'principle of the unity of the deposit' as a pragmatic solution.[282] Martinus Mouton submitted his own views, but did not address the issue of shared resources.[283] However, in an earlier work, Mouton agreed with the Secretariat on the adoption of a principle on protective perimeter and unity of deposit.[284] He traced the rule to the analogous practice of states, specifically Germany and the Netherlands in their Boundary Treaty of Aix-la-Chappelle of 26 June 1816,[285] and Norway and Sweden in *Grisbadarna Arbitration*.[286] Germany and the Netherlands drew a perimeter along parts of their land boundary that was straddled by coal deposits,[287] whereas Norway and Sweden accepted an arbitration award that drew a boundary line in such a way

[279] 499 UNTS (1958) 311.

[280] UN Doc A/CONF62/122, 7 October 1982.

[281] A/CN4/32 (n 24). This proposal was not endorsed by the Special Rapporteur to the ILC. See UN Doc A/CN4/42, Second Report of the Special Rapporteur, JPA François, 10 April 1951; Fourth Report of the Special Rapporteur, UN Doc A/CN4/60, 19 February 1953; UN Doc A/CN4/79, Sixth Report of the Special Rapporteur, 1 March 1954; UN Doc A/CN4/97, Corr 1 and Add 1–3, Regime of the High Seas and Regime of the Territorial Sea, 27 January 1956.

[282] Comment of de Azcarraga in JPA Francois, Fourth Report on the Regime of the High Seas, A/CN4/60 (n 24) 74.

[283] See UN Doc A/CONF13/25, Recent developments in the technology of exploiting the mineral resources of the continental shelf, by M Mouton, 3 January 1958.

[284] M Mouton, *The Continental Shelf* (Leiden, Nijhoff, 1952) 421–22.

[285] (1816–17) 66 *Consolidated Treaty Series* 187–204.

[286] Arbitral Award Rendered on October 23, 1909, in the Matter of the Delimitation of a Certain Part of the Maritime Boundary between Norway and Sweden (*Grisbadarna Arbitration*) 11 Reports of International Arbitral Awards 155.

[287] Articles 19–20 of the Treaty of Aix-la-Chappelle (n 69).

as to preserve the Grisbadarna bank and its mineral resources as a unit.[288] Thus, for Mouton, the principle arose from customary law or analogous and limited practices.

Among the individual members of the ILC, Manley Hudson agreed with the Secretariat, but only with respect to the adoption of a protective perimeter as a matter of pragmatism.[289] Faris Bey-el-Khoury also agreed with the adoption of a protective perimeter: 'Moslem law [under which a] well dug in the desert enjoyed an easement ... [for it] was forbidden to dig another well within a radius of 300 meters.'[290] Other experts agreed with the proposal of the Secretariat based on rational choice.[291]

The ILC did not carry the proposal of the Secretariat in any of its draft articles on the continental shelf.[292] In its commentary to the draft Article 8 on compulsory dispute settlement, the ILC specifically referred to 'disputes arising in connexion with the existence of common deposits situated across the surface boundaries of the submarine areas, a problem which has arisen in some countries in the relations of owners of adjoining oil deposits'.[293] Thus, the ILC prescribed not a one-size-fits-all rule on shared resources, but a case-by-case dispute settlement based on general principles developed by domestic courts on the rule of capture.

The First LOSC did not adopt a provision on shared resources in the 1958 Convention on the Continental Shelf.[294] It also rejected compulsory arbitration as there was no existing body of laws that could be applied to any dispute over the continental shelf.[295]

At the Third LOSC in 1974–82, South Korea suggested that, in situations where adjacent or opposite states are unable to agree on the delimitation of

[288] *Grisbadarna Arbitration* (n 274) 6–7.

[289] YBILC, 1951, vol 1, paras 130, 287.

[290] YBILC, 1950 (n 259), paras 62, 234.

[291] Comments, A/CN4/60 (n 281); YBILC, 1951, vol I, 16 May–27 July 1951, paras 130, 287.

[292] UN Doc A/CN4/49, Draft Articles on the Continental Shelf and Related Subjects Prepared by the International Law Commission, 30 July 1951; UN Doc A/2456, Draft Articles on the Continental Shelf in Report of the International Law Commission covering the work of its fifth session, 1 June–14 August 1953, 212–20; UN Doc A/2934, Report of the International Law Commission covering the work of its seventh session, 2 May–8 July 1955; UN Doc A/3159, Report of the International Law Commission covering the work of its eighth session, 23 April–4 July 1956, paras 7–33.

[293] A/2456 ibid, para 90, 217; see A/CN4/97 (n 269) para 21, 4. Draft art 8 became art 73 of the Articles Concerning the Law of the Sea. Article 73 provides for compulsory arbitration by the ICJ unless the parties agree on another method of dispute settlement. The commentary to art 73 no longer referred to the problem of shared resources. See UN Doc A/CN4/104, Report of the International Law Commission on the Work of its Eighth Session, 23 4 July 1956, Official Records of the General Assembly, Eleventh Session, Supplement No 9, 256–301.

[294] (1965) 499 UNTS 311.

[295] See UN Doc A/CONF13/C3/SR26-30, Summary Records of the 26th to 30th Meetings of the Third Committee, 24 February–27 April 1958, 75; UN Doc A/CONF13/C4/SR31-35, Summary Records of the 31st to 35th Meetings of the Fourth Committee, 99. Instead of compulsory ICJ jurisdiction, an Optional Protocol of Signature concerning the Compulsory Settlement of Disputes was adopted. See 450 UNTS 169 (1958).

their overlapping maritime claims, the 'joint development schemes … suggested by the [ICJ] in its 1969 decision on the North Sea continental shelf case' should be adopted.[296] In 1978, Korea and Japan entered into a joint development agreement pending an agreement on their maritime boundary.[297]

The interim measure that was deliberated upon and eventually adopted by the Third LOSC in UNCLOS[298] enjoins claimant states to 'make every effort to enter into provisional arrangements of a practical nature', during which they shall not engage in any activity that will hamper the reaching of a final agreement.[299] This provision has been interpreted to mean that joint development or international unitisation as a provisional arrangement is not mandatory, and that other provisional measures are available to the parties.[300]

The 1958 and 1982 LOSCs did not expressly provide for the rights and obligations of states in relation to shared resources.[301] Rather, the principle of sovereign rights under Article 2 of the 1958 Convention on the Continental Shelf and Article 77 of UNCLOS countenance unilateralism insofar as they recognise in the coastal states the inherent and exclusive right to employ every means to win petroleum resources from the seabed, without there being any prior restraint, except those to which they may have given consent.[302]

Fifty years after the ILC Secretariat proposed the adoption of a principle of the unity of deposit, the ILC Committee on Shared Natural Resources in 2000 began work on the codification of customary law on the subject.[303] The ILC Committee sought information from various governments regarding state practice in 'the exploration and exploitation of transboundary oil and gas

[296] UN Doc A/CONF62/C2/SR17, Summary records of meetings of the Second Committee 17th meeting, 26 July 1974, paras 29–30.

[297] Agreement between Japan and the Republic of Korea concerning Joint Development (n 275).

[298] See Report of the Chairman of Negotiating Group 7, UN Doc NG7/45, 22 August 1979; Report of the Chairman of Negotiating Group 7, UN Doc A/CONF62/L47, 24 March 1980, 77–78; A/CONF62/122 (n 268) 167, 169.

[299] Articles 74 and 83 UNCLOS, 1833 UNTS 897.

[300] T Mensah, 'Joint Development Zones as an Alternative Dispute Settlement Approach in Maritime' in R Lagoni and D Vignes (eds), *Maritime Delimitation* (Dordrecht, Martinus Nijhoff, 2006) 147; V Becker-Weinberg, *Joint Development of Hydrocarbon Deposits in the Law of the Sea* (New York, Springer, 2014) 100–02.

[301] 63 *Int'l L Ass'n Rep CONF (n 23)*; T Daintith, *Finders Keepers? How the Law of Capture Shaped the World Oil Industry* (New York, Routledge, 2010) 394, 406–07, 433; C Redgwell and L Rajamani, 'Energy Underground: What's International Law Got to Do with it?' in D Zillman, A McHarg, L Barrera-Hernandez and A Bradbrook, *The Law of Energy Underground* (Oxford, Oxford University Press, 2014) 108; E Benvenisti, *Sharing Transboundary Resources: International Law and Optimal Resource Use* (Cambridge, Cambridge University Press, 2002) 104. Eyal Benvenisti noted that there is neither a conventional nor a customary source of rules on shared resources.

[302] M Loja, 'Who Owns the Oil That Traverses a Boundary on the Continental Shelf in an Enclosed Sea? Seeking Answers in Natural Law through Grotius and Selden' (2014) 27 *Leiden Journal of International Law* 896–98.

[303] UN Doc A/55/10, Report of the International Law Commission, 1 May–9 June and 10 July–18 August 2000, 141; UN Doc A/CN4/533 and Add 1, First Report on Shared Natural Resources, Special Rapporteur, 30 April and 30 June 2003, 122.

resources or for any other cooperation for such oil or gas', including unitisation and joint development agreements.[304] It posed the following questions to various governments:

(1) Do you have any agreement(s), arrangement(s) or practice with your neighbouring State(s) regarding the exploration and exploitation of transboundary oil and gas resources or for any other cooperation for such oil and gas?
(2) Are there any joint bodies, mechanisms or partnerships (public or private) involving exploration, exploitation or management of transboundary oil or gas?[305]

Various states responded to the questionnaire in writing,[306] while others gave statements before the Sixth Committee of the General Assembly.[307] The majority of the states opposed codification by the ILC due to a lack of existing custom as a source of international law. Others urged the ILC to identify common principles and best practices for the guidance of host governments and petroleum corporations.[308] Some of the states which did not immediately oppose codification found sufficient state practice in existing bilateral agreements,[309] while others sought further studies on the nature and extent of practices in dealing with disputes over shared resources.[310] South Africa urged the ILC to 'survey the practice of inter-State and private contracts' to identify general trends for

[304] UN Doc A/CN4/L717, 17 July 2007, 3; Paper on Oil and Gas of the ILC Special Rapporteur on Shared Natural Resources, UN Doc A/CN4/608 (18 February 2009).

[305] A/CN4/L717, ibid. The second question implies that the practice of petroleum corporations is relevant.

[306] A/CN4/607 and Add 1 (n 236) 105–26.

[307] See UN Doc A/C6/62/SR22, 4 December 2007; UN Doc A/C6/62/SR24, 13 December 2007; UN Doc A/C6/62/SR25, 10 December 2007; UN Doc A/C6/63/SR16, 10 November 2008; UN Doc A/C6/63/SR17, 11 November 2008; UN Doc A/C6/64/SR18, 9 December 2009; UN Doc A/C6/64/SR20, 17 December 2009; UN Doc A/C6/64/SR21, 22 December 2009; UN Doc A/C6/64/SR22, 8 February 2010; A/C6/64/SR23, (n 19).

[308] (Italy) A/C6/62/SR22 (n 295) para 83; (Norway) A/C6/63/SR16 (n 295) paras 29–30. Norway states that bilateral arrangements between states over their transboundary deposits are a practical solution and ensures legal certainty, but as each transboundary situation is unique and complex, '[i]t might be more productive for the Commission to note the existence of such practice rather than to attempt … [at] codification' (ibid). See also (Czech Republic) A/C6/64/SR20 (n 295) para 44; and (Vietnam) A/C6/64/SR21 (n 295) para 5.

[309] (Sweden and Egypt) A/C6/62/SR22, ibid paras 32, 66; (the Netherlands) A/C6/62/SR24 (n 295), para 45; (Indonesia), A/C6/62/SR25 (n 295) paras 36–37; (Libya) A/C6/63/SR17 (n 295) para 17.

[310] (Uruguay, Guatemala and Germany) A/C6/62/SR22, ibid paras 68, 72 and 80; (Mexico, Romania, the Democratic Republic of Congo, the Russian Federation, the Syrian Arab Republic and Portugal) A/C6/62/SR24 (n 295) 139, paras 11, 20, 30, 81, 93, 104, 109 and 111; (New Zealand, Thailand) A/C6/62/SR25 (n 295) 139, paras 14 and 51; (Poland) UN Doc A/C6/63/SR17, (n 295) para 50; and A/C6/64/SR21 (n 295) para 79. Germany urged that further studies be undertaken given that each transboundary situation is unique and yet global regulation is needed; see A/C6/64/SR20 (n 295) para 37. Mexico noted that there is an 'emerging obligation under international law to enter into unitization agreements' and the ILC should 'identify the elements of such agreements' (see A/C6/63/SR17 (n 295) para 7).

the purpose of drawing guidelines for the future.[311] Speaking for all Nordic countries, Norway invited the ILC to study the 'interface between unitization agreements concluded between States and the establishment of joint ventures with unitization arrangements between the oil companies concerned on each side of the boundary'.[312]

Table 3.1 below summarises the views of the various states on the codification of customary international law (CIL) on shared resources and their choice of criteria for identifying such a norm.

Table 3.1 Identification of CIL on shared resources

Country	Source	Criteria
Australia	Sovereign will	No CIL; issue involves the essential bilateral interests of states[313]
Canada	Sovereign will	No CIL; highly technical and politically sensitive matter is reserved for bilateral agreement[314]
China	Sovereign will	No CIL; issue involving the permanent sovereignty of states over their natural resources is reserved for bilateral agreement[315]
DRC	Sovereign will	No CIL; the issue is reserved for bilateral agreement[316]
France	Sovereign will	No CIL; the politically sensitive matter is reserved for bilateral agreement[317]
Greece	Sovereign will	No CIL; the matter is reserved for bilateral negotiations[318]
Hungary	Sovereign will	No CIL; there is no urgency for codification[319]
Indonesia	Sovereign will	No CIL; the issue is reserved for bilateral agreement[320]
Iran	Sovereign will	No CIL; the issue is reserved for bilateral cooperation[321]

(continued)

[311] A/C6/64/SR21 (n 295) para 81.
[312] A/C6/63/SR16 (n 295) paras 29–30.
[313] A/CN4/607 (n 236) 125; A/C6/64/SR21 (n 295) 15–16; A/C6/63/SR17 (n 295) 5.
[314] A/CN4/607 (n 236) 106, 125; A/C6/64/SR21 (n 295) 5; A/C6/63/SR16 (n 295) para 52; A/C6/63/SR17 (n 295) paras 29 and 39; UN Doc A/C6/62/SR23, 6 December 2007, para 18; UN Doc A/CN4/595, 26 March 2008, para 230.
[315] A/C6/62/SR22 (n 295) para 61.
[316] ibid para 30.
[317] A/C6/64/SR21 (n 295) 5, para 25.
[318] A/C6/64/SR17 (n 295) 143, para 44; A/C6/64/SR21 (n 295) para 42.
[319] A/C6/64/SR18 (n 295) para 61.
[320] A/C6/62/SR25 (n 295) paras 35–37.
[321] A/C6/62/SR25 (n 295) para 45.

Table 3.1 *(Continued)*

Country	Source	Criteria
Israel	Sovereign will	No CIL; this politically sensitive matter is reserved for bilateral negotiations[322]
Japan	Sovereign will	No CIL; codification/universalisation based on custom would be counterproductive as each situation is unique[323]
Libya	Practice	Joint exploration is a source of norms if it leads to discoveries[324]
Malaysia	Sovereign will	No CIL; the issue involves the sovereignty of states[325]
Mexico	Principles	As stated in the *North Sea Cases*, there are analogous principles that can be codified[326]
Myanmar	Sovereign will	No CIL; the issue implicates the principle of sovereign rights[327]
Norway	Sovereign will	No CIL as each practice is influenced by distinct factors; reserved for bilateral agreement[328]
The Philippines	Sovereign will	No CIL; the issues can be resolved through a bilateral joint development agreement[329]
Poland	Practice	There are analogous practices that are relevant[330]
Romania	Practice	There is sufficient analogous practice that can be codified[331]
South Africa	Practice	Inter-state and private contracts should be included in the survey of practice[332]
South Korea	Sovereign will	No CIL; the issue involves a strategic resource which is reserved for bilateral agreement[333]

(continued)

[322] A/C6/64/SR23 (n 17) para 8.
[323] ibid 6; A/C6/64/SR17 (n 295) para 1.
[324] A/C6/64/SR17 (n 295) para 17.
[325] ibid para 39.
[326] A/C6/62/SR24 (n 295) para 11. Mexico cited equitable principles as declared in the *North Sea Cases*, the precautionary principle, the principle of equitable and reasonable use, the obligation to cooperate in exploration and exploitation, and the *sic utere tuo ut alienum non laedas* principle.
[327] A/C6/64/SR21 (n 295) para 5.
[328] A/C6/63/SR16 (n 295) paras 29–30.
[329] A/C6/64/SR23 (n 17) paras 28, 30.
[330] A/C6/62/SR26 (n 303) paras 18–20.
[331] ibid para 20.
[332] A/C6/63/SR16 (n 295) paras 80–81.
[333] A/CN4/607 and add 1 (n 236) 107; UN Doc A/C6/62/SR26, Summary Records of the 26th Meeting of the Sixty-second Session of the Sixth Committee, 13 December 2007, para 8; A/CN4/595 (n314) para 52.

Table 3.1 *(Continued)*

Country	Source	Criteria
Turkey	Sovereign will	No CIL; this highly technical and politically charged matter is not suitable for universal codification[334]
UK	Sovereign will	No CIL; pragmatism and technical guidance rather than a universal rule is necessary[335]
US	Sovereign will	No CIL; this politically sensitive matter is reserved for bilateral agreement rather than universal codification[336]
Venezuela	Sovereign will	No CIL; the matter is too technical to be subject to universal regulation[337]

In view of the objections from governments, the Special Rapporteur[338] and the Working Group[339] recommended the discontinuance of efforts to codify international law on shared resources. The ILC[340] and the Sixth Committee[341] agreed to this.

Table 3.1 above indicates that, in opposing the codification of custom or general principles on shared resources, the various governments invoked the sovereign will of the state as the only source of norms.[342] They deny consensus on a customary norm at the same time as they validate sovereign will as the only source of international law by citing the complexity and technicality of the subject matter of oil and gas resources, the politically charged nature of disputes over these resources, and a lack of urgency to adopt a rule of general application.

It could be argued that these are not criteria for identifying but are rather justifications for denying the existence of a custom and preferring convention as a source of norms. They reflect idiosyncratic preferences rather than descriptive tools of the genealogy of rules. The strategic importance of a resource seems to automatically negate the emergence of a sense of obligation to comply with a norm on shared resources as a custom. Complexity, urgency and expediency negate the sufficiency and uniformity of practice in any norm on shared resources. These elements are highly subjective characterisations of the state of facts surrounding a dispute rather than neutral and precise signals of the

[334] A/C6/64/SR23 (n 17) para 17.
[335] ibid paras 39, 44; A/C6/64/SR20 (n 295) 7.
[336] A/CN4/607 and add 1 (n 236) 126; A/C6/64/SR21 (n 295) 15.
[337] ibid para 44.
[338] UN Doc A/CN4/621, 9 March 2010, Shared Natural Resources: feasibility of future work on oil and gas: paper prepared by Shinya Murase.
[339] UN Doc A/65/10, 2010, Report of the International Law Commission, May–August 2010, para 384, p 344.
[340] ibid para 377, p 343.
[341] UN Doc A/CN4/638, 19 January 2011, Topical summary of the discussion held in the Sixth Committee of the General Assembly during its sixty-fifth session, prepared by the Secretariat.
[342] See *SS Lotus Case* (n 229) 18.

existence or non-existence of the identifying criteria of a customary norm. The very same considerations could justify recourse to non-legal standards, such as established engineering or economic principles on oil and gas conservation.

Geomorphological diversity of shared resources is a common argument against the existence of a customary norm on shared resources.[343] The UK and Norway admit to extensive practice in international unitisation in the North Sea, but deny any accompanying sense of obligation to apply this as a rule in every instance, given that the structure of each shared resource is unique.[344] Yet, in petroleum laws and contracts, there is an increasing standardisation of international unitisation/joint development clauses, and these are applicable to every discovery of a shared resource. Norway, as well as South Africa,[345] drew attention to this phenomenon and urged the ILC to study its significance.

To summarise, as proposed by the Secretariat in 1950, the principle of unity of deposit and the rule on protective perimeters were derived not from any emerging custom or a priori principle, but from the function of the regime of the continental shelf and the exclusive economic zone. The perceived function of this regime is to enable the exploitation of offshore resources to the extent allowed by modern technology and to regulate these activities for the purpose of resource conservation in the name of humankind. The ILC did not adopt these proposed principles; rather, it suggested that disputes over shared resources be subjected to compulsory arbitration based on analogous principles that have been enunciated by domestic courts. At the First and Third LOSCs, the member states did not adopt any provision on shared resources or on compulsory arbitration, citing the lack of a body of norms that can be applied or codified. Before the ILC Committee on Shared Natural Resources and the Sixth Committee of the General Assembly, member states again opposed codification on the ground that there is no sufficient practice or sense of obligation to adhere to a particular practice. They cited the politically strategic, technically complex and geomorphologically unique nature of the resource as an obstacle to the crystallisation of customary international law and a justification for reliance on bilateral agreements as the only source of norms.

In its comments on the proposed codification of international law on shared oil and gas resources, Mexico cited the *North Sea Cases* to argue that unity of deposit is an equitable principle:

> In its judgment in the North Sea Continental Shelf cases (Federal Republic of Germany/Denmark; Federal Republic of Germany/Netherlands), the International Court of Justice had referred to equitable exploitation of transboundary deposits that took account of geological and geographical factors and the unity of the deposits

[343] See the views of Canada and the US vis-a-vis the views of Romania, Poland and Indonesia in Table 3.1.

[344] See the views of the UK and Norway in Table 3.1.

[345] South Africa itself has no petroleum law authorising its petroleum agency or corporations to negotiate and enter into international unitisation agreement.

> in question. The Court had held that it was not a question of applying equity simply as a matter of abstract justice, but of applying a rule of law which itself required the application of equitable principles.[346]

As such, according to Mexico the principle can be applied to resolve disputes over shared resources. Yet, in the *North Sea Cases*, the ICJ noted some level of state practice, but did 'not consider that unity of deposit constitutes anything more than a factual element which it is reasonable to take into consideration in the course of the negotiations for a delimitation'.[347] Since the *North Sea Cases*, there have been a number of arbitrations that grappled with the identification of rules applicable to disputes over shared resources.

ii. International Tribunals

To date, there have been six conciliations, arbitrations and adjudications where the parties and tribunals referred to rules applicable to disputes over shared oil and gas and other natural resources. These are *Grisbadarna Arbitration*, the *Gulf of Maine* and *North Sea Cases*, *Iceland v Norway*, *Eritrea v Yemen* and *Guyana v Suriname*. *Grisbadarna Arbitration* and *Gulf of Maine* dealt with fishery/lobster stocks that traversed actual or potential boundaries, but the views of the Tribunals in these cases are often cited as also relevant to offshore petroleum. *Iceland v Norway*, *Eritrea v Yemen* and *Guyana v Suriname* involved disputes over oil and gas resources. This section focuses on the method and criteria that were applied by the parties and tribunals in ascertaining whether certain norms were part of international law.

a. *Grisbadarna Arbitration*

The Tribunal in *Grisbadarna Arbitration* recognised that Sweden has exclusive rights to lobster fishing on the banks of Grisbadarna, and Norway on Skjöttegrunde.[348] It then drew a boundary that did not cut through the parties' lobster shoals.[349] However, the Tribunal did not identify the source of the rights of Sweden and Norway to the preservation of the unity of their respective fish stocks, except to say that there is 'a well-established principle of the law of nations that the state of things that actually exists and has existed for a long time should be changed as little as possible'.[350] In effect, the principle is a pre-existing principle and is presumed to still exist and apply.

[346] See A/C6/64/SR22 (n 295) para 22; A/C6/62/SR24 (n 295) para 11.
[347] *North Sea Cases* (n 133) para 97.
[348] *Grisbadarna Arbitration* (n 274) 6–7.
[349] ibid.
[350] ibid 6.

b. The *Gulf of Maine Case*

In *Gulf of Maine*, the US argued that its boundary should be drawn according to equitable principles to ensure an equitable result.[351] Among the rules that are based on equitable principles is that the 'boundary should facilitate resource conservation and management'.[352] The US argued that resource conservation is based on equitable principles according to the ruling in *Grisbadarna Arbitration*, in which the boundary was adjusted to preserve the integrity of a resource stock and to place said stock under the management of a single state.[353] Citing the *North Sea Cases*, it equated resource conservation with unity of deposit and argued that, as such, resource conservation is a relevant factor to be taken into account in maritime delimitation because it guarantees an equitable outcome:

> [I]n citing the unity of deposits as a factor relevant for delimiting the continental shelf, the Court in the North Sea Continental Shelf cases underscored the need to conserve and to manage continental shelf resources. The principle of resource conservation and management thus is well-recognized for purposes of continental shelf delimitation.[354]

Yet, as Canada pointed out in its Counter-Memorial, the *North Sea Cases* referred to unity of deposit as a mere factual element.[355]

Canada agreed that conservation is based on equitable principles applicable to a shared fish stock.[356] However, what is equitable depends on agreement. Thus, a boundary line can cut across an identified resource stock, but the same shall be exploited jointly by the claimant states rather than being managed by one state.[357] It identified the principle of conservation as a source according to the criterion of state practice, as noted by the Tribunal and the separate opinion of Judge Jessup in the *North Sea Cases*.[358] Canada cited the 'firmly settled practice that agreements delimiting the continental shelf include stipulations requiring some form of cooperation in the management and exploitation of transboundary oil and gas deposits'.[359] It also cited 'common sense and equity' to validate that preservation of a fish stock is part of the principle of conservation.[360]

351 Memorial of the United States of America, *Gulf of Maine Case* (n 238) vol II, 92–93. In addition to the principle of conservation, the fact of occupation was also invoked by the US, in that Georges Bank had been subjected to exclusive fishing, development and domination by US nationals since independence. *Gulf of Maine Case* (n 238) 18, 259–63.

352 ibid 95–96.

353 ibid paras 248–51.

354 ibid para 248.

355 Counter-Memorial of Canada, *Gulf of Maine Case* (n 238) vol III, paras 503–06.

356 ibid.

357 ibid paras 501, 503

358 ibid paras 503–04.

359 ibid para 505.

360 ibid paras 503–06.

The Tribunal in *Gulf of Maine* noted that both the US and Canada pointed to resource conservation and unity of deposit being based on equitable principles applicable to maritime delimitation[361] and fisheries jurisdiction.[362] However, no party was able to establish the existence of such rules of general principle as international law[363] – specifically, that unity of deposit was an existing rule applicable to the Georges Bank.[364] Rather, the applicable rule is that delimitation shall be based on equitable consideration, as provided under the 1958 Convention on the Continental Shelf, the 1982 UNCLOS and general customary international law, as applied in international arbitrations and adjudications.[365] However, the factors to be considered are not identified in the conventions. The existing customary rule is not substantive but procedural, for it 'merely contains a general requirement of the application of equitable criteria and the utilization of practical methods of implementing them'.[366] Any substantive rule, such as on the specific factors worthy of equitable consideration, should be based on a special agreement between the parties'.[367] The Tribunal declared that the US failed to prove the existence of a special agreement or custom that would warrant the application of preservation of the integrity of the resource stock on Georges Bank as a rule in maritime delimitation.[368] Thus, the Tribunal drew a boundary line that cut through Georges Bank, although it reminded the parties that this should not disrupt their long history of cooperation.[369]

[361] *Gulf of Maine Case* (n 238) paras 97–100, 233–34.
[362] ibid paras 109–12.
[363] ibid paras 109–11, 157.
[364] ibid paras 109–13, 240.
[365] ibid paras 82–96.
[366] ibid paras 109–10.
[367] ibid para 114.
[368] ibid paras 168, 235, 240–41. In the *North Sea Cases*, the Tribunal appeared to give states carte blanche in the choice of factors that are fit for equitable consideration. See *North Sea Cases* (n 133) para 93). In contrast, in *Libya v Malta*, the tribunal restricted the choice of equitable factors to those relevant to the function of the continental shelf as defined in the law of the sea conventions (n 17, para 48). Moreover, the *Gulf of Maine Case* adds special agreement as a source of rules on the choice of equitable factors. Thomas Cottier similarly interprets the *Gulf of Maine* arbitration to mean that special agreements are a source of authority for the international tribunal to take into account certain relevant principles, circumstances and concepts in drawing maritime boundaries. See T Cottier, *Equitable Principles of Maritime Boundary Delimitation: The Quest for Distributive Justice in International Law* (Cambridge, Cambridge University Press, 2015) 600.

Cameroon v Nigeria is relevant, although it did not involve the question of whether a maritime boundary should take into account the potential or actual presence of shared resources. The issue in this case was whether oil concessions unilaterally granted by the parties should be taken into account in the determination of the boundary of their overlapping maritime claims. The tribunal held that, in themselves, oil concessions cannot influence the tribunal's determination of the boundary unless the same are 'based on express or tacit agreement between the parties'. See *Case Concerning the Land and Maritime Boundary between Cameroon and Nigeria (Cameroon v Nigeria; Equatorial Guinea Intervening)*, Judgment of 10 October 2002, para 304.
[369] *Gulf of Maine Case* (n 238) para 240.

The US and Canada in *Gulf of Maine* referred to the statements of the Tribunal in the *North Sea Cases* regarding unity of deposit.[370] Various individual authors have also cited the *North Sea Cases* to argue that unity of deposit is a principle that is applicable to disputes over shared resources,[371] that it is an emerging principle[372] or that it is one of several relevant geophysical/economic factors to be considered in the course of maritime delimitation.[373]

c. The *North Sea Cases*

The Tribunal in the *North Sea Cases* had a limited jurisdiction: to identify the rules that the parties can apply in their boundary negotiations.[374] It examined various possible sources of these rules[375] and concluded that the appropriate sources are 'mutual agreement and … equitable principles'.[376] It noted that in continental shelf and exclusive economic zone legislation and agreements involving the parties, they expressly stated that their overlapping areas shall be delimited by mutual agreement and according to equitable principles.[377] These practices of the parties are based on 'two beliefs': that no one-size-fits-all method of delimitation will prove satisfactory; and, rather, that delimitation 'should be carried out by agreement (or by reference to arbitration) … and effected on equitable principles'.[378] These practices are consistent with Article 6 of the 1958 Convention on the Continental Shelf.[379]

However, as Germany was not a party to the 1958 Convention and as there was no existing convention from which to draw rules of delimitation,[380]

[370] Memorial of the United States (n 340) paras 247–251; Counter-Memorial of Canada (n 344) paras 503–504.

[371] G Garcia Sanchez and R McLaughlin, 'The 2012 Agreement on the Exploitation of Transboundary Hydrocarbon Resources in the Gulf of Mexico: Confirmation of the Rule or Emergence of a New Practice?' (2015) 37 *Houston Journal of International Law* 711–12; A Hakim, *The Middle Eastern States and the Law of the Sea* (Manchester, Manchester University Press, 1979) 130–31.

[372] D Anderson, *Modern Law of the Sea Selected Essays* (Leiden, Nijhoff, 2008) 411–12.

[373] R Bundy, 'Natural Resource Development (Oil and Gas) and Boundary Disputes' in G Blake et al (eds), *The Peaceful Management of Transboundary Resources* (Leiden, Nijhoff, 1995) 24; A Bastida et al 'Cross-border Unitization and Joint Development Agreements: An International Law Perspective' (2006) 28 *Houston Journal of International Law* 371, 381–82; J Weaver et al, 'Unitizing Oil and Gas Fields around the World: A Comparative Analysis of National Laws and Private Contracts' (2006) 28 *Houston Journal of International Law* 86–88.

[374] ibid paras 1–2, 84.

[375] Such as convention (*North Sea Cases*, ibid para 34); natural law (ibid para 37); custom (ibid para 60); and codification or crystallisation (ibid paras 83–85).

[376] *North Sea Cases*, ibid paras 47, 55 and 85.

[377] According to the Tribunal, the concepts of 'delimitation by mutual agreement and delimitation in accordance with equitable principles, have underlain all the subsequent history of the Subject … and various other State proclamations of the period, and after, and in the later work on the subject'. See *North Sea Cases*, ibid para 47.

[378] ibid para 55.

[379] ibid.

[380] ibid paras 27, 83.

equitable principles is the only remaining source.[381] The question was: what legal rules can be drawn from equitable principles?[382] For the Tribunal, there was no rule specifying imperative factors; rather, every relevant factor must be taken into account to ensure that 'a reasonable result is arrived at'.[383] In other words, there is no substantive rule that one particular factor vis-a-vis another must be taken into consideration; instead, there is only a procedural rule that all relevant factors must be considered during the delimitation and that such procedure must serve the purpose producing a reasonable result[384]

Thus, while unity of deposit is a relevant factor to be considered during delimitation,[385] its relative weight would depend on whether there is 'risk of prejudicial or wasteful exploitation', given that the purpose of the continental shelf and the exclusive economic zone is reasonable exploitation.[386] Otherwise, unity of deposit is merely a 'factual element which it is reasonable to take into consideration in the course of delimitation'.[387] The parties are free to agree on a particular delimitation of their overlapping area, but they may also opt for joint exploitation, 'the latter solution appearing particularly appropriate when it is a question of preserving the unity of a deposit'.[388]

In his separate opinion, Judge Jessup agreed that rules consistent with equitable principles are applicable to the parties' boundary negotiations,[389] and this means that the presence and location of oil deposits should be taken into account, as this was the motivation of the parties to the arbitration.[390] He cited bilateral agreements that incorporate a unity of deposit clause[391] as well as national legislations that authorise 'ministerial action' to pave the way for international unitisation.[392] He concluded that unity of deposit, 'even if it is

[381] ibid para 88.

[382] *North Sea Cases*, ibid paras 88–90. The Tribunal inquired whether equidistance as a rule was mandated by equity. The Tribunal discarded equidistance for the same would in fact result in inequity (ibid para 89). Thereafter it examined whether appurtenance (ibid para 95), concavity/convexity of the coastlines (ibid para. 96) and unity of deposit (ibid para 97) are applicable.

[383] ibid paras 90 and 92–93.

[384] The practices cited by the Tribunal are (1) art 4 of the Agreement between the Government of the United Kingdom of Great Britain and Northern Ireland and the Government of the Kingdom of Norway (n 19); (2) art 1 of the Agreement between the Government of the Kingdom of the Netherlands and the Government of the United Kingdom of Great Britain and Northern Ireland relating to the exploitation of single geological structures extending across the dividing line on the continental shelf under the North Sea [1967] Treaty Series No 24; and (3) art 5 of the Supplementary Agreement to the Treaty Concerning Arrangements for Co-operation in the Ems Estuary (Ems-Dollard Treaty), 509 UNTS 142 (1964).

[385] *North Sea Cases* (n 133) paras 92–94.

[386] ibid para 97.

[387] *North Sea Cases* (n 133).

[388] ibid para 99.

[389] Separate Opinion of Judge Jessup, *North Sea Cases*, ibid 67.

[390] ibid 67–80, 84.

[391] ibid 81–83. Judge Jessup cited state practice in unitisation in the North Sea, the Baltic Sea and the Persian/Arabian Gulf, and analogous practice in international rivers.

[392] Separate Opinion of Judge Jessup, ibid 84. Jessup also cited the work of Onorato (n 256), 85; and J Morris, 'The North Sea Continental Shelf: Oil and Gas Legal Problems' (1968) 2 *International Lawyer* 191.

not considered to reveal an emerging rule of international law, may at least be regarded as an elaboration of the factors to be taken into account in the negotiations … [of] the Parties'.[393] For him, existing practices point to both equitable principles and emerging customary law as a source of a substantive rule that unity of deposit should be taken into account in boundary-making.

Judge Ammoun discussed unity of deposit from a formalist perspective.[394] His separate opinion may have guided the Tribunal in *Gulf of Maine*, which, it should be recalled, required a special agreement to warrant the application of unity of a resource stock as an equitable factor. Judge Ammoun agreed that equitable principles are a source of the requirement that the parties must take special circumstances into account in their boundary negotiations.[395] The trouble is that these special circumstances are not defined in the text of positive law and consist of an extreme variety of 'legal and material factors'.[396] In particular, unity of deposit is a mere economic factor that is irrelevant to boundary-making, unless the parties voluntarily agree to treat it as a relevant factor.[397] For Judge Ammoun, boundary-making should not depend on economic factors such as unity of deposit or the presence and location of oil, as otherwise boundary-making would amount to apportionment rather than delimitation of the continental shelf, in violation of the inherent continental shelf and the exclusive economic zone rights of coastal states.[398] Furthermore this would result in the constant rectification of boundaries every time oil is discovered.[399]

In their pleadings, the parties acknowledged that the rule is that unity of deposit is a special circumstance that should be taken into consideration in boundary delimitation. For Germany, the rule was based on a pre-existing 'principle of the just and equitable share',[400] while for Denmark and the Netherlands, the presence of 'indivisible deposits of mineral oil or natural gas' was a special circumstance only if treated as such in a special agreement among the parties.[401]

[393] Separate Opinion of Judge Jessup, *North Sea Cases* (n 133). Jessup considered unity of deposit a significant factor on the ground that it was apparent in the pleadings of the parties that their main objective was to obtain access to petroleum resources in the disputed area and, at the same time, ensure equitable and reasonable exploitation of these resources (67–80).

[394] ibid.

[395] Separate Opinion of Opinion of Judge Fouad Ammoun, ibid 101.

[396] ibid 148.

[397] ibid 149.

[398] ibid.

[399] ibid. Similar to Judge Amoun's view, Judge Tanaka's position is that complications would arise from drawing boundaries based on equitable factors, such as unity of deposit. Tanaka favoured application of the positive rule of equidistance. See Separate Opinion of Judge Tanaka, ibid 192.

[400] Memorial Submitted by the Government of the Federal Republic of Germany, ibid paras 35–37 and 80.

[401] Counter-memorial Submitted by the Government of the Kingdom of Denmark, ibid 211; Counter-memorial Submitted by the Government of the Kingdom of the Netherlands, ibid 364. According to Elferink, before the arbitration, Germany had proposed joint development, but Denmark, the Netherlands and their respective concessionaires opposed the idea. See A Elferink, *The Delimitation of the Continental Shelf between Denmark, Germany and the Netherlands: Arguing Law, Practicing Politics?* (Cambridge, Cambridge University Press, 2013) 364, 368, 371.

The outcome of this arbitration is that the parties adopted continental shelf and exclusive economic zone boundary agreements containing similarly worded and detailed provisions on unity of deposit and its enforcement through arbitration.[402] The agreements require that the parties or their contractors/operators agree on regulations governing the exploitation of shared resource or, if no such regulation is agreed upon, that an arbitration tribunal should formulate regulations based on equity.[403] A similar recommendation on unity of deposit was adopted by the Commission in the conciliation between Iceland and Norway.

d. *Iceland v Norway*

The Conciliation Commission in *Iceland v Norway* was specifically instructed by the parties to make recommendations regarding their continental shelf boundary, taking special circumstances into account.[404] A unanimous Conciliation Commission drew a boundary line and, at the same time, designated a zone for the joint exploitation of resources.[405] It expressly stated that the reasons for the recommendations are political and economic – that is, to 'further promote cooperation and friendly relations' between the parties, alleviate Iceland's total dependence on oil imports and encourage resource development.[406] It recommended that if petroleum resources are found to traverse the boundary, the parties should adopt the 'usual unitization … procedures',[407] although it did not identify the source of any rule requiring the adoption of such procedures.

In their 1981 continental shelf and exclusive economic zone boundary agreements, Iceland and Norway adhered to the Commission's recommendations[408] but clarified that the source of unitisation procedures would be a separate agreement of the parties.[409] In 2011, the parties defined their principles of unitisation in a framework agreement, which will be discussed in Chapter 4.[410]

[402] Articles 2 and 5 of the 1971 Germany-Denmark Boundary Agreement; arts 2 and 5 of the 1972 Germany-Netherlands Boundary Agreement (n 270).

[403] Articles 2 (2) and (4) of the Germany-Denmark Boundary Agreement, ibid; arts 2(2) and (4) pf the Germany-Netherlands Boundary Agreement, ibid.

[404] Conciliation Commission on the Continental Shelf area between Iceland and Jan Mayen: Report and Recommendations to the Governments of Iceland and Norway, Decision of June 198 (1981) 20 *International Legal Materials* 797, 799, 823.

[405] ibid 840.

[406] ibid 826.

[407] ibid 838–39.

[408] Article 8 of the Agreement on the Continental Shelf between Iceland and Jan Mayen, 2 June 1982, 2124 UNTS 262. The states parties agreed to participation rights in each other's exclusive economic zone as well as a commitment to negotiate in relation to a shared resource.

[409] ibid.

[410] Agreement between Norway and Iceland Concerning Transboundary Hydrocarbon Deposits, 3 October 2011, 2888 UNTS 13. This agreement outlines the provisions to be included in any unitisation agreement between the two states (art 2.3 and art 3).

e. *Eritrea v Yemen*

Unlike the Conciliation Commission in *Iceland v Norway*, the jurisdiction of the Tribunal in *Eritrea v Yemen* was broadly defined: to render an award on maritime delimitation in accordance with international law.[411] While the Tribunal's award was confined to an all-purpose single boundary,[412] its statements on the impact of this boundary on existing and future petroleum offshore contracts are novel.[413] To begin with, the statements are not part of the *dispositif* of the case, yet they speak of the parties being 'bound to inform one another and to consult one another on any oil and gas and other mineral resources that may be discovered that straddle the single maritime boundary between them or that lie its immediate vicinity'.[414] The Tribunal noted that, 30 years since the views in the *North Sea Cases* on unity of deposit, 'there has grown up a significant body of cooperative State practice in the exploitation of resources that straddle maritime boundaries'.[415] Unity of deposit is all the more appropriate in the Red Sea, a semi-enclosed narrow body of water bordered by the parties, whose peoples have 'a common rule as well as a common religion'.[416]

The foregoing statements prompted Reisman to comment that the Tribunal in *Eritrea v Yemen* seems to have 'inferred an obligation-based on historical connections, friendly relations, and state practice'.[417] Indeed, the Tribunal concluded that there was a significant body of state practice on unity of deposit merely on the basis of the views of some experts, such as Hazel Fox, while ignoring the contrary views of other experts.[418] Moreover, far from stating that there is customary law, Fox et al had concluded that there were yet no customary rules on shared resources, and that the parties must adopt rules by way of special agreement.[419]

[411] *Eritrea v Yemen* (n 292) para 6.

[412] ibid ch VI.

[413] ibid ch III.

[414] ibid para 86.

[415] ibid para 84. The Tribunal cited Fox (n 23); and M Miyoshi, *The Joint Development of Offshore Oil and Gas in Relation to the Maritime Boundary Delimitations* (Durham, International Boundaries Research Unit, 1999).

[416] *Eritrea v Yemen* (n 292) para 85.

[417] W Reisman, 'Eritrea-Yemen Arbitration (Award, Phase II: Maritime Delimitation)' (2000) 94 *American Journal of International Law* 721, 723.

[418] See I Brownlie, 'Legal Status of Natural Resources in International Law (Some Aspects)' (1979) 162 *Recueil des Cour* 289; Bundy (n 361) 39. Bundy agrees that there is customary rule on negotiation and consultation in relation to a shared resource, but not on unitisation or joint development. See also I Townsend-Gault and W Stormont, 'Offshore Petroleum Joint Development Arrangements: Functional Instrument? Compromise? Obligation?' in Blake (n 361) 53, 58. See also S Vinogradov, 'The Legal Status of the Caspian Sea and its Hydrocarbon Resources' in G Blake, M Pratt, C Schofield and J Brown (ed), *Boundaries and Energy: Problems and Prospects* (New York, Kluwer, 1998), 146.

[419] Fox (n 23) 35.

Eritrea and Yemen have not reached a formal cooperation agreement.[420] Nonetheless, Eritrea revised its petroleum regulation to authorise its energy ministry to make decisions on international unitisation,[421] while Yemen has not adopted a similar regulation.[422]

f. *Guyana v Suriname*

In *Guyana v Suriname*, Suriname accused Guyana of breaching its obligation under UNCLOS 'by authorizing its concession holder to drill an exploratory well in a known disputed maritime area'.[423] Articles 74(3) and 83(3) of UNCLOS provide that the parties to a maritime dispute shall 'make every effort to enter into provisional arrangements of a practical nature' and to 'not … jeopardize or hamper the reaching of a final agreement'. The question was whether these provisions imposed an obligation to refrain from issuing petroleum concessions and conducting exploratory surveys.

The Tribunal declared that the purpose of Articles 74(3) and 83(3) is to 'pave the way for provisional utilization of disputed areas pending delimitation so as to avoid the suspension of economic development in a disputed maritime area'.[424] In light of this purpose, the provisions impose an obligation to negotiate a provisional arrangement in good faith, such as international unitisation or joint development.[425] At the same time, they do not impose an obligation to refrain from 'acts which, although unilateral, would not have the effect of jeopardizing or hampering the reaching of a final agreement on the delimitation of the maritime boundary'.[426] The Tribunal held that both unilateral activities and activities based on consent are permissible:

> The Tribunal is of the view that unilateral acts which do not cause a physical change to the marine environment would generally fall into the second class. However, acts that do cause physical change would have to be undertaken pursuant to an agreement

[420] In 2014, the countries' energy ministries were reportedly in talks on a mode of cooperation in oil and gas exploration and production in the Red Sea. See 'Yemen, Eritrea Seek to Boost Oil, Minerals Cooperation', *Yemen News Agency (SABA)*, 26 September 2014, sabanews.net/en/news369639.htm.

[421] Article 27 of Legal Notice No 45/2000, Revised Regulations on Petroleum Operations, extwprlegs1.fao.org/docs/pdf/eri203351.pdf.

[422] Unlike other countries that have adopted a general legal framework for petroleum activities, Yemen authorises its energy ministry to enter into production sharing agreements which are then ratified into law by the legislature. See, for example, art 33 of the Production Sharing Agreement between Ministry of Oil and Mineral Resources and Occidental of Yemen (Block 75) et al, 31 May 2007, resourcecontracts.org/contract/ocds-591adf-0281884724/view#. In 2010, Yemen passed a new mining law applicable to the continental shelf and the exclusive economic zone. The law does not contain a provision on unitisation. See Law No (22) of 21 November 2010 Concerning Mines & Quarries, extwprlegs1.fao.org/docs/pdf/yem185121E.pdf.

[423] *Guyana v Suriname* (n 115) para 161 (2c).

[424] ibid paras 460–61.

[425] ibid para 462–64.

[426] ibid para 466.

> between the parties to be permissible, as they may hamper or jeopardise the reaching of a final agreement on delimitation. A distinction is therefore to be made between activities of the kind that lead to a permanent physical change, such as exploitation of oil and gas reserves, and those that do not, such as seismic exploration.[427]

The Tribunal declared that the foregoing definition of state obligations under UNCLOS is based on 'the jurisprudence of international courts and tribunals on interim measures … [specifically the] ICJ's decision in the Aegean Sea case between Greece and Turkey'.[428] Yet, in the *Agean Sea Continental Shelf Cases*,[429] the ICJ decision was based on Article 41 of the ICJ Statute on irreparable damage, not UNCLOS, and the ground for denial of an interim measure was based on the finding that even if Greece suffers some prejudice resulting from unilateral exploration surveys by Turkey, the damage would still be 'capable of reparation' and therefore not irreparable.[430]

Moreover, the interpretation of the Tribunal in *Guyana v Suriname* that Articles 74(3) and 83(3) of UNCLOS contemplate negotiation in good faith for joint exploration and exploitation is far from settled. In *The Philippines v China*, the Tribunal was presented with evidence that the Philippines and China (as well as Vietnam) had adopted a Tripartite Agreement for Joint Marine Seismic Undertaking in the Agreement Area in the South China Sea (JMSU) as a provisional arrangement,[431] but the Philippines withdrew from the arrangement[432] over the protest from China.[433] This tribunal did not address the question of

[427] ibid.

[428] ibid para 468.

[429] *Aegean Sea Continental Shelf, Interim Protection, Order of 11 September 1976* [1976] ICJ Rep 3, para 30.

[430] ibid para 33.

[431] A Tripartite Agreement for Joint Marine Seismic Undertaking in the Agreement Area in the South Sea was signed on 14 March 2005 in Manila, the Philippines, by and among the China National Offshore Oil Corporation (CNOOC), the Vietnam Oil and Gas Corporation (PETROVIETNAM) and the Philippine National Oil Company (PNOC). See mfa.gov.cn/ce/ceph/eng/zt/nhwt/t187333.htm. The parties regarded the joint survey as a provisional arrangement, to wit:

> The three parties affirm that the signing of the Tripartite Agreement will not undermine the basic positions held by their respective Governments on the South China Sea issue and will contribute to the transformation of the South China Sea into an area of peace, stability, cooperation, and development in accordance with the 1982 United Nations Convention on the Law of the Sea and the 2002 ASEAN-China Declaration on the Conduct of Parties in the South China Sea.

In an official statement affirming the Joint Marine Seismic Undertaking, the Chinese Foreign Ministry referred to the agreement as 'an important measure to implement the Declaration on the Conduct of Parties in the South China Sea'. See 'Foreign Ministry Spokesman Liu Jianchao's Comment on the Joint Marine Seismic Undertaking Accord Signed by the Oil Companies of China, Vietnam and the Philippines', 16 March 2005, fmprc.gov.cn/ce/cgit/eng/fyrth/t187607.htm#.

[432] A legislator filed a petition for certiorari docketed as *Bayan Muna Party List vs President Gloria Macapagal-Arroyo et al*, GR No 182734, 21 May 2008. This case has not been resolved.

[433] Foreign Ministry Spokesperson Hua Chunying's Remarks on the Philippines' Statement on the South China Sea, Ministry of Foreign Affairs of the People's Republic of China, fmcoprc.gov.hk/eng/xwdt/wjbt/ t1059343.htm.

whether the Philippine withdrawal from JMSU constituted a violation of its obligation to negotiate a provisional arrangement.[434] Thus, contrary to *Guyana v Suriname*, there is no clear obligatory rule on good faith negotiation for joint exploration or exploitation as a provisional arrangement.

To summarise, the Tribunal in *Guyana v Suriname* did not engage in source-ascertainment; rather, it adopted a method of interpretation using as a reference the purpose of Articles 74(3) and 83(3) of UNCLOS and drawing out the best rule to achieve the purpose. It reinforced this interpretation by citing state practice and 'jurisprudence of international courts and tribunals'.[435]

The Special Chamber of the International Tribunal on Law of the Sea (ITLOS) in *Ghana v Côte D'Ivoire*[436] interpreted Articles 74(3) and 83(3) of UNCLOS in a way that extends the scope of permissible unilateral activities on disputed waters to include any unilateral activity, regardless of nature and extent, performed by a party before 'realizing that that area was also claimed' by another state.[437] The ICJ in *Somalia v Kenya* further expanded the scope of unilateral activities to include even those undertaken after knowledge of an opposing claim, provided 'these activities are not of the kind that could lead to permanent physical change in the marine environment'.[438]

To summarise, in the foregoing cases, international courts and tribunals identified the rules to be applied to disputes over shared resources according to whether there is a bilateral agreement and custom. In the absence of either agreement or custom, they presumed a pre-existing principle, or relied on state practice reinforced by jurisprudence on the usefulness of a particular practice towards attaining the purpose of the regime of the continental shelf and the exclusive economic zone. They circle the wagons by layering upon each other's jurisprudence.

iii. Other Institutions

The tribunals in the *North Sea Cases* and *Eritrea v Yemen* cited the works of Ranier Lagoni et al under the ILA and Hazel Fox et al under the British Institute of International and Comparative Law (BIICL) on the extent of state practice in unitisation and joint development. These authors ascertained whether, with respect to a shared resource, there is: (1) an obligation to refrain from unilateral

[434] PCA Case No 2013-19 In the Matter of the South China Sea Arbitration, 12 July 2016, pcacases.com/web/sendAttach/2086. The Tribunal declared certain unilateral activities of China in the disputed waters as a breach of its substantive obligations under UNCLOS to not pre-empt the outcome of the arbitration (ibid 473–77).

[435] J d'Aspremont, 'The International Court of Justice, the Whales, and the Blurring of the Lines between Sources and Interpretation' (2017) 27 *European Journal of International Law* 1027–41.

[436] *Dispute Concerning Delimitation of the Maritime Boundary between Ghana and Côte d'Ivoire in the Atlantic Ocean (Ghana v Côte d'Ivoire)*, Judgment, 23 September 2017.

[437] ibid para 631.

[438] ibid para 207.

activities; and (2) an obligation to negotiate a cooperation agreement.[439] They examined state practice found in maritime boundary agreements and joint development agreements, and in analogous regimes.[440] They excluded national petroleum laws, regulations and contracts, purportedly due to their lack of relevance to international law.[441]

Lagoni discounts any pre-existing principle imposing on states an obligation to exercise restraint or to negotiate. Such obligation must be set out in a boundary agreement.[442] If the boundary agreement has a unity of deposit clause, this gives rise to the obligation of the parties to notify and inform about any potential or actual shared resource, and to negotiate in good faith with a view to reaching an agreement on the joint exploitation thereof.[443] If there is no unity of deposit clause, customary law imposes the same obligation to inform and negotiate.[444] Indicators of the existence of customary law as a source of the obligation to inform and negotiate are 'the virtually uniform practice of States to include resource deposit clauses, which are of fundamentally norm-creating character, into their delimitation agreements'[445] and *opinio juris*, as evidenced by the incorporation of unity of deposit clauses into boundary agreements.[446] In effect, he engaged in double-counting[447] for the practice of incorporating a unity of deposit clause is also evidence of a conviction that there is an obligation to notify and inform.

Whether or not the boundary agreement has a unity of deposit clause, there are substantive norms that can be derived from *sic utere tuo ut alienum non laedas* or the no-harm principle.[448] Lagoni deduced this principle from UNCLOS, specifically the provisions recognising that a coastal state has equal and exclusive sovereign rights to exploit the resources on the seabed that are found on its side of a maritime boundary. He interpreted these provisions to mean that sovereign rights of a coastal state shall not be interfered with by another state. These sovereign rights are violated when an opposite or adjacent state uses directional or

[439] ILA (n 23) 530–48. For Lagoni, unitisation and joint development are only one of several kinds of provisional measures. Another kind of provisional measure is unilateral – ie, states unilaterally desist from issuing new exploration or production licences in areas of overlapping claims or suspend existing licences or concessions. As regards the relevance of the presence of resources in the process of delimitation, only identified or identifiable and commercially significant resources are legally relevant.

[440] ibid 510.

[441] ibid 512, 559. According to Lagoni, 'the contractual relations of the natural or juridical persons involved in the operations' have no international law content (ibid 559). See also Fox (n 23) 53–70.

[442] ibid 530–33.

[443] ibid 533.

[444] ibid 538.

[445] ibid

[446] ibid. Lagoni also cited analogous practice in other kinds of transboundary resources. See ILA (n 23) 544–45.

[447] ILC (n 9) Conclusion No 3.

[448] ILA (n 23) 530–33.

horizontal drilling and pierces the defined boundary.[449] In contrast, these rights are not violated if the opposite or adjacent state drills into a shared resource without piercing the defined boundary, unless such activity causes a reduction in the portion of the resource that is found on the side of the other state.[450] In sum, there is no positive obligation to engage in joint exploitation, but there is an obligation not to cause harm.

The foregoing obligations bind contractors/operators as non-state actors, in that their activities would engage the host state's international responsibility for allowing its continental shelf and the exclusive economic zone or territory to be used in a manner that harms the sovereign rights of another state.[451]

Fox et al did not identify legal rules or trace their genealogy, but rather formulated model provisions for states to be incorporated into their joint development agreement.[452] Their methodology consisted of deriving model provisions from existing joint development and other cooperation agreements[453] and from the views of experts.[454] They also referred to agreements on subject matters other than oil and gas, such as the Moon Treaty.[455]

Fox et al proposed an international unitisation clause that authorises contractors/operators to agree on a unit development plan applicable either within the joint development zone or across the boundary between the zone and the continental shelf and the exclusive economic zone of one party.[456] This particular provision seems to be based on custom. Fox et al characterise the previous industry practice in unitisation as a mere pragmatic response to the rule of capture rather than a requirement of law.[457] Sole-country unitisation is mandatory in

[449] ibid 530–31.
[450] ibid 531.
[451] ibid 538–39.
[452] Fox (n 23) 10–12.
[453] ibid ch 2.
[454] H Fox (ed), *Joint Development of Oil and Gas*, vol II (London, British Institute of International and Comparative Law, 1990) pt II.
[455] Fox (n 23) 87–110.
[456] The model clause reads as follows:

> Art 18. (1) If any single geological petroleum structure or petroleum field extends across any dividing line, not being one covered by paragraph 2 below, the States Parties shall consult together in accordance with articles 23 and 24 as appropriate. (2) If any single geological petroleum structure or petroleum field extends across the dividing line between any development or contract areas within the Zone or across the dividing line between the Zone and any undisputed exclusive maritime area of one of the States Parties, and the part of such structure or field which Is situated on one side of the said dividing line is exploitable, wholly or in part, from the other side of the said dividing line, the States Parties shall, on failure of the contractors (if any) to agree among themselves, seek to reach agreement as to the manner in which the structure or field shall be most effectively exploited and the manner in which the proceeds deriving therefrom shall be apportioned.

See Fox (n 442) 17.
[457] Fox (n 23) 320–21.

most petroleum jurisdictions,[458] while international or cross-border unitisation is mandated in some maritime boundary agreements and joint development agreements.[459] These authors agree with Lagoni et al that state practice indicates the existence of a customary procedural rule to notify and inform and to negotiate in good faith.[460] They also cite analogous state practice – in the form of agreements on the joint exploitation of fisheries and other common resources, including those in the international seabed, the Arctic, the Antarctic and the Moon[461] – but they do not justify the transposition of such regime of common goods/resources to oil and gas, which is held by individual sovereign states under their exclusive sovereign rights.

Fox et al maintain that 'there is at present no clear rule of customary law which requires a State to inform and consult' in relation to a shared resource in a disputed area.[462] They arrived at this conclusion because of the conflicting views of experts[463] rather than on the basis of their independent assessment of existing indicators, particularly in the light of their transposition of the regime of common goods to the regime of oil and gas.

The Association of International Petroleum Negotiators (AIPN) through Bastida et al examined the contractual, national and international regimes that apply to shared resources[464] but limited their question to whether, in the absence of a treaty source, customary law and general principles are a source of rules on shared resources.[465] They referred to various joint development agreements, international unitisation agreements between states as well as those between contractors, and framework unitisation agreements, covering the period from 1976 to 2005,[466] but did not make an independent assessment of the significance of these agreements as source of rules. Rather, they relied on the views rendered by other authors 10–20 years ago and reiterated the latter's conclusion that there is no existing customary law or general principles of law that can serve as the source of rules.[467] They characterised existing practices as a mere trend

[458] ibid.

[459] H Fox, 'Summary of Conference Discussions and the Research Team's Response' in Fox (n 442) 27; Fox (n 23) 33-34, 61, 322. See, for example, art 4 of the Convention on the Delimitation of the Continental Shelves of the Two States in the Bay of Biscay, 5 April 1975, 996 UNTS 344 (1976).

[460] Fox (n 23) 33.

[461] ibid 87–110.

[462] ibid 35.

[463] ibid 34–35, citing Onorato (n 256) 85, 101; W Onorato, 'A Case Study on Joint Development: The Saudi Arabia/Kuwait Partitioned Neutral Zone' (1985) 10 *Energy* 539, 541; and M Miyoshi, 'The Basic Concept of Joint Development of Hydrocarbon Resources on the Continental Shelf'' (1988) 3 *International Journal of Estuarine and Coastal Law* 10–11.

[464] Weaver et al (n 361) 9; Bastida et al (n 361). The two studies were later consolidated and published as J Weaver, D Asmus, E Bastida, J Ross, S Mahmud and T Wälde, 'International Unitisation of Oil and Gas Fields: The Legal Framework of International Law, National Laws, and Private Contracts – AIPN' (2007) 5 *Oil, Gas and Energy Law* 2,

[465] Asmus et al, ibid 375.

[466] ibid 379–80, 391–420.

[467] ibid 380–81, 420–21.

that states and petroleum corporations regard unitisation as a pragmatic and rational mode of exploitation.[468]

The views of the individual experts who were cited by Bastida et al will be discussed next. In general, they focused on the existence of customary law as source of rules on shared resources. Although the majority relied on the criteria of state consent/intent, the pioneering author William Onorato adopted the criteria of substantive validity and effectiveness.

C. The Efforts of Scholars to Identify International Law on Shared Resources

At around the same time that the ILC Secretariat proposed the incorporation of a principle of unity of deposit into the regime of the continental shelf, Hersch Lauterpacht wrote that, with respect to 'pools of deposits situated across the surface boundaries of [their] respective submarine areas', there is a general principle requiring states to respect perimeter zones and cooperate in the exploitation of the common pool.[469] He referred to it as 'limiting principles … that there must be no deliberate waste to the injury of the neighbor and that the owner must not wantonly perform acts injurious to the common reservoir or calculated to destroy it'.[470] He identified this general principle based on its local application by administrative agencies and domestic courts, as well as its laudable purpose of resource conservation for the next generation. This purpose of the regime is consistent with its original conceptualisation by the US when it claimed jurisdiction over the continental shelf in order to address the 'phenomenon of common pools independent of political boundaries'.[471] Hugh Waldock agreed that the Truman Proclamation was 'intended to protect resources within the United States which might be tapped from the high seas'.[472]

In contrast to Lauterpacht, Juraj Andrassy found no pre-existing principle or customary law restraining sovereign states from the unilateral exploitation of a shared resource.[473] Prior discovery and drilling by one state cannot prevent the other state from tapping into the same structure, even if this would lead to

[468] ibid 421–22. It cited Ong (n 256) 771; and I Gault, 'Petroleum Development Offshore: Legal and Contractual Issues' in N Beredjick, T Wälde and I Townsend Gault (eds), *Petroleum Investment Policies in Developing Countries* (New York, Kluwer, 1988).

[469] H Lauterpacht (1950), 'Sovereignty over Submarine Areas' 27 *British Yearbook of International Law* 376, 410.

[470] H Lauterpacht, *International Law* (Cambridge, Cambridge University Press, 1977) vol III, pt 2-6, fn 1, 180.

[471] Lauterpacht (n 459).

[472] See H Waldock, 'The Legal Basis of Claims to the Continental Shelf' (1950) 36 *Transactions of the Grotius Society* 124.

[473] J Andrassy, 'Le Droit International de Voisinage', 79 *Collected Courses of The Hague Academy of International Law* (Leiden, Brill, 1951), 27.

conflict and wastage.[474] Andrassy suggested that competing states should agree on some form of collaboration or sharing quota.[475]

In 1968, Onorato drew attention to the need to ascertain sources of rules governing shared resources.[476] Noting the lack of treaty and customary law sources,[477] he turned to general principles of law[478] as defined by national laws and court cases on the sole-country unitisation of oil and gas,[479] as well as analogous practices in inter-state cooperative exploitation of common resources such as fisheries.[480] From the foregoing sources, he derived the rules that: (1) a shared resource is under the joint ownership of the superjacent states; (2) cooperative development of the resource is required; (3) the international rule of capture is prohibited;[481] and (4) the presence of the resource and the necessity to exploit it as a single unit does not constitute a special circumstance that would cause the maritime boundary to be drawn in such a way as to ascribe the resource to the ownership of a single state.[482] He concluded that international tribunals would be able to discern a 'rule of law requiring co-operative development of an international petroleum deposit' from 'municipal petroleum practice and from custom and practice in international apportionment of analogous resources as well as the sparse actual practice on [shared resources]'.[483]

Ten years later, Onorato would reiterate that there is a body of procedural and substantive rules[484] on shared resources and that these can be drawn from the municipal laws of oil-producing nations relating to apportionment of common petroleum deposits with particular reference to the established principle of 'unitisation' or 'unit production'; provisions of international law relating to apportionment of international common natural resources having physical properties analogous to those of petroleum; and principles and rules on the apportionment of international common petroleum deposits emerging from existing state practice which might be considered 'general practices accepted as law' on the question or which reflect the *opinio juris* in the matter of apportionment.[485]

[474] ibid.

[475] ibid.

[476] Onorato (n 256) 85, 88–89.

[477] ibid 89.

[478] ibid.

[479] ibid 89–93.

[480] ibid 93–97. Another author transposed the legal regime of international rivers to oil and gas. See A Utton, 'Institutional Arrangements for Developing North Sea Oil and Gas' (1968) 9 *Virginia Journal of International Law* 68–69.

[481] Onorato (n 256) 101.

[482] ibid 86–87.

[483] ibid 100–01.

[484] Onorato (n 256) 325–28. See also W Onorato, 'Joint Development of Hydrocarbon Resources: An Overview of Precedents in the North Sea' (1981) 6 *Energy* 1311; W Onorato, 'A Case Study in Joint Development: The Saudi Arabia-Kuwait Partitioned Neutral Zone' (1985) 10 *Energy* 539; I Shihata and W Onorato, 'The Joint Development of International Petroleum Resources in Undefined and Disputed Areas' (1996) 11 *ICSID Review* 299.

[485] ibid 328.

A contemporary work by Joseph Morris reached the opposite conclusion: in the North Sea, the rule of capture, which countenances unilateral activities, prevails because it is based on leading municipal case law in both civil and common law systems.[486] There are domestic conservation regulations under which 'voluntary conservation practices are encouraged … failing which, the state has the power to require compliance with a development scheme which must be fair and equitable to all licensees'. However, the transposition of these conservation practices to the inter-state level requires an international agreement. It presupposes 'that part of the oil field is on one side and part is on the other side of the median line'. This can be ascertained only 'if commercial wells are drilled on both sides of the median line … otherwise the rule of capture will apply'.[487] If only one state is engaged in petroleum activities on one side of the medial line, the other state would be in no position to complain, even if those activities might cause the migration of resources across the median line.

Other authors have disagreed with Onorato's finding of a general customary rule on joint exploitation, but in identifying the rules applicable to shared resources, they have also relapsed into deformalisation. One group maintains that there is a customary rule, but only of notification, consultation and negotiation on joint exploitation of a shared resource, and that such a procedural rule serves as a prior restraint on unilateral exploitation.[488] Another group denies that there is a customary procedural or substantive rule. Any prior restraint on the sovereign rights of a state to exploit its resource must be based on agreement.[489]

Masahiro Miyoshi identified custom as a source of the obligation to inform and negotiate by reference to the views of other commentators[490] and by interpretation of the intention behind the requirements of UNCLOS to adopt provisional measures and the scope of the concept of sovereign rights under the law of the sea conventions.[491]

[486] Morris (n 380) 205–10. Vasco Becker-Weinberg discounts regional custom as a source of restraints on states in the exercise of sovereign rights over a shared resource. See Becker-Weinberg (n 288).

[487] ibid 211–13.

[488] See R Lagoni, 'Oil and Gas Deposits across National Frontiers' (1979) 73 *American Journal of International Law* 2, 215; Ong (n 256) 795; Miyoshi (n 453) 18; Roughton (n 256) 374.

[489] Daintith (n 289) 370–72, 394, 433; P Cameron, 'The Rules of Engagement: Developing Cross-border Petroleum Deposits in the North Sea and the Caribbean' (2006) 55 *International and Comparative Law Quarterly* 559–85; P Cameron, 'Cross-border Unitisation in the North Sea' (2007) 5 *Oil Gas & Energy Law* 2, 9–11; P Blyschak, 'Offshore Oil and Gas Projects amid Maritime Border Disputes: Applicable Law' (2013) 6 *Journal of World Energy Law & Business* 226. See also Special Unit for South-South Cooperation United Nations Development Programme, *Effective Hydrocarbon Management: Lessons from the South* (New York, United Nations Development Program, 2009) 30.

[490] Miyoshi (n 403) 4. In an earlier publication, Miyoshi reported that at the conclusion of an international workshop among experts, it was summarised that there is 'no international rule of capture … [as] nations … have duties: a) to consult with each other; b) to share information about the resources; c) to negotiate in good faith to reach an equitable agreement on the sharing of these resources; and d) to refrain from taking resources clearly within the other nation's jurisdiction'. See Miyoshi (n 453) Appendix 3, 18.

[491] Miyoshi (n 403) 5.

David Ong, on the other hand, inferred the existence of a primary customary rule not to engage in international rule of capture, and a corollary rule to inform and negotiate on joint exploitation[492] from the following circumstances: (1) the absence of any provision in the law of the sea conventions that authorises unilateral exploitation;[493] (2) the rejection of unilateralism by states that practise joint development;[494] and (3) the authoritative opinions of other commentators.[495] He applied by analogy UN General Assembly resolutions on the protection of the environment surrounding certain global commons.[496] In a subsequent publication, he clarified that the obligation to inform and negotiate arises from a soft law source formed by UN General Assembly resolutions on the analogous topic of human rights and the environment.[497]

Scholars in the field of natural resources and energy law also addressed the question of international law governing disputes over shared resources. The writers in these fields are divided between those who maintain that the rule of capture is the prevailing norm and those who assert that there is an existing obligation to negotiate and cooperate.

For Terence Daintith, the general rule is that coastal states have the right to engage in the unilateral exploitation of a shared resource. He based this view on: (1) the statements of the Tribunal in *Guyana v Suriname* that unilateral drilling is legitimate;[498] (2) an interpretation of the scope of sovereign rights under UNCLOS;[499] and (3) actual practice among major oil producers, such as France and the US.[500]

Daintith may have overlooked the fact that while Suriname's petroleum instruments are silent on the status of shared resources,[501] Guyana's petroleum

[492] Ong (n 256) 777–78.

[493] ibid 777.

[494] ibid 778.

[495] ibid.

[496] ibid 777, 781, citing UN GA Resolution No 3129 (XXVJIJ). Co-operation in the Field of the Environment Concerning Natural Resources Shared by Two or More States, 13 December 1973. It reads as follows:

1. *Considers* that it is necessary to ensure effective co-operation between countries through the establishment of adequate international standards for the conservation and harmonious exploitation of natural resources common to two or more States in the context of the normal relations existing between them;
2. *Considers further* that co-operation between countries sharing such natural resources and interested in their exploitation must be developed on the basis of a system of information and prior consultation within the framework of the normal relations existing between them.

[497] D Ong, 'South-East Asian State Practice on the Joint Development of Offshore Oil and Gas Deposits' in Blake (n 361) 92.

[498] Daintith (n 289) 433–34.

[499] ibid.

[500] ibid 398–400.

[501] See art 9.9 of the Production Sharing Contract for Petroleum Exploration, Development and Production relating to Block 45 Offshore Suriname between STAATSOLIE MAATSCHAPPIJ SURINAME NV (hereinafter referred to as 'Staatsolie') and Kosmos Energy Surinam, 13 December 2011, sec.gov/Archives/edgar/data/1509991/000110465913080961/a13-19720_1ex10d21.htm.

law adopts international unitisation, even as its contracts reiterate Guyana's ownership of disputed resources.[502] Moreover, France's 1974 boundary agreement with Spain includes a standard unity of deposit clause, with a right to compensation in the event that the parties or their contractors are shown to have drained part of a shared resource.[503] A similar agreement on compensation can be found in the boundary agreements of Greece with Albania[504] and Italy.[505] In providing for compensation, the parties clearly do not countenance the rule of capture along their boundary. Moreover, as discussed earlier, notwithstanding practice in the rule of capture onshore, the US issued the Truman Proclamation as a measure of self-protection against the rule of capture in the international context.[506]

The International Boundaries Research Unit (Durham University) published *The Peaceful Management of Transboundary Resources* (1995), in which two chapters addressed the question on the sources of international law applicable to shared resources within either a disputed area or a delimited area.[507] Rodman Bundy argues that there is a prevailing international rule of capture, and relies on the practice of Iran and the United Arab Emirates (UAE).[508] The Sassan or Abu Al Bu Khoosh-ABK field straddles the maritime boundary of these two countries[509] and has been exploited separately by them. When armed conflicts forced Iran to suspend operations,[510] the UAE continued operations and experienced a surge in production due to the substantial migration of oil from the

[502] Under art 31.1 of its contracts, Guyana reiterates its ownership of petroleum resources in disputed areas. See Ratio Energy Limited, Ratio Guyana Limited, Kaieteur Block, PSA, 2015, resourcecontracts.org/contract/ocds-591adf-2701587320/view#/pdf; and Tullow Guyana BV, Eco Oil and Gas Limited, Orinduik Block, PSA, 2016, resourcecontracts.org/contract/ocds-591adf-2603001790/view#/pdf.

[503] Article 4 of the France-Spain Convention on the Delimitation of the Continental Shelves of the Two States in the Bay of Biscay (n 461). See also art 3 of the Agreement between the Government of the French Republic and the Government of the Italian Republic regarding the Delimitation of the Territorial Seas and Zones under National Jurisdiction between France and Italy (signed 21 March 2015), Lathrop (n 23) 11. Article 3 holds the state/contractor engaging in the rule of capture liable for compensation to the other state/contractor. Although the settlement/enforcement mechanism is not defined, this provision on compensation indicates that the parties object to the rule of capture.

[504] Article 3 of the Agreement between the Hellenic Republic and the Republic of Albania on the Delimitation of Their Respective Continental Shelf Areas and Other Maritime Zones to Which They are Entitled under International Law, signed 27 April 2009, Lathrop (n 23) 4470.

[505] Article 2 of the Agreement between the Hellenic Republic and the Italian Republic on the Delimitation of the Zones of the Continental Shelf Belonging to each of the Two States, 12 November 1980, Lathrop (n 23) 1598.

[506] See Memorandum of Conversation by Mr Eugene H Dooman, Special Assistant to the Assistant Secretary of State (Dunn), 12 May 1945, in Formulation of United States Policy on the Resources of the Continental Shelf (n 18) 1505; Memorandum by Mr Eugene H Dooman, 15 June 1945, ibid 1511.

[507] Bundy (n 361) 23.

[508] ibid 24–25.

[509] Offshore Boundary Agreement between Iran and (UAE) Dubai, signed 31 August 1974, Lathrop (n 23) 1538. Article 2 is the standard provision on shared resources with a clause establishing a protective perimeter.

[510] Bundy (n 361) 24.

dormant side of Iran.[511] For Bundy, the UAE was justified in draining oil from Iran's side under the prevailing international rule of capture.[512]

The international rule of capture arises from several sources, which Bundy identified using the device of assertion, interpretation and analogy. He identified a customary law source by the mere assertion that 'the exploitation of international oil and gas reserves … [is] based … on the law of capture'.[513] Treaty sources are identified by the interpretation of the text of the boundary agreement of the two countries.[514] According to Bundy, Iran and the UAE adopted the provision that neither shall drill within a 125-kilometre protective perimeter from their boundary and that both shall endeavour to reach agreement on the exploitation of Sassan.[515] Bundy interpreted these provisions to mean that:

> [T]he parties had absolutely no obligation to reach agreement or to coordinate production; they only had to endeavour to do so … [and in] practice, only a modest amount of co-ordination was achieved … [through] a joint committee … established primarily as a conduit for the exchange of technical information relating to the field.[516]

Bundy acknowledged that there is a customary duty to inform and negotiate, it arises mainly from joint development agreements or, at the very least, from a soft law regime created by UN General Assembly resolutions on the environment as a common good.[517]

The foregoing interpretation of boundary agreements appears counter-intuitive, as it could also be argued, as Lagoni did in the previous section, that the incorporation of resource clauses, as opposed to their general absence in past boundary agreements, indicates that the parties do not countenance unilateral exploitation. Iran's boundary agreements with Bahrain, Oman and Qatar provide for both resource cooperation and a protective perimeter.[518] The boundary agreement of Iran with Bahrain expressly prohibits directional drilling.[519] Similarly, Iran's exclusive economic zone boundary agreement with Oman

[511] ibid.
[512] ibid.
[513] ibid.
[514] ibid 24–26.
[515] Offshore Boundary Agreement between Iran and UAE (n 499).
[516] Bundy (n 361) 26.
[517] ibid 28–38.
[518] Article 2 of the Agreement Concerning Delimitation of the Continental Shelf between Iran and Bahrain, 14 May 1972, 826 UNTS 234; art 2 of the Offshore Boundary Agreement between Iran and (UAE) Dubai (n 499); arts 4 and 5 of the Agreement on the Delimitation of the Maritime Boundary in the Sea of Oman between the Islamic Republic of Iran and the Sultanate of Oman (with chart), 16 September 2016, Reg No 54173; art 2 of the Agreement Concerning Delimitation of the Continental Shelf between Iran and Oman, 28 May 1975, 972 UNTS 265; art 2 of the Agreement concerning the Boundary Line Dividing the Continental Shelf between Iran and Qatar, 10 May 1970, Lathrop (n 23) 1516.
[519] Agreement Concerning Delimitation of the Continental Shelf between Iran and Bahrain, ibid.

provides that they shall notify each other regarding any petroleum activity within 250 metres of their boundary, and if the activity involves drilling a well, the same shall be solely exploratory.[520] While Iran's 1969 boundary agreement and exchange of letters with Saudi Arabia do not contain a shared resource clause, they prohibit oil and gas drilling using an installation within 500 metres of the boundary, as well as directional drilling outside the boundary, except upon mutual consent and after exchange of information.[521] The boundary agreement between Argentina and Uruguay allows unilateral petroleum activities, provided the parties agree to a proportionate sharing and avoid 'causing appreciable damage' to each other.[522] The agreement between the Netherlands and Denmark is slightly different, as it does not countenance unilateral activities; rather, they must negotiate on the location of installations, structures and drilling sites along their boundary.[523]

Richard Barnes asserts the opposite: there is no international rule of capture;[524] instead, there is an obligation to cooperate.[525] However, there is no obligation to adopt a certain nature and extent of cooperation, such as a joint property regime,[526] although 'international law strongly urges this' because of the 'physical nature of the resource' and 'the fact that cooperation is a more stable and proper means of regulating a resource'.[527] Barnes reinforces the views of experts with an interpretation that UNCLOS 'prohibits the coastal state from exercising any rights over the continental shelf in such a way that infringes or constitutes an unjustifiable interference with … the rights … of other States'.[528]

Peter Cameron takes the middle ground in finding only a soft law regime consisting of rules of engagement rather than procedural and substantive rules in relation to a shared resource.[529] There rules of engagement stem from what he calls a 'relevant principle of international law' of cooperation.[530] This principle is formed by UN General Assembly resolutions, bilateral agreements, international judicial decisions and the views of experts.[531] The principle requires states

[520] Article 4 of the Agreement on the Delimitation of the Maritime Boundary in the Sea of Oman (n 507).

[521] Article 4 of the Agreement Concerning Sovereignty Over Al-'Arabiyah and Farsi Islands and Delimitation Of Boundary Line Separating Submarine Areas between the Kingdom of Saudi Arabia and Iran; Exchange of Letters, 24 October 1968, 696 UNTS 195.

[522] Article 71 of the Agreement between the Government of Argentina and the Government of Uruguay relating to the Delimitation of the River Plate and the Maritime Boundary between Argentina and Uruguay, 12 February 1974, 1295 UNTS 293.

[523] Article 2 of the Agreement between the Government of the Kingdom of the Netherlands and the Government of the Kingdom of Denmark concerning the Delimitation of the Continental Shelf under the North Sea between the Two Countries, 1 August 1967, 604 UNTS 209.

[524] R Barnes, *Property Rights and Natural Resources* (Oxford, Hart Publishing, 2009) 270–82.

[525] ibid 276.

[526] ibid 277.

[527] ibid 281.

[528] ibid 274–75, citing arts 78(2) and 79 of UNCLOS.

[529] Cameron (n 479) 561.

[530] ibid 561–63.

[531] ibid

to consult and negotiate, but does not clearly define the scope and content of such cooperation;[532] it does not compel states to reach a specific type of agreement within a specific period.[533] In the event of a breakdown in negotiations, the parties can either prolong negotiations or engage in unilateral exploitation.[534] Such loose procedures or rules of engagement indicate that the existing state practice 'lack[s] … the psychological or subjective element of acceptance of the specific obligation as binding in law'.[535] This view is similar to that of Thomas Mensah, who considered state practice in joint exploitation to be motivated by pragmatism, in that it enables states to gain economic benefits from a disputed area while negotiating for a more final settlement.[536]

According to Cameron, the foregoing limitations of soft law can be mitigated by the adoption of framework agreements, similar to those that have been adopted in the North Sea, the Gulf of Mexico and the Caribbean Sea. Framework agreements apply to present and future shared resources, thus eliminating the need to negotiate and conclude an agreement each and every time a shared resource is discovered. They incorporate procedural mechanisms and substantive rules regarding the exploitation of a shared resource. They adopt modes of cooperation, including those that directly involve petroleum corporations.[537]

Cameron did not comment on the normative significance of these framework agreements, not even as a model for other states to adopt.[538] He made no comment about their standard provision on the participation of contractors and operators in the formulation of unitisation operating agreements and the simplified system by which these implementing agreements are approved by the respective petroleum agencies of the state parties.[539] In his view, a unitisation or joint development agreements between states are the starting point for resolving disputes over shared resources.[540]

Ernst Smith et al find bilateral joint development agreements to be necessary in order for there to be a joint exploration or exploitation of shared resources.[541] They note that best practices in the petroleum industry merely prescribe

[532] ibid 560.
[533] ibid 564.
[534] ibid 561.
[535] ibid 564.
[536] Mensah (n 288) 150.
[537] Cameron (n 479) 577–83.
[538] Cameron (n 478).
[539] In an earlier book chapter, Cameron agreed with Fox that non-state actors are not a proper subject of international law on shared resources. See P Cameron and R Nowinski, 'Joint Development Agreements: Legal Structure and Key Issues' in R Beckman et al (eds), *Beyond Territorial Disputes in the South China Sea Legal Frameworks for the Joint Development of Hydrocarbon Resources* (Cheltenham, Edward Elgar, 2013) 169–71.
[540] P Cameron and M Stanley, *Oil, Gas and Mining: A Sourcebook for Understanding the Extractive Industry* (New York, World Bank Group, 2017) 135–36.
[541] E Smith et al (eds), *Materials on International Petroleum Transactions* (Colorado, Rocky Mountain Mineral Law Foundation, 1993).

unitisation as a pragmatic arrangement or soft law.[542] Catherine Redgwell and Lavanya Rajamani[543] as well as Claude Duval[544] agree that inter-governmental agreements are the main source of norms.

Others relied on the provisions of UNCLOS and the ruling in *Guyana v Suriname* as the source of rules on shared resources. Tim Martin, for instance, summarised the provisions of UNCLOS that implicate oil and gas activities on the continental shelf[545] and concluded that, with respect to shared resources, the only source of rules are bilateral joint development and unitisation agreements.[546] With respect to petroleum corporations, they have no standing to directly challenge the claim of a foreign state or the latter's contractors to the same resource; their protection lies only in the terms of their contracts with the host state, such as by way of expanding the scope of *force majeure*,[547] similar to the provision found in the model contract of Qatar.[548] He suggested that petroleum corporations should protect themselves from resource disputes by ensuring that their respective host states issue 'matching concessions' in favour of a single operator or contractor.[549] Marianthi Pappa also inquired into the rights and obligations petroleum corporations operating in contested waters. He argues that, being non-state actors, petroleum corporations are not subject to Articles 74(3) and 83(3) of UNCLOS, as interpreted in *Guyana v Suriname*;[550] they are governed only by domestic law.[551] Thus, they 'cannot be held liable for breaching international law of the sea when operating in contested waters' and they have no legal recourse if their licence is cancelled by their respective host states should they opt to negotiate for cooperation.[552] In contrast, Paul Blyschak found bilateral joint development and unitisation agreements to be a source of the rights and obligations of petroleum corporations.[553] Bastida (AIPN) agrees that there is trans-nationalisation of the concept of sole-country unitisation in that, while

[542] ibid 271.

[543] Redgwell and Rajamani (n 289) 107–08, 118–19.

[544] C Duval, H Le Leuch, A Pertuzio and J Weaver, *International Petroleum Exploration and Exploitation Agreements: Legal, Economic and Policy Aspects* (New York, Barrows, 2009) 207.

[545] T Martin, 'Energy and International Boundaries' in K Talus (ed), *Research Handbook on International Energy Law* (Cheltenham, Edward Elgar, 2014) 181–87.

[546] ibid 188–90.

[547] ibid 194–95.

[548] Article 37 of the Model Development & Production Sharing Agreement of 2002 between the Government of Qatar and Contractor (North Field), *Barrows* ME, Supplement No 155. Article 37 provides that where the operations of a contractor 'will result in a dispute over a boundary line with a neighbouring state or states, the GOVERNMENT may set limits on the conduct of the Petroleum Operations … If the GOVERNMENT should set limits on the area of operations … the CONTRACTOR shall have full recourse to the provisions of Force Majeure'.

[549] T Martin, 'Dispute Resolution in the International Energy Sector: An Overview' (2011) 4 *Journal of World Energy Law & Business* 356.

[550] M Pappa, 'Private Oil Companies Operating in Contested Waters and International Law of the Sea: A Peculiar Relationship' (2018) 16 *Oil, Gas & Energy Law* 10–21.

[551] ibid 24.

[552] ibid 24–26.

[553] Blyschak (n 478) 222–23.

originating in the US, it is now being practised in other parts of the world[554] and even in situations involving shared resources of sovereign states.[555] She refers to these developments as a mere 'trend towards an international consensus on an acceptable practice'.[556]

Another group of authors looked beyond UNCLOS and bilateral agreements. For Alex Wawryk, through trans-nationalisation, domestic legal principles on sole-country unitisation[557] are now part of international energy law, which is identified as follows:

> It encompasses a concept of international governance and regulation that is broader than that of traditional international law, being a conglomeration of, and complex interaction between, the rules of custom, treaties, national and regional laws, the principles of intergovernmental organizations (IGOs) and non-government organizations (NGOs) and codes of conduct and guidelines of industry associations, which together regulate the various facets of oil exploration, production, transport, consumption and trade a number of broad and disparate sources of principles and norms that regulate the allocation of rights and duties concerning the exploitation of petroleum resources between individuals, between individuals and governments, and between states ... [and] encompasses a concept of international governance and regulation that is broader than that of traditional international law.[558]

Highet Keith cast a wider net and identified 'analogous' conventions, such as on straddling fish stocks and the international seabed as the common heritage of humankind as a source of norms.[559]

Finally, Sanchez and Mclaughlin acknowledge that the US-Mexico transboundary framework agreement contains a resolutory provision under which the parties may engage in unilateral exploitation if no field unitisation is agreed upon within a fixed period.[560] Nonetheless, even with the lack of express provisions in UNCLOS[561] and the absence of customary law,[562] the parties have

[554] Bastida et al (n 361) 420.

[555] ibid.

[556] ibid. Timothy Tyler et al finds that the transnationalisation of petroleum laws on unitisation, such as through its incorporation in model contracts, does not create rights and obligations. These model contracts are merely a guide in transboundary negotiations. See T Tyler et al, 'Developing Arctic Hydrocarbon Resources: Delineating and Delimiting Boundaries for Field Development in the Arctic' in M Nordquist, J Norton Moore, A Chircop and R Long (eds), *The Regulation of Continental Shelf Development: Rethinking International Standards* (Dordrecht, Martinus Nijhoff, 2013) 344–48.

[557] A Wawryk, 'Petroleum Regulation in an International Context: The Universality of Petroleum Regulation and the Concept of *Lex Petrolea*' in Hunter (n 29) 14.

[558] ibid 6.

[559] H Keith, 'Conflict Avoidance through Prior Agreement: Offshore Delimitation Agreements, Offshore/Onshore Unitization and/or Joint Development Agreements' (1996) 11 *ICSID Review-Foreign Investment Law Journal* 292–94. Keith saw the usefulness of petroleum instruments to pre-empt disputes over access to shared resources.

[560] Sanchez and Mclaughlin (n 359) 683.

[561] ibid 700–05.

[562] ibid 721–26

an obligation to exercise restraint based on the history of economic cooperation between Mexico and the US.[563]

III. CHAPTER SUMMARY

This chapter has demonstrated that since 1950, the identification of international law on shared resources has been characterised by deformalisation. Source-ascertainment is substituted with other devices. Through textual interpretation, rules are extrapolated from the provisions of UNCLOS, bilateral boundary agreements as well as agreements involving other natural resources, such as a common fish stock. Borrowing of regimes governing the global commons replaces source-ascertainment. It is often justified by merely labelling shared resources and global commons as analogous. It is a convenient device when the global commons is governed by a treaty, such as the Moon Treaty. Ascertaining customary international law involves a mere review of verbal evidence – namely, expert opinion and statements from the ICJ. A tally of treaties and legislations is often cited, but without an examination of their actual invocation and application in state practice. The bare assertion of the existence or non-existence of custom replaces a detailed examination of evidence of actual practices and a conviction of the obligatory nature of such practices. Some took for granted that there is a customary rule arising from a history of bilateral cooperation in general. Equitable principles are either merely presumed to exist or defined by 'analogous' domestic laws and court cases. International energy law as a mixed bag of treaty law, custom, regional agreements, national legislation and administrative regulations has also been declared a source of norms without further examination, especially of the incompatibility of the norms they generate. The identifying criteria are a combination of the formal and informal. While a written agreement is regarded as the primary indicator, less objective and formal indicators are applied, such as the strategic nature of the resource being governed by the norm, the purpose of the norm in relation to the broader continental shelf regime, validations of the substance of the norm by the a priori principle of conservation for the common good, and plain state practice in the norm, at times reinforced by jurisprudence. These efforts to identify international law on shared resources retreated into deformalisation even as, with the exception of Wawryk, they disregarded the practices of non-state actors as relevant materials.

In contrast, this book places non-state actors and their agreements within the frame of inquiry. At the same time, it asks whether their agreements can be a source of international legal norms. Chapter 4 addresses the question through a case study of international agreements on shared resources between petroleum

[563] ibid 726–34.

agencies and corporations as non-state actors. It examines petroleum instruments to ascertain whether objective criteria have been developed by which such international agreements can be ascertained as a source of legal rules. Chapter 5 outlines the role of China National Offshore Oil Corporation (CNOOC) in managing the territorial, maritime and resource disputes of China in the South China Sea and the East China Sea. It makes a preliminary assessment of the possibilities and limits of such a mode of resolving disputes in those parts of Asia.

4

The Identification of International Agreements between Non-state Actors as a Source of International Law

A Case Study

As discussed in Chapter 1, this book acknowledges that international agreements are negotiated and concluded between non-state actors to manage disputes involving their host states. It inquires whether such agreements are susceptible to identification as a source of international law, and whether formal criteria outside of Article 38 of the ICJ Statute are available by which such identification can be made. Chapter 2 surveyed the descriptive and predictive concepts and tools of the positivist, pluralist and postmodernist approaches to the identification of international law. Chapter 3 reviewed the application of the positivist and pluralist approaches to the specific question of international law on shared resources. It also demonstrated that deformalisation beset these efforts.

This chapter applies the tools of postmodern legal positivism to describe and analyse data from a case study of international agreements involving non-state actors – specifically, international agreements that petroleum agencies and corporations negotiate and conclude to manage disputes between their host states over shared resources. It ascertains whether formal, objective and external criteria are available by which the agreements can be identified as a source of legal rules.

Section I of this chapter defines the parameters of the case study, while the following sections present the findings from the case study and address the question of whether international agreements between non-state actors are identifiable as a source of international legal rules.

I. THE PARAMETERS OF THE CASE STUDY

This preliminary section defines the parameters of the case study. It describes the types of petroleum instruments that are used as research materials and identifies the relevant provisions in these instruments. It then outlines the application of the theoretical and conceptual tools of postmodern legal positivism to the relevant provisions of the petroleum instruments.

A. Petroleum Instruments as Research Materials

This case study examined the petroleum instruments of 100 countries over the period from 1937 to 2021. The petroleum instruments were obtained from several repositories:

(1) Official websites of petroleum agencies and national petroleum corporations.[564]
(2) National and regional digital libraries and archives of Qatar and the Arabian Gulf.[565]
(3) Barrows Basic Oil Laws and Concession Contracts (hereinafter Barrows).[566]
(4) Oil, Gas and Energy Law (OGEL) Legal & Regulatory Documents by Country.[567]
(5) The United Nations Food and Agricultural Organization (FAO) Mineral Resources and Energy database.[568]
(6) The database at ResourceContracts.org.[569]
(7) The database at the Extractive Industries Transparency Initiative (EITI).[570]
(8) The US Securities and Exchange Commission (SEC) database of company filings.[571]

[564] See, for instance, the official website of the Ministry of Industry, Energy and Mines of the Republic of Tunisia, which publishes a database of petroleum contracts – see catalog.industrie.gov.tn/dataset?groups=contrats-petroliers. The UK Oil and Gas Authority provides access to all petroleum contracts issued from 1923 through 2020 at: arcg.is/08OryT0. Not all governments provide access to petroleum contracts.

[565] The Arabian Gulf Digital Archives of the United Arab Emirates is available at agda.ae/en, while the Qatar Digital Library is available at qdl.qa/en.

[566] These are published by Barrows Company Inc, New York. The Barrows materials used in this study came from the open shelves of the Main Library, University of Dundee, UK. The author visited the library between 2 and 20 May 2015. Basic Oil Laws and Concession Contracts are published by region. The materials used in the case study are published under Asia and Australasia (hereinafter *Barrows* A&A), Central America and the Caribbean (hereinafter *Barrows* CAC), Europe (*Barrows* Europe), the Middle East (*Barrows* ME), and South and Central Africa (*Barrows* SCA).

[567] The materials are available by subscription at ogel.org/news.asp?key=536. Copies of the materials used in this book are with the author.

[568] The database maintained by the UN Food Agriculture Organization is available at fao.org/faolex/collections/en/?search=adv&subj_coll=Mineral%20resources%20and%20Energy and contains energy and mineral resources laws and regulations.

[569] The database at resourcecontracts.org/countries is maintained by the World Bank, the Columbia Center on Sustainable Investment and the Natural Resource Governance Institute.

[570] The database at eiti.org/countries is maintained by member countries and companies of Extractive Industries Transparency Initiative.

[571] See, for example, 7 November Production Sharing Agreement between Joint Exploration, Exploitation and Petroleum Services Company ('Joint Oil') and Canadian Superior Energy Inc, 27 August 2008, sec.gov/Archives/edgar/data/1177470/000134100412001088/soq_6k.htm.

These repositories are accessible to the public, although Barrows and the OGEL require a subscription, while the SEC imposes certain restrictions. Most are written in English, while some are written in languages that can be translated into English using Google Translate. The translations are unofficial. The selection of the 100 countries was based on the accessibility of their petroleum instruments.

Petroleum instruments consist of specific provisions in bilateral agreements, laws, regulations, contracts, official statements and records of ceremonial acts, all of which constitute the regulatory framework of investment in and development of petroleum resources.[572] They are part of public or administrative law as they are employed by the state, acting *jure imperii*, to regulate a strategic resource for the national interest.[573] They are also transnational law instruments in that they 'contain similar clauses and similar structures, regardless of the country or region in the world' in which they are issued.[574] At the same time, they generally interact with public and private international law when they: (1) regulate activities on the continental shelf, the exclusive economic zone, international rivers, land frontiers and boundaries therein, where international standards on such matters as sovereign rights or economic jurisdiction, labour, safety, artificial installations, environmental protection and good governance also apply;[575] (2) involve states and international petroleum corporations and international organisations, such as the World Bank and the Asian Development Bank (ADB);[576] and (3) engage global networks of capital, infrastructure/pipelines

[572] W Onorato, *Legislative Frameworks Used to Foster Petroleum Development Policy Research Working Paper No 1420* (New York, Legal Department, World Bank, 1995), 3. Some countries like Bahrain and Cuba do not have petroleum laws or regulations that are of general application. Petroleum operations are governed by the contract approved by the legislative body. See, for example, Bahrain's Law No 24 for the year 2009, Approving the Development and Production Sharing Agreement on Development of Bahrain Field between the Government of the Kingdom of Bahrain, Occidental Petroleum Corporation of the USA, Mubadala of the United Arab Emirates, cited at noga.gov.bh/noga/legislation-details.aspx?id=64, but without the text.

[573] R Higgins, 'The Taking of Property by the State: Recent Developments in International Law' (1982) 176 *Recueil de Cours* 306; T Daintith, 'Regulation by Contract: The New Prerogative' (1979) 32 *Current Legal Problems* 53–59; AFM Maniruzzaman, 'The New Generation of Energy and Natural Resource Development Agreements: Some Reflections' (1993) 11 *Journal of Energy and Natural Resources Law* 234–41; Duval et al (n 547) 23.

[574] Talus et al (n 30) 181–93; T Hewitt, 'An Asian Perspective on Model Oil and Gas Services Contracts' (2010) 28 *Journal of Energy and Natural Resources Law* 331–32.

[575] A Jennings, *Oil and Gas Exploration Contracts* (London, Sweet & Maxwell, 2002) 20–23; C Redgwell, 'Mind the Gap in the GAIRS: The Role of Other Instruments in LOSC Regime Implementation in the Offshore Energy Sector' (2014) 29 *International Journal of Marine and Coastal Law* 606–15; C Garcıa-Castrillon, 'Reflections on the Law Applicable to International Oil Contracts' (2013) 6 *Journal of World Energy Law & Business* 2–4.

[576] M Bunter, *The Promotion and Licensing of Petroleum Prospective Acreage* (New York, Kluwer, 2002) 1–26; Smith (n 544) 23–35. An example is the involvement of the World Bank in the creation of the institutional framework for cross-border unitisation of the shared resources of Senegal and Mauritania. See World Bank Grant No IDA D273-MR, 'Supporting Gas Project Negotiations and Enhancing Institutional Capacity Project, Financing Agreement between Islamic Republic of Mauritania and International Development Association', 19 April 2018, documents1.worldbank.org/curated/en/763991524577707623/pdf/Official-Documents-Financing-Agreement-for-Grant-D273-MR-Closing-Package.pdf.

and markets.[577] To illustrate the interaction of petroleum instruments with international law, the petroleum contracts of Ghana and Suriname incorporate the anti-bribery convention of the Organisation for Economic Co-operation and Development (OECD),[578] while the petroleum contracts of the Republic of Guinea incorporate international human rights standards.[579]

In this case study, the relevant provisions of petroleum instruments intersect with international law as they deal with resources that are situated on disputed maritime zones or along defined boundaries, and they address conflicting claims between states to possession and ownership of the resources.[580] These provisions expressly acknowledge the status of shared resources and adopt criteria for delineating legal rules, as opposed to non-legal rules, that can be applied to resolve disputes over these resources.

In particular, the bilateral delimitation and resource cooperation agreements that are relevant to the case study are those that indicate whether shared resources shall be governed by rules of international law and adopt criteria to identify the sources of these rules. The relevant provisions of boundary agreements are those that authorise the petroleum agencies and corporations of the states parties to implement prescriptive resource clauses. In Article 4 of their 1978 continental shelf boundary agreement, Italy and Tunisia authorise their

[577] Wawryk (n 560) 3–5.

[578] Article 44 (8.2) of the Production Sharing Contract between Staatsolie Maatschappij Suriname NV and Kosmos Energy Suriname (Block 42), 13 December 2011, resourcecontracts.org/contract/ocds-591adf-4815087699/view#/pdf; and art 21 (1.2) of the Unitization and Unit Operating Agreement, Ghana National Petroleum Corporation et al, covering the Jubilee Field Unit located Offshore the Republic of Ghana, 13 July 2009, resourcecontracts.org/contract/ocds-591adf-0771447862/view#/pdf. See generally P Cameron, *International Energy Investment Law: The Pursuit of Stability* (Cambridge, Cambridge University Press, 2012). In ch 8, Cameron discusses the overlap between the regimes of international energy investment law, international human rights law and international environmental law.

[579] Article 10 of Simfer SA, Rio Tinto Mining & Exploration Limited, Concession, 2011, resourcecontracts.org/contract/ocds-591adf-2396569119/view#/pdf.

Peter Muchlinski's view is that internationalisation of a petroleum instrument depends on the choice of law clause; see Muchlinski (n 49), 12. Muchlinksi overlooks the fact that petroleum instrument implement municipal laws and incorporate international law (including customs and principles of justice and equity) as well as industry practice. See art 6 of the Muscat Agreement (n 25), which identifies mutual consent, custom and equity as sources of international norms on shared resources:

> In the event of the discovery of an extension of any geological petroleum structure, individual oil or gas field … cross the delimitation line … the following provisions shall apply: (1) Exploitation of the aforementioned resources shall be undertaken by mutual agreement of the two States Parties. These resources shall be divided according to the then prevailing rules and customs of international law as well as the principles of justice and equity. (2) A zone of 125 metres width on either side of the delimitation line defined in article 3 of this Agreement shall not be exploited by either State Party except by mutual consent.

[580] See, for example, Ethiopia's 1986 Model Petroleum Agreement, *Barrows SCA* Supplement No 85. Article 9.1.3 states that, with respect to a shared resource, the rights of the contractor shall be subject to the 'special rules and conditions' that the petroleum agency may find 'necessary to comply with the general principles of international law and satisfy obligations under an agreement with an adjacent state with respect to the production of such petroleum deposits'.

'competent authorities ... [to] endeavour to reach agreement as to the manner in which [shared] resources are to be exploited, after consulting with possible licence-holders'.[581] Equatorial Guinea and Nigeria provided in their 2002 maritime boundary agreement that their 'relevant government entities, in association with the relevant concession holders [shall] establish appropriate unitisation and other arrangements', but the same shall take effect only after the boundary treaty comes into force.[582] In a protocol agreement, the two governments approved the commercial arrangements that their petroleum agencies and corporations had entered into.[583]

Another type of treaty provision confirms a prior agreement between the petroleum agencies and corporations of the states parties. In 2003, the petroleum agencies of Venezuela and Trinidad and Tobago entered into a memorandum of understanding on their countries' shared resources.[584] Their authority was confirmed by their governments in the latter's framework treaty.[585]

The relevant provisions in petroleum laws and regulations are those that declare whether rules of international law shall govern disputes over shared resources and adopt rules to identify the source thereof. The petroleum law of Guatemala expressly provides that disputes over shared resources shall be resolved through a bilateral agreement 'concluded with the formalities of the law'.[586] Mali's petroleum law requires prior government authorisation before

[581] Agreement between the Government of the Italian Republic and the Government of the Tunisian Republic Relating to the Delimitation of the Continental Shelf between the Two Countries, 6 December 1978, Lathrop (n 23) 1621.

[582] Article 6 of the Treaty between the Federal Republic of Nigeria and the Republic of Equatorial Guinea Concerning their Maritime Boundary, 29 June 2002, Lathrop (n 23) 2666

[583] Article 1 of the Protocol in Implementation of art 6.2 of the Treaty between the Federal Republic of Nigeria and the Republic of Equatorial Guinea Concerning their Maritime Boundary, 29 June 2002, Lathrop (n 23) 3624–25, 3630.

[584] Letter of Intent and Memorandum of Understanding dated 12 August 2003 Concerning the Procedure for Unitization of Hydrocarbon Reservoirs That Extend across the Delimitation Line between the Republic of Trinidad and Tobago and the Bolivarian Republic of Venezuela, 12 August 2002, *Barrows* CAC, Supplement No 129.

[585] Framework Treaty Relating to the Unitisation of Hydrocarbon Reservoirs That Extend across the Delimitation Line between the Republic of Trinidad and Tobago and the Bolivarian Republic of Venezuela, 16 August 2010, 2876 UNTS 3.

[586] Article 62 of the Reglamento General de la Ley de Hidrocarburos, 15 December 1983, mem.gob.gt/wp-content/uploads/2015/06/1_Ley_de_Hidrocarburos_y_su_Reglamento.pdf; art 62 of the Decreto Ley Numero 109–83, Ley de Hidrocarburos, sice.oas.org/Investment/NatLeg/GTM/Hidrocarburos_s.pdf. The unofficial translation of their common provision (art 62) reads as follows:

> In the event that one or more deposits extend outside the limits of the national territory, their exploitation may be the subject of an international treaty, concluded with the formalities of the law, in order to exploit any deposit jointly with the corresponding country, if technical and economic reasons justify it. [The Spanish text reads: En caso de que uno o más yacimientos se extiendan fuera de los límites del territorio nacional, su explotación podrá se objeto de un tratado internacional, celebrado con las formalidades de ley, a fin de explotar cualquier yacimiento en forma conjunta con el país correspondiente, si razones de orden técnico y económico así lo justifican.]

a licensee may enter into an international agreement over a specific shared resource,[587] whereas under the law of Venezuela, government approval after the petroleum agency or corporation has concluded an agreement with its foreign counterpart would suffice.[588] The US transboundary law expressly withholds from the petroleum agency authority to negotiate any agreement over shared resources with its counterpart in Cuba.[589] Other laws merely approve specific agreements of the petroleum agency or corporation[590] or generally confirm the existence of such an agreement.[591] Petroleum regulations are issued by petroleum agencies to either implement existing laws on shared resources or to introduce a new rule, such as Indonesia's petroleum regulation, which recognises

[587] Article 43 of the Code des Hydrocarbures, Loi No 2015-035 du 16 juillet 2015, extwprlegs1.fao.org/docs/pdf/mli153041.pdf.

[588] Decreto No 10, Decreto con Rango y Fuerza de Ley Orgánica de Hidrocarburos Gaseosos, Gaceta Oficial de la Republica de Venezuela No 36793, 23 September 1999, pdvsa.com/images/pdf/marcolegal/LEY_ORGANICA_DE_HIDROCARBUROS_GASEOSOS.pdf. Under art 21, Venezuela authorises the contractor to negotiate and agree with its foreign counterparts on the unitisation of a shared resource, subject to approval by the petroleum agency and parliament. The unofficial translation of the Spanish text reads as follows:

> When the same gaseous hydrocarbon reservoir extends under the areas indicated in Article 1 of this Law and under areas that are part of the domain of neighbouring countries, the agreements that the owners acting in Venezuela must enter into for their exploitation with those of neighbouring countries will require the approval of the Ministry of Energy and Mines, as well as the Congress of the Republic. In the absence of a timely agreement, the Ministry of Energy and Mines will adopt the necessary measures, including the revocation of the exploitation right, to safeguard the interests of the Republic. [The Spanish text reads: Cuando un mismo yacimiento de hidrocarburos gaseosos se extienda bajo las áreas indicadas en el artículo 1° de esta Ley y bajo áreas que formen parte del dominio de países limítrofes, los convenios que para su explotación deban celebrar los titulares que actúen en Venezuela con los de los países limítrofes, requerirán la aprobación del Ministerio de Energía y Minas, así como del Congreso de la República. A falta de oportuno acuerdo, el Ministerio de Energía y Minas adoptará las medidas necesarias, incluida la revocatoria del derecho de explotación, para salvaguardar los intereses de la República.]

This was amended by art 21 of the Hydrocarbons Organic Law (Official Gazette N° 37323, dated 13 November 2001) Decree N° 1510, 2 November 2001 and art 43, Ley Orgánica de Hidrocarburos, 24 May 2006, pdvsa.com/images/pdf/marcolegal/LEY_ORGANICA_DE_HIDROCARBUROS.pdf. These provisions require an international unitisation agreement before petroleum activities affecting shared resources can be undertaken. Under the 2001 law, the agreement shall be concluded between the contractor and its foreign counterpart, subject to the approval of the petroleum agency and Congress. Pending negotiation or approval, the national government shall adopt interim measures. The 2006 law also requires an international unitisation agreement, but does not expressly state whether the petroleum agency or the corporation can act as parties to the agreement.

[589] Transboundary Hydrocarbon Agreements (n 31) para d.

[590] Code Pétrolier 2019, Loi n°2019-03 du 1er février 2019, droit-afrique.com/uploads/Senegal-Code-2019-petrolier.pdf. Through this law, Senegal ratified the international unitisation agreement that the petroleum corporations of Senegal and Mauritania entered into.

[591] A few months after the petroleum agency of Angola entered into a memorandum of understanding with the petroleum agency of the DRC, Angola passed a law adopting such a mode of negotiation and agreement on shared resources. See art 64.8 of Law No 10/04, 12 November 2004, faolex.fao.org/docs/pdf/ang81903E.pdf.

international agreements that the petroleum minister may enter into regarding the exploitation of a shared resource.[592]

Model contracts are incorporated into regulations,[593] although some are issued separately to guide petroleum corporations during licensing rounds.[594] Model contracts contain what the host government considers as threshold provisions[595] which 'are principally derived from internationally accepted petroleum practices under similar conditions' and are presumed to be acceptable to petroleum corporations.[596] In some jurisdictions, provisions in model contracts are deemed to be incorporated into the actual contracts.[597] The provisions in model contracts that are relevant to the case study are those that either interpret or implement a provision on shared resources in international agreements[598] and national petroleum laws and regulations,[599] or introduce a rule de novo.[600]

Petroleum contracts are legal arrangements whereby a host state, as putative owner of the petroleum resource in situ,[601] grants a petroleum corporation

[592] See Regulation on Upstream Oil and Gas Business Activities No 35, 2004, *Oil Gas and Energy Law Documents* (copy with the author). Article 43 provides that, with respect to a shared resource, its 'resolution shall be determined by the Minister based on the continental shelf agreement between the Government of the Republic of Indonesia and the Government of the other country concerned and on considerations of optimum benefit to the state'. All the maritime boundary agreements of Indonesia require a bilateral agreement on shared resources.

[593] See Second Schedule attached to the Petroleum (Production) Regulations, UK, 13 May 1935, *Barrows Europe*, vol 1, no 1, c-5.

[594] See, for example, Model Exploration and Production Sharing Contract, Republic of Cyprus, 2 June 2016, mcit.gov.cy/mcit/mcit.nsf/7DF75846053512BDC2257F6A002284E7/$file/Model_EPSC%20(02%20June%202016).pdf, which was issued in connection with the country's third licensing round.

[595] Smith (n 544) 281; Talus (n 548) 469. See, for example, art 3 of the UK Petroleum (Production) (Continental Shelf and Territorial Sea) Regulations (1964) 3 *International Legal Materials* 621.

[596] Talus (n 548) 467. For instance, the petroleum contract issued by the Republic of Guinea expressly states that it is based on the 2002 AIPN model contract. See Operating Agreement between SCS Corporation and Dana Petroleum (E&P) Limited based on the 2002 Model Form International Operating Agreement of AIPN, 28 January 2010, sec.gov/Archives/edgar/data/937136/000114420410004433/v172634_ex10-1.htm. The petroleum contract issued by Ireland is only five pages long, but art 2.3 incorporates all the provisions of Licensing Terms for Offshore Oil and Gas Exploration, Development & Production 2007, gov.ie/pdf/75206/?page=null.

[597] Bunter (n 579) 49–56. For instance, the UK model clauses are generally non-negotiable, unless the petroleum authority deems it fit to modify or exclude the model clauses from an actual contract. See art 4 of the UK Petroleum Act 1998 c 17, legislation.gov.uk/ukpga/1998/17/enacted/data.pdf.

[598] Art 9.1.4 of the 1986 Model Petroleum Agreement (n 580).

[599] See, for example, art 28 of Angola's 2005 Model Production Sharing Agreement, *Oil Gas & Energy Law Documents* (copy with the author), which implements art 64 of Law No 10/04 (n 591).

[600] Model Contract (English), Guinea Ecuatorial de Petroleos, PSA, 1982, resourcecontracts.org/contract/ocds-591adf-0907900772/view#/text. This model contract introduced a provision requiring the contractors to agree with their foreign counterparts on how to exploit a shared resource (s 12.4). No such provision can be found in the existing law. See Code des hydrocarbures 1981 (abrogé) Loi n°1981-07 du 16 juin 1981, droit-afrique.com/upload/doc/guinee-equatoriale/GE-Code-hydrocarbures-1981-abroge-ESP.pdf.

[601] Sovereign rights in the law of the sea conventions do not include ownership by the state of petroleum resources in situ on the continental shelf. See A Ronne, 'Energy Law in Denmark' in M Roggenkamp (ed), *Energy Law in Europe: National, EU and International Law and Institutions* (Oxford, Oxford University Press, 2001) 32. However, all the 100 countries in the dataset claim ownership of the resource

the right to explore and produce petroleum for a certain consideration.[602] The relevant contracts in the data set pertain to offshore operations (beyond the territorial sea) rather than onshore operations (land and territorial sea), and they implement a provision on shared resources in an existing treaty, law or regulation,[603] or introduce a new one altogether.[604]

Finally, the dataset contains official statements and guidelines dealing with shared resources. Official statements either expressly define the status of shared resources or report an official act confirming the status of the resource. An example of the former are the separate statements issued by Israel and Cyprus regarding ongoing negotiations between their petroleum agencies on the joint exploration/exploitation of their shared resources.[605] The second type of official statements includes the report published by the governments of Senegal and Mauritania regarding the signing by their respective petroleum agencies of an inter-governmental agreement on shared resources, and the attestation of the agreement by their respective heads of government.[606] Official guidelines include

in situ. Whether such uniform and widespread practice modifies the principle of sovereign rights is the subject of a separate study on customary norms in the law of the sea regime.

602 G Barrows, *Worldwide Concession Contracts and Petroleum Legislation* (Tulsa, PenWell Books, 1983) 9–15. The differences among concession agreements, production-sharing agreements and service contracts are not relevant.

603 See s 10 of the License for Exploration and Production of Hydrocarbons No 2014/01, 22 January 2014, orkustofnun.is/gogn/Frettir/licence-2014-01-cnooc-eykon-petoro.pdf, which provides that 'if a hydrocarbon resource extends over into the continental shelf of another state, the licensee shall comply with instructions of Orkustofnun [energy agency] in accordance with … the Hydrocarbon Act … [and] the agreement between Iceland and Norway concerning transboundary hydrocarbon deposits'.

Moreover, in their joint development agreement, Japan and Korea bound themselves to incorporate treaty provisions into the joint operating agreement between their contractors. See art 5 of the Agreement between Japan and the Republic of Korea concerning Joint Development (n 275).

604 Annex 8 of the Concession Contract of 21 December 1967 between Petromin and AGIP Saudi Arabia, 21 December 1967, *Barrows* ME, Supplement No 21. Article 10(8) provides that, with respect to a shared resource, the rights-holders shall enter into an agreement with their foreign counterparts. However, should such agreement not be reached, then the 'GOVERNMENT shall permit PETROMIN to take all reasonable measures to prevent drainage and migration of its rightful reserves caused by operations beyond the concession boundary'.

This contractual provision preceded the statutory provision on shared resources. In 1968, Saudi Arabia issued a decree declaring ownership of resources in the Red Sea and acknowledging that it 'may exercise its rights in exploring or mining these resources … by way of sharing with the neighbouring governments which have similar rights recognized by the government of the Saudi Arabia Kingdom in common zones'. See s 3 of the Royal Decree No M-27, 7 September 1967, extwprlegs1.fao.org/docs/pdf/sau159314.pdf.

605 Since 2014, the petroleum agencies of Israel and Cyprus have been negotiating a framework agreement on their shared resource involving the Aphrodite (Cyprus) and Ishai (Israel) fields. Cyprus' licensee Noble Energy suspended its operations in Aphrodite field pending negotiation on the framework agreement. See Israel-Cyprus Joint Statement, 24 July 2016, gov.il/en/departments/news/spokejoint240716. Lebanon protested against the negotiations between Israel and Cyprus. See HE General Michel Sleiman, President of the Republic of Lebanon, Address at the 66th Session of the General Assembly of the United Nations, 21 September 2011, gadebate.un.org/sites/default/files/gastatements/66/LB_en.pdf.

606 Signature d'une convention de coopération entre notre pays et le Sénégal, 9 February 2018, fr.ami.mr/Depeche-43672.html.

those issued by Norway and the UK relating to the formulation of field development plans according to their framework transboundary agreement.[607]

The following discussion in this chapter will examine the relevant provisions of the petroleum instruments. The purpose is to ascertain whether they record certain formal criteria by which to ascertain whether international agreements that are negotiated and concluded between petroleum agencies or corporations are a source of legal rules on shared resources. The examination of the petroleum instruments shall be undertaken using the tools of postmodern legal positivism.

B. The Application of Postmodern Legal Positivism

The theoretical and conceptual tools of postmodern legal positivism shall be applied to present and analyse the petroleum instruments. To recall the discussion in Chapter 1 and Chapter 2, postmodern legal positivism situates international law-making in social processes, but identifies international law based on formal criteria or rules of recognition. The identifying criteria are themselves dynamic as they develop through the social practices of law applying authorities.

In the previous chapter, the practices of domestic and international courts, individual judges and experts in the ILC as law-applying authorities were discussed. In this preliminary section, the focus will be on the role of petroleum agencies, petroleum corporations and their industry networks, as well as sovereign states, specifically the US and the UK, in the formulation of specific provisions in petroleum instruments relating to shared resources

i. The Role of Petroleum Agencies, Corporations and Associations

Initially, the role of petroleum agencies, corporations and associations was limited to advising governments on domestic regulations relating to the rule of capture. They eventually influenced the incorporation of provisions on shared resources in boundary agreements and petroleum laws and contracts.

During the period of self-regulation of the US petroleum industry,[608] petroleum corporations and associations advised the government on the formulation

[607] UK-Norway Guidelines for Development of Trans-boundary Oil and Gas Fields, npd.no/globalassets/1-npd/regelverk/forskrifter/en/transboundary-fields-1016.pdf. This outlines the steps to be taken following the discovery of a shared resource. Article 1.2 requires the contractors to enter into an agreement for approval by their respective governments.

[608] *Jennison v Kirk*, 98 US 453, 457. US mineral laws were applied to oil and gas leases. In effect, the 'customs of miners, as enforced and moulded by the courts and sanctioned by the legislation of the State' became the basis of early regulation of commercial petroleum production. See the Act to Authorize the Entry and Patenting of Lands Containing Petroleum and Other Mineral Oils under the Placer-Mining Laws of the United States, 11 February 1897, Chap 216, 29 Stat 526. There was no existing regulation appropriate for oil and gas drilling in the Gulf of Mexico in 1938. See Statement

of measures to address wastage arising from the application of the rule of capture.[609] As early as 1909, self-protection vis-a-vis the rule of capture was the subject of debate in the industry and government.[610] Henry Doherty (Cities Service Oil Company) and other operators opposed the rule of capture[611] on the ground that oil is the most important munition of war and its wastage is a threat to the 'common defence'.[612] Doherty urged the federal government to adopt regulations on sole-country unitisation dictated by natural conservation principles.[613] The American Petroleum Institute (API) also promoted unitisation through the formulation of model contracts, but regarded it merely as a rational choice based on good international petroleum industry practice.[614] Unitisation was subsequently adopted as a domestic regulation in the public domain (federal lands, submerged lands and the outer continental shelf),[615] but not on private lands.[616]

Petroleum agencies, corporations and associations also shaped international regulations on shared resources. Following the Truman Proclamation, Bahrain and Saudi Arabia negotiated the settlement of their seabed frontier in the Persian/Arabian Gulf. The concessionaire Arabian American Oil Company (ARAMCO) proposed 'some kind of sharing of any oil that might be found',[617] while Bahrain Petroleum Company (BAPCO) proposed a joint zone which would be jointly exploited by itself and ARAMCO.[618] The arrangement proposed by ARAMCO

of William Embry Wrather, Director, Geological Survey, Department of the Interior in *Hearings before a Special Committee Investigating Petroleum Resources, United States Senate Seventy-Ninth Congress, First Session, June 19, 20, 21, 22, and 25, 1945* (Washington DC, Government Printing Office, 1946) 360–80.

[609] American Petroleum Institute (API) Bulletin No 132, 10 December 1920, 54–59. See Address by Henry l Doherty in Federal Oil Conservation Board, *Complete Record of Public Hearings, 10 and 11 February* (Washington DC, Government Printing Office, 1926) 25–33.

[610] Letters dated 24 October 1908 and 6 November 1908 of the Director of the Geological Survey to the Secretary of the Interior regarding wastage resulting from competitive drilling; and Letter of the Secretary of Interior to the President, 17 September 1909, regarding wastage arising from competitive drilling, in M Ball (1916), 'Petroleum Withdrawals and Restorations Affecting the Public Domain' *United States Geological Survey Bulletin No 623,* 113–16, 134–35.

[611] Letter of President Coolidge Constituting the Federal Oil Conservation Board, 19 December 1924, in United States, Federal Oil Conservation Board, *Federal Oil Conservation Board Complete Record of Public Hearings (1927), 10 and 11 February 1926* (Washington DC, Government Printing Office, 1926) viii-ix.

[612] Address by Doherty (n 610) 28, 32.

[613] ibid 32–33.

[614] API, *Model Form of Unit Operating Agreement* (New York, API, 1957).

[615] Department of the Interior, *Report II-IV of the Federal Oil Conservation Board to the President of the United States, January 1928* (Washington DC, Government Printing Office, 1928) 17–24. See 30 Code of Federal Regulations, Chapter II, Subchapter B, Part 250, Subpart M – Unitization, 1 July 2013, gpo.gov/fdsys/pkg/CFR-2013-title30-vol2/pdf/CFR-2013-title30-vol2-part250-subpartM.pdf1.

[616] Address of ML Requa, Vice-President of the Sinclair Consolidated Oil Corporation, API Bulletin No 132 (n 611) 59.

[617] Tuson (n 251) 527–28.

[618] ibid 531.

was incorporated into the 1958 frontier agreement of the two countries.[619] In the North Sea, the petroleum corporations were involved in formulating the unity of deposit clause in boundary agreements[620] as well as regulations implementing treaty provisions on shared resources.[621]

Like the API, the AIPN[622] and the World Bank[623] have promoted model laws, regulations and contracts, and have commissioned studies to define good international petroleum industry practices with respect to shared resources. Good international petroleum industry practices have been cited as a source of rules on shared resources.[624]

ii. The Role of the US, the UK and Other States

As Lauterpacht and Waldock noted in 1950, the Truman Proclamation was 'intended to protect resources within the United States which might be tapped from the high seas'.[625] The US invoked the principle of self-protection against the rule of capture in the international context[626] and analogous practices in other seas.[627] In its notification to various governments of the application of the Truman Proclamation to areas beyond its territorial sea,[628] the US explained that

[619] ibid 535. See Saudi Arabia and Bahrain Frontier Agreement, 22 February 1958, 1733 UNTS 3:

> Art 2 The said area, as delimited above, is in the sector belonging to the Kingdom of Saudi Arabia. In accordance with the desire of His Highness the Ruler of Bahrain and with the agreement of His Majesty the King of Saudi Arabia, oil resources there shall be exploited in the manner chosen by His Majesty, on the understanding that the Government of Bahrain shall be accorded one half of the net revenues accruing to the Government of Saudi Arabia as a result of such exploitation. This shall be without prejudice to the right of sovereignty and administration of the Government of Saudi Arabia over the area stipulated above.

[620] Elferink (n 401) 133–34.

[621] A Kemp, *The Official History of North Sea Oil and Gas*, vol 1 (New York, Routledge, 2012) 104–06.

[622] See AIPN, Model Form International Unitization and Unit Operating Agreement (2020, subscription required).

[623] World Bank, *Vietnam's Petroleum Sector: Technical Assistance for the Revision of the Existing Legal and Regulatory Framework* (Washington DC, World Bank, December 2003) 48, openknowledge.worldbank.org/handle/10986/17456. This outlines the role of PetroVietnam and the Prime Minister in the negotiation and conclusion of agreements on shared resources.

[624] See art 26.1 of the Exploration and Production Sharing Agreement of Oman (undated), Oil, Gas and Energy Law Legal & Regulatory Documents (copy with the author).

[625] Lauterpacht (n 473); Waldock (n 474).

[626] Formulation of United States Policy on the Resources of the Continental Shelf and on Coastal Fisheries (n 18) 1505 and 1511.

[627] It cited state practice in 'Ceylon and India, off Bahrein, off Ireland, off Tunis and in other parts of the Mediterranean, off the coasts of Australia, and elsewhere' of acquiring 'by occupation and contiguity rights of the land beneath the high seas provided that the freedom of navigation is not thereby impaired'. See ibid 1502.

[628] The governments notified were Cuba, Mexico, Canada, the UK, the Soviet Union, the Netherlands, Norway, Denmark, France, Iceland, and Portugal. See Memorandum by Mr Eugene H Dooman, Special Assistant to the Assistant Secretary of State (Dunn), to Mr William Phillips, Special Assistant to the Secretary of State 15 June 1945, in ibid 1510.

advances in petroleum technology had enabled foreign states to engage in petroleum operations 'in the Coast of Mexico and off the coast of California',[629] and since petroleum resources in the Gulf of Mexico 'often form part of a pool or deposit extending seaward from within the state [US]',[630] the utilisation of the part of the pool that was offshore might affect the other part that was onshore or within US territory.[631] Through the Proclamation, the US can 'assert the necessary control over … operations off the coast of the United States … [and] guard against the depletion of [its] mineral resources'.[632] The law will forestall 'the draining of pools of oil within the United States by operations carried on at some distance from the coasts of [the] country'.[633]

Thus, in issuing the Truman Proclamation, the US was not merely legislating; it was identifying and applying sources of norms governing the continental shelf. The sources it invoked were the principle of self-protection and an analogous state practice.

The UK influenced the formulation of provisions on shared resources in concession agreements involving British petroleum corporations in the Persian/Arabian Gulf. In 1936, Petroleum Concessions Ltd proposed the adoption of the following provision on joint interest in the neutral zones:

> Art 4. … if hereafter any neutral zone is created adjacent to the territory of the State, wherein the Shaikh shall have a co-equal and joint interest, the Shaikh hereby agrees to grant to the Company an oil concession over such neutral zone on terms to be agreed between the Shaikh, the Company and the joint ruler of such neutral zone.[634]

This proposed provision found its way into various concession agreements.[635]

[629] ibid 1505 and 1511.

[630] ibid 1501. An example was the first offshore field drilled by the US in 1896 in Summerland, California, which was found to be an extension of an onshore field discovered in 1894. See M Adams, C John, R Kelly, A LaPointe and R Meurer, 'Mineral Resource Management of the Outer Continental Shelf' (1975) *Geological Survey Circular* 2–3.

[631] Formulation of United States Policy on the Resources of the Continental Shelf and on Coastal Fisheries (n 18).

[632] ibid 1505.

[633] ibid 1508.

[634] See Letter of Petroleum Concessions Limited to Under Secretary of State, India Office, 30 January 1936, regarding terms of concession contracts, including on shared resources in neutral zones, in CONFIDENTIAL 86/7-II B-35 OIL TRUCIAL COAST & OMAN, British Library: India Office Records and Private Papers, IOR/R/15/1/672, 172–244, qdl.qa/archive/81055/vdc_100000000193.0x000286, 162–315.

[635] Article 4 of the Petroleum Concession Limited Agreement with the Shaikh of Sharjah, 17 September 1937 in Coll 30/151 'Oil: Sharjah Political Agreement, and Commercial Concession', British Library: India Office Records and Private Papers, IOR/L/PS/12/3886, 76, qdl.qa/archive/81055/vdc_100000000648.0x0001c6; art 4 of the Agreement between His Excellency Shaikhk Ahmad Bin Rashid, Ruler of Umm-al-Qaiwain Arabia and Petroleum Concessions Limited (n 247); art 4 of the Agreement between the Ruler of Ras-Al-Khaimah Shaikh Sultan Bin Salim and Petroleum Concession Limited, 21 June 1954 in Coll 30/110(2) 'Oil: Oil concessions on the Trucial Coast. Negotiations with Sheikhs Ras-al-Khaimah Agreement Abu Dhabi' [26r] (51/917), British Library: India Office Records and Private Papers, IOR/L/PS/12/3836, 51, qdl.qa/archive/81055/vdc_100050244071.0x000036.

Following the issuance of the Truman Proclamation, the UK drafted the texts of the continental shelf and fisheries zone proclamations, which the various rulers in the Persian/Arabian Gulf then adopted.[636]

Other states exercised their law-applying authority when they objected to the codification of international law on shared resources. Chapter 3 detailed that their objections was based on the view that there is no custom to be codified for existing practices do not fulfil the two-element criteria of Article 38 of the ICJ Statute. During the first LOSC, they rejected draft Article 8, on compulsory arbitration of disputes over shared resources, also on the ground that there are no applicable customary rules that could be applied by any arbitration tribunal.

The foregoing social practices in the application of the law are recorded in provisions of petroleum instruments. For the case study here, the relevant provisions are those that declare whether shared resources are subject to self-regulation or domestic law or international law. Those petroleum instruments that consider shared resources to be governed by the rules of international law identify traditional, non-traditional and mixed sources.[637] The traditional sources are bilateral agreements, whether in the form of joint development or unitisation or profit-sharing. The non-traditional sources are international agreements that are negotiated and entered into between petroleum agencies and corporations.

Furthermore, the relevant provisions in petroleum instruments adopt identifying criteria. For example, Guatemala's petroleum law requires that the inter-state agreement on shared resources must be celebrated with all the formalities imposed by law.[638] The 1999 petroleum law of Venezuela also requires ratification of international unitisation agreements involving its licensees.[639] The boundary treaty between Denmark and the Faroe Islands details the procedure and substance of any inter-governmental unitisation agreement.[640]

The inclusion of this provision was negotiated through British colonial officials. Every British petroleum corporation operating in the Persian/Arabian Gulf signed a side political agreement with the UK government, according to which the corporation may negotiate terms, not directly with the host rulers, but through identified British colonial officials. See art 1-2 and art 4-5 of the Agreement Relating to the Debai Oil Concesssion between the United Kingdom and Petroleum Concessions Limited, 5 February 1937, British Library: India Office Records and Private Papers, IOR/L/PS/18/B456, 1-10, qdl.qa/archive/81055/vdc_100000000833.0x000012; Sharjah Oil Concession and Connected Documents, Sep 1937-May 1938 (India Office Confidential Prints, Memos B444, B445, B458, B467) [153r] (25/62), British Library: India Office Records and Private Papers, IOR/R/15/1/749/2, 309, qdl.qa/archive/81055/vdc_100035849170.0x00006f.

[636] See File 39/23 I (n 73) 59–66; File 39/23 II Negotiations for Seabed Oil in Bahrain, Trucial Coast and Qatar, British Library: India Office Records and Private Papers, IOR/R/15/2/890, 3, 11, 13, 33, 39, qdl.qa/archive/81055/vdc_100000000241.0x000161.

[637] Other petroleum instruments cite equitable principles, regional custom and good international petroleum industry practice. These were discussed in ch 3.

[638] Decreto Ley Numero 109–83 (n 588).

[639] Art 21 of Decreto No 310 (n 588).

[640] Article 3 of the Agreement between the Government of the Kingdom of Denmark, together with the Government of the Faroes, on the one hand, and the Government of Iceland, on the other hand, relating to the Maritime Delimitation in the area between the Faroe Islands and Iceland, 29 April 2008, Lathrop (n 23) 4561.

iii. Petroleum Instruments as Record of Identifying Criteria

Out of the 100 countries in the case study, eight adopt in their petroleum instruments sole-country unitisation: Brazil, Côte d'Ivoire,[641] Gabon, Kenya, Myanmar, Peru, South Africa and Sri Lanka. Sole-country unitisation involves the licensees of a single host state, and their rights and obligations are defined by the national laws of that state. For instance, Kenya's petroleum law[642] and contracts[643] require licensees whose petroleum fields traverse the boundaries of their contract areas to work the fields as a single unit subject to the country's petroleum regime. Sole-country unitisation does not address the status of shared resources across a maritime zone or boundary.

The remaining 92 countries acknowledge in their petroleum instruments the potential or actual presence of shared resources, and regard disputes over them as the proper subject matter of the rules of international law. For example, in the face of opposing claims from Suriname and Venezuela, Guyana maintains in its petroleum contracts sole ownership of its resources on the continental shelf, but acknowledges that the resolution of disputes shall be performed according to the rules of international law.[644] Thus, in its provisional arrangement with Barbados, Guyana agreed that in 'the area of bilateral overlap' in the outer limits of their respective exclusive economic zones, there shall be no petroleum activities until 'decisions over jurisdictional issues' have been made through a written agreement on joint management between their respective petroleum agencies, but such joint management shall be governed by the terms and conditions defined in a written bilateral agreement or exchange of diplomatic notes.[645] At the same time, in its petroleum law, Guyana recognises that international agreements that are negotiated and concluded by its petroleum agencies and corporations shall

[641] The national petroleum corporations of Ghana and Côte d'Ivoire have agreements on joint exploration and exploitation, but the texts are not available. Moreover, these agreements appear to involve resources found wholly on the side of Côte d'Ivoire. See Reply of Ghana, *Ghana v Côte D'Ivoire* (n 436) 65–70.

[642] See, for example, art 63 of the Petroleum Exploration, Development and Production Bill 2015, kenyalaw.org/kl/fileadmin/pdfdownloads/bills/2015/PetroleumExplorationDevelopmentandProduction Bill2015.pdf.

[643] See, for example, art 30 of the 2015 Model Production Sharing Contract, erc.go.ke/images/docs/Model_Production_Sharing_Contract_2015-210115.pdf.

[644] See Petroleum Prospecting License between the President of the Cooperative Republic of Guyana and Esso Exploration and Production Guyana Limited, 14 June 1999, resourcecontracts.org/contract/ocds-591adf-2947803650/view#/pdf. Article 31.1 acknowledges the possibility that part of the contract area or its resources will be claimed by other states; however, Guyana assures the contractor that it has sovereignty over the contract area and that it 'shall continue to assert its rights to the entire contract area and seek to resolve current and future claims, if any, by other States'.

[645] Articles 3 and 6 of the Treaty between the Republic of Guyana and the State of Barbados Concerning the Exercise of Jurisdiction in Their Exclusive Economic Zones in the Area of Bilateral Overlap within Each of Their Outer Limits and Beyond the Outer Limits of the Exclusive Economic Zones of other States, 5 May 2004, Lathrop (n 23) 587.

also govern disputes over shared resources.[646] In effect, while Guyana asserts sovereign rights over shared resources, it acknowledges that disputes over them shall be resolved based on rules of international law. Moreover, it recognises that these rules are derived from a traditional source (international agreements involving claimant states) and a non-traditional source (international agreements that are negotiated and concluded by their respective petroleum agencies and corporations).

a. A Traditional Source

The following 29 countries expressly provide in their treaties and laws that the source of rules on shared resources shall be bilateral agreements between states: Algeria,[647] Argentina,[648] Australia,[649] Cambodia,[650] Costa Rica,[651] Cuba,[652]

[646] Petroleum (Exploration and Production) Act, Chapter 65:10, 1986, parliament.gov.gy/documents/acts/8170-act_no._3_of_1986_petroleum_(exploration_and_production)_act_1986.pdf. Article 69(1) reads as follows:

> The Minister may (a) for the purpose of giving effect to any treaty … or (b) in the interests of peace and good relationship with other countries, issue to any licensee directions in respect of all or any of the following matters …
> (iii) where only part of a petroleum reservoir is located in such production area and the other or any other part of the petroleum reservoir is located in any country other than Guyana and there are one or more persons lawfully entitled to recover petroleum from such part of the petroleum reservoir as is located in such country other than Guyana, requiring the licensee to enter into an agreement in writing with any such person or persons, within such time as may be specified therefor in the direction, for the unit development of that petroleum reservoir.

[647] Article 5 of the Agreement on Provisional Arrangements for the Delimitation of the Maritime Boundary between the Republic of Tunisia and the People's Democratic Republic of Algeria, 23 November 2003, 2238 UNTS 208 (2007). The only role of the licensee is to inform the petroleum agency regarding the potential or actual presence of a shared resource. See art 105 of Law No 19-13, 11 December 2019, *Journal Officiel de la Republique Algerienne* N° 79, 4, joradp.dz/FTP/JO-FRANCAIS/2019/F2019079.pdf.

[648] Article 2-4 of the UK-Argentina Joint Declaration of Cooperation over Offshore Activities in the South West Atlantic, 27 September 1995, 35 *International Legal Materials* 301. Argentina notified the UN Secretary-General of the termination of this joint declaration due to repeated unilateral activities of the UK. See Letter dated 28 March 2007 from the Permanent Mission of Argentina to the United Nations addressed to the Secretary-General, UN Doc A/61/827, 30 March 2007.

[649] Sections 53–55 and 191 of the Offshore Petroleum and Greenhouse Gas Storage Act 2006 No 14, extwprlegs1.fao.org/docs/pdf/aus64464volume1.pdf in relation to arts 7 and 8 of the Treaty between Australia and the Democratic Republic of Timor-Leste Establishing Their Maritime Boundaries in the Timor Sea, 30 August 2019, dfat.gov.au/sites/default/files/treaty-maritime-arrangements-australia-timor-leste.pdf.

[650] Article 3 of the Agreement on Historic Waters of Vietnam and Kampuchea, 7 July 1982, Lathrop (n 23), 2364; art 33 of the Model Contract, PSA, 2004, resourcecontracts.org/contract/ocds-591adf-0311756882/view#/pdf.

[651] Article 4 of the Convention on the Delimitation of Maritime and Submarine Areas between the Republics of Costa Rica and Ecuador signed 12 March 1985, Lathrop (n 23) 825.

[652] Article 4 (g) of the Agreement between the Commonwealth of the Bahamas and the Republic of Cuba for the Delimiting Line between their Maritime Zones, 2831 UNTS 2 (2012).

Ghana,[653] Greece,[654] Grenada,[655] Guatemala,[656] Honduras,[657] India,[658] Japan,[659] Liberia,[660] Mauritius,[661] Mozambique,[662] Nicaragua,[663] Oman,[664] the Republic of Guinea,[665] São Tomé and Príncipe,[666] the Seychelles,[667] Sierra Leone,[668] Spain,[669]

[653] Article 35 of Ghana's Petroleum (Exploration and Production) Act 2016, petrocom.gov.gh/wp-content/uploads/2018/12/Act-9190001.pdf.

[654] Article 2 of the Agreement between the Hellenic Republic and the Italian Republic (n 507).

[655] Article 7 of the Treaty between the Republic of Trinidad and Tobago and Grenada on the Delimitation of Marine and Submarine Areas, 27 April 2010, Lathrop (n 23) 4716.

[656] Decreto Ley Numero 109–83 (n 588).

[657] Article 3 of the Treaty between the Government of the Republic of Honduras and the Government of the United Mexican States on Maritime Delimitation, 30 November 2006, Lathrop (n 23) 4210.

[658] Article 4 of the Agreement between the Government of the Republic of India and the Government of the Kingdom of Thailand on the Delimitation of Seabed Boundary between the Two Countries in the Andaman Sea, 15 December 1978, Lathrop (n 23) 440.

[659] Japan-Korea Joint Development Agreement (n 275); Law of 14 June 1978 to Implement the Agreement regarding Joint Development of the Southern Part of the Continental Shelf Adjacent to Japan and the Republic of Korea, *Barrows* A&A, Supplement No 60.

[660] Article 29.1 of the Act to Amend and Restate the New Petroleum Law of Liberia, 5 October 2016, lpra.gov.lr/images/Laws_and_Regulations/Petroleum_EP_Law_2016_Final_1.pdf.

[661] Treaty Concerning the Joint Management of the Continental Shelf in the Mascarene Plateau Region, 13 March 2012, 2847 UNTS 307; Treaty Concerning the Joint Exercise of Sovereign Rights over the Continental Shelf in the Mascarene Plateau Region, 12 March 2012, 2847 UNTS 277.

[662] Article 7 of the Agreement between the United Republic of Tanzania and the People's Republic of Mozambique, signed 28 December 1988, Lathrop (n 23) 898.

[663] Law No 286, Special Law on the Exploration and Exploitation of Hydrocarbon, 12 June 1998, *Oil Gas & Energy Law Documents* (copy with the author). Article 47 provides that 'in cases where the deposits are shared with neighboring countries, the unitization agreements shall be negotiated between the governments involved for a joint exploitation'. See also Concession Agreement for the Exploration and Exploitation of Hydrocarbons, 'Perlas' Prospect, 24 March 2009, sec.gov/Archives/edgar/data/822746/000114420411029215/v222400_ex10-8.htm. Clause 25(3) provides for inter-state agreement on shared resources with the technical assistance of the contractors.

[664] Article 6 of the International Boundary Agreement between the Sultanate of Oman and the Republic of Yemen, 17 December 1992, 1709 UNTS 432; art 4 of the Agreement to Mark the Maritime Borders between the Republic of Yemen and the Sultanate of Oman, 10 April 2004, Lathrop (n 23) 3909.

[665] Article 38 of the Portant Code Petrolier de la Republique de Guinee, 8 August 2014, mines.gov.gn/assets/uploads/2016/03/Code-Petrolier.pdf. The unofficial translation of art 38 reads:

> In the event that a field extends into the territory of another state, [Republic of Guinee] will approach the state in question to try to agree on the most effective way of coordinating oil operations and on the principles of allocation of Hydrocarbon volumes. [The French text reads: Au cas où un gisement s'étendrait sur le territoire d'un autre état, l'Etat se rapprochera de l'état en question pour tenter de s'accorder sur la manière la plus efficace de coordonner les opérations pétrolières et sur les principes d'allocation des volumes d'Hydrocarbures.]

[666] Treaty Concerning the Joint Management of the Continental Shelf in the Mascarene Plateau Region (n 743); Treaty Concerning the Joint Exercise of Sovereign Rights over the Continental Shelf in the Mascarene Plateau Region (n 743).

[667] ibid.

[668] Oil/Gas-Petroleum Exploration and Production Act (2011), 25 July 2011, sierra-leone.org/Laws/2011-07.pdf. Article 62 (cross border petroleum operations) states:

> (1) Where a petroleum reservoir extends into the territory or continental shelf of another state, the State shall seek to reach agreement with that state for the most efficient coordination of petroleum operations in connection with the petroleum reservoir and the apportionment of the petroleum reserve.

[669] Article 4 of the France-Spain Delimitation Convention (n 449).

Sweden,[670] Suriname,[671] Thailand,[672] Timor Leste,[673] Turkey[674] and Yemen.[675] There is no provision in their petroleum instruments recognising international agreements that are directly negotiated and concluded between petroleum agencies and corporations. The parties with authority to negotiate and conclude the agreements are states. For example, under Nicaragua's petroleum law, agreements on shared resources shall be between governments.[676] India's petroleum agency issued a regulation that adopts international unitisation as a good international petroleum industry practice, but reserved the authority to negotiate and conclude the agreement to the state,[677] which is consistent with the country's boundary treaties.[678] The 2011 petroleum law of Sierra Leone provides that '[w]here a petroleum reservoir extends into the territory or continental shelf of another state, the State shall seek to reach agreement with that state' on the exploitation and apportionment of the shared resource.[679]

The practice of Oman and Yemen departs from unilateralism and adopts both self-restraint and bilateral agreement. The two countries agreed under Article 6 of their 1992 boundary treaty that 'in the event of the discovery of common natural resources, agreement shall be reached on the manner of their exploitation and division'.[680] In their 2009 boundary agreement, they expressly

[670] Article 3 of the Agreement between the Kingdom of Sweden and the German Democratic Republic about the Delimitation of the Continental Shelf, 20 December 1978, Lathrop (n 23) 2036.

[671] Article IV of the Declaration between France and Suriname concerning Cooperation in the Maritime Domain, 8 November 2017, Lathrop (n 23) Report No 3-11.

[672] Article 3 of the Agreement between the Government of the Republic of India, the Government of the Republic of Indonesia and the Government of the Kingdom of Thailand Concerning the Determination of the Trijunction Point and the Delimitation of the Related Boundaries of the Three Countries in the Andaman Sea, 2 March 1979, Lathrop (n 23) 1386. See also Memorandum of Understanding between the Royal Government of Cambodia and the Royal Thai Government Regarding the Area of their Overlapping Maritime Claims to the Continental Shelf, 18 June 2001, Lathrop (n 23) 3743. Under arts 1 and 2, the parties declared the intention to negotiate on the joint development of resources within a defined area. The terms of the joint development agreement shall be drawn by a technical team. See also Memorandum of Understanding between the Kingdom of Thailand and Malaysia (n 23).

[673] Treaty between Australia and the Democratic Republic of Timor-Leste (n 645).

[674] Article 4(2) of the Memorandum of Understanding between the Government of the Republic of Turkey and the Government of National Accord-State of Libya on Delimitation of the Maritime Jurisdiction Areas in the Mediterranean, 8 December 2019, UN Registration No 56119.

[675] International Boundary Agreement between the Sultanate of Oman and the Republic of Yemen (n 662); Agreement to Mark the Maritime Borders between the Republic of Yemen and the Sultanate of Oman (n 662).

[676] Article 47 of Law No 286 (n 661).

[677] Directorate General of Hydrocarbon, Ministry of Petroleum, Good International Petroleum Industry Practices (GIPIP), 19 February 2016, dghindia.gov.in/assets/downloads/GIPIP.pdf. The directorate declares sole-country unitisation and cross-border unitisation as good international petroleum industry practices. It recognises that cross-border unitisation typically involves the licensees, but it should take place only after the host states have agreed to a maritime boundary.

[678] India-Indonesia-Thailand Boundary Agreement (n 669)

[679] Article 62 of the Oil/Gas-Petroleum Exploration and Production Act (n 666).

[680] International Boundary Agreement between the Sultanate of Oman and the Republic of Yemen (n 662).

prohibited under Article 4 the '[drilling of] a well on any side of the border line … if any part of its productive sections lies less than 250 metres from the said border line unless commonly agreed by both parties'.[681] Only an agreement between the states parties shall have legal effect on existing licences. Qatar adopts self-restraint rather than unilateralism, provided that the opposite or adjacent state reciprocates.[682]

Other instruments limit the role of petroleum agencies and corporations to technical consultation.[683] In 2001, the petroleum minister of Cambodia and the foreign minister of Thailand entered into a provisional agreement establishing a joint technical committee that would negotiate the terms of joint development and maritime delimitation for adoption by the governments.[684] Most joint development authorities are composed of petroleum agencies and corporations.[685]

[681] Agreement to Mark the Maritime Borders between the Republic of Yemen and the Sultanate of Oman (n 662).

[682] Model Development & Production Sharing Agreement (n 548). Article 37.1 provides as follows:

> Physical Limits on Petroleum Operations: The CONTRACTOR shall keep the GOVERNMENT, through QP, fully informed as to the specific areas from time to time for the conduct of the Petroleum Operations. The CONTRACTOR shall be free to conduct the Petroleum Operations within the boundaries of the Contract Location and elsewhere as provided in this Agreement except that, if there has been an expansion of the Contract Location in accordance with article 5.5 and the GOVERNMENT has reason to believe that activities in a specific area of the expanded Contract Location will result in a dispute over a boundary line with a neighbouring state or states, the GOVERNMENT may set limits on the conduct of the Petroleum Operations within that specific area of the Contract Location provided that 37.1.1. the GOVERNMENT can only set limits if and to the extent that similar limitations are laid down for the operations of other contractors working under similar circumstances in the same vicinity as the Contract Location.

[683] Article 2 of the Agreement between Albania and Italy for the Determination of the Continental Shelf of Each of the Two Countries, 18 December 1992, 26 *Law of the Sea Bulletin* 54; Treaty between the Republic of Trinidad and Tobago and Grenada on the Delimitation of Marine and Submarine Areas (n 653).

[684] Cambodia-Thailand Memorandum of Understanding (n 669). Under arts 1 and 2, the parties declared the intention to negotiate on the joint development of resources within a defined area. The terms of the joint development agreement shall be drawn by a technical team. It is reported that this agreement has been terminated, but no copy of an official statement regarding the termination could be obtained. See 'Termination of the Memorandum of Understanding between the Royal Thai Government and the Royal Government of Cambodia regarding the Area of their Overlapping Maritime Claims to the Continental Shelf', 9 November 2009, ryt9.com/es/mfa/88839.

[685] Article 2-4 of the UK-Argentina Joint Declaration of Cooperation (n 740); (Japan-Korea) 1974 Joint Development Agreement (n 714); (Mauritius-Seychelles) Treaty Concerning the Joint Management of the Continental Shelf in the Mascarene Plateau Region (n 743); Treaty Concerning the Joint Exercise of Sovereign Rights over the Continental Shelf in the Mascarene Plateau Region, Lathrop (n 743); (Nigeria-Sao Tome and Principe) Nigeria-Sao Tome and Principe Joint Development Authority Model PSC, grip.st/docs/27---DT%20-%2027%20_JDA.pdf; (Thailand-Malaysia) Memorandum of Understanding between the Kingdom of Thailand and Malaysia on the Establishment of a Joint Authority, Lathrop (n 23) 1105; (Australia-Timor Leste) art 6, Timor Sea Treaty (n 645).

The laws and treaties of Bangladesh,[686] Bahrain,[687] Bolivia (onshore)[688] and South Korea[689] are silent on the status of shared resources. To fill this gap, their petroleum agencies and corporations issued contracts and regulations that provide for inter-state unitisation agreements.[690] Korea amended its existing petroleum contract to provide that shared resources shall be subject to inter-state agreement, to be negotiated with the technical assistance of the petroleum corporation.[691] In Bolivia, the petroleum agency issued a regulation applying the 'Laws of the Republic and International Law Standards' to shared resources.[692]

b. A Non-traditional Source

The petroleum instruments of the 59 other countries in the case study recognise a non-traditional source of legal rules on shared resources – namely, international agreements that are negotiated and concluded between petroleum agencies and corporations across a maritime zone or boundary. The boundary agreement between Nigeria and Equatorial Guinea authorises the parties' petroleum

[686] Bangladesh Petroleum Act (Act No 32), 2016, dpp.gov.bd/upload_file/gazettes/36878_71554.pdf.

[687] Agreement Concerning Delimitation of the Continental Shelf between Iran and Bahrain (n 521). Article 2 contains a broad resource cooperation clause, but adds a perimeter zone and a prohibition against directional drilling.

[688] Ley No 1689 del 30 de Abril de 1996, biblioteca.unmsm.edu.pe/redlieds/Recursos/archivos/Legislacion/Bolivia/ley1689_hidrocarburos.pdf. Bolivia is land-locked.

[689] The law in force at the time in question was the Sea Bottom Mineral Resources Development Law, Law 2184, 1 January 1970, *Barrows* A&A, Supplement No 29. The original contract dated 24 December 1970 also had no provision on shared resources; see *Barrows* A&A, Supplement No 33. The joint development agreement with Japan is dated 1974.

[690] (Bangladesh) Model Production Sharing Contract 2008, *Barrows* A&A, Supplement No 178. Under art 33.5, the government shall, upon consultation with the contractor, represent the contractor in an international unitisation agreement. The terms of the unitisation agreement shall bind the contractor. (Bahrain): Concession Contract of 15 December 1970 between Superior Oil Inc and the Ruler of Bahrain, *Barrows* ME, Supplement No 32. Article 44 prohibits the contractor from any form of exploration or exploitation activity other than surveying along the boundary. Each petroleum contract is approved by way of legislation. There is no petroleum law of general application. Other contracts are listed in the website of the National Oil and Gas Authority at noga.gov.bh/noga/legislation.aspx, but the text has not been made public.

[691] Amendment of 24 September 1970 to the Wendell Phillips Contract of 24 September 1970 (Concerns Possible Boundary Dispute), *Barrows* A&A, Supplement No 48. The amendment provides that 'in the event of a dispute regarding the boundaries or sovereignty of the agreement area between the Korean government and any other government' and if the dispute causes delays in the operations of the contractor, the latter shall be relieved from its payment obligation (art 2). The contractor 'will cooperate fully with the government in reaching a mutually satisfactory resolution in accordance with the settlement which may be arrived at for the said dispute in the shortest possible time' (art 3). The law in force at that time (the Sea Bottom Mineral Resources Development Law, Law 2184, 1 January 1970, *Barrows* A&A, Supplement No 29) and the original contract had no provision on shared resources. The original contract is dated 24 December 1970 in *Barrows* A&A, Supplement No 33. The joint development agreement with Japan is dated 1974.

[692] Article 24 of the Unitization Regulation (n 25).

agencies and corporations to reach an international unitisation agreement.[693] A subsequent protocol ratified 'four confidential associated commercial agreements signed by the concession holders on each side and approved by … [their respective] governments'.[694] Germany's boundary treaties with Denmark (1971) and the Netherlands (1972) provide that, with respect to shared resources, an arrangement may be 'concluded wholly or in part between [their] beneficiaries … or persons having a right to extract such natural resources', subject to the approval of the governments.[695]

Under the petroleum laws of Benin and Mali, their licensees may come to an agreement with their foreign counterparts,[696] but the same must be approved

[693] See Treaty between the Federal Republic of Nigeria and the Republic of Equatorial Guinea Concerning Their Maritime Boundary (n 582). Article 6.2 states that 'the Contracting Parties shall authorise the relevant government entities in association with the relevant concession holders to establish appropriate unitisation and other arrangements' to enable a shared resource to be developed, provided '[s]uch arrangements shall not be effective until the entry into force of this Treaty'.

[694] Protocol (n 583). Article 2 approved and authorised the implementation of a unitisation agreement between the licensees of Nigeria's Block 102 and Equatorial Guinea's Block B. Each government ensures compliance with the unitisation agreement. Amendments formulated by the licensees must be approved by the respective petroleum agencies (art 3).

[695] Article 2 (1) and (3) of the Agreement between the Federal Republic of Germany and the Kingdom of Denmark Concerning the Delimitation of the Continental Shelf under the North Sea, 28 January 1971, Lathrop (n 23) 1809; art 2(1) and (3) of the Treaty between the Kingdom of the Netherlands and the Federal Republic of Germany Concerning the Delimitation of the Continental Shelf under the North Sea, 7 December 1972, Lathrop (n 23) 1844, which uses the term 'regulation' rather than 'arrangement' and 'entitled party' rather than 'beneficiary'.

[696] Their laws are similarly worded. For Benin, see Loi N° 2019-06 du 15 Novembre 2019, sgg.gouv.bj/doc/loi-2019-06. The unofficial English translation of art 87 reads as follows:

> The State may invite the Holder of an exploitation authorisation relating to a commercial field whose limits extend beyond the territory to a perimeter covered by an authorisation or a hydrocarbon exploitation title issued to a foreign holder to conclude with the latter a boundary unitisation agreement concerning the permits. The signing of this unitisation agreement is subject to the conclusion of an international agreement between the Republic of Benin and the neighbouring state concerned with regard to the conditions and modalities of exploitation of this commercial deposit. [The French text reads: L'État peut inviter le Titulaire d'une Autorisation d'Exploitation portant sur un Gisement Commercial dont les limites s'étendent au-delà du territoire national sur un périmètre couvert par une autorisation ou un titre d'exploitation d'Hydrocarbures délivré à un Titulaire Étranger à conclure avec ce dernier un Accord d'Unitisation limitrophe concerné let permet. La signature de cet accord d unitisation est subordonnée a la conclusion d'un accord international entre la République de Benin et l'état limitrophe concerné relativement aux conditions et modalités d'exploitation de ce gisement commercial.]

For Mali, see Code des hydrocarbures (n 587). The unofficial English translation of art 43 reads as follows:

> The state may invite the holder of an authorisation exploitation relating to a commercial deposit whose limits extend beyond the national territory on a perimeter covered by an authorisation or an operating permit of hydrocarbons delivered to a foreign holder by a state neighbour, to conclude with the latter a unitisation agreement on this commercial deposit, insofar as the legislation of the neighbouring state allows it. The signing of this unitisation agreement is subject to the conclusion of an international agreement between the Republic of Mali and the neighbouring state concerned with regard to the terms and conditions of operation of this commercial

by their respective host governments in the form of a separate inter-state agreement.[697] Cyprus' 2007 petroleum law also authorises its petroleum corporation to reach an agreement with its foreign counterpart, subject to the written approval of the petroleum agency.[698]

These agreements are recognised in petroleum regulations and contracts. Ethiopia's model contracts from 1986 through 2011 allow the petroleum corporation to reach an international unitisation agreement with its foreign counterpart, subject to approval by the petroleum agency; yet, Ethiopia's petroleum law during that same period was silent on the status of shared resources.[699] Under Brunei's model and actual petroleum contracts, Brunei National Petroleum Company Sendirian Berhad or PetroleumBRUNEI shall negotiate international unitisation agreements, notwithstanding the lack of a corresponding provision in its petroleum law.[700] The amendment to Saudi Arabia's 1967 petroleum contract allows AGIP Saudi Arabia to enter into an international unitisation agreement.[701] In the preceding cases, no provision on non-traditional sources can be found in the existing treaties and laws.[702]

The petroleum instruments of other countries that recognise a non-traditional source of rules on shared resources are discussed in section II below. For the purpose of this section, the significance of the foregoing instruments is

deposit. The application decree specifies, as necessary, the modalities of application of the provisions of this article. [The French text reads: L'État peut inviter le titulaire d'une autorisation d'exploitation portant sur un gisement commercial dont les limites s'étendent au-delà du territoire national sur un périmètre couvert par une autorisation ou un titre d'exploitation d'hydrocarbures délivré à un titulaire etranger par un État voisin, à conclure avec ce dernier un accord d'unitisation portant sur ce gisement commercial, dans la mesure où la législation de l'État voisin le permet. La signature de cet accord d'unitisation est subordonnée à la conclusion d'un accords international entre la République du Mali et l'État voisin concerné relativement aux conditions et modalités d'exploitation de ce gisement commercial. Le décret d'application précise, en tant que de besoin, les modalités d'application des dispositions du présent article.]

[697] ibid.

[698] Hydrocarbons (Prospection, Exploration and Exploitation) Regulations, 2007 and 2009, Official Gazette, Suppl III(I):26 1 2007 13 3 2009. Article 21(1) and (5) requires written approval by the petroleum agency of any international unitisation agreement concluded by the contractor.

[699] Section 9.1.3 of the 1986 Model Petroleum Agreement (n 580); s 9.1.4 of the 2011 Model Petroleum Production Sharing Agreement (n 2) in relation to Proclamation No 295/1986, A Proclamation to Regulate Petroleum Operations, 26 March 1986, 45 *Negarit Gazeta* 6, 62.

[700] Article 11.5 of the Production Sharing Agreement for Block L (n 15) vis-a-vis the Petroleum Mining Act Cap 44, 2002, agc.gov.bn/AGC%20Images/LAWS/ACT_PDF/cap044.pdf.

[701] Article 10.8 of the Concession Contract of 21 December 1967 (n 605). This preceded s 3 of Royal Decree No M-27 (n 605).

[702] See, for example, Agreement Relating to the Joint Exploitation of the Natural Resources of the Sea-Bed and Sub-soil of the Red Sea in the Common Zone between Saudi Arabia and Sudan, 26 August 1974, 952 UNTS 198. This provides for an inter-state agreement and established a joint commission headed by their relevant agencies. The agreement between Sudan and South Sudan on oil matters opts for an inter-state agreement on shared resources. See art 9 of the Agreement between the Government of the Republic of South Sudan and the Government of the Republic of Sudan on Oil and Related Economic Matters, 27 September 2012, peacemaker.un.org/sites/peacemaker.un.org/files/SD%20SS_120927_Agreement%20on%20oil%20and%20related%20economic%20matters.pdf.

that they record the practice of states themselves, either bilaterally or unilaterally, whereby international agreements between petroleum agencies and corporations are identified as a source of international law on shared resources.

Several countries in the case study accept both traditional and non-traditional sources. The Bahamas' boundary treaty with Cuba contains a standard resource clause which requires an inter-state agreement,[703] while its own petroleum law contemplates an international agreement being negotiated by its petroleum agency, in consultation with other agencies.[704] Under Iceland's 2001 law, the petroleum agency is authorised to direct the petroleum corporation to reach a unitisation agreement with its foreign counterpart.[705] Yet, Iceland's continental shelf boundary agreement and framework transboundary agreement with Norway contemplate inter-state agreement, and do not mention direct negotiations between its petroleum agency or licensee and their counterparts across the boundary.[706] Under Lebanon's 2018 petroleum contract, shared resources shall be subject to a 'government-to-government' agreement as well as agreement between the right-holder and 'any private sector or right-holder in the other country'.[707] The agreement between petroleum corporations across the boundary 'shall be subject to the prior approval of the Council of Ministers'.[708] Moreover, while Libya's 2019 memorandum of understanding with Turkey requires an inter-state agreement on shared resources,[709] its own boundary agreement with Malta allows direct consultation between their competent authorities.[710] Similarly, Nigeria has an inter-state agreement with São Tomé and Príncipe over a defined joint development zone,[711] while its boundary agreement

[703] Agreement between the Commonwealth of the Bahamas and the Republic of Cuba (n 649).

[704] Act No 2 of 2016, An Act to Provide for the Exploration and Production of Petroleum and for Matters Incidental Thereto, 1 March 2016, extwprlegs1.fao.org/docs/pdf/bha169530.pdf. Under art 26, upon being notified of an actual or potential shared resource, the petroleum agency shall prohibit any activity affecting the resource without its written authorisation. It shall consult with other agencies and decide on the appropriate steps to be taken.

[705] Act on Prospecting, Exploration and Production of Hydrocarbons No 13, 13 March 2001, nea.is/media/olia/Act-No-13-2001-14102014.pdf. Section 19 provides that the energy authority shall oblige the licensees to 'take part in [any] cooperation' arrangement over a shared resource as may be agreed upon between Ireland and a neighbouring country.

[706] Agreement between Norway and Iceland Concerning Transboundary Hydrocarbon Deposits (n 410); Agreed Minutes Concerning the Right of Participation Pursuant to art 5 and art 6 of the Agreement of 22 October 1981 between Iceland and Norway on the Continental Shelf in the Area between Iceland and Jan Mayen, 3 November 2008, 85 *Law of the Sea Bulletin* 27; Agreement on the Continental Shelf between Iceland and Jan Mayen (n 408).

[707] Article 21.5 of the Total E&P Liban, Eni Lebanon, Novatek Lebanon, Production Agreement (n 3).

[708] ibid.

[709] Memorandum of Understanding between the Government of the Republic of Turkey and the Government of National Accord-State of Libya (n 669).

[710] Article 3 of the Agreement between the Republic of Malta and the Great Socialist People's Libyan Arab Jamahariya Implementing Article III of the Special Agreement and the Judgment of the International Court of Justice, 11 December 1987, 22, Lathrop (n 23) 1661.

[711] Treaty between the Federal Republic of Nigeria and the Democratic Republic of São Tomé and Príncipe on the Joint Development of Petroleum and Other Resources in Respect of Areas of the Exclusive Economic Zone of the Two States, 16 January 2003, Lathrop (n 23) 3649.

with Equatorial Guinea authorises their competent authorities to conclude an international agreement relating to a specific shared resource.[712]

Under the maritime boundary treaty between Russia and Norway in the Barents Sea and the Arctic Ocean, their shared resources shall be governed by a hierarchy of agreements: first, Annex II of the treaty, which defines the general area where a possible cooperation on shared resources can be agreed upon and the parameters of any such future interstate unitisation agreement; second, the unitisation agreement between the states parties, which shall delineate the specific shared resource and apportion reserves; and, third, a joint operating agreement among the affected licensees, which shall 'regulate the exploitation of the transboundary hydrocarbon deposit' in accordance with both Annex II of the boundary treaty and the field-specific inter-state unitisation agreement.[713] On the other hand, Russia's maritime boundary agreement with Kazakhstan provides that the 'authorized organizations of the Parties will sign an agreement on the framework for joint activities ... to include the terms for use of the subsoil resources'.[714] Yet, Kazakhstan's petroleum law recognises only inter-state agreements.[715]

Other similar petroleum instruments that recognise non-traditional or mixed traditional and non-traditional sources of rules are discussed in section II below.

To summarise, this preliminary section has explained how the theoretical and conceptual tools of postmodern legal positivism guide the presentation and analysis of petroleum instruments as a record of how states, domestic and international courts, and petroleum agencies, corporations and associations invoke and apply certain criteria by which the rules of international law on shared resources can be identified. The relevant practices that are recorded in

[712] Treaty between the Federal Republic of Nigeria and the Republic of Equatorial Guinea and Protocol (n 582).

[713] Article 5 in relation to Annex II, Treaty between the Kingdom of Norway and the Russian Federation concerning Maritime Delimitation and Cooperation in the Barents Sea and the Arctic Ocean, 7 July 2011, Lathrop (n 23) 5189.

[714] Article 2 of the Seabed Boundary Agreement between the Republic of Kazakhstan and the Russian Federation Protocol to the Agreement between the Republic of Kazakhstan and the Russian Federation on Demarcation of the Seabed in the Northern Caspian Sea for the Purpose of Exercising Sovereign Rights to the Use of Subsoil Resources of 6 July 1998, Kazakhstan approval 14 November 2002; Russian approval 7 April 2003, Lathrop (n 23) 4022.

[715] Decree No 454, Statute on the Ministry of Oil and Gas of the Republic of Kazakhstan, 20 May 2010, OGEL Documents (copy with the author). Article 89 provides as follows:

1. If, as a result of conducted exploration or production, the subsoil user discovers that the field is a cross-border field, the subsoil user shall immediately notify the competent authority thereof.
2. If no relevant international treaties of the Republic of Kazakhstan have been entered into with the state on the territory or under the jurisdiction of which a part of a given cross-border field is located, the competent authority may demand that exploration or production at the cross-border field be suspended until a relevant agreement with that state is reached.

the petroleum instruments are as follows: first, in 91 countries in the case study, the petroleum instruments provide that disputes over shared resources shall be governed by rules of international law; second, in 33 of these countries, the petroleum instruments recognise only the traditional source of rules – that is, international agreements between states; and, third, in the remaining 59 countries, the petroleum instruments also recognise a non-traditional source of rules consisting of international agreements that are negotiated and concluded between petroleum agencies or corporations to manage disputes between their states over shared resources.

Section II below will detail the findings from the case study on the criteria for the formal identification of the non-traditional source of rules.

II. THE MAIN FINDINGS FROM THE CASE STUDY

The following are the key findings from the case study. First, as detailed in section I above, international agreements between petroleum agencies and corporations are recognised as a non-traditional source of the rules of international law on shared resources.

Second, international agreements between petroleum agencies and corporations can be identified as a source of precisely defined rules using the criterion of authority:

(1) The provisions of treaties, laws, regulations and contracts expressly grant to petroleum agencies and corporations authority to negotiate and conclude international agreements on any or all of the following distinct aspects of the exploration and exploitation of shared resources: the delineation of a shared resource; the modalities of cooperation or coordination; and the allocation of costs, production and proceeds.
(2) Treaties, laws and official statements impliedly grant authority by approving agreements that a petroleum agency or corporation had entered into, even without an existing and express grant of authority to do so.

Third, international agreements between petroleum agencies or corporations can be identified as a source of binding rules using the criterion of legality:

(1) The provisions of treaties, laws, regulations and contracts expressly provide that the agreements shall produce rules with legal force upon ratification or approval of the agreement.
(2) Through official statements, governments approve confidential agreements entered into by their petroleum agencies or corporations, and confirm that these agreements shall have legal effect.

The first key finding was already detailed in section I above. In this section, the second and third key findings will be discussed in full.

A. The Identification of International Agreements between Non-state Actors as a Source of International Law Based on Authority

As discussed in section I above, the petroleum instruments of 59 countries in the case study provide that the exploration and exploitation of shared resources shall be governed by the rules of international law. They acknowledge that certain international agreements that are negotiated and concluded between petroleum agencies and corporations are a source of such rules. In this section, the focus is on whether there are formal criteria by which to ascertain that the agreements generate legal rather than non-legal rules. This subsection details the identifying criterion of authority. The relevant provisions in treaties, laws, regulations, contracts and official statements dealing with shared resources expressly or impliedly grant authority to the petroleum agency or corporation to negotiate and agree on specific terms and conditions relating to distinct aspects of the exploration and exploitation of shared resources. Using the criterion of authority, the rules generated by the agreements can be precisely defined.

i. Express Grant of Authority

An express grant of authority is provided in maritime boundary agreements, provisional agreements, national petroleum laws, regulations and contracts. The authority granted is for petroleum agencies and corporations to negotiate and conclude agreements on the designation of a shared resource, the specific mode of cooperation, and the sharing of costs, output and earnings.

a. Express Grant under a Treaty

Generally, the authority granted to the petroleum agency or corporation under a treaty is limited to the formulation of the mode of cooperation or coordination and the allocation of costs, production and proceeds. The delineation of the shared resource is reserved to the state. Under Article 2(3) of the separate maritime boundary agreements of Germany with Denmark and the Netherlands, the authority of their respective licensees is activated only upon a prior determination by both governments or, in the event of disagreement, by an arbitral tribunal that a shared resource exists.[716] Italy's maritime boundary agreements with Yugoslavia and Tunisia respectively require a prior confirmation by both governments that a shared resource exists before their competent authorities may begin negotiations.[717]

[716] 1971 Agreement between the Federal Republic of Germany and the Kingdom of Denmark (n 693); 1972 Treaty between the Kingdom of the Netherlands and the Federal Republic of Germany (n 693).

[717] Article 2 of the Agreement between Italy and Yugoslavia Concerning the Delimitation of the Continental Shelf between the Two Countries in the Adriatic Sea, 21 January 1970, Lathrop (n 23)

In other instances, the authority granted is specific to a shared resource that is already defined in the treaty itself. This is true in the boundary agreements between Nigeria and Equatorial Guinea[718] and in the provisional agreement between Malaysia and Vietnam relating to their overlapping maritime zones in the South China Sea.[719] Libya's boundary agreement with Tunisia[720] is supplemented by a confidential agreement identifying the '7th of November block' as a shared resource and recognising 'Joint Oil' as a legal entity that has been established between their national petroleum corporations with an exclusive right to explore for, develop and produce from the block.[721]

In some treaties, the states parties designate the shared resource and apportion costs, production and proceeds, leaving to their petroleum agencies and corporations the formulation of the commercial terms of cooperation. Thus, the inter-governmental agreement between Senegal and Guinea-Bissau delineated the common zone and fixed resource sharing at 85% for Senegal and 15% for Guinea Bissau.[722] At the same time, they established an 'international agency' with 'exclusive mineral or oil titles' in the zone and 'privileges and immunities that are ordinarily granted to international organizations and their officers'.[723]

1634; art 4 of the Agreement between the Government of the Italian Republic and the Government of the Tunisian Republic (n 583).

Italy considers the boundary agreement in the Adriatic Sea still to be in effect, despite the disintegration of Yugoslavia. Meanwhile, under art 43, para 2 of its 1994 Maritime Code, Croatia recognises the boundary through state succession to the treaty. Gerald Blake and Dusko Topalovic deem all the successor states to Yugoslavia to be automatically bound by the treaty – see G Blake and D Topalovic, 'The Maritime Boundaries of the Adriatic Sea' (1996) 1 *Maritime Briefing* 8, 16.

718 Treaty between the Federal Republic of Nigeria and the Republic of Equatorial Guinea (n 582).

719 Article 8 of the Memorandum of Understanding between Malaysia and the Socialist Republic of Vietnam for the Exploration and Exploitation of Petroleum in a Defined Area of the Continental Shelf Involving the Two Countries, 4 June 1993, Lathrop (n 23) 2341.

720 Agreement between the Great Libyan Arab Socialist People's Jamahariya and the Republic of Tunisia to Implement the Judgment of the International Court of Justice in the Tunisia-Libya Continental Shelf Case, 11 April 1989, Lathrop (n 23) 1679. The decision being implemented is *Continental Shelf (Tunisia/Libyan Arab Jamahiriya)*, Judgment [1982] ICJ Rep 18.

721 See 7 November Block Production Sharing Agreement (n 573), which provides as follows:

> WHEREAS, all Petroleum existing within the Contract Area as defined in Article 1 of this Petroleum Agreement, are national riches of GSPLAJ where located on the Libyan side of the delimitation line of the continental shelf and of TUNISIA where located on the Tunisian side of the delimitation line of the continental shelf; and
> WHEREAS, First Party, pursuant to the Agreement between GSPLAJ and TUNISIA for the establishment of Joint Oil has the exclusive right to explore for, develop and produce Petroleum in and throughout the Contract Area …; and
> WHEREAS, National Oil Corporation of GSPLAJ ("NOC") and Entreprise Tunisienne d'Activites Petrolieres ('ETAP') of TUNISIA have executed Articles of Association of Joint Oil dated December 7, 1988 (the 'Articles of Association').

722 Articles 1-2 of the Management and Cooperation Agreement between the Government of the Republic of Senegal and the Government of the Republic of Guinea-Bissau, 21 December 1995, Lathrop (n 23) 2257.

723 Articles 6 and 8 of the Protocol of the Agreement having reference to the organization and operation of the Agency of Management and Cooperation between the Republic of Senegal and the Republic of Guinea-Bissau instituted by the Accord of 14 October 1993, 21 December 1995.

Its members are the heads of state or their representatives, and its authority includes the formulation of operational regulations and terms of commercial activities.[724] The cooperation agreement between Mauritius and the Seychelles already defined the joint management area and apportioned costs and revenues at 50% each.[725] The only role left to the relevant agencies as part of a joint ministerial council is to resolve operational issues.[726]

Limited authority is granted to the petroleum agencies under Annex II of the Russia-Norway boundary agreement. Such matters as resource designation and cost/production allocation shall already be provided for in the unitisation agreement between the states parties themselves.[727] A similar arrangement is found in the boundary agreement between Norway and Iceland, where the states parties retain the authority to designate the shared resource and set the allocation of costs, production and proceeds.[728] These terms and conditions are deemed to be part of the joint operating agreement between their petroleum agencies and corporations.[729] The Russia-Kazakhstan boundary agreement itself identifies three shared resources, and allocates production and proceeds.[730] Only the mode of cooperation remains to be agreed upon by the petroleum agencies and corporations.

In contrast, Norway's framework agreement with the UK provides that the agreement between their licensees shall cover such matters as the delineation of the shared resource to be exploited and the 'apportionment of the reserves between the licensees of each government'.[731] Under their framework treaty, the US and Mexico allow their executive agencies to designate a shared resource, but they must do so within 60 days, otherwise the authority shall be exercised by the representatives of the states parties.[732] Moreover, the executive agencies shall agree on cost and production allocations within 30 days, otherwise such authority shall be exercised by the states parties.[733]

The framework treaty between Trinidad and Tobago and Venezuela established a joint committee composed of their petroleum agencies, and vested the committee with the authority to delineate the shared resource and to allocate cost

[724] ibid arts 9–11.

[725] Articles 3–4 of the Treaty Concerning the Joint Management of the Continental Shelf in the Mascarene Plateau Region between the Government of the Republic of Seychelles and the Government of the Republic of Mauritius (with annexes), 18 June 2012, UN Reg I-49783.

[726] ibid art 5.

[727] Article 1(1) and (3) and 1(6)(c) of Annex II, Treaty between Norway and Russia (n 712).

[728] Articles 2, 3(1) and (3) of the Agreement between Norway and Iceland Concerning Transboundary Hydrocarbon Deposits (n 410).

[729] ibid art 3(7).

[730] Article 2 of the Seabed Boundary Agreement between the Kazakhstan and Russia (n 715) in relation to arts 3–5 of the Protocol to the Agreement (n 714).

[731] Article 3.3 of the Framework Agreement between the Government of the United Kingdom of Great Britain and Northern Ireland and the Government of the Kingdom of Norway Concerning Cross-boundary Petroleum Co-operation, 10 July 2007, 2491 UNTS 3.

[732] Articles 5, 6, 8 and 14 of the US-Mexico Transboundary Agreement (n 22).

[733] ibid arts 8 and 9.

and production.[734] Pursuant to this treaty, their petroleum agencies concluded a unitisation agreement identifying the Loran-Manatee field as a shared resource and agreeing to a 'hydrocarbon distribution' of 73.06% (Venezuela) and 26.94% (Trinidad and Tobago).[735]

In 2005, Canada and France signed a transboundary agreement which requires an inter-state agreement on the delineation of a shared resource and its joint exploitation.[736] At the same time, the 'mineral title holders' on both sides of a specific field shall conclude a unitisation agreement with provisions on: '(a) combining their respective rights in the hydrocarbon resources of that transboundary field; (b) sharing the costs and benefits relating thereto; and (c) operating the transboundary field as a single unit'.[737] This transboundary agreement shall take effect after France and Canada align their respective laws. Nonetheless, this is a departure from France's earlier boundary agreement with Italy[738] and Canada's boundary agreement with Denmark,[739] both of which recognise only bilateral agreements between states.

To summarise, the foregoing treaties recognise international agreements between petroleum agencies and corporations as a source of legal rules on shared resources. They adopt the identifying criterion of authority granted upon these non-state actors. Generally, the treaties reserve to the states parties any decision on the delineation of the shared resource or its apportionment. The authority of the petroleum agency or corporation is limited to the operational aspects of cooperation. Other treaties grant full authority to the petroleum agency or corporation, including the delineation of the shared resource and its distribution.

[734] Articles 3 and 5 of the Trinidad-Tobago Framework Treaty (n 585).

[735] Articles 2–4 of the Unitisation Agreement for the Exploitation and Development of Hydrocarbon Reservoirs of the Loran-Manatee Field that Extends across the Delimitation Line between the Republic of Trinidad and Tobago and the Bolivarian Republic of Venezuela (with annexes), 16 August 2010, 2876 UNTS 55.
Subsequent geopolitical developments, specifically US sanctions on Venezuela, caused the parties to rescind the agreement and agree on the independent development of the field according to a predetermined recovery factor. See Statement by Prime Minister Dr the Honourable Keith Rowley on the Agreement for the Development of the Loran-Manatee Field, 7 February 2020, opm.gov.tt/17522-2.

[736] Articles 3 and 4 of the Agreement between the Government of Canada and the Government of the French Republic Relating to the Exploration and Exploitation of Transboundary Hydrocarbon, signed 15 May 2005;,Lathrop (n 23) Report No 2-22.

[737] ibid art 5. The agreement is not yet in force as neither government has revised its respective legislation to make way for international unitisation. In 2016, Canada passed the Energy Safety and Security Act, SC 2015, c4, 26 February 2016, laws.justice.gc.ca/eng/acts/O-7/section-29-20160227.html?wbdisable=true. Article 48.1-48.27 applies to transboundary resources. A transboundary resource is as 'a pool, extending beyond the National Energy Board's jurisdiction' (s 29). There is no record of any new legislation by France.

[738] Article 3 of the Agreement between the Government of the French Republic and the Government of the Italian Republic (n 505). The two countries agreed to negotiate an agreement over petroleum fields that are already in production but are found to traverse their boundary. They did not assign any role to their licensees, notwithstanding that the latter have been producing from these fields.

[739] Article 5 of the Agreement between the Government of the Kingdom of Denmark and the Government of Canada Relating to the Delimitation of the Continental Shelf between Canada and Greenland, 13 March 1974, Lathrop (n 23) 380.

b. Express Grant under a Law

In general, laws expressly provide that petroleum agencies and corporations may negotiate and conclude international agreements if their host states have agreed in principle to cooperate rather than engage in unilateral activities in relation to a shared resource. The grant of authority is not unilateral, but bilateral. However, unlike in the preceding sub-section (section II.A.i.a) where the bilateral agreement names the petroleum agencies and corporations as the parties to agreements on shared resources, in this section the bilateral agreement broadly states that shared resources shall be subject to an agreement between the states parties. The law then interprets the broad provision to mean that the agreement shall be negotiated and concluded between the petroleum agencies or corporations of the states parties.

For example, Indonesia's petroleum law provides that the authority of the petroleum agency would depend 'on the continental shelf agreement between the government of the Republic of Indonesia and the government of the other country concerned and on considerations of optimum benefit to the state'.[740] Its petroleum agency would have scope for negotiation with the petroleum agency of Vietnam because the two countries provide under Article 4 of their boundary treaty that they 'shall seek to reach agreement' on the joint exploitation of a shared resource in the South China Sea.[741] Article 4 does not specifically name the petroleum agencies of the states parties as the participants in the negotiations. However, Indonesia's petroleum law interprets Article 4 to mean that an agreement with Vietnam on shared resources can be initiated and signed by their petroleum agencies. In contrast, the petroleum agency of Indonesia would have no authority to negotiate with the petroleum agency of the Philippines, as the boundary treaty between the two countries pertains only to their exclusive economic zone in the Sulawesi Sea and has no provision on shared resources.[742]

Similarly, the petroleum law of Iceland requires that 'an agreement of cooperation regarding exploration and production from the hydrocarbon resource has been reached between the State and the Icelandic State' before the petroleum agency 'may oblige the licensees on the Icelandic continental shelf to take part in the cooperation'.[743] Finally, under the petroleum laws

[740] Articles 40 and 43 of the Upstream Oil and Gas Business Activities (n 592).

[741] Agreement between the Government of the Socialist Republic of Vietnam and the Republic of Indonesia Concerning the Delimitation of the Continental Shelf Boundary, 29 May 2007, Lathrop (n 23) 4301.

[742] Agreement between the Government of the Republic of the Philippines and the Republic of Indonesia Concerning the Delimitation of the Exclusive Economic Zone Boundary, 1 August 2019, Lathrop (n 23) 4947.

[743] Article 19 of the Act on Prospecting, Exploration and Production of Hydrocarbons (n 703).

of Barbados,[744] Mexico[745] and the Republic of Congo,[746] the authority of their respective petroleum agencies and corporations to conclude international agreements on identified shared resources can be exercised only if their respective governments are parties to a general or special agreement on joint exploration and exploitation.

Under the laws of Denmark, Benin and Mali, the authority of the petroleum agency is recognised, but it may be exercised in relation to an identified shared resource only on the basis of a specific government authorisation. Thus, Denmark's continental shelf law provides that upon the identification of a shared resource, the petroleum agency shall be authorised by a special legislative committee to enter into 'an agreement on the coordination of exploration and production … with the relevant country'.[747] The laws of Benin[748] and Mali[749] are similarly worded, and both provide that upon the identification of a shared resource, the 'State may invite' the licensee to conclude a unitisation agreement. Like Benin and Mali, Niger is a landlocked state, but faces Lake Chad. Its petroleum regulation also grants the petroleum agency with the authority to decide

[744] Chapter 282a Offshore Petroleum, 1 LRO 2007, barbadosparliament-laws.com/en/ShowPdf/282A.pdf. Article 41 (5) provides as follows:

> (5) Where a discovery extends into the sovereign territory of another State and an agreement on the coordination of exploration and production is made between the Crown and the other State, the Designated Authority may by written notice (a) require a licensee whose license area includes part of the discovery to participate in such coordination; and (b) specify the terms and conditions applicable to such coordination.

[745] Ley de Hidrocarburos, 11 August 2014, dof.gob.mx/nota_detalle.php?codigo=5355989&fecha=11/08/2014. Under art 3 in relation to art 42, the exploration and exploitation of a shared resource shall be 'carried out under the terms of the treaties and agreements to which Mexico is a party, celebrated by the President of the Republic and ratified by the Chamber of Senators'. Under art 42, the 'Energy Secretary … [shall] instruct the unification of extraction' of shared resources according to the terms of international treaties. Hence, its petroleum laws recognise only inter-state agreements. However, in order to implement the US-Mexico Transboundary Agreement, it passed a law incorporating the treaty *in toto* into national legislation. See Decreto Promulgatorio del Acuerdo entre los Estados Unidos Mexicanos y los Estados Unidos de América relativo a los Yacimientos Transfronterizos de Hidrocarburos en el Golfo de México, firmado en Los Cabos el veinte de febrero de dos mil doce, dof.gob.mx/nota_detalle.php?codigo=5352990&fecha=18/07/2014.

[746] Hydrocarbons Code Law No 28-2016, 12 October 2016, droit-afrique.com/uploads/Congo-Code-2016-Hydrocarbures.pdf. The French text of art 61 reads as follows:

> Si le gisement s'etend sur perimetre situe à l'exeterieur du territorire national, un permis d'exploitation est attribut sur la parties du gisement se trougant à l'interieur du territoire national. Un accord d'exploitation conjointe est conclu, le cas echeant, entre les deux Etats et les contracteurs concernes. [Unofficial English translation: If the deposit extends over a perimeter located outside the national territory, an exploitation permit is granted for the parts of the deposit located inside the national territory. A joint operating agreement is concluded, if necessary, between the two states and the contractors concerned.]

[747] Consolidated Act on the Use of the Danish Subsoil (n 14).

[748] Article 13.4.1 of the 2020 Model Contract, Décret N° 2020-568 du 2 Décembre 2020, sgg.gouv.bj/doc/decret-2020-568.

[749] Code des Hydrocarbures (n 587).

on joint exploitation subject to confirmation of its decisions by the council of ministers.[750]

In contrast, under the petroleum laws of Angola[751] and the Bahamas,[752] regardless of whether there is a bilateral agreement to cooperate, their petroleum agencies and corporations may already coordinate and propose possible cross-border arrangements. The authority of these agencies may be exercised upon the identification of a shared resource. In 2013, Vietnam passed a law promulgating a model contract, section 18.2.2 of which mandates the licensee to negotiate:

> If any proven accumulation of petroleum extends … into … another country, then the contractor and the contractors concerned in such adjacent areas must negotiate in order to reach agreement on unitized development in order to jointly appraise, develop and produce such accumulation of Petroleum by a method generally agreed within the petroleum industry, and in accordance with same the costs and revenue arising shall be shared at an equitable ratio.[753]

The licensee may negotiate upon proof of the existence of a shared resource and according to good industry practice. The 2015 law of Vietnam is slightly different, in that it requires not only the identification of a shared resource, but also the declaration that this is commercially viable before the petroleum agency and the licensee may propose a unitisation plan to the Prime Minister.[754]

No prior bilateral agreement on cooperation or a field-specific legislative authority is necessary under the laws of the Dominican Republic,[755] Equatorial

[750] Décret N°2007-082 /PRN/MME du 28 mars 2007, inis.iaea.org/collection/NCLCollectionStore/_Public/44/129/44129362.pdf. Section 171 provides that the petroleum agency has the authority to decide on the delineation of a shared resource, its joint exploitation and equitable allocation. The licensee shall comply with the decision of the petroleum agency upon approval by the Council of Ministers. The petroleum law itself is silent on the status of shared resources. See Code Pétrolier, Loi n°2007-01 du 31 Janvier 2007, droit-afrique.com/upload/doc/niger/Niger-Code-2007-petrolier.pdf.

[751] Law No 10/04 (n 591). Article 64.8 provides that 'in the event of unitization under paragraph 1 in respect of an area … of a neighboring country, the supervising Ministry, by means of a proposal by the National Concessionaire shall submit the strategy to be pursued in order to render the production of the Petroleum in question possible [for] the approval of the Government'.

[752] Act No 2 of 2016 (n 703). Article 26 on cross-border operations provides: '(1) If a discovery extends over the maritime boundary of The Bahamas into the territory of another country the Minister shall be notified in writing within seven days. (2) Subject to subsection (1), no further activity shall be carried out without the prior approval of the Minister in writing. (3) Subject to subsection (2) the Minister shall in consultation with the relevant authorities take such steps as considered fit'.

[753] Decree No 33-2013-ND-CP, Decree Promulgating Standard Petroleum Production Sharing Contract, 22 April 2013, thuvienphapluat.vn/van-ban/Doanh-nghiep/Decree-No-33-2013-ND-CP-approving-the-model-contract-of-contracts-of-oil-and-183362.aspx.

[754] Law No 95/2015/ND-CP, Decree Detailing some Article of the Petroleum Law, 16 October 2015, thukyluat.vn/vb/decree-no-95-2015-nd-cp-detailing-some-articles-of-the-petroleum-law-47ded.html#TaiVe.

[755] Hydrocarbon Exploration and Production Regulation, Law No 83-16, 23 March 2016, bndh.gob.do/wp-content/uploads/2016/04/Decree-establishing-the-Rules-of-Exploration-and-Production-of-.pdf.

Guinea,[756] Guyana,[757] Lebanon,[758] the Netherlands,[759] Norway,[760] Tanzania,[761] the US[762] and Venezuela.[763] Under the 1966 petroleum regulation and the 1998 petroleum law of the UK, the authority of the petroleum agency does not depend on a prior bilateral agreement on joint exploration or exploitation. Upon being

[756] Article 56, Hydrocarbons Law No 8/2006 (n 3). See also Petroleum Regulations of the Republic of Equatorial Guinea, 20 June 2013, sonagas-ge.com/wp-content/uploads/2012/12/ley_001_en.pdf, which provide as follows:

> Article 118. International Unitization. 1. In the event that one or more of the adjacent areas referred to in Article 111 is situated outside the territory of Equatorial Guinea, the Ministry shall initiate negotiations with the government with jurisdiction over that adjacent area with a view to reaching an agreement acceptable to all parties for the development and production of the discovery concerned. 2. That agreement must be approved by each of the governments involved. Production from the discovery concerned shall not commence until those approvals have been obtained.

[757] Article 69(1) of the Petroleum (Exploration and Production) Act (n 646). The petroleum agency may exercise the authority either to implement a treaty or in the interests of peace.

[758] Offshore Petroleum Resources Law, Law 132 24/8/2010, lpa.gov.lb/Library/Assets/Gallery/asdasdas/Laws/OPRL%20-%20English.pdf. Article 38(1) provides that 'if the reservoir straddles the delimitation line of the continental shelf or territorial waters subject to the jurisdiction of another nation state … [the] right holders shall seek to reach agreement on the most efficient coordinated way of Petroleum Activities'.

This is probably the only instrument that recognises shared resources in the territorial sea.

[759] Law of 23 September 1965, Containing Regulations Governing the Exploration for and the Production of Minerals in or on the Part of the Continental Shelf situated under the North Sea (Continental Shelf Mining Law), 23 September 1965, *Barrows* Europe, Supplement No 8. Section 11 provides that to every license 'may also be attached the regulations that … [if] a deposit which in the opinion of [the] Minister extends beyond the boundary of the relevant part of the continental shelf, render the cooperation requested by [the] Minister in the bringing-about of an agreement between the holder and the party entitled to produce that mineral in an adjoining area, under which production shall be effected in joint consultation'. See also Mining Act of the Netherlands, 1 January 2003, nlog.nl/sites/default/files/2019-02/2019-01-01%20Translation%20Mijnbouwwet%20in%20English.pdf. Article 42(2) provides that the Minister can oblige the licence holder 'to co-operate in reaching an agreement between the licence holder and the party entitled to produce minerals or terrestrial heat in the adjacent area'. The obligations under the law shall apply to the licence holder.

[760] Act No 72 (n 16), which provides as follows:

> Sec 4-7. Coordinated petroleum activities. If a petroleum deposit extends … on the continental shelf of another state, an agreement shall be sought on the most rational coordination of petroleum activities … and on the distribution of the petroleum deposit … Agreements on coordinated exploration drilling shall be notified to the Ministry. Agreements on coordinated extraction activities … shall be submitted to the Ministry for approval. If no agreement is reached within a reasonable time, the Ministry may decide how such coordinated petroleum activities are to take place, including allocating the deposit.

[761] Petroleum Act, 18 September 2015, tpdc.co.tz/wp-content/uploads/2016/02/SHERIA-PETROLEUM-ACT-2015-Updated-version-15-6.pdf. Article 78 states that:

> (5) Where petroleum accumulation extends beyond the jurisdiction of this Act, the Minister, upon advice of [Petroleum Upstream Regulatory Authority] PURA, shall carry out strategies to render unit development in cooperation with the foreign country of jurisdiction on which the accumulation extend with a view to ensure the correct apportionment of the accumulation and the most efficient coordination of petroleum operation.

[762] Paragraph b(1) and (2) of the Transboundary Hydrocarbon Agreements (n 31).

[763] Decreto No 310 (n 588); Hydrocarbons Organic Law (n 588).

satisfied of the existence of a shared resource and the expediency of working and developing it as 'a unit in cooperation by the licensee and all other persons having an interest in any part of the oil field', the petroleum agency may 'give to the licensee such directions as [it]may think fit', even if these would entail a revision or revocation of a development plan.[764]

To summarise, the foregoing petroleum laws recognise that the rules of international law shall govern shared resources, and that a source thereof are international agreements involving petroleum agencies and corporations with the authority to negotiate and agree on all key aspects of its exploration and exploitation. As a rule, while general authority is granted under the law, it may only be exercised if there is an express treaty obligation on the part of the state to cooperate. However, under other laws, the authority granted is broad enough in that it does not depend on a pre-exiting treaty obligation.

c. Express Grant under a Regulation or Contract

Earlier, the 1966 petroleum regulation and the 1998 petroleum law of the UK were cited as a record of the authority of its petroleum agency and licensees to manage disputes over shared resources. However, even before these instruments were issued, the petroleum agency asserted authority to make decisions regarding the unit development of a shared resource. As early as 1965, the petroleum contract issued by the UK provided:

> D. 1 Directions as to oil fields across boundaries – Where the minister is satisfied that any strata in the licensed area or any part thereof form part of an oil field, other parts whereof are in an area to which the minister's powers to grant licenses pursuant to the act of 1934 or the act of 1964 do not apply and the minister is satisfied that it is expedient that the oil field should be worked and developed as a unit in cooperation by the licensee and all other persons having an interest in any part of the oil field, the minister may from time to time by notice in writing give to the licensee such directions as the minister may think fit as to the manner in which the rights conferred by this licensee shall be exercised.[765]

This provision has been incorporated into the UK regulation and law,[766] and it continues to be part of offshore licences.[767] The Frigg field[768] and Statfjord

[764] See art 20, sch 4 of the Petroleum (Production) Regulations, 8 August 1966, *Barrows* Europe, Supplement No 10. Article 5 of sch 1 of the Petroleum Act 1998 (n 598) incorporated sch 4 of the Petroleum (Production) Regulations 1966.

[765] License No P084, Minister of Power and Shell et al, 25 November 1965, dataogauthority.blob.core.windows.net/external/Redacted_Licence_Docs/P084_LICENCE_Redacted.pdf.

[766] Petroleum Act 1998 (n 598) in relation to the Petroleum (Production) Regulations 1966 (n 755).

[767] See art 28 of Licence P2607, Oil and Gas Authority and Hartshead Resourced Ltd, 19 January 2021, dataogauthority.blob.core.windows.net/external/Redacted_Licence_Docs/P2607_Licence_Redacted.pdf.

[768] Frigg Field Unitisation Agreement (n 276).

field[769] unitisation agreements were negotiated and signed by the petroleum agencies of the UK and Norway.[770]

Vietnam's 2013 decree was also preceded by an actual contract whereby the petroleum agency asserted authority to direct the concessionaire in seeking an international agreement on shared resources. Article 33.2 of a 1978 petroleum contract provides that if a shared resource is detected, then 'the state shall assist the concessionaire in seeking a fair and equitable agreement with the other sovereign power(s) and holder(s) of the concession(s) granted thereby'.[771] This particular provision on the authority of the petroleum corporation is not found in subsequent contracts.[772] The 2013 decree restored this authority by providing that the affected 'contractors ... must negotiate to reach a unified development agreement to jointly evaluate, develop and exploit' the shared resource.[773]

However, in 2015, Vietnam passed a law shifting authority to the petroleum agency as well as narrowing its scope:

> Art. 67(5). In case the oil and gas discovery with commercial potential of contractual area reaches the area of adjacent lot which is managed by another country, the contractor shall coordinate with the Vietnam Oil and Gas Group to send a document specifying the reasons and handling plan to the Ministry of Industry and Trade. Within 45 days after receiving such document, the Ministry of Industry and Trade shall coordinate with the Ministries and sectors to prepare the plan and report to the Prime Minister for consideration and decision.[774]

Under this 2015 law, it is the Prime Minister who ultimately decides whether the petroleum agency or the licensee may enter into an international unitisation agreement. Later, in Chapter 5, the discussion will turn to joint exploration between Vietnam's national petroleum corporation and China National Offshore Oil Corporation (CNOOC) on the basis of a confidential framework agreement that has been periodically reviewed and approved by their governments.

A similar practice has been adopted by Iraq. Under Iraq's 2007 and 2011 laws, it is the 'Council of Ministers [that shall take] the necessary measures to protect the interests of all the Iraqi people and discoveries in the fields of

[769] Agreement Relating to the Exploitation of the Statfjord Field Reservoirs and the Offtake of Petroleum therefrom (with annexes), 30 January 1981, 1254 UNTS 380.

[770] See Kemp (n 620) 104–05, 112, 280–81, 285; A Kemp, *The Official History of North Sea Oil and Gas*, vol 2 (New York, Routledge, 2012) 462–63.

[771] Petroleum Contract dated 15 September 1978 for Blocks 01 and 02 TLD between La Societe du Petrole et du Gaz du Viet Nam & the Bow Valley Canadian, *Barrows* A&A, Supplement No 76.

[772] See 2005 Model Petroleum Production Sharing Contract attached to Decree No 139-2005-ND-CP, 11 November 2005, *Barrows* A&A, Supplement No 172; art 18.2 of the Model Petroleum Production Sharing Contract of 2007 between Vietnam Oil & Gas Corporation and Contract, *Barrows* A&A, Supplement No 178.

[773] Decree No 33/2013/ND-CP (n 757).

[774] Law No 95/2015/ND-CP (n 745).

petroleum, which extends beyond the borders of the Republic'.[775] Yet, under Iraq's 2018 model petroleum contract, it is the regional oil company of the petroleum agency that 'shall be the party representing [the] contractor in any international unitization and redetermination agreement', which shall be binding on the contractor.[776] The authority of the regional oil company does not depend on a prior bilateral agreement or a field-specific legislative grant. In the above instances, no prior treaty defining a shared resource or declaring a mode of cooperation is necessary.

In contrast, under the petroleum contracts of Malaysia, there must be an existing boundary agreement before the national petroleum corporation may exercise authority to negotiate and conclude international unitisation agreements. The contracts provide as follows:

> Art 17. Where international boundaries are involved, Petronas shall, after consulting [the] contractors, be the party representing the contract area in the international unitisation agreement, and the terms and conditions agreed to by Petronas (after consulting contractors) shall bind contractors.[777]

No similar provision can be found in the petroleum laws of Malaysia.[778] Malaysia and Vietnam only have a provisional agreement,[779] while Malaysia and Brunei have boundary agreements,[780] one of which is confidential.[781] The statement issued by Malaysia regarding its confidential boundary agreement with Brunei declares that

[775] Iraq Oil and Gas Law 2007, *Oil, Gas & Energy Law Documents* (copy with the author). Article 11 states that: '[The] Council of Ministers shall adopt the necessary measures to protect the interests of the Republic of Iraq in Petroleum Discoveries extending beyond the borders of the Republic. In such cases efforts shall be made to seek joint solutions with the said neighbouring countries.' See also Oil and Gas Law for 2011, OGEL Documents (copy with the author). Article 25 provides that the 'Council of Ministers [shall] take the necessary measures to protect the interests of all the Iraqi people and discoveries in the fields of petroleum, which extends beyond Iraq's borders'.

[776] Development and Production Contract No __[Area] for [Name of Area] between [Regional Oil Company] of the Iraqi Ministry of Oil and [Contractor], ieiti.org.iq/mediafiles/articles/doc-566-2018_12_04_10_12_46.pdf.

[777] Production Sharing Contract dated 3 May 1980 between Petronas, Petronas Carigali, Oceanic and BP Petroleum, *Barrows* A&A, Supplement No 98; Sun Contract dated 11 December 1987 between Petroliam Nasional Berhad and Sun Malaysia Petroleum Company, Champlin Malaysia Inc, and Petronas Carigali Sdn Bhd (Offshore Block PMI), *Barrows* A&A, Supplement No 109; 1989 Offshore Standard Production Sharing Contract, Barrows A&A, Supplement No 107; 1991 Model Contract for Exploration and Production of Petroleum Offshore Malaysia (Deepwater Blocks A & B), *Barrows* A&A, Supplement No 115; 1998 Model Contract (R/C PSC) between Petroliam Nasional Berhad and Petronas Carigali Sdn, Bhd and Contractor, *Barrows* A&A, Supplement No 143.

[778] See Petroleum Development Act 1974 Act 144, 1 October 1974, as amended up to June 2013, agc.gov.my/agcportal/uploads/files/Publications/LOM/EN/Act%20144%20-%20Petroleum%20Development%20Act%201974.pdf; Petroleum Mining Act 1966, with amendments up to 1 January 2006, Oil, Gas & Energy Law Documents (copy with the author).

[779] Memorandum of Understanding between Malaysia and the Socialist Republic of Vietnam (n 717).

[780] Statutory Instruments 1958 No 1517, Overseas Territories, North Borneo (Definition of Boundaries) Order in Council, 1958; Statutory Instruments 1958 No 1518, Overseas Territories, Sarawak (Definition of Boundaries) Order in Council, 1958.

[781] See Statement on the Exchange of Letters between Malaysia and Brunei Darussalam dated 16 March 2009, kln.gov.my/archive/content.php?t=7&articleid=735675.

certain blocks in the area of their overlapping claims 'now belongs to Brunei … [h]owever for this area the agreement includes a commercial arrangement under which Malaysia will be allowed to participate on a commercial basis, to jointly develop the oil and gas resources in this area for a period of 40 years'. On the basis of these provisional agreements, Malaysia's Petroliam Nasional Berhad or Petronas entered into separate agreements with Vietnam Oil and Gas Group or PetroVietnam[782] and the Brunei National Unitisation Secretariat (BNUS).[783]

No prior delimitation is required under the contracts of Cyprus and Albania. Under its regulation and contract, Cyprus grants the petroleum agency and licence-holder the authority to negotiate and conclude a unit development agreement, notwithstanding that bilateral negotiations are ongoing; however, in the event of conflict, the bilateral agreement shall prevail.[784] A broader authority is enjoyed by the petroleum agencies of Albania, which may 'negotiate with the competent agency of the foreign government having jurisdiction to agree upon a unit development scheme' and this will bind the contractor.[785] A subsequent bilateral agreement will also bind the contractor.[786] The regulations and contracts of Brunei,[787]

[782] There is no publicly available official record or statements regarding the agreements; there are only secondary materials that cite each other and without reference to a primary source. See N Chow-Bing, 'Prospects for Sino–Malaysian Joint Development in the South China Sea: Lessons from Malaysia's Experiences' in H Qi and S Xue (eds) *Cooperative Development in the South China Sea: Policies, Obstacles, and Prospects* (New York, Routledge, 2020) 61–63.

[783] See Joint Statement on the 17th Annual Leaders' Consultation between Brunei Darussalam and Malaysia, 8 December 2013, mfa.gov.bn/Lists/Press%20Room/news.aspx?ID=30&ContentTypeId=0x01040055E31CAE71A9C144B21BBB007363093500B667C4949BC69D4394F4AC8FA016E767. The two governments confirmed in para 5 'the signing of Heads of Agreement for Gumusut/Kakap and Geronggong/Jagus-East Fields to establish a joint development based on a provisional production and cost sharing, and the signing of the Heads of Agreement for Kinabalu West NAG and Maharajalela North Fields to formalise the unitization arrangement and way forward on these straddling fields'.

[784] Article 21 of the Hydrocarbons (Prospection, Exploration and Exploitation) Regulations (n 698).

[785] Annex D-2, s 7.4 of the Petroleum Agreement for the Production, Development and Exploration of Petroleum in Delvina Block, 8 August 2007, between Albpetrol Sh A and Stream Oil & Gas Limited, downloads.openoil.net/contracts/al/al_Delvina-Block_dd20070808_Petro-Agree_Albpetrol_Stream.pdf.

[786] ibid.

[787] Model Petroleum Agreement of Brunei Darussalam between the Authority and Company A, and Company B, and Company C, 22 May 2002, *Barrows* A&A, Supplement No 151:

> Article 10.6 … Where international boundaries are involved the authority shall after consulting the operator be the party representing the agreement area in any international unitisation agreement and all terms and conditions agreed thereto by the authority after consultation with the operator shall bind the operator.

The actual contracts that were issued in 2002 identify the authority as PetroleumBrunei. They provide as follows:

> Article 11.5 International Unitisation … (a) PetroleumBrunei may, if it so elects, but only after consulting with the contractor, represent the contractor parties in any international unitisation negotiations …
> (d) During the course of such negotiations, PetroleumBrunei shall (i) endeavour to involve the contractor at each stage, and (ii) make no commitment on any material provisions without the prior agreement of the contractor … (f) Subject to PetroleumBrunei complying with its obligations of this art 11.5, all terms of an international unitisation agreement agreed by PetroleumBrunei shall bind the contractor.

Cameroon,[788] Chad[789] and Eritrea[790] provide that their respective petroleum agencies or corporations shall negotiate with their foreign counterparts on the delineation of a shared resource. The authority of the licensee of Tanzania is to primarily notify the petroleum agency of a potential or actual shared resource and to recommend coordinated activities.[791]

Likewise, despite the absence of a corresponding provision in their petroleum laws, the contracts and regulations of Belize,[792] Ecuador[793] and Ethiopia[794] authorise their respective petroleum agencies and corporations to enter into an international unitisation agreement with their foreign counterparts. Such

See Production Sharing Contract of 2003 between Brunei National Petroleum Corporation and Shell Deepwater Borneo Ltd, Diamond Energy Exploration & Production (Brunei Deepwater) BV and Conoco Philippes (UK), Ltd, Block K, *Barrows* A&A, Supplement No 174; art 11.5 of the Production Sharing Agreement for Block L (n 15).

[788] See Décret d'Application du Code Pétrolier Décret n°2000/465 du 30 juin 2000, droit-afrique.com/upload/doc/cameroun/Cameroun-Decret-2000-465-application-Code-petrolier.pdf. Article 114 provides that the petroleum agency shall have authority to negotiate on the delineation of a shared resource and the equitable distribution of proceeds.

[789] Contrat de Partage de Production entre la Republique du Tchad et le Consortium Mashak Petroleum LLC-Clogoil Systems, observatoire.td/upload/contrats/CPP1%20MASHAK.pdf. According to its unofficial English translation, art 13.4 provides that the petroleum agency shall decide on the delineation of a shared resource and instruct the licensee accordingly. Chad's petroleum law itself recognises only sole-country unitisation. See Decree No 10-796 PR-PM-MPE, 30 September 2010, extwprlegs1.fao.org/docs/pdf/cha161463.pdf.

[790] Legal Notice No 24/1995 Regulations on Petroleum Operations, 11 July 1995, *Barrows*, Supplement No 134. Article 27 provides as follows:

> (1) Where the Minister is satisfied that any strata in the licensed area or any part thereof form part of an oil field, other parts whereof are in an area which lies outside the jurisdiction of Eritrea and the Minister is satisfied that it is expedient that the oil field should be worked and developed as a unit in cooperation by the contractor and all other persons having an interest in any part of the oil field, the Minister may from time to time by notice in writing give to the contractor such directions as the minister may think fit.

[791] Article 32 of the Model Production Sharing Agreement between the Government of the United Republic of Tanzania and Tanzania Petroleum Development Corporation and ABC Ltd for Any Area (2013), tpdc.co.tz/pdfstuff/Model%20Production%20Sharing%20Agreement%20(2013).pdf.

[792] Article 22.5 of the 2007 Belize Model Production Sharing Agreement, estpu.gov.bz/images/GPD/Legal%20Regime/Belize%20Model%20Production%20Sharing%20Agreement.pdf. It applies the rules on sole-country unitisation to international unitisation. This entails the contractor collaborating with its foreign counterpart (art 22.2) and presenting a unitisation agreement for approval by the government (art 22.3). In addition, the government shall adopt special rules to enforce this agreement (art 22.5 and 22.6). No similar provision can be found in its petroleum law; see Petroleum Act Chapter 225, Revised Edition 2000, 5 July 1991, *Barrows* CAC, Supplement No 128.

[793] Service Provision for the Hydrocarbons (Crude Oil) Exploration and Exploitation Contract, in the Block … of the Ecuadorian Amazon Region, *Oil, Gas & Energy Law Documents* (copy with the author). Article 13.9 deals with 'binational common oilfields' by providing that the 'Secretary [of hydrocarbon], in coordination with the equivalent entity … will perform its biggest efforts to arrange an agreement that allow to exploit such discovery, according to the legal normative of each country, and respecting the sovereignty and property of the hydrocarbons resources of each country'. This provision pertains to an onshore area parts of which are disputed with Peru.

[794] Ethiopia 1986 Model Petroleum Agreement (n 580); Ethiopia 2011 Model Contract (n 2).

authority is merely implicit in the petroleum contracts of Gambia[795] and Ireland,[796] which provide that the petroleum agency may delineate a shared resource and decide on whether this should be developed as a unit 'in cooperation by the licensee and all other persons having an interest in [it]'. It is not necessary that there is a prior bilateral agreement before the petroleum agency may decide on these matters.

It may be recalled that as early as 1937 and 1945, the petroleum contracts of the UAE already incorporated an authorisation to petroleum corporations to enter into a cooperation arrangement with the licensees of the joint rulers of the neutral zone.[797] In contrast, in 1957, Saudi Arabia's petroleum contract merely obliged the contractor to acknowledge the share of Kuwait in any production in the two countries' neutral zone.[798] By 1967, Saudi Arabia amended its petroleum contract with Petromin to authorise rights-holders to agree to an international arrangement regarding shared resources.[799] Other petroleum contracts in the Persian/Arabian Gulf merely restored to the rulers the discretion to limit petroleum operations that might affect shared resources.[800] Moreover, in this

[795] See art 24.1 of Petroleum License, 24 May 2012, between the Republic of the Gambia and Camac Energy Block A5 (Gambia) Ltd, resourcecontracts.org/contract/ocds-591adf-5888157546/download/pdf.

[796] Licensing Terms for Offshore Oil and Gas Exploration, Development & Production 2007 (n 596). Article 33 provides that the petroleum agency has authority to delineate a shared resource and to decide on whether it 'should be worked and developed as a unit in co-operation by the licensee or lessee and all other persons having an interest in any part of the field'. Ireland's petroleum law has no provision on shared resources; see Petroleum and Another Minerals Development Act 1960, irishstatutebook.ie/eli/1960/act/7/enacted/en/html.

[797] Petroleum Concession Limited Agreement with the Shaikh of Sharjah and Others (n 636); Agreement between His Excellency Shaikhk Ahmad Bin Rashid, Ruler of Umm-al-Qaiwain Arabia and Petroleum Concessions Limited (n 636).

[798] Agreement dated 10 December 1957 between the Government of Saudi Arabia and Japan Petroleum Trading Company Ltd for Exploitation of the Saudi Arabian Offshore Portion of the Neutral Zone, *Barrows* ME, Supplement No 65. Article 4 states that 'one half of all petroleum produced within the Concession Area shall be deemed to have been produced from the Shaikh's (Kuwait's) undivided one half share in the Petroleum resources in the said Area and one half shall be deemed to have produced from the undivided one half share therein belonging to the Government of the Kingdom of Saudi Arabia'. It implements the boundary treaty between Saudi Arabia and Kuwait. The contract area belongs to Saudi Arabia, but the rights of Kuwait to the shared resource are recognised.

[799] Concession Contract of 21 December 1967 (n 605).

[800] Offshore Concession Agreement and Operating Agreement between the Government of Abu Dhabi and Maruzen Oil Co, Ltd, etc, 6 December 1967, *Barrows* ME, Supplement No 24. Article 43 provides that the concession company shall be free to operate within the limits of its concession area 'save that where operations in a specific area might in the opinion of the Ruler result in disputes with neighboring States; the Ruler may lay down operating limits within the Concession Area. In these circumstances the Companies shall not operate outside the operating limits as defined by the Ruler except with the written approval of the Ruler'. See also art 42 of the Agreement dated 31 January 1970 between the Abu Dhabi Government and Middle East Oil Co, Ltd, *Barrows* ME, Supplement No 46; art 42 of the 1973 Model Agreement, *Barrows* ME, Supplement No 36.

With respect to contracts applicable to the neutral zone, they provide that 'one half of all petroleum produced within the concession area shall be deemed to have been produced from' the undivided half of the joint owner. See art 4 of the Offshore Concession Agreement between the Government of Kuwait and Arabian Oil Co Ltd (Japan Petroleum Trading Co Ltd), July 1958, *Barrows* ME, vol II, B-8.

region, the boundary agreements from 1969 to 1974 did not grant authority to petroleum corporations to act as parties to international agreements on shared resources.[801]

In summary, even in the absence of an express grant under a treaty or law, certain petroleum regulations and contracts provide that rules of international laws shall govern the shared resources of states. They identify international agreements between petroleum agencies and corporations as a source of these rules. The scope of their authority includes the delineation of a shared resource, the definition of the specific mode of cooperation or coordination, and the allocation of costs, production and proceeds. The authority granted usually depends on the existence of an agreed boundary traversing the shared resource. Other regulation and contracts do not impose such a precondition.

ii. Implied Grant of Authority

There are six international agreements that have been concluded between petroleum agencies and corporations and have been published in full. These agreements involve the petroleum agencies and corporations of Angola and the Republic of Congo, Trinidad and Tobago and Venezuela, Angola and the Democratic Republic of Congo (DRC), Cyprus and Egypt, Mauritania and Senegal, and Iran and Azerbaijan. The agreements were concluded despite a lack of an express authority of the parties under an existing treaty or law. However, the agreements were subsequently acknowledged and approved by the governments in a treaty or law.

a. The Angola-Republic of Congo Agreements

In 2001, the Minister of Petroleum of Angola and the Minister of Hydrocarbons of the Republic of Congo signed a protocol of agreement on the 'unitization of prospects 14K, in the Republic of Angola, and A-IMI, in the Republic of the Congo' within a defined unitisation zone, and to an equal sharing of costs and production.[802] They adopted the legal and fiscal terms of the petroleum contract

[801] See Offshore Boundary Agreement between Iran and (UAE) Dubai (n 626). Article 2 is the standard clause on shared resources with a provision establishing a protective perimeter. See also Agreement for Settlement of the Offshore Boundary and Ownership of Islands between the Emirates of Qatar and Abu Dhabi, 20 March 1969, *Barrows* ME, Supplement No 28. Articles 6 and 7 provide that the parties equally own the al-Bunduq field, but Abu Dhabi Marine Areas (ADMA) shall develop it in accordance with the terms of its concession with the Ruler of Abu Dhabi. All royalties and profits shall be divided between Qatar and Abu Dhabi. See also Saudi Arabia-Sudan Agreement (n 701).

[802] Articles 2, 6.3 and 7.3 of the Protocol of Agreement dated 10 September 2001 between the Republic of the Congo and the Republic of Angola Approving Offshore Unitization Zone 14K & A-IMI, Lathrop (n 23) 4288. The zone is defined in a map which forms part of the agreement (art 3).

issued by Angola over block 14K.[803] This protocol agreement was ratified by the Republic of Congo on 14 March 2002[804] and by Angola on 21 May 2002.[805]

The petroleum agencies further agreed to appoint Chevron-Texaco as unit operator and to constitute the inter-state management body.[806] This was approved by the Republic of Congo,[807] while there is no available record of approval by Angola. From 2005 to 2007, the petroleum agencies and all the affected licensees of Congo and Angola signed a Participation Agreement which defined, among other things, the interest held by each licensee. The Republic of Congo approved this participation agreement,[808] while there is no record of its approval by Angola. Angola and the Republic of Congo passed new laws in 2004[809] and 2016[810] respectively, granting their petroleum agencies general authority to negotiate and conclude international agreements on shared resources.

b. The Trinidad and Tobago-Venezuela Agreements

Article 7 of the 1991 boundary treaty between Trinidad and Tobago and Venezuela provides that if a shared resource is identified, the state parties shall 'seek to reach an agreement' on its exploitation and apportionment.[811] In 2003, their petroleum agencies implemented Article 7 by entering into a Letter of Intent and a Memorandum of Understanding declaring the presence of a shared resource across the boundary, and identifying the scope and procedure of negotiations between Venezuela's national petroleum corporation Petróleos de Venezuela SA (PDVSA) and the licensees of Trinidad and Tobago for unitisation.[812]

The preamble to the 2007 framework treaty on unitisation between the states parties confirmed the letter of intent and the memorandum of understanding between their petroleum agencies.[813] The framework treaty defined the principles that would underlie specific unitisation agreements and directed the petroleum

[803] ibid.

[804] See Ordinance No 2-2002 dated 20 February 2002 and Decree No 2002-172 dated 20 March 2002, Special Issue, *Journal Officiel de la République du Congo*, March 2003, sgg.cg/JO/2003/congo-jo-2003-02-sp.pdf.

[805] Republic of Angola Council of Ministers Resolution No 7/02 of 21 May 2002 Approving Protocol of Agreement between Angola and Congo on the Unitization of Prospects 14K and A-IMI, Lathrop (n 23) 428.

[806] Accord dated 26 March 2002 and Agreement Relative to the Inter-state Management Body dated 27 November 2002, Special Issue, *Journal Officiel de la République du Congo* (n 794).

[807] See Decree No 2002-176, 3 April 2002 and Decree No 2002-379, 23 December 2002 Special Issue, *Journal Officiel de la République du Congo* (n 794).

[808] Decree No 2008-157, 25 June 2008, *Journal Officiel de la Republique du Congo No 28*, 10 July 2008, 1271.

[809] Law No 10/04 (n 591).

[810] Hydrocarbons Code Law No 28-2016 (n 746).

[811] Article 7 of the Treaty between the Republic of Trinidad and Tobago and the Republic of Venezuela on the Delimitation of Marine and Submarine Areas, 1654 UNTS 301.

[812] Letter of Intent and Memorandum of Understanding (n 584).

[813] See the preambular clauses in the Trinidad and Tobago-Venezuela Framework Treaty (n 585).

agencies to agree on such matters as the delineation of the shared resource[814] and the distribution of costs, production and proceeds.[815] On the same date on which the framework treaty took effect, a unitisation agreement specifically for the Loran-Manatee field was signed by their petroleum agencies.[816] The petroleum agencies agreed on such key terms as the delineation of the shared resource (Article 2) and the distribution of the 'hydrocarbon volume' (Article 4).

There is no provision in the petroleum law or regulation in Trinidad and Tobago authorising the petroleum agency to negotiate an international unitisation agreement,[817] whereas, since 1999, Venezuela's petroleum law already gave the petroleum agency such authority.[818]

c. The Angola-Democratic Republic of Congo Agreements

In 2003, the petroleum agencies of Angola and the DRC entered into a memorandum of understanding on three blocks in their undelimited maritime zones and declared that each country would have a 50% interest in each block.[819] The blocks are identified in the attached map.[820] Angola's Council of Ministers ratified the agreement in 2005,[821] while the DRC ratified it in 2007.[822]

Thereafter, the same petroleum agencies entered into an agreement defining a broader Common Interest Maritime Zone rather than individual blocks[823] and dividing interest in the zone equally between the two countries.[824] The authority of the petroleum agencies was confirmed when their governments ratified the agreement.[825]

[814] ibid art 3.2

[815] ibid arts 2.3 and 3.2.

[816] Unitisation Agreement for the Exploitation and Development of Hydrocarbon Reservoirs of the Loran-Manatee Field (n 735). This agreement took effect on the same date that it was signed (art 7).

[817] Petroleum Chap 62:01, Act No 46, Act to Consolidate and Amend the Law Relating to Petroleum so as to Make Better Provision for the Exploration for, and the Development and Production of, Petroleum, and for Matters Consequential or Incidental, 30 December 1969, as amended up to 2016, laws.gov.tt/ttdll-web2/revision/download/90976?type=act.

[818] Decreto No 310 (n 588); Hydrocarbons Organic Law (n 757).

[819] Memorando de Entendimento para uma Exploração Petrolífera Comum das Águas Profundas da Bacia Inferior do Congo, 18 June 2003, saflii.org/ao/legis/num_act/mdepuepcdpdbidc886.pdf.

[820] ibid annexes 1–3.

[821] See Ministério dos Petróleos, Resolução No 19/04, de 30 de Julho 2004, saflii.org/ao/legis/num_act/mdepuepcdpdbidc886.pdf.

[822] Law No 07/004, 16 November 2007, 48 *Journal Officiel de la République Démocratique du Congo* 30 November 2007, extwprlegs1.fao.org/docs/pdf/bi-85744.pdf.

[823] Agreement on the Exploration and Production of Hydrocarbons in the Common Interest Maritime Zone between the Democratic Republic of the Congo and the Government of the Republic of Angola, 23 July 2008, Lathrop (n 23) 4277–80. This expanded the common zone to encompass 'North of block 1, South of block 14, North of block 31 of the Angolan petroleum concession'.

[824] ibid arts 3 and 5.

[825] ibid.

d. The Cyprus-Egypt Agreements

In their 2004 maritime boundary treaty,[826] Cairo and Egypt agreed under Article 2 to 'cooperate in order to reach an agreement' on any shared resource. Interpreting this provision as authority to negotiate and conclude an agreement, their petroleum agencies entered into a memorandum of understanding in 2005 and a framework unitisation agreement in 2012.[827] This 2012 agreement was not ratified according to its terms under Article 9.3 and was replaced in 2013 by another framework agreement on broad principles governing the determination of a shared resource and its apportionment (Article 4.2). Their governments confirmed the authority of the petroleum agencies by ratifying the 2013 framework agreement and bringing it into effect in 2014.[828]

e. The Senegal-Mauritania Agreements

Like Angola and the DRC, Senegal and Mauritania do not have a maritime boundary agreement. They have no law or contract granting their petroleum agencies or licensees the authority to directly negotiate on shared resources.[829] However, with the discovery of potential shared resources, their heads of state verbally and in principle agreed on joint exploitation.[830] In 2016, their licensees entered into a memorandum of understanding regarding negotiations on the delineation, assessment, development and exploitation of the shared resource. The text of this agreement is not available to the public, but its execution is reported in Law No 2018-21 of Senegal.[831]

In 2018, the petroleum agencies of the two countries signed an agreement on the unitisation of Grand Tortue/Ahmeyim, specifically Block C-8 (licensed by Mauritania) and Block Saint Louis (licensed by Senegal),[832] providing for a

[826] Agreement between the Republic of Cyprus and the Arab Republic of Egypt on the Delimitation of the Exclusive Economic Zone (with annexes), 7 March 2004, 2488 UNTS 3.

[827] Framework Agreement between the Republic of Cyprus and the Arab Republic of Egypt Concerning the Development of Cross-median Line Hydrocarbons Resources, 27 January 2012, *Efimerida tis Dimokratias* No 4156, Part I, Supplement III, 27 January 2012, 32–44, extwprlegs1.fao.org/docs/pdf/bi-110369.pdf.

[828] Framework Agreement between the Republic of Cyprus and the Arab Republic of Egypt (n 277) preambular clause.

[829] For Mauritania, see Law No 2010–33 dated 20 July 2010 Instituting Code of Crude Hydrocarbons, petrole.gov.mr/IMG/pdf/code_des_hydrocarbures_in_english.pdf; Exploration and Production Contract between the Islamic Republic of Mauritania and Kosmos Energy Mauritania Bloc C8, 5 April 2012, sec.gov/Archives/edgar/data/1509991/000110465913080961/a13-19720_1ex10d17.htm. For Senegal, see Code Pétrolier 2019 (n 590).

[830] See paras 1 and 2 of the Explanatory Statement, Law No 2018-21, 14 June 2018, 63 *Official Journal of the Republic of Senegal* 7119, 57.

[831] ibid para 3. The licensees-parties were Pétroles du Sénégal (Petrosen), Société Mauritanienne des Hydrocarbures et de Patrimoine Minier (SMHPM) and Kosmos Energy.

[832] Article 2 of the Interstate Cooperation Agreement on the Development and Exploitation of the Grand Tortue/Ahmeyim Field Reservoirs between the Islamic Republic of Mauritania and the Republic of Senegal, signed 9 February 2018 by the Minister of Petroleum and Energy of Senegal

provisional equal distribution of costs and production.[833] The agreement was ratified by the government of Mauritania under Law No 2019-12 and Law No 2019-014, all dated 20 February 2019,[834] and the government of Senegal under Law No 2018-21.[835]

f. The Iran-Azerbaijan Agreements

The petroleum agencies of Iran and Azerbaijan agreed to 'jointly exploit Block 1 and Block 2, located in the relevant sectors to be delimited between the Republic of Azerbaijan and the Islamic Republic of Iran, through their national oil companies … on a 50/50 basis'.[836] A map of the blocks is attached to the agreement. The President of Azerbaijan approved the agreement and ordered its implementation.[837] There is no document of a similar written approval by Iran currently available.

g. Confidential Agreements

Unlike the foregoing agreements whose texts have been published, other agreements involving petroleum agencies and corporations are confidential. The existence of the agreements and the authority of their parties are merely cited in a subsequent inter-state agreement or reported in government statements. Thus, the unitisation agreements entered into by the licensees of Equatorial Guinea and Nigeria are confidential, but the existence of the agreements and their legal effects are confirmed under Article 2 of the protocol agreement between the two governments.[838] Iran's petroleum agency and corporation have a memorandum of understanding with those of Iraq regarding the two countries' Naft Shahr and Khorramshahr joint oilfields (onshore), but the agreement is merely reported without the text being quoted by Iran's petroleum agency.[839] A more formal recognition was issued by Malaysia and Brunei with respect to the authority of the Brunei National Unitisation Secretariat (BNUS) and

and the Minister of Petroleum, Energy and Mines of Mauritania, 63 *Official Journal of the Republic of Senegal* 7119, 58.

[833] ibid art 6.

[834] *Official Journal of the Islamic Republic of Mauritania No 1433*, 15 March 2019, 162–64.

[835] Law No 2018-21 (n 826).

[836] Section 1 of the Understanding Memorandum on Joint Development of Relevant Blocks in the Caspian Sea between the Ministry of Energy of the Republic of Azerbaijan and the Ministry of Oil of the Islamic Republic of Iran, 23 April 2018, e-qanun.az/framework/38588.

[837] Decree of the President of the Republic of Azerbaijan on approval of the Memorandum of Understanding between the Ministry of Energy of the Republic of Azerbaijan and the Ministry of Oil of the Islamic Republic of Iran on joint development of relevant blocks in the Caspian Sea (ibid).

[838] Protocol Agreement (n 583).

[839] 'Iran, Iraq Strike Understanding for Development of Joint Oilfields', 7 April 2019, en.shana.ir/news/288279/Iran-Iraq-Strike-Understanding-for-Development-of-Joint-Oilfields.

Petronas to negotiate on the unitisation of four identified fields: 'Kinabalu West NAG (KN) and Maharajalela North Fields (MLJ) and (ii) Gumusut/Kakap (GK) and Geronggong/Jagus-East (GRG/JGE)'.[840] CNOOC and Vietnam National Petroleum Corporation also signed a confidential framework agreement on oil and gas cooperation in the Beibu/Bac Bo Gulf in 2005.[841] Their authority is merely confirmed in regular joint statements issued by their governments.[842]

Other confidential agreements are purportedly confirmed by official acts. However, the text of these official acts are themselves not available to the public. A case in point is the Cooperation Agreement on Oil Exploration within the Common Regime Area (ARC) between the petroleum agencies of Colombia and Jamaica. This agreement is reported to be a treaty in force by the Ministry of Foreign Affairs of Colombia.[843] Another is the memorandum of understanding between the governments of Turkmenistan and Azerbaijan on Joint Exploration and Development of Hydrocarbon Resources of the Dostluk Field in the Caspian Sea, the signing[844] and ratification[845] of which are merely officially reported by the governments, but without their texts. It is also merely reported that the petroleum agencies of Libya and Malta entered into a memorandum of understanding on joint exploration.[846]

To summarise, petroleum agencies and corporations negotiate and conclude international agreements on the determination of the perimeter, the mode of cooperation, and the allocation of costs, production and proceeds in relation to a shared resource. Even without express authorisation under a treaty, the petroleum agencies and corporations initiated negotiations and concluded the agreements. However, their authority to act as the parties was implicitly recognised in the subsequent law, treaty or official statement issued by the respective governments approving the agreement.

[840] Paragraph 5 of the Joint Statement on the 22nd Annual Leaders' Consultation between Malaysia and Brunei, 5 March 2019, mfa.gov.bn/Lists/Press%20Room/news.aspx?id=736&source=http://www.mfa.gov.bn/site/home.aspx.

[841] 'CNOOC and PetroVietnam Signed a Framework Agreement on Oil and Gas Cooperation in the Beibu Gulf', 1 November 2005, gov-cn.translate.goog/jrzg/2005-11/01/content_88855.htm?_x_tr_sch=http&_x_tr_sl=zh-CN&_x_tr_tl=en&_x_tr_hl=fil&_x_tr_pto=op,sc.

[842] See 'Vietnam, China Renew Joint Exploration Agreement', 20 June 2013, en.nhandan.vn/highlights/item/1808402-pm-vows-to-realise-socio-economic-development-plan.html.

[843] 'Jamaica: Agreements Currently in Force', cancilleria.gov.co/en/Jamaica.

[844] 'Meeting of the Presidents of Turkmenistan and Azerbaijan', 21 January 2021, mfa.gov.tm/en/news/2449. This states that negotiations were conducted by the petroleum agencies and corporations, but the memorandum of understanding was signed by the foreign ministers of both countries.

[845] See 'Parliament of Turkmenistan Ratifies MoU on Dostluk Field', 23 February 2021, meclis.gov.az/documents/263-VIQ.pdf.

[846] It was reported that on 2 September 2013, the energy ministers of Libya and Malta signed a memorandum of understanding on energy cooperation, but the text has not been made available to the public. See Annual Report 2013 of the Ministry for Foreign Affairs of the Government of Malta, 9. Libya reported that 'the two countries had agreed to opt for joint oil exploration'. See 'Libya and Malta Agree Oil Deal; Will Collaborate on Exploration', 2 September 2013, english.libyanembassy.org/?p=5827 (copy with the author).

iii. Section Summary

This section has presented the second key finding from the case study: that international agreements between petroleum agencies and corporations can be identified as a source of rules using the criterion of authority. This criterion is discernible in the provisions of treaties, laws, regulations and contracts that expressly grant to petroleum agencies and corporations the authority to negotiate and conclude international agreements on distinct aspects of the exploration and exploitation of shared resources. The criterion can also be drawn from the provisions of treaties, laws and official statements that impliedly grant authority by approving agreements that a petroleum agency or corporation had entered into, even without an existing positive authority to do so.

The grant of authority is either conditional or unconditional and broad or narrow. Authority is conditional if the petroleum agency or corporation may negotiate and conclude an agreement, but only in accordance with an existing treaty of maritime delimitation or provisional cooperation. This conditionality ensures certainty and consistency in the rules promulgated by the agreements. In other cases, no prior delimitation or cooperation agreement is necessary; the petroleum agency or corporation has scope for negotiation on the terms of the agreement. The authority granted may include any or all of the following matters: the delineation of the shared resource; the adoption of modes of cooperation; and/or the allocation of costs and benefits. Thus, based on the provisions of petroleum instruments, authority is an available criterion for identifying international agreements between petroleum agencies and corporations as a source of precisely delineated and clearly defined rules of conduct in relation to shared resources. In other words, by reference to the authority granted to the petroleum agency or corporation, it can be ascertained that their agreements engender specific rules applicable to distinct aspects of the exploration and exploitation of shared resources, and, as such, they can be separated from economic, geopolitical, moral and other rules of conduct.

B. The Identification of International Agreements between Non-state Actors as a Source of International Law Based on Legality

Section II.A found that the petroleum instruments of 59 countries in the case study apply the criterion of authority to indicate that international agreements involving petroleum agencies and corporations are a source of clearly defined rules. This section further finds that the petroleum instruments use a distinct language to signal that the agreements shall generate rules that are also legally binding. The legal effect of the agreements is unmistakable. Under the US transboundary law, the agreements between licensees across the US-Mexico maritime boundary may entail a modified application of US laws and regulations to the affected licence areas.[847] The petroleum law of the Dominican Republic provides that an existing licence may be revoked to give way to an international unitisation agreement that has been entered into by the petroleum agency.[848] The 2022 model petroleum contract of Gambia grants the licensee the procedural right to appeal the instructions of the petroleum agency regarding the implementation of an international agreement on shared resources.[849]

However, such legal effects shall become applicable only upon compliance with certain forms or procedures of approval that the laws themselves prescribe. Thus, the more important question to be addressed shortly is as follows: what are the linguistic and procedural formalities by which it could be ascertained that an international agreement entered into by a petroleum agency or corporation is a source of legal rules? The petroleum instruments are surveyed below and are divided into two general categories: those that expressly require ratification or approval and those that only impliedly require approval.

i. Express Requirement of Ratification or Approval

The six published international agreements between petroleum agencies that were discussed in section II.A all provide that the agreements shall take effect upon ratification according to a prescribed form or approval in a general manner. The same requirement can be found in treaties, laws, contracts and regulations.

a. As Required in Published International Agreements between Petroleum Agencies and Corporations

Article 16 of the protocol agreement between the petroleum agencies of Angola and the Republic of Congo provide that the unitisation of block 14K and block A-IMI shall take effect once their governments have exchanged written notifications of 'ratification by the competent institutions of both States'.[850] Accordingly, Ordinance No 2-2002 of 20 February 2002,[851] Decree No 2002-172

[847] Paragraph b (2) of the Transboundary Hydrocarbon Agreements (n 31).

[848] Hydrocarbon Exploration and Production Regulation, Law No 83–16, 23 March 2016, bndh.gob.do/wp-content/uploads/2016/04/Decree-establishing-the-Rules-of-Exploration-and-Production-of-.pdf. Chapter 5, art 23 provides as follows:

> In the event a hydrocarbon deposit extends to … neighboring countries, this will require entering into an agreement, and subsequent approval by the Dominican State, pursuant to the legal and constitutional provisions in force corresponding to international agreements. The Dominican state may adopt the necessary measures to protect the interest of the Dominican Republic, including, among others, revoking the right of allowing production in the deposit in question.

[849] Article 27 of the Model Petroleum Exploration, Development and Production Licence 2022, mope.gm/download-file/559cb33c-8843-11ec-86ec-022a5fa1767e.

[850] Protocol(n 800).

[851] Ordinance No 2-2002 (n 802).

of 20 March 2002[852] and Decree No 2008-157 of 25 June 2008[853] were issued by the Council of Ministers and the President of the Republic of Congo ratifying the protocol agreement, the agreement creating an inter-state unitisation committee and the participation agreement, respectively, all entered into by its petroleum agency and that of Angola. On the part of Angola, through Resolution No 07/02, its Council of Ministers and President ratified the protocol agreement.[854] A similar requirement of exchange of ratification instruments is provided under Article 9.3 of the framework agreement between the petroleum agencies of Cyprus and Egypt,[855] and Article 8 of the memorandum of understanding between Azerbaijan and Iran.[856]

Pursuant to paragraph 8 of the memorandum of understanding between their petroleum agencies, Angola issued Resolution No 19/04,[857] while the DRC issued Law No 07/004, both ratifying the agreement. The subsequent agreement of the two petroleum agencies of these countries establishing a common interest zone also took effect within six months of its ratification.[858] Moreover, the parties implemented Article 7 of the agreement by establishing a joint working group to formulate the terms of cooperation in the common interest zone.[859] Similarly, in accordance with Article 50 of the inter-governmental cooperation agreement between their petroleum agencies, the governments of Mauritania and Senegal ratified it in separate laws.[860] Thereafter, the government of Senegal amended existing contracts over the area and instructed the licensees and the unit operator to conduct operations according to the unitisation agreement.[861] A simpler process was adopted by the petroleum agencies of Trinidad and Tobago and Venezuela. Their memorandum of understanding[862] and the unitisation agreement for the Loran-Manatee field[863] provide that the agreements shall take effect upon signature.

[852] ibid.

[853] Decree No 2008-157 (n 806).

[854] Resolution No 07/02 (n 803).

[855] Framework Agreement (n 277).

[856] Memorandum of Understanding (n 834).

[857] Resolution No 19/04 (n 819).

[858] Agreement on the exploration and production of hydrocarbons in the common interest maritime zone (n 823).

[859] 'Angola and RDC Analyze Cooperation in the Domain of Hydrocarbons', 25 September 2021, mirempet.gov.ao/ao/noticias/angola-e-rdc-analisam-cooperacao-no-dominio-dos-hidrocarbonetos.

[860] See nn 832 and 833.

[861] Projet de Décret Autorisant l'exploitation par les Compagnies Petrolieres BP Sénégal Investments Limited, Kosmos Energy Investments Sénégal Limited et Petrosen de la Parcellé Sénégalaise Parcelle B issue du Bloc de Saint Louis Offshore Profond et Comprise dans le Périmètre de l'United le la Zone Grant Tortue/Ahmeyim, issued by the petroleum agency, itie.sn/wp-content/uploads/2021/06/4e-Decret-2019-595-autorisant-BP-Kosmos-PETROSEN-dexploiter-la-parcelle-senegalaise-B-pour-GTA.pdf. It recognised the following participation interests: 60% BP Senegal Investment Limited; 30% Kosmos Energy; 10% Petrosen.

[862] Article 11 of the Memorandum of Understanding (n 584).

[863] Article 7 of the Unitisation Agreement (n 808).

b. As Required in Inter-state Agreements, Laws, Regulations and Contracts

The UK-Norway framework transboundary treaty provides that the agreement between their licensees on the delineation of a shared resource and the allocation of costs and production must be approved by the two governments.[864] Approval is presumed unless the licensees are 'notified to the contrary, by either government, within 60 days'. The petroleum agencies of the UK and Norway detailed the requirements for approval of their licensees' agreement.[865] Unlike the foregoing consensus mechanism under the UK-Norway framework treaty, a consent mechanism is provided for by the US-Mexico framework treaty. Agreements between their licensees on the delineation of a shared resource and on production allocation shall require approval by the petroleum agencies and national governments.[866] The agreement is deemed to be rejected if one of the petroleum agencies does not issue written notice of approval, rejection or modification within 120 days from receipt of the proposed agreement.[867]

The boundary treaties of Germany with Denmark and the Netherlands are more broadly worded, as both provide that any arrangement entered into by their licensees shall take effect only upon the separate consent of their respective governments.[868] It is not clear whether such consent shall be expressed in a parallel treaty or in separate ratification instruments. Nigeria and Equatorial Guinea simply provide in their maritime boundary treaty that their licensees may enter into an agreement on shared resources, but '[s]uch arrangement shall not be effective until the entry into force of the treaty' – that is, the maritime boundary treaty itself. France and Canada provide in their proposed bilateral treaty on shared resources that there be a prior agreement between states or a determination by an expert of the presence of a shared resource, and that a subsequent agreement between their licensees on such matters as the allocation of costs and benefits and the specific mode of cooperation shall take effect only following the written approval of the two governments.[869] In their provisional agreement, Barbados and Guyana authorise their petroleum agencies to enter 'a written agreement on joint management' of the two countries' 'area of bilateral overlap in the outer limits of their respective exclusive economic zones', but the

[864] Article 3.2.3 of the UK-Norway Framework Agreements (n 728).

[865] Sections 1 and 2, of the Guidelines for Development of Trans-Boundary Oil and Gas Fields (n 718).

[866] Articles 4, 5, 6(1) and 6(4) of the US-Mexico Transboundary Agreement (n 22),

[867] ibid.

[868] 1971 Agreement between the Federal Republic of Germany and the Kingdom of Denmark (n 693); 1972 Treaty between the Kingdom the Netherlands and the Federal Republic of Germany (n 693).

[869] Article 3-5 of the Canada-France Agreement (n 736), which is not yet in force.

terms and conditions thereof must be agreed upon the two countries in a 'written bilateral agreement or exchange of diplomatic notes'.[870]

The practice of Vietnam varies. Its memorandum of understanding with Malaysia did not delimit the two countries' overlapping claims, but it defined a cooperation area and distributed costs and benefits equally.[871] It then expressly authorised Petronas and PetroVietnam to 'enter into a commercial arrangement … provided that the terms and conditions … shall be subject to the approval of the Government of Malaysia and the Government of the Socialist Republic of Vietnam'.[872] On the other hand, Vietnam's maritime boundary treaty with China in the Gulf of Beibu/Bac Bo requires the consent of both states regarding the designation of the shared resource and equitable sharing of its benefits.[873] Yet, as Chapter 5 will show, PetroVietnam and CNOOC have a joint exploration agreement over a designated area, and this arrangement was regularly approved by the two governments in a series of joint statements.

Certain petroleum laws that recognise international agreements between petroleum agencies and corporations generally do not specify how or when the agreements will have legal effect. Indonesia's petroleum law prescribes a substantive criterion, namely 'considerations of optimum benefit to the state',[874] while the laws of Barbados and Guyana require adherence with the written terms and conditions imposed by the petroleum agency,[875] while those of Iceland require adherence the provisions of an existing treaty.[876] The petroleum law of Tanzania adopts a procedural criterion consisting of regular consultation by the petroleum agency with the Petroleum Upstream Regulatory Authority in order to ensure efficient coordination and equitable apportionment with the petroleum agency of the other state.[877] Other less objective criteria are the perception of

[870] Articles 3 and 6 of the Treaty between the Republic of Guyana and the State of Barbados Concerning the Exercise of Jurisdiction in Their Exclusive Economic Zones in the Area of Bilateral Overlap within Each of Their Outer Limits and Beyond the Outer Limits of the Exclusive Economic Zones of other States, 5 May 2004, Lathrop (n 23) 587.

[871] Articles 1 and 2 of the Malaysia-Vietnam Memorandum of Understanding (n 717).

[872] ibid art 3.

[873] Article 7 of the Agreement between the People's Republic of China and the Socialist Republic of Viet Nam on the Delimitation of the Territorial Seas, Exclusive Economic Zones and Continental Shelves of the Two Countries in Beibu Gulf/Bac Bo Gulf (with maps), effective 30 June 2004, 2336 UNTS 179.

[874] Articles 40 and 43 of the Upstream Oil and Gas Business Activities (n 592).

[875] See art 41(5), ch 282a of the Offshore Petroleum of Barbados (n 739); and art 69(1) of the Petroleum (Exploration and Production) Act of Guyana (n 646).

[876] Article 19 of the Act on Prospecting, Exploration and Production of Hydrocarbons (n 703).

[877] Petroleum Act, 18 September 2015, tpdc.co.tz/wp-content/uploads/2016/02/SHERIA-PETROLEUM-ACT-2015-Updated-version-15-6.pdf. Article 78 states as follows:

> (5) Where petroleum accumulation extends beyond the jurisdiction of this Act, the Minister, upon advice of PURA[the Petroleum Upstream Regulatory Authority], shall carry out strategies to render unit development in cooperation with the foreign country of jurisdiction on which the accumulation extend with a view to ensure the correct apportionment of the accumulation and the most efficient coordination of petroleum operation.

the petroleum agency as to what is 'fit' (the Bahamas)[878] and compliance by the agreement with the laws of each country on sovereignty over petroleum resources (Ecuador).[879]

Other petroleum laws adopt a more formal criterion for legality. Under the petroleum laws of Benin,[880] Mali[881] and the Republic of Congo,[882] any international agreement involving their respective petroleum agencies or licensees must be ratified by way of subsequent parallel inter-state agreements. Equatorial Guinea also requires in its petroleum law that, prior to any production from the shared resource, the international agreement entered into by the petroleum agency shall be approved by the governments that hold an interest in the shared resource.[883] However, it is not clear whether approval must be jointly issued, such as by way of a treaty. Ratification under Venezuela's petroleum law is no less formal: there must be both approval by the petroleum minister and ratification by Congress.[884]

Angola's law requires mere government approval of the agreement.[885] For the Dominican Republic, no less than the 'subsequent approval by the Dominican State, pursuant to the legal and constitutional provisions in force corresponding to international agreements' is necessary.[886] Lebanon prescribes approval in the form of 'a decision by the Council of Ministers on the basis of a proposal by the Minister based upon the opinion of the Petroleum Administration.'[887] In contrast, under the petroleum laws of the Netherlands,[888] Denmark,[889] Norway[890] and Cameroon,[891] approval may be rendered by the agency that has jurisdiction over the petroleum activity.

Petroleum regulations and contracts also adopt a certain language to signal that international agreements involving petroleum agencies and corporations are a non-traditional but identifiable source of legal rules on shared resources.

878 Article 26 of the Act to Provide for the Exploration and Production of Petroleum and for Matters Incidental Thereto (n 703).

879 Article 13.9 of the Service Provision for the Hydrocarbons (Crude Oil) Exploration and Exploitation Contract (n 788).

880 Loi No 2019-06 du 15 Novembre 2019 (n 695).

881 Code des Hydrocarbures (n 587).

882 Article 61 of the Hydrocarbons Code Law No 28-2016 (n 746).

883 Petroleum Regulations of the Republic of Equatorial Guinea (n 750).

884 Decreto No 310 (n 588).

885 Law No 10/04 (n 591).

886 Hydrocarbon Exploration and Production Regulation (n 848).

887 Article 38(1) of the Offshore Petroleum Resources Law (n 752).

888 Law of 23 September 1965 (n 753)

889 Consolidated Act on the Use of the Danish Subsoil (n 14).

890 Section 4-7 of Act No 72 (n 16).

891 Section 82 of Law No 2019/008 of April 25, 2019 on the Petroleum Code, snh.cm/images/publications/Code%20petrolier.pdf. Prior to this law, the 2000 petroleum regulation provided that the agreement entered into by the licensee shall have binding effect if the licensee complied with the instructions of the petroleum agency. See arts 114-16 of the Décret d'Application du Code Pétrolier (n 782).

Under the petroleum contract of Belize, there must be approval by the government and promulgation of special rules in order to give legal effect to the agreement.[892] For the DRC, approval shall be in the form of the concurrence by the state itself with the decision of the petroleum agency or corporation to enter into an international unitisation agreement.[893]

On the other hand, approval by the petroleum agency is sufficient under the petroleum regulations and contracts of Cyprus,[894] Ethiopia,[895] Equatorial Guinea[896] and Tanzania.[897] In addition to approval by the petroleum agency, compliance with the latter's subsequent written instructions is required under the 2007 model contract of Ireland[898] and the 2012 petroleum contract of Gambia[899] for the purposes of implementation of the agreement.

A less formal criterion is prescribed in the model and petroleum contract of Brunei, as mere consultation with the licensee and its involvement in the negotiations being led by the petroleum agency are sufficient.[900] Under Albania's petroleum contract, in the course of negotiations with its foreign counterpart, the petroleum agency must bear in mind the interest of the licensee.[901]

To summarise, the relevant provisions of treaties, laws, regulations and contracts expressly adopt the criterion of legality to identify international agreements between petroleum agencies and corporations as a source of rules on shared resources. They provide that upon ratification or approval by the governments involved, either through the issuance of a ratification instrument or the

[892] Belize Model Production Sharing Agreement (n 787).

[893] Article 9.5 of the Contrat de Partage de Production entre La Republique Democratique du Congo et L'Association Nessergy Ltd./Cohydro sur L'offshore Profond Gongolais (Couloir Maritime) (n 947).

[894] Article 21 of the Hydrocarbons (Prospection, Exploration and Exploitation) Regulations (n 698).

[895] Ethiopia 1986 Model Petroleum Agreement (n 582); Ethiopia 2011 Model Contract (n 2).

[896] Triton Equatorial Guinea, Inc., Block F, PSA, 1997, resourcecontracts.org/contract/ocds-591adf-7317531109/view#/pdf. Section 12.4 provides that the petroleum agency shall direct the contractor to enter into an international unitisation agreement, subject to the provisions of existing treaties. Under s 12.5, the contractor has 180 calendar days to agree and proceed to operate under a cooperation arrangement, subject to the approval of the petroleum agency.

[897] Article 32 of the Model Production Sharing Agreement (n 786).

[898] Articles 32.1 and 33.2 of the Licensing Terms for Offshore Oil and Gas Exploration, Development & Production 2007 (n 596). Ireland's petroleum law has no provision on shared resources; see Petroleum and Another Minerals Development Act, 1960, irishstatutebook.ie/eli/1960/act/7/enacted/en/html.

[899] See Article 24.1 of the Petroleum License, 24 May 2012, between the Republic of the Gambia and Camac Energy Block A2 (Gambia) Ltd, sec.gov/Archives/edgar/data/1402281/000135448812003921/cak_ex108.htm.

[900] Production Sharing Contract of 2003 between Brunei National Petroleum Corporation and Shell Deepwater Borneo Ltd (n 782).

[901] Sec 6.14.4, Bankers Petroleum Albania Ltd, Block F, PSA, 2010, resourcecontracts.org/contract/ocds-591adf-5095341388/view#/pdf, which provides that, with respect to a shared resource, 'AKBN [National Agency of Natural Resources] shall undertake to negotiate with the competent agency of the foreign government having jurisdiction to agree upon a Unit Development Scheme, bearing in mind the interests of the CONTRACTOR', and subject to the right of the contractor to appeal the decision. The agreement must be consistent with the international obligations of Albania.

conclusion of a parallel treaty, or the issuance of a general approval by the petroleum or designated agency, such agreements shall produce rules that have legal and binding effect, including the revocation or modification of affected licences.

ii. Implied Requirement of Approval

Unlike the above published agreements which are formally approved, confidential agreements involving petroleum agencies and corporations are confirmed to exist and are approved either in a subsequent treaty or an official statement of the governments. The unitisation agreements entered into by the licensees of Equatorial Guinea and Nigeria are confidential, and their existence and legal effects are confirmed under Article 2 of the protocol agreement between their governments.[902] It is reported that the petroleum agencies of Kuwait and Iraq have entered into a memorandum of understanding on joint oilfields and that on the part of Kuwait, the agreement was approved by its Council of Ministers through the issuance of Amiri Decree No 217 (2007).[903]

A less formal approval was issued by Malaysia and Brunei with respect to the confidential unitisation agreement between Petronas and Brunei National Unitisation Secretariat and Petronas (BNUS). The two governments issued the following joint statement:

> 11. The Leaders welcomed the formalisation of the Unitisation Agreement (UA) between the Brunei National Unitisation Secretariat and PETRONAS, which would be a landmark agreement and signifies the strong cooperation between the two sides. The UA will provide a positive momentum to the oil and gas cooperation between both countries.[904]

In an official statement in 2005, the governments of China and Vietnam jointly announced their approval of a confidential framework agreement on oil and gas cooperation between CNOOC and PetroVietnam.[905] Approval of the amendment and extension of the agreement was also merely announced in a joint statement:

> The two sides welcomed the amendments to an agreement on joint survey in the defined area in the [Beibu/Bac Bo] Gulf signed between the two nations' relevant businesses, which expands the defined area and extend the term of the agreement as well as promoting joint exploration for oil and gas composition across the delimitation line in the [Beibu/Bac Bo] Gulf for positive progress.[906]

[902] Protocol Agreement (n 583).

[903] See 'Kuwait Okays Oil Field Work with Iraq', *Oil & Gas Journal*, 11 September 2017, ogj.com/articles/2017/09/kuwait-okays-oil-field-work-with-iraq.html.

[904] See Joint Statement on the 23rd Annual Leaders' Consultation between Brunei and Malaysia, 4–5 April 2021, mfa.gov.bn/Lists/Press%20Room/news.aspx?id=904&source=http://mfa.gov.bn/site/home.aspx.

[905] CNOOC and PetroVietnam signed a framework agreement (n 840).

[906] The amendment and map are confirmed by the two governments in 'Vietnam, China Issue Joint Statement', 21 June 2013, en.nhandan.vn/_mobile_politic/item/1813002-vietnam-china-issue-joint-statement.html.

The text of the agreement and the amendment is not available. Agreements involving CNOOC are further discussed in Chapter 5.

A mere announcement by the petroleum agency of Iran signifies the existence and legal effect of the memorandum of understanding involving itself, Iran's petroleum corporation and their counterparts in Iraq.[907] The cooperation agreement between the petroleum agencies of Colombia and Jamaica is also merely announced as an 'agreement currently in force'.[908]

In summary, based on the foregoing petroleum instruments, it can be said that an identifying criterion of legality can be applied even with respect to confidential agreements entered into by petroleum agencies or corporations. Confirmation of the existence of the agreement and approval of its terms are expressed in that instrument to give legal effect to the agreements.

iii. Transparency

The secrecy of some of the agreements discussed above raises difficulties in their identification as a source of rules. Secret treaties between states persist to this day,[909] notwithstanding the requirement of registration of treaties with the United Nations Secretary-General.[910] Secret treaties are concluded between states that make a formal decision to conceal the instrument, in whole or in part, for security and other reasons.[911] Informal agreements that are adopted as a quick response to security issues are often hidden agreements.[912]

Benedict Kingsbury considers publicness, including transparency, to be an indispensable element of legality,[913] while d'Aspremont finds publicness to be a substantive criterion for the purposes of determining the validity of the contents of agreements, insofar as third parties are concerned.[914] For Pauwelyn, the criterion of publicness requires the exercise of value judgement that has no place in neutral source-ascertainment.[915]

Based on the petroleum instruments in the case study, transparency does not appear to be a criterion for the identification of the agreements as a source of legal rules. In fact, all the petroleum contracts impose confidentiality when it comes of maps, plans and scientific data.[916] Prior to publication, petroleum

[907] 'Iran, Iraq Strike Understanding for Development of Joint Oilfields' (n 838).
[908] 'Jamaica: Agreements Currently in Force' (n 838).
[909] See A Pribran, *The Secret Treaties of Austria-Hungary, 1879–1914* (Cambridge, MA, Harvard University Press, 1920)
[910] Article 102 of the UN Charter, 1 UNTS 16. See M Hudson, 'The Registration and Publication of Treaties' (1925) 19 *American Journal of International Law* 273–75.
[911] R Caddell, 'Treaties, Secret' in R Wolfrum (ed), *Max Planck Encyclopedia of Public International Law* (*MPEPIL* online) (copy with the author).
[912] Lipson (n 41) 523.
[913] Kingsbury (n 120) 30–31.
[914] D'Aspremont (n 113) 120–21.
[915] Pauwelyn (n 46) 137–38.
[916] See, for example, art 23 of the Anadarko Algeria Corporation, Sonatrach, PSA, 1989, reourcecontracts.org/contract/ocds-591adf-9645096819/view#/pdf; art 6, Occidental of Yemen (Block 75) (n 422).

contracts are redacted with respect to key provisions on financial terms and geophysical data of petroleum operations.[917] Even the protocol agreement between Equatorial Guinea and Nigeria that approved the unitisation agreements between their licensees expressly provides that these agreements shall remain confidential.[918] Article 5 of the 2018 memorandum of understanding between the Philippines and China states that any agreement between their licensees shall be confidential.[919]

While concealment of the text of international agreements does not make them non-existent, their validity can be challenged by those who had no participation in the negotiation of its terms, but whose interests are adversely affected.[920] The confidential framework agreement between Petronas and BNUS is a case in point. The agreement is part of a package of deals at the center of which is the 2009 exchange of letters between Malaysia and Brunei regarding: (1) the future delimitation of their maritime zones; (2) the relinquishment by Malaysia of ownership over two blocks in these zones; and (3) the joint exploitation of two other blocks.[921] Concealment of the text of the exchange of letter triggered public protests in Malaysia.[922] Similar protests were held in the Philippines regarding the secrecy of the text of the JMSU.[923]

Indeed, there are special linguistic and procedural criteria that require reasonable disclosure of the text of the agreements. Under the petroleum regulation of Norway, the petroleum agency shall act as observer in the joint authority that might be created by the licensees to implement joint exploitation.[924] The evident purpose is to ensure that the public interest is protected. The US transboundary law imposes stringent documentary requirements to be submitted to various government departments.[925] These procedural requirements clearly entail some form of disclosure of the contents of the agreements. An analogous

[917] See Petroleum Contract between CNOOC and Primeline for Contract Area 33/07 in the East China Sea, resourcecontracts.org/contract/ocds-591adf-6266688800/download/word.

[918] Article 10 of the Protocol in Implementation of art 6.2 of the Treaty between the Federal Republic of Nigeria and the Republic of Equatorial Guinea (n 583).

[919] Memorandum of Understanding on Cooperation on Oil and Gas Development between the Government of the People's Republic of China and the Government of the Republic of the Philippines, 27 November 2018, fmprc.gov.cn/mfa_eng/wjdt_665385/2649_665393/t1616644.shtml.

[920] See S Ratner, 'Drawing a Better Line: UTI Possidetis and the Borders of New States' (1996) 90 *American Journal of International Law* 597.

[921] Exchange of Letters between Malaysia and Brunei Darussalam (n 776).

[922] 'Ministry: Two Oil-Rich Blocks Claimed by Malaysia Now Brunei's', *The Star Online*, 4 May 2010, thestar.com.my/news/nation/2010/05/04/ministry-two-oilrich-blocks-claimed-by-malaysia-now-bruneis/#V6rrcTOau28bLeEp.99.

[923] Senate Resolution No 319: Joint marine seismic agreement/Spratly Islands, 14th Congress, 5 March 2008, Congressional Record, Plenary Proceedings, legacy.senate.gov.ph/lis/bill_res.aspx?congress=14&q=SRN-319.

[924] Section 82 of the Regulations to Act Relating to Petroleum Activities, Royal Decree 27 June 1997, as amended up to 2012, npd.no/en/Regulations/Regulations/Petroleum-activities. (n 965).

[925] Paragraph b of the Transboundary Hydrocarbon Agreements (n 31).

study found that agreements involving transboundary oil and gas pipelines[926] adopt the common principles of freedom of production and transit of oil and gas.[927] Transparency of transit is a necessary element of freedom of transit. However, there are exceptions, such the transboundary pipeline agreements in the Middle East, where secrecy was found to be necessary in order to forestall security threats.[928]

Thus, transparency is a governance rather a source-ascertainment criterion. The petroleum instruments in the case study do not expressly require publication. On the contrary, as mentioned above, the protocol agreement between Equatorial Guinea and Nigeria states that the commercial agreements between their licensees shall remain confidential. The 2009 exchange of letters and the subsequent framework unitisation agreement involving Malaysia and Brunei have remained confidential, despite public protests. Lack of publication does not negate the legality of the rules as between the parties, although it does make analysis difficult, as Chapter 5 will show.

iv. Section Summary

In this section, the third key finding from the case study was presented: international agreements between petroleum agencies or corporations can be identified as a source of binding rules using the criterion of legality. The petroleum instruments in the case study apply the criterion of legality by providing that the agreements shall have legal effect following their ratification or approval. They have legal effects in that they can cause changes in existing petroleum laws, regulations and contracts. They can create rights, such as the right of the licensee to notification, consultation, participation in decision-making and even to an appeal. They impose an obligation on these licensees to conduct operations according to the terms of the agreements or the instructions of the petroleum agency. These legal effects set in after the agreements are ratified or approved according to a form or procedure prescribed by the petroleum instrument. Formal ratification shall be rendered through the issuance of separate ratification instruments by the governments involved, as though the agreements were treaties. Ratification can also take the form of a joint approval by these governments as expressed in a parallel agreement. A more general approval can be rendered directly by the governments, without any prescribed form or procedure, or by the petroleum agency or other designated agency. Approval is also implied from certain treaties, laws or official statements confirming and

[926] See R Leal-Arcas, *Energy Transit Activities: Collection of Intergovernmental Agreements of Oil and Gas Transit Pipelines and Commentary* (Brussels, Energy Charter Secretariat, 2015).

[927] Freedom of transit is the absence of interruption in transit, even where ownership of the energy in production and transit is disputed, unless such activities imperil public health and safety (ibid 8–15).

[928] ibid 49–56.

sanctioning agreements that have been negotiated and concluded by petroleum agencies or corporations even without an express and prior grant of authority. Using the criterion of legality as applied in the petroleum instruments, it is possible to ascertain that a set of rules originating from international agreements that have been negotiated and concluded between petroleum agencies or corporations shall have legal and binding force.

The above findings from the case study support the generalisation that authority and legality are formal criteria that can be applied to identify international agreements between petroleum agencies or corporations as a source of clearly defined and legally binding rules on shared resources. Addressing the main question raised in this book, it can therefore be concluded that international agreements between non-state actors are susceptible to formal ascertainment as a source of international law.

III. CHAPTER SUMMARY

This chapter has presented a case study in order to address the main question of whether international agreements between non-state actors can be objectively identified as a source of international law. The case study is on international agreements between petroleum agencies or corporations to manage disputes over shared resources. The research materials consist of certain provisions in petroleum instruments, consisting of treaties, laws, regulations and contracts, of 100 countries. The descriptive and predictive tools of postmodern legal positivism were applied to present and analyse the research materials. According to postmodern legal positivism, the objective criteria for the identification of sources of international law can be discerned from the social conventions of law-applying authorities. In the case study, these social practice and conventions are recorded in certain types of provisions in petroleum instruments.

Section I demonstrated that petroleum instruments are a record of the social conventions of states, courts, agencies, industry leaders and key corporations and associations that engage in the practice of asserting and advocating for the application of certain set of criteria for identifying international legal rules with respect to shared resources. The first main finding laid out in this section is that the petroleum instruments of 92 countries acknowledge that disputes over shared resources are governed by rules of international law. In 33 of these countries, the petroleum instruments recognise international agreements between states as the only source of these rules. However, in the other 59 countries, the petroleum instruments also recognise international agreements between petroleum agencies and corporations as a non-traditional source of said rules. These specific findings from the case study lead to the conclusion that there is available evidence of the recognition of non-traditional sources of the rules of international law. Non-traditional sources co-exist rather than replace the traditional sources of inter-state agreement or custom.

Section II examined whether, in recognising international agreements between petroleum agencies and corporations as a non-traditional source of rules, the petroleum instruments adopted certain criteria to demarcate the rules promulgated by the agreements as legal vis-a-vis the mass of political, economic or even moral norms that are also relevant to activities affecting shared resources. The second finding, which was also presented in this section, is that the petroleum instruments adopt the criterion of authority to identify clearly defined and precisely delineated rules emanating from the agreements and to demarcate them from broad political, economic and moral norms. The criterion of authority pinpoints the actors tasked to negotiate and delimits the scope of their negotiation according to how broad or narrow the procedural and substantive rules they can formulate and the range of activities that those rules can govern. Certainty in the rules is ensured by the enumeration of the activities subject for negotiation, specifically the determination and redetermination of the shared resource, the allocation of costs, production and proceeds and the specific mode of cooperation, including the distribution of jurisdictions. From this particular finding in the case study, it can be concluded that the adoption of the criterion of authority enables the identification of rules of international law from international agreements between non-state actors.

Section II also detailed the third finding: that the petroleum instruments record the adoption of the criterion of legality – that is, they expressly provide that the rules promulgated by the agreements shall have legal and binding force only following the ratification or approval of the agreement, whether through the issuance of a ratifying instrument, or the conclusions of a parallel inter-state agreement, or the issuance of an official statement confirming the agreement. The performance of these positive observable acts provide a tangible signal that the rules laid down by the agreement between petroleum agencies and corporations shall have legal effect as though they emanate from agreements between states.

To conclude and address the main question raised in this book, there are international agreements between non-state actors that are amenable to formal identification as a source of international law.

The significance of the above findings and conclusion would be better appreciated in the context of existing territorial, maritime or resource disputes, and the potential capacity of government agencies and corporations to focus these disputes away from securitisation or militarisation and towards socio-economic management. Chapter 5 looks at how CNOOC engages with PetroVietnam in the Beibu/Bac Bo Gulf; the Japan Oil, Gas and Metals National Corporation (JOGMEC) in the East China Sea; and PetroleumBrunei, PetroVietnam, the Philippine National Offshore Oil Corporation (PNOC) and Forum Energy (a Philippine licensee) in the South China Sea.

5

China National Offshore Oil Corporation and the Management of Resource Disputes in the South China Sea and the East China Sea

Chapter 4 examined the petroleum instruments of 59 countries to find out whether international agreements that are negotiated and concluded between petroleum agencies and corporations can be objectively identified as a source of international legal rules on shared resources. This chapter will focus on arrangements and agreements involving CNOOC in the Gulf of Beibu/Bac Bo, South China Sea and the East China Sea. The discussion is preliminary as most of the agreements are confidential. Moreover, since 2020, the author has been working as a consultant to the Philippine Secretary of Energy as co-Vice Chair in the Intergovernmental Joint Steering Committee under the 2018 Memorandum of Understanding on Cooperation on Oil and Gas Development between the Government of the Republic of the Philippines and the Government of the People's Republic China. As such, she is constrained by the confidentiality clause in her consultancy contract from disclosing the contents of proposals and counterproposals and transcripts of formal meetings and informal negotiations, except those details that are already in the public domain.

The discussion will cover engagements between CNOOC and PetroVietnam, CNOOC and Forum Energy, CNOOC and PetroleumBrunei, and CNOOC and JOGMEC.

I. THE GULF OF BEIBU/BAC BO

The territorial (land boundary), maritime and resource dispute between China and Vietnam in the Gulf of Beibu/Bac Bo dates back several centuries.[929]

[929] L Hiep and A Tsvetov (eds), *Vietnam's Foreign Policy under Doi Moi* (Singapore, Yusof Ishak Institute 2018) 73–74.

This deteriorated into clashes, mainly over fisheries, in the 1970s.[930] In 2000, the two states agreed to a delimitation of their territorial sea, exclusive economic zone and continental shelf in a part of the gulf. Under Article 7, they undertook to reach an agreement on the manner in which a shared resource shall be 'effectively exploited' and the 'equitable sharing of the benefits arising from such exploitation'.[931] This treaty took effect in 2004 and, beginning in 2005, CNOOC and PetroVietnam entered into a series of agreements on joint exploration preparatory to the implementation of Article 7.[932] These agreements are reported in 2013 in NhanDan, the Central Organ of the Communist Party of Vietnam:

> Petrovietnam and the CNOOC signed and implemented a framework agreement on oil and gas co-operation in the agreed offshore area of the Beibu/Bac Bo Gulf in 2005. Based on the outcomes of the framework agreement, the two sides then signed the official agreement on November 6, 2006, which was approved by both Governments and has been in effect since January 2, 2007.[933]

The 2013 report went on to state that 'Petrovietnam, and the China National Offshore Oil Corporation (CNOOC) renewed their agreement on joint exploration' and expanded the 'exploration area from 1,541 km^2 to 4,076 km^2'. It also published a map of the original and expanded joint exploration areas.

The report is accompanied by an image showing that the heads of state of China and Vietnam attested to the signing of the agreement.

This agreement expired in 2016. There is no official statement on the outcome of the joint surveys or on any further extension of the agreement. However, it is reported that the two sides are in discussions about cooperative activities in an undelimited area of the gulf.[934]

Even in the absence of the text of the agreements, several features are discernible. First, CNOOC and PetroVietnam interpreted Article 7 of the delimitation treaty as authority to negotiate the joint exploration agreement. Second, their authority includes the designation of the area for joint exploration, provided that this is situated along the maritime boundary. Third, the agreement took effect following approval by their governments, although the only available evidence of such approval consists of joint statements and official reports, including of the attestation made by their heads of state. Finally, the agreements are of limited duration; their renewal or extension depends on beneficial outcomes for the two states.

[930] G Xue, 'Improved Fisheries Co-operation: Sino-Vietnamese Fisheries Agreement for the Gulf of Tonkin' (2006) 21 *International Journal of Marine and Coastal Law* 220–21.

[931] Beibu/Bac Bo Gulf Treaty (n 873).

[932] 'Vietnam, China Renew Joint Exploration Agreement' (n 842).

[933] ibid.

[934] B de Tréglodé, 'Maritime Boundary Delimitation and Sino-Vietnamese Cooperation in the Gulf of Tonkin' (2016) 3 *China Perspectives* 39. See the map published in the official electronic newspaper of Vietnam in 'Vietnam, China Survey the Agreement Area outside the Mouth of the Gulf of Tonkin', 19 December 2015, baochinhphu.vn/print/viet-nam-trung-quoc-khao-sat-khu-vuc-thoa-thuan-vung-ngoai-cua-vinh-bac-bo-102195699.htm.

Figure 5.1 Diagram of the agreed area for joint exploration in the Tonkin Gulf

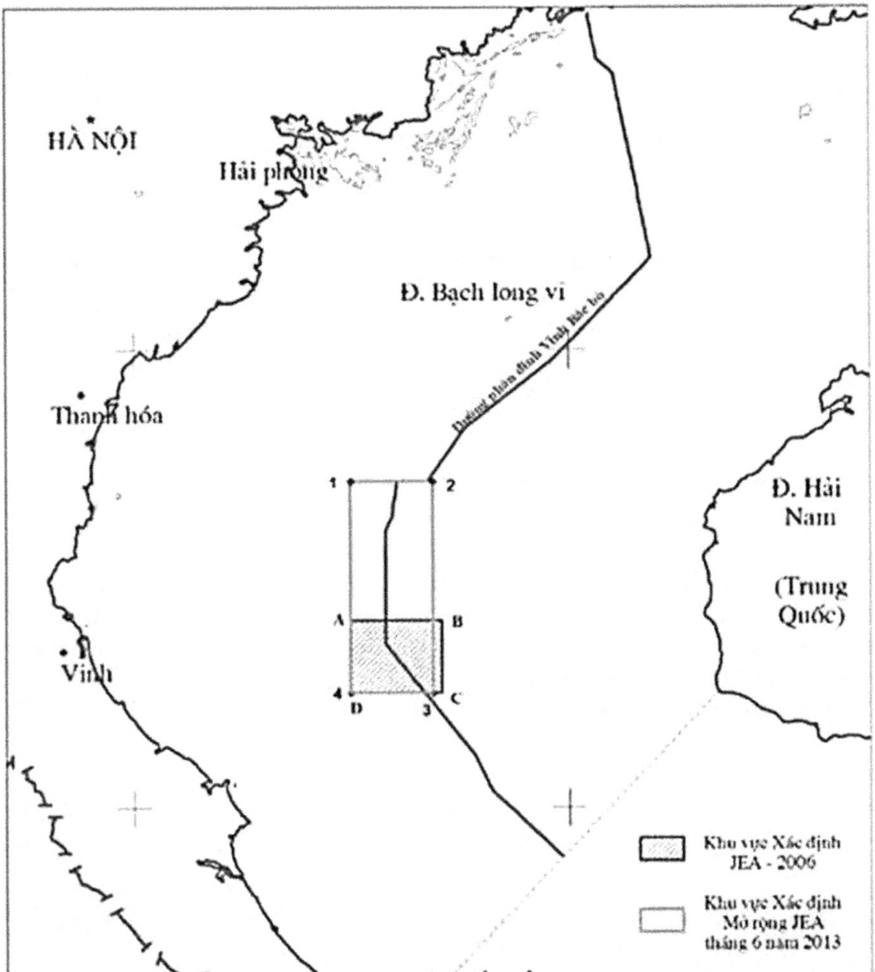

Source: NhanDan Online, Central Organ of the Communist Party of Vietnam

II. THE SOUTH CHINA SEA

At around the same time that CNOOC and PetroVietnam agreed to a joint exploration of a defined area in the Beibu/Bac Bo Gulf, CNOOC, PetroVietnam and PNOC agreed in 2005 to a joint survey of a portion of the South China Sea.[935] In 2018, China and the Philippines entered into a memorandum of understanding on oil and gas cooperation.[936]

A. The CNOOC-PetroVietnam-PNOC Joint Marine Seismic Undertaking

The full text of the CNOOC-PetroVietnam-PNOC joint survey agreement has not been made available to the public.[937] However, as summarised in the joint statement issued by the parties and officially reported by their governments, the key provisions are as follows: first, the parties shall undertake joint research as a pre-exploration activity 'in accordance with the seismic work programmes approved by the parties'; second, the joint research shall 'cover an area of about 143,000 square km which is defined by specific geographic coordinates'; third, the agreement shall be for a term of three years; and, fourth, the agreement shall 'not undermine the basic positions held by their respective Governments on the South China Sea issue'. The coordinates and the map of the agreement area have not been published. However, a number of scholars have adopted unofficial and unconfirmed maps of the area without reference to the coordinates.[938]

The agreement was signed by the national petroleum corporations in the presence of the Chinese and Vietnamese ambassadors, and was presented to the Philippine President.[939] The foreign ministries of the three governments announced the agreement.[940] However, the Philippine Senate eventually opposed the JMSU on the ground that it failed to comply with the constitutional

[935] CNOOC/PETROVIETNAM/PNOC Tripartite Agreement (n 431).

[936] 2018 Memorandum of Understanding (n 920).

[937] The JMSU was preceded by three Philippine-Vietnam Joint Oceanographic Marine Scientific Expedition in the South China Sea (JOMSRE-SCS). After China protested against these activities, the parties adopted the JMSU. See S Balme and M Sidel (eds), *Vietnam's New Order: International Perspectives on the State and Reform in Vietnam* (Basingstoke, Palgrave Macmillan, 2007) 77.

[938] See International Crisis Group, 'Stirring up the South China Sea (IV): Oil in Troubled Waters' (2016) *Asia Report* N°275, Map 4. See also B Milligan, 'Legal and Policy Options for the Provisional Joint Management of Maritime Spaces Subject to Overlapping Jurisdictional Claims' (PhD thesis, University of Wollongong, 2012) fig 3.25.

[939] 'Oil Companies of China, the Philippines and Vietnam Signed Agreement on South China Sea Cooperation', 15 March 2005, ph.china-embassy.org/eng/sgdt/t187333.htm.

[940] 'Foreign Ministry Spokesman Liu Jianchao's Comment on the Joint Marine Seismic Undertaking Accord' (n 431); 'Tripartite Agreement for Joint Marine Seismic Undertaking in the Agreement Area in the South China Sea', 14 March 2005, mofa.gov.vn/en/tt_baochi/pbnfn/ns050314164241/view; 'Secretary Romulo Heralds RP-China-Vietnam Agreement on Joint Seismic Survey of the South China Sea', Press Release, SFA-AGR-149–05 (2005)', 17 March 2005, daf.gov.ph/news/pr/pr2005/mar/pr149.htm.

requirement of Senate concurrence to treaties.[941] PNOC defended bypassing Senate concurrence and explained that the 'JMSU is not a treaty' and that mere 'approval of the respective governments of the three oil companies was required to make the commercial agreement binding'.[942] Consequently, the Philippines allowed the agreement to lapse on 30 June 2008, with only '11,704 line kilometers 2D seismic data acquired from October 2007 to April 2008'.[943]

The foregoing internal dispute in the Philippines over the requirements for giving legal effect to the JMSU stems from the absence of any provision in Philippine treaties, laws, regulations and contracts dealing with shared resources.[944]

B. CNOOC-Forum Energy

On 2 March 2011, Chinese patrol vessels prevented a seismic survey from being undertaken by Forum Energy, the contractor of Service Contract 72 of the Philippines in the South China Sea.[945] This prompted the Philippine government to approve applications for the declaration of 'force majeure' and place exploration activities in Service Contract 72 and four other service contract areas in the South China Sea under moratorium.[946]

While the moratorium was in place, the foreign ministers of China and the Philippines entered into a memorandum of understanding on oil and gas cooperation. While the agreement provides under Article 4 that it 'does not create rights or obligations under international or domestic law', it declares that the two governments have 'decided to negotiate on an accelerated basis arrangements to facilitate oil and gas exploration and exploitation in relevant maritime areas consistent with applicable rules of international law' (Article 2) and 'without prejudice to the respective legal positions of both governments' (Article 4). Towards this end, the agreement adopts a working mechanism with two key features.

First, there shall be two levels of negotiations. At the level of the Intergovernmental Joint Steering Committee, the members shall be the foreign

[941] Senate Resolution No 319: Joint Marine Seismic Agreement/Spratly Islands, 14th Congress, 5 March 2008; Congressional Record, Plenary Proceedings of the 14th Congress, First Regular Session, House of Representatives, Vol 4, No 66, 10 March 2008 at 194.

[942] Joint Statement of former Energy Secretary Vince Perez and former PNOC President Eduardo V Manalac, 9 March 2008, archives.pia.gov.ph/?m=12&sec=reader&fi=p080309.htm&no=10.

[943] 'Philippine National Oil Corporation, PNOC@35 Expanding its Horizons', Annual Report (2008), 4, pnoc.com.ph/wp-content/uploads/2021/05/2008-Annual-Reports.pdf.

[944] See generally M Loja, 'Is the Rule of Capture Countenanced in the South China Sea? The Policy and Practice of China, the Philippines and Vietnam' (2014) 32 *Journal of Energy & Natural Resources Law* 483–508.

[945] See *The Philippines v China* (n 343) para 656.

[946] Memorandum from the Secretary of Energy re Service Contracts in the West Philippine Sea, 25 June 2012.

ministers (as co-chair), the energy ministers (as co-vice-chair) and representatives of an equal number of other relevant agencies (Article 3.a). The committee shall 'negotiate and agree' on the following matters: the cooperation area(s), the cooperation arrangements, and the working groups for the cooperation areas (Article 3.b).

Second, at the level of the Inter-entrepreneurial Working Group(s), the members shall be 'enterprises authorized by the two governments' (Article 3.a). Each working group shall 'negotiate and agree on inter-entrepreneurial technical and commercial arrangements that will apply in the relevant working area' (Article 3.b). For this purpose, the two governments declared that:

> C) China authorizes China National Offshore Oil Corporation as the Chinese enterprise for each Working Group. The Philippines will authorize the enterprise(s) that has/have entered into a service contract with the Philippines with respect to the applicable working area or, if there is no such enterprise for a particular working area, the Philippine National Oil Company-Exploration Corporation (PNOC-EC), as the Philippine enterprise(s) for the relevant Working Group.

The two governments committed to agree on a cooperation arrangement within 12 months. To date, no agreement has been reached.

The Inter-governmental Joint Steering Committee met only once on 28 October 2019. No negotiation took place and no working group was established. In contrast, CNOOC and Forum Energy engaged in informal negotiations in the period from 17 October 2019 to 21 December 2020. Their informal discussions included the delineation of the entire cooperation area as well as certain terms of cooperation. The only committee members present were those from the foreign ministry of China. Forum Energy is the contractor of Service Contract No 72. It has been promoting the idea of a vast integrated energy hub covering almost 60% of the Philippine exclusive economic zone in the South China Sea.

On 15 October 2020, the Philippine President lifted the moratorium on oil and gas activities in the South China Sea, including in Service Contract 72.[947] The energy secretary explained that the lifting of the moratorium was a 'concrete and explicit … enforcement of sovereign rights consistent with our [the Philippines'] real gains in the South China Sea Arbitral Award'.[948] This development brought to the fore two threshold issues affecting the negotiations: first, which area could be offered for negotiation as the broader cooperation area or a specific working area under the 2018 memorandum of understanding; and, second, what was the authority of any enterprise, such as Forum Energy, to negotiate the terms of cooperation relating to a cooperation area or a working area.

[947] 'Pres. Duterte Okays Lifting of Oil Exploration Moratorium in WPS', 15 October 2020, doe.gov.ph/press-releases/pres-duterte-okays-lifting-oil-exploration-moratorium-wps?withshield=1.

[948] Statement of DOE Secretary Alfonso G Cusi on Ensuring PH Energy Security through the Resumption of Oil and Gas Activities and the Licensing of New Contract Areas in the WPS, 16 July 2021, doe.gov.ph/press-releases/statement-doe-secretary-alfonso-g-cusi-ensuring-ph-energy-security-through-resumption.

The first issue relates to the Arbitral Award in *The Philippines v China*. Under the award, only the Philippines has an entitlement to an exclusive economic zone in the area of the Spratly Islands.[949] China's claim to entitlement based on the nine-dash lines was declared contrary to UNCLOS.[950] Moreover, all other claimant states (China, Vietnam and Malaysia) may be entitled to, at most, 12 nautical miles of territorial sea emanating from each rock that they respectively occupy (but which remain contested by other claimants, including the Philippines).[951] The designation of the cooperation area has been made even more complex by the presence of these rocks and pockets of territorial seas within the Philippine exclusive economic zone. As pointed out in the Arbitral Award, the Philippines admitted that the territorial seas of these rocks are automatically enclaved from its 200-nautical mile continental shelf and exclusive economic zone:

> (b) The Philippines' Rights in the Exclusive Economic Zone
>
> 683. The Philippines submits that the waters, seabed and subsoil of the South China Sea within 200 M of the Philippine coast, but beyond 12 M from any high-tide feature within the South China Sea, constitute the EEZ and continental shelf of the Philippines under Articles 57 and 76 of the Convention because none of the maritime features claimed by China generates entitlement to an EEZ or continental shelf.[952]

Hence, there is no overlap between these pockets of territorial seas and the Philippine continental shelf and exclusive economic zone. The question is whether or not the cooperation area or working area(s) may be designated along the interface of the two distinct maritime zones. The history of joint development or international unitisation agreements offers no guidance on this, as there has been no case where the subject matter is a shared resource that straddles the territorial sea of one state and the continental shelf and exclusive economic zone of another state. The fundamental disparity in the nature of the right to full territorial sovereignty over the territorial sea vis-a-vis mere functional sovereign rights over the continental shelf and exclusive economic zone is well established.[953]

Another difficulty in the designation of the cooperation area or working areas is brought about by the continued adherence by China and the Philippines to the concept of an offshore archipelago in the South China Sea. China refers to its offshore archipelago in the Spratly Islands as Nansha Qundao,[954]

949 *The Philippines v China* (n 343) para 1203A(3)(d).
950 ibid para 1203B(2).
951 ibid paras 683 and 1203B(6).
952 ibid.
953 See *Territorial and Maritime Dispute (Nicaragua v Colombia)*, Judgment [2012] ICJ Rep 624, paras 177–78.
954 Position Paper of the Government of the People's Republic of China on the Matter of Jurisdiction in the South China Sea Arbitration Initiated by the Republic of the Philippines, 7 December 2014, para 20.

while the Philippines refers to it as the Kalayaan Island Group (KIG). The Philippines demarcated the KIG in 1978 by drawing straight boundary lines around it and declaring that it has its own 'sea-bed, sub-soil, continental margin and air space'.[955] For China, Nansha Qundao as a single unit is entitled to a territorial sea, continental shelf and exclusive economic zone.[956]

In *The Philippines v China*, the Arbitral Tribunal declared that UNCLOS precludes China, which is a continental state, from claiming Nansha Qundao as an offshore archipelago.[957] It likewise denied the Philippines an entitlement to an offshore archipelago such as the KIG:

> In any event, however, even the Philippines could not declare archipelagic baselines surrounding the Spratly Islands. Article 47 of the Convention limits the use of archipelagic baselines to circumstances where 'within such baselines are included the main islands and an area in which the ratio of the area of the water to the area of the land, including atolls, is between 1 to 1 and 9 to 1'. The ratio of water to land in the Spratly Islands would greatly exceed 9:1 under any conceivable system of baselines.[958]

Yet, in 2020, while purporting to interpret *Philippines v. China*, the Philippine Supreme Court declared that, under Article 76 of UNCLOS, the KIG is a territorial unit with 'its own seabed, subsoil, continental margin, and air space'.[959] This ruling of the Philippine Supreme Court inexplicably departs from the ruling of the Arbitral Tribunal that no feature in the Spratly Islands is entitled to a continental shelf or exclusive economic zone under Article 76.[960]

China also continues to employ the narrative of an offshore archipelago in the Spratly Islands.[961] Given the two parties' departure from the Arbitral Award on the question of an offshore archipelago, the cooperation area or working areas to be designated under the 2018 Memorandum of Understanding would have to be situated within, technically speaking, disputed archipelagic and therefore territorial waters that are subject to the claims not just of China and the Philippines, but also of Vietnam and Malaysia. As Taiwan occupies Itu Aba and this feature falls within Nansha Qundao and the KIG, respectively, its participation would also have to be sought.

The second threshold issue is that, under the Philippine petroleum law, the Philippine petroleum agency has sole regulatory jurisdiction over oil and

[955] Section 1 of Presidential Decree No 1596, officialgazette.gov.ph/1978/06/11/presidential-decree-no-1596-s-1978.

[956] Position Paper (n 955).

[957] *The Philippines v China* (n 343) para 573.

[958] ibid para 574.

[959] *Republic v Provincial Government of Palawan*, GR Nos 170867 & 185941 (Resolution), 21 January 2020.

[960] *The Philippines v China* (n 343) paras 382–84, 625–26, 643–48.

[961] Statement by Spokesperson of the Chinese Embassy in the Philippines on the Presence of Alleged Chinese Maritime Militia Vessels at Niu'e Jiao, 22 March 2021, fmprc.gov.cn/ce/ceph/eng/sgdt/t1863034.htm.

gas activities, including in offshore areas such as the South China Sea.[962] This statutory authority may be amended only by a subsequent law. Thus, it was not amended by the 2018 Memorandum of Understanding. Therefore, it is doubtful whether Forum Energy or any enterprise would derive from the Memorandum of Understanding an authority to offer any area for informal negotiation with CNOOC, much less one which is well beyond Service Contract 72. The existing regulatory regime would have to be amended first to give authority to negotiate to a contractor such as Forum Energy. Otherwise, only the petroleum agency would have colourable authority to engage in the negotiation.

C. CNOOC-PetroleumBrunei

In a joint statement dated 5 April 2013, Brunei and China declared that:

> 10. The Leaders agreed to support relevant enterprises of the two countries to carry out joint exploration and exploitation of maritime oil and gas resources following the principle of mutual respect, equality and mutual benefit. Such cooperation shall not be interpreted as to prejudice the position of the respective countries in relation to maritime rights and interest.[963]

The foregoing commitment is reiterated in the 2018 joint statement of the two governments.[964] There is no record that an agreement has been concluded between their relevant enterprises, namely CNOOC and PetroleumBrunei.

It is remarkable that underlying the commitment to engage in joint exploration and exploitation is an implicit acknowledgement on the part of Brunei that its maritime zones in the South China Sea overlap with those of China. The overlap could only emanate from China's controversial nine-dash line, as China's coast is neither adjacent nor opposite to that of Brunei. Such implicit acceptance by Brunei appears to have been maintained even after the Arbitral Tribunal in *The Philippines v China* declared in 2016 that China's claim to a maritime entitlement on the basis of its nine-dash lines are 'contrary to the Convention [UNCLOS] and without lawful effect to the extent that they exceed the geographic and substantive limits of China's maritime entitlements under the Convention'.[965]

[962] Section 5 of Presidential Decree No 87 and Section 4 of the Republic Act No 7638 (1992), Department of Energy, Compendium of Energy Laws, Circulars and other Issuances, doe.gov.ph/sites/default/files/pdf/issuances/2018_compendium_volume_2_upstream.pdf.

[963] Joint Statement between the People's Republic of China and Brunei Darussalam, 5 April 2013, fmprc.gov.cn/mfa_eng/wjdt_665385/2649_665393/201304/t20130409_679342.html.

[964] Joint Statement between Brunei Darussalam and the People's Republic of China, 19 November 2018, para 11, mfa.gov.bn/Lists/Press%20Room/news.aspx?id=710.

[965] *The Philippines v China* (n 343) para 1203B(2).

III. THE EAST CHINA SEA

After several years of tension over Chunxiao/Shirakaba field in the East China Sea, China and Japan announced on 18 June 2008 that they have reached an 'in-principle consensus' on joint development in an undelimited area, including the Chunxiao/Shirakaba field.[966] Taiwan protested against its exclusion from the agreement.[967]

The full text of the agreement has not been available to the public. While the two governments published a joint statement dated 18 June 2008, their respective publications differ in the choice of words and tenor. For example, according to the version published by the Foreign Ministry of Japan, their leaders 'agreed to cooperate without compromising their legal positions in the transitional period until the delimitation [of the overlapping claims in the East China Sea] is realized',[968] and their agreement is the first step. On the other hand, the Foreign Ministry of China simply declared that 'China and Japan have reached principled consensus on the East China Sea issue through consultation on equal footing', that they 'agreed through serious consultations that the two sides will conduct cooperation in the transitional period prior to delimitation without prejudicing their respective legal positions' and that they had taken initial steps and would continue to consult.[969]

The two versions of the joint statement do not diverge in their definition of the agreed cooperation area.[970] Moreover, both provide that the parties shall engage in the joint exploration of the defined area and thereafter agree on the portion where they shall engage in what Japan refers to as 'collaborative development' and China as 'joint development'. Both agreed to enter into bilateral agreements on joint development in accordance with their respective domestic procedures.

With respect to the Chunxiao/Shirakaba field itself, both versions of the joint statement acknowledge that China has undertaken the production of this field. The two versions then state that Chinese enterprises operating the field welcome the participation of Japanese enterprises in the development of the field and that such participation shall be in accordance with the prevailing laws of China.[971]

[966] Y Song, 'Peaceful Proposals and Maritime Cooperation between Mainland China, Japan, and Taiwan in the East China Sea: Progress Made and Challenges Ahead' (2016) 22 *Asian Yearbook of International Law* 25, 29.

[967] Y Hwang and E Frettingham, 'Sovereignty and Identity: Taiwan's Claims in the South China Sea' in Y Hwang and E Frettingham, *Maritime and Territorial Disputes in the South China Sea Faces of Power and Law in the Age of China's Rise* (New York, Routledge, 2021) 78–80.

[968] 'Japan-China Cooperation in the East China Sea', Japan-China joint press release, 18 June 2008, mofa.go.jp/mofaj/area/china/higashi_shina/press.html.

[969] 'China and Japan Reach Principled Consensus on the East China Sea Issue', 18 June 2008, mfa.gov.cn/ce/cenz//eng/xw/t466729.htm.

[970] The coordinates of the cooperation area are identified in the joint statement.

[971] See Shirakaba (Chinese name: 'Spring Akatsuki'), Understanding of Oil and Gas Field Development, 18 June 2008, in 'Japan-China Cooperation' (n 969).

The fundamental difference between the versions lies in the language used in relation to when the Chunxiao/Shirakaba agreement between their enterprises will take effect. The Japanese version reads as follows:

> The two governments will confirm this, agree on the necessary exchange statement, and strive to conclude it as soon as possible. Both sides will take the necessary domestic procedures to conclude the agreement.[972]

On the other hand, the version published by China reads as follows:

> The governments of China and Japan have confirmed this, and will work to reach agreement on the exchange of notes as necessary and exchange them at an early date. The two sides will fulfill their respective domestic procedures as required.[973]

Thus, for China, pending formalisation, approval of the agreement among all the enterprises involved is already presumed, while for Japan, approval has yet to be made. Nonetheless, it is apparent that both require a government approval for the purposes of giving effect to the agreement.

IV. CHAPTER SUMMARY

This chapter has highlighted the significance of the findings and conclusion of the case-study in Chapter 4. In the Gulf of Tonkin, the South China Sea and the East China Sea, petroleum agencies and corporations are at the forefront of negotiations of agreements for managing disputes over shared resources. Similar to the practices discussed in Chapter 4, the practices of CNOOC in relation to PetroVietnam, PNOC and JOGMEC indicate the adoption of the identifying criteria of authority and legality for the purposes of establishing that the agreements involving these parties shall produce rules with legal effect. These agreements are a viable mode of reversing the securitisation of resources disputes in the South China Sea. With respect to Forum Energy and PetroleumBrunei, there is uncertainty regarding their authority to negotiate on certain aspects of the exploration and exploitation of shared resources.

[972] ibid.

[973] See Understanding on the Participation of Japanese Legal Person in the Development of Chunxiao Oil and Gas Field in Accordance with Chinese Laws, 18 June 2008, in 'China and Japan Reach Principled Consensus' (n 970).

6

Conclusion

CHAPTER 4 LAID out four concrete findings regarding the identification of international agreements between petroleum agencies and corporations as a source of international law on shared resources.

First, petroleum instruments are a record of the social conventions of states, courts, agencies, industry leaders, and key corporations and associations that engage in the practice of applying certain sets of criteria for identifying international legal rules with respect to shared resources. The petroleum instruments of 59 countries recognise that international agreements that are negotiated and concluded between petroleum agencies and corporations are a non-traditional source of such rules.

Second, in recognising international agreements between petroleum agencies and corporations as a non-traditional source of rules, the petroleum instruments further adopted criteria to demarcate the rules promulgated by these agreements as legal vis-a-vis the mass of political, economic or even moral norms that might be relevant to but not binding on activities affecting shared resources.

Third, one criterion that can be found in the petroleum instructions of 59 countries is that of authority. Authority to negotiate and agree on distinct aspects of the exploration and exploitation of shared resources ensures that clearly defined and precisely delineated rules emanating from the agreements can be identified. The criterion of authority enables the demarcation of these rules from broad political, economic and moral norms.

Fourth, the petroleum instruments also record the adoption of the criterion of legality. The rules promulgated by the agreements have legal and binding force upon government approval, whether rendered formally or formal in a general manner. As approval requires a positive act, it sufficiently signals when an agreement shall have legal effect.

Based on the above findings, it can be generalised that international agreements between non-state actors are amenable to formal ascertainment as a source of international law.

Chapter 5 demonstrated the significance of the above findings and conclusion. In the context of heightening tensions in the Gulf of Beibu/Bac Bo, the South China Sea and the East China Sea, the availability of agreements between CNOOC, PetroVietnam, PNOC and JOGMEC as a non-traditional source of legal rules forestalls the militarisation of resource disputes in these waters.

In addition, the findings and conclusion establish that, as was discussed in Chapter 2, postmodern legal positivism offers useful conceptual and theoretical tools for the purposes of explaining and analysing emerging realities in international law. It is unlike the mainstream state-centric and consent-based approach of positivism and the purpose-driven and value-laden pluralistic approach, which, as was shown in Chapter 3, retreat into deformalisation when faced with new realities.

While this book confined its data-gathering and textual analysis to certain provisions on shared resources in petroleum instruments, its outcome addresses the broader question raised in Chapter 1: whether international agreements between non-state actors can be identified as a source of international law using objective criteria. The methodology it employed can therefore be replicated to make better sense of the place of non-state actors in the international legal system.

Appendix

The petroleum instruments that were used in the case study are presented in the table below. They were issued by 100 countries over the period from 1937 to 2021. They are presented by country, treaty, law, regulation and contract. Those petroleum instruments that contain a provision dealing with disputes over shared resources are shaded. The titles of the instruments are found in the notes.

Table of Petroleum Instruments

Country	Treaties		Laws		Regulations and contracts	
1. Albania	(Italy) 1992[974] (Gre) 2009[975]			1993[976]	2010[977] 2007[978]	1993[979] 2012[980]
2. Algeria	(Tunisia) 2003[981]		2019[982]	1986[983] 1988[984]		1989[985]
3. Angola	(RC) 2001,[986] (DRC) 2008[987]	(Nam) 2002[988]	2004[989]		2003[990] 2005[991] 2010[992] 2012[993]	1973[994] 1991[995]
4. Argentina	(Uru) 1974[996] (UK) 1995/2007[997]	(Chile) 1985[998]		1967[999] 2014[1000]		1985[1001] 2015[1002]
5. Australia	(Tim) 2019[1003] (Pap) 1978/1985[1004] (Ind) 1997[1005]		2006[1006]			
6. Azerbaijan	(Iran) 2018[1007] (Turkmenistan) 2021[1008] (Kazakhstan) 2003[1009]					2018[1010]
7. The Bahamas	(Cuba) 2012[1011]		2016[1012]	1971[1013]		2016[1014]
8. Bahrain	(SA) 1958[1015] (Iran) 1972[1016]			1970[1017]		
9. Bangladesh				1974[1018]	2008[1019]	1993[1020]
10. Barbados	(Guy) 2004[1021]		2007[1022]	2013[1023]		
11. Belize[1024]				2000[1025]	2007[1026] 2000–2010[1027]	1992[1028] 2003[1029]
12. Benin	(Nig) 2006[1030]		2019[1031]	2006[1032]	2020[1033]	1997[1034]
13. Bolivia				1996[1035] 2005[1036]	2003[1037]	2006[1038]

(continued)

(Continued)

Country	Treaties		Laws		Regulations and contracts	
14. Brazil		(Uru) 1975[1039] (Fr Gui) 1981[1040]		1997[1041] 2010[1042]		2016[1043] 2004[1044] 2008[1045] 2017[1046]
15. Brunei	(Mal) 2009[1047]	1958[1048]		1948[1049] 1963[1050] 2002[1051]	2002[1052] 2003[1053] 2006[1054] 2019[1055]	
16. Cambodia	(Viet) 1992[1056] (Th) 2001[1057]			1991[1058]		1991[1059] 2004[1060]
17. Cameroon		(Nig) 1975[1061]		1999[1062]	2000[1063]	2007[1064]
18. Canada	(Den) 1974[1065] (France) 2005[1066]			2015[1067] 1985[1068] 1988[1069]		
19. Chad				2010[1070] 2007[1071]	2018,[1072,1073]	
20. China	(Viet) 2004[1074] (Phil) 2018[1075]			2016[1076] 1986[1077]	2005[1078] 2013[1079]	1982[1080] 1985–98[1081] 1993[1082] 2005–12[1083]
21. Colombia	(Hon) 1986[1084] (Jam) 1993[1085]	(Ec) 1975[1086] (Pan) 1976[1087] (CR) 1977[1088] (DR) 1978[1089] (Ha) 1978[1090]		1999[1091] 2001[1092]	2008[1093]	2004[1094] 2009[1095] 2011[1096] 2013[1097] 2019[1098]
22. Costa Rica	(Ec) 1984[1099]	(Pan) 1982[1100] (see Col)		1994[1101]		1994[1102] 1999[1103] 1989[1104]
23. Cuba	see Bah (2012)[1105]	(Mex) 1976[1106] (Haiti) 1978[1107] (Hon) 2013[1108] (Jam) 1995[1109] (US) 2015[1110]				1993[1111] 1995–99[1112]
24. Cyprus	(Eg) 2003[1113] 2014[1114] (Is) 2011[1115] (Leb) 2007			2007[1116]	2007[1117] 2007[1118] 2016[1119]	1962[1120] 2012[1121]
25. Denmark	(Nor) 1965[1122] (Neth) 1966[1123] (UK) 1966[1124] 1999[1125] (Ger) 1971[1126] (Iceland/ Faroes) 2008[1127] see Can (1974)		2011[1128]	1950[1129]	2018[1130]	1963[1131]

(continued)

(Continued)

Country	Treaties		Laws		Regulations and contracts	
26. The Dominican Republic		(Col) 1979[1132] (Ven) 1982[1133]	2016[1134]		2016[1135]	
27. DRC	see Angola (2008)			1981[1136]	2005[1137]	
28. Ecuador	see Costa Rica (1984)	Peru 1975, 1994[1138]		2017[1139]	2012[1140]	1999[1141]
29. Equatorial Guinea	(Nig) 2000–02[1142]	(Sen) 1993[1143] (ST) 1999[1144]	2006[1145]	1981[1146]	1982[1147] 1997[1148] 2013[1149]	1998[1150] 2006[1151]
30. Eritrea			2000[1152]	1995[1153]	1997[1154]	
31. Ethiopia				1986[1155]	1986[1156] 1994[1157] 2011[1158]	1973[1159]
32. France	(It) 2015[1160] (Sp) 1994[1161] see Canada (2005)	(UK) 1977–2014[1162] (Sey) 2011[1163]				1947 and 1955[1164]
33. Gabon		(STP) 2001[1165]		2014[1166]		1995[1167] undated[1168] 2006[1169]
34. Gambia		(Sen) 1976[1170]		2004[1171]	2012[1172] 2014[1173] 2022[1174]	
35. Germany	(Neth) 1960[1175] 1962[1176] 1972[1177] see Den (1971) (Swe) 1978[1178]			1980[1179]		1972[1180]
36. Ghana			2016[1181]	1984[1182]		2000[1183] 2002[1184] 2005[1185] 2008[1186] 2006[1187] 2009[1188] 2016[1189]
37. Greece	see Al (2009) (It) 1980[1190]			2011[1191]		2014[1192] 2014[1193] 2017[1194]
38. Grenada	(T&T) 2010[1195]			1989[1196]		1996[1197]
39. Guatemala			1983[1198]			1983[1199] 2005[1200] 2005[1201] 2009[1202] 1976[1203]

(continued)

(Continued)

Country	Treaties		Laws		Regulations and contracts	
40. Guinea Bissau	(Sen) 1960[1204] 1995[1205]			1982[1206] 2006[1207]		2011[1208]
41. Guyana	see Bar (2004)		1986[1209]	1997[1210]	1999[1211] 2015[1212] 2016[1213]	1986[1214]
42. Honduras	see Col (1986) (Mex) 2006[1215]	(see Cuba) (UK) 2002[1216]		1984[1217] 2013[1218]		2013[1219]
43. Iceland	(Nor) 1981[1220] 2008[1221] 2011[1222] see Den/Faroes (2008)		2001[1223]		2013[1224] 2014[1225]	2009[1226]
44. India	(Th) 1978[1227] (Indo, Th) 1979[1228] (Maldives) 1978[1229] (Sri) 1976[1230]				2016[1231]	2005[1232]
45. Indonesia	(Th) 1973[1233] 1975[1234] (Mal) 1973[1235] (Pap) 1973[1236] (Vn) 2007[1237] see India (1979)			2001[1238]	2004[1239]	1963[1240] 2013[1241] 1980[1242] 2003[1243]
46. Iran	see Bahrain (1958) (SA) 1958[1244] (Qat) 1970[1245] (UAE) 1974[1246] (Oman) 1974,[1247] 2016[1248] (Iraq) 2019[1249]			1974[1250] 1987[1251] 2014[1252]		1969[1253] 2016[1254]
47. Iraq	(Ku) 2017[1255] see Iran (2019)	(Ku) 1993[1256]	2011[1257]	1971[1258] 1985[1259]		1969[1260] 1974[1261]
48. Ireland	(UK) 1990–2014[1262]			1960[1263]	1992–2007[1264]	
49. Israel	see Cyprus (2011)	(Jor) 1996[1265]		1953[1266] 2016[1267]	2016[1268]	
50. Italy	(Yu) 1968[1269] (Tun) 1978[1270]	see Fr		1967[1271] 1957[1272]		
51. Ivory Coast				1970[1273] 1996[1274] 2014[1275]		1990[1276] 2017[1277]
52. Japan	(Kor) 1974[1278]		1974[1279]			

(continued)

(Continued)

Country	Treaties		Laws		Regulations and contracts	
53. Kazakhstan	(Ru) 2002[1280] (Azer) 2003[1281]		2010[1282]			2007[1283]
54. Kenya		(Tan) 2009[1284]		1986[1285] 2015[1286]		2012[1287] 1986[1288]
55. Korea	see Japan (1974)			1970[1289] 1984[1290]	1970[1291]	1981[1292] 1985[1293]
56. Kuwait	(SA) 1961[1294] 2001[1295] see Iraq (2017)			1973[1296]	1958[1297]	
57. Lebanon			2010[1298]		2015[1299] 2018[1300]	2010[1301]
58. Liberia			2016[1302]	2000[1303]		2009[1304] 2013[1305] 2015[1306]
59. Libya	(Malta) 1986[1307] 2013[1308] (Tun) 1989[1309] (Tur) 2019[1310]			1965[1311] 1972[1312] 2012[1313]	2008[1314]	2012[1315]
60. Malaysia	(Th) 1982–90[1316] (Vn) 1993[1317] (Bru) 2009, 2019–21[1318]		1990[1319]	1974[1320] 2006[1321]	1980–2000[1322] 2009[1323]	1968[1324]
61. Mali			2015[1325]	2004[1326]		undated[1327]
62. Malta	see Lib (1986)			1958[1328]		1969[1329]
63. Mauritania	(Senegal) 2016[1330] 2018[1331]	(Cape Verde) 2003[1332]	2019[1333]	2002[1334] 2010[1335]		2011[1336] 2012[1337]
64. Mauritius	(Sey) 2012[1338]			1970[1339]		
65. Mexico	(US) 2014[1340]	(see Hon) (see Cuba) (US) 1997[1341]	2014[1342]			2012[1343] 2018[1344]
66. Mozambique	(Tan) 2011[1345]			2014[1346]		2015[1347] 2016[1348]
67. Myanmar		(Th) 1982[1349]				1974[1350] 1992[1351]
68. The Netherlands	(UK) 1965[1352] see Germany (1960)	(see Den) (Bel) 1996[1353]	1965[1354] 2003[1355]			2012[1356]
69. Nicaragua		(see Cs Rica)	1998[1357]	1958[1358]	1998–2000[1359] 2009[1360]	1998[1361]

(continued)

(Continued)

Country	Treaties		Laws		Regulations and contracts	
70. Nigeria	(STP) 2003[1362] 2005[1363] see Eq Gui (2000–01) see Benin (2009)			1969[1364]	2003[1365]	1969[1366] 2007[1367] 2011[1368]
71. Norway	(UK) 1965,[1369] 2005[1370] see Den/ Greenland (1965) see Iceland (1981) (Ru) 2011[1371]		1996[1372]	1972[1373] 1965[1374]	1997[1375] undated[1376]	1969[1377] 1969[1378] 2004[1379]
72. Oman	(Pak) 2000[1380] (Yem) 1992[1381] 2004[1382]			1975[1383] 2011[1384]		undated[1385]
73. Peru		(Chile) 1954[1386] (Ec)		1993[1387]		2020[1388]
74. The Philippines		Indo 2019[1389] (see Ch)		1949[1390] 1972[1391] 1983[1392]	2005[1393]	2019[1394]
75. Qatar	see Iran (1970) (UAE) 1969[1395]	(SA) 1965[1396] 2008[1397]		2007[1398]	1997[1399] 2002[1400]	
76. Rep of Congo	(Angola) 2002[1401]		2016[1402]			
77. Rep of Guinea			2014[1403]	1995[1404]		2006[1405] 2010[1406]
78. Russia	see Nor (2011) see Kaz (2002)	(Swe) 1989[1407]		1992[1408]		1994[1409]
79. São Tomé and Príncipe	(see Nigeria)	(Gab) 2001[1410] (Eq Guinea) 1999		2009[1411]	2003	2010[1412] 2016[1413]
80. Saudi Arabia	(Sud) 1974[1414] (see Bah) (see Iran) (see Kuwait)		1968[1415]		1967[1416]	
81. Senegal	(see GnBs) (see Maur)	(CV) 1993[1417] (see Gambia)	2019[1418]		(see Maur)	1998[1419] 2012[1420]
82. The Seychelles	(see Mauritius) (Com) 2012[1421]	(Tan, Com) 2012[1422] (Tan) 2002[1423]		1976[1424] 2012[1425]		2013[1426]
83. Sierra Leone			2011[1427]	2001[1428]		2012[1429]

(continued)

(Continued)

Country	Treaties		Laws		Regulations and contracts	
84. South Africa				2002[1430]		2002[1431] 2019[1432]
85. Spain	(see Fr)			1958[1433] 1998[1434]		1958[1435]
86. Sri Lanka				2003[1436]		2008[1437] 2013[1438]
87. Suriname				1986[1439] 1990[1440]		2011[1441] 2015[1442]
88. Sweden	(see Ger) 1978	(SU) (Fin) 1995[1443] (Est) 2000[1444]		1966[1445] 1991[1446]		
89.						
90. Tanzania	(see Sey) (Comoros) 2011[1447]	(see Moz) (see Kenya)	2015[1448]	1980[1449]	2013[1450]	
91. Thailand	(see Malaysia, Camb, India, Indo) (Vn) 1997[1451]	(see Myanmar)		1967[1452] 1971[1453]	(see Mal) 2009	
92. Timor Leste	(see Australia)		2005[1454]	2005[1455]		2020[1456]
93. Trinidad and Tobago	(Ven) 1991–2010[1457] (see Grenada)			1969[1458] 1986[1459] 2010[1460]		
94. Tunisia	(see Alg) (see Italy) (see Libya)		1999[1461]		(see Libya) 2008	1955[1462] 2013[1463]
95. Turkey	(see Libya)	1998 (Bulgaria)[1464]		1973[1465] 2014[1466]		
96. UAE (Abu Dhabi, Dubai, Sharjah, Umm)[1467]	see Qatar (1969) see Iran (2003)	(Abu/Dub) 1974[1468]			1937[1469] 1945[1470] 1967–73[1471]	
97. The UK	see Ar, Den, Neth, Nor (various dates)		1966[1472]	1918[1473] 1934[1474] 1964[1475]	1976–2008[1476] 1979[1477] undated[1478] 2017[1479]	
98. The US	(see Mex) (see Cuba)	(Cub, Mex, Ven) 1978	2013[1480] 1945[1481]	1953[1482]	2016[1483]	
99. Venezuela	(Neth) 1978[1484] see T&T (1991–2010)	(US) 1980[1485] (Fr) 1983[1486] (DR) 1982	1999[1487] 2001[1488] 2006[1489]			1969[1490]
100. Vietnam	(see China, Mal, Cam, Ph, Indo, Thailand)		2015[1491]	1993[1492] 2000[1493]	1978[1494] 2013[1495]	
101. Yemen	(see SA) (see Om)	(see SA)		2010[1496]		2007[1497]

[974] Article 2, Agreement between Albania and Italy for the Determination of the Continental Shelf of Each of the Two Countries, 18 December 1992, 26 *Law of the Sea Bulletin* 54.

[975] Article 3, Agreement between the Hellenic Republic and the Republic of Albania on the Delimitation of their Respective Continental Shelf Areas and Other Maritime Zones to which they are entitled under International Law, signed 27 April 2009, C Lathrop (ed), *International Maritime Boundaries* (Leiden, Brill, 2011), 4470 (hereinafter 'Lathrop'). Albania revoked its consent.

[976] Article 11, Petroleum Law (Exploration and Production) No 7746, 28 July 1993, *Oil, Gas & Energy Law Documents* (hereinafter '*OGEL* Documents'; copy with the author).

[977] Sec 6.14.4, Bankers Petroleum Albania Ltd, Block F, PSA, 2010, resourcecontracts.org/contract/ocds-591adf-5095341388/view#/pdf.

[978] Annex D-2, s 7.4, Petroleum Agreement for the Production, Development and Exploration of Petroleum in Delvina Block, 8 August 2007, between Albpetrol Sh A and Stream Oil & Gas Limited, downloads.openoil.net/contracts/al/al_Delvina-Block_dd20070808_Petro-Agree_Albpetrol_Stream.pdf.

[979] Petroleum Regulation of 1993, *OGEL* Documents.

[980] Clause B.10, Terms and Conditions for Application under Production Sharing Contract (PSC) and Legal Framework, akbn.gov.al/wp-content/uploads/2016/08/Terms-and-conditions.pdf.

[981] Article 5, Agreement on Provisional Arrangements for the Delimitation of the Maritime Boundary between the Republic of Tunisia and the People's Democratic Republic of Algeria, 23 November 2003, 2238 UNTS 208 (2007).

[982] Article 105, Law No 19-13, 11 December 2019, *Journal Officiel De La Republique Algerienne* N° 79, 4, joradp.dz/FTP/JO-FRANCAIS/2019/F2019079.pdf.

[983] Law No 86 of Algeria Relating to Exploitation and of Transportation of Hydrocarbons, 14 August 1986, French text *OGEL* Documents (copy with the author).

[984] Decree No 88-34, 16 February 1988, relating to exploitation of the hydrocarbons of Algeria, *OGEL* Documents (copy with the author).

[985] Agreement for exploration and exploitation of liquid hydrocarbons between Sonatrach and Anadarko Algeria Corporation, 23 October 1989, resourcecontracts.org/contract/ocds-591adf-9645096819/view#/pdf.

[986] Protocol of Agreement dated 10 September 2001 between the Republic of the Congo and the Republic of Angola Approving Offshore Unitization Zone 14K & A-IMI, Lathrop (n 2) 4288.

[987] Agreement on the Exploration and Production of Hydrocarbons in the Common Interest Maritime Zone between the Democratic Republic of the Congo and the Government of the Republic of Angola, 23 July 2008, Lathrop (n 2) 4277–80.

[988] Treaty between the Government of the Republic of Angola and the Government of the Republic of Namibia regarding the Delimitation and Demarcation of the Maritime Borders between the Republic of Angola and the Republic of Namibia, signed 4 June 2002, in J Charney, D Colson, L Alexander and R Smith (eds), *International Maritime Boundaries*, vol 5 (Leiden, Nijhoff, 2005) 3709.

[989] Article 64.8, Law No 10/04, 12 November 2004, faolex.fao.org/docs/pdf/ang81903E.pdf.

[990] Memorandum of Understanding, 30 July 2004, saflii.org/ao/legis/num_act/mdepuepcdpd-bidc886.pdf.

[991] Article 27, Model Production Sharing Agreement, 2005, resourcecontracts.org/contract/ocds-591adf-3213850251/view#/pdf.

[992] Article 26, Risk Services Agreement between Sonangol and Cie Angola Block 21 Ltd et al, 24 February 2010, resourcecontracts.org/contract/ocds-591adf-0839745741/view#/pdf.

[993] Article 27, Production Sharing Contract between Sociedade Nacional de Combustíveis de Angola, Empresa Pública – (Sonangol, EP) and Cie Angola Block 20 Ltd Sonangol Pesquisa E Produção, SA Bp Exploration Angola (Kwanza Benguela) Limited China Sonangol International Holding Limited in the Area of Block 20/11, 20 December 2011, resourcecontracts.org/contract/ocds-591adf-0014595575/view#/pdf.

[994] Model Contract, Offshore, Concession, 1973, resourcecontracts.org/contract/ocds-591adf-0100189184/view#/pdf.

[995] Model Contract, Sociedade Nacional de Combustiveis de Angola Empresa Publica (Sonangol, EP), Deep Water Blocks, Concession, 1991, resourcecontracts.org/contract/ocds-591adf-4291933927/view#/pdf.

[996] Article 71, Agreement between the Government of Argentina and the Government of Uruguay Relating to the Delimitation of the River Plate and the Maritime Boundary between Argentina and Uruguay, 12 February 1974, 1295 UNTS 293.

[997] Article 2-4, UK-Argentina Joint Declaration of Cooperation over Offshore Activities in the South West Atlantic, 27 September 1995, 35 ILM 301. Argentina notified the UN Secretary-General of the termination of this joint declaration due to repeated unilateral activities by the UK. See Letter dated 28 March 2007 from the Permanent Mission of Argentina to the United Nations addressed to the Secretary-General, UN Doc A/61/827, 30 March 2007.
[998] Treaty of Peace and Friendship between Argentina and Chile, effective 6 May 1985, Lathrop (n 2) 736–41.
[999] Article 27, Ley N° 17.319, 23 June 1967, as amended by Ley N° 27.007, 31 October 2014, servicios.infoleg.gob.ar/infolegInternet/anexos/15000-19999/16078/texact.htm.
[1000] Article 5, Ley 27.007, Ley N° 17.319, Modificación, Sancionada Octubre 29 de 2014, iesc.gov.ar/iesc/Include/documents/legales/H_ley_27007_modif_17319.pdf.
[1001] Decreto N° 1.443/1985, Hydrocarbon Regulations, servicios.infoleg.gob.ar/infolegInternet/anexos/225000-229999/228204/norma.htm.
[1002] President Petroleum SA, CNO-8 Puesto Guardian, Concession, 2015, resourcecontracts.org/contract/ocds-591adf-0673203082/view#/.
[1003] Treaty between Australia and the Democratic Republic of Timor-Leste Establishing their Maritime Boundaries in the Timor Sea, 30 August 2019, dfat.gov.au/sites/default/files/treaty-maritime-arrangements-australia-timor-leste.pdf.
[1004] Article 6, Treaty between Australia and the Independent State of Papua New Guinea Concerning Sovereignty and Maritime Boundaries in the Area between the Two Countries, including the Area known as Torres Strait, and Related Matters, 15 February 1985, Lathrop (n 2) 937.
[1005] Article 9, Treaty between the Government of Australia and the Government of Indonesia Establishing an Exclusive Economic Zone Boundary and Certain Seabed Boundaries, signed 14 March 1997, Lathrop (n 2) 2714.
[1006] Offshore Petroleum and Greenhouse Gas Storage Act 2006 No 14, extwprlegs1.fao.org/docs/pdf/aus64464volume1.pdf.
[1007] Understanding Memorandum on Joint Development of Relevant Blocks in the Caspian Sea between the Ministry of Energy of the Republic of Azerbaijan and the Ministry of Oil of the Islamic Republic of Iran, 23 April 2018, e-qanun.az/framework/38588.
[1008] Memorandum of Understanding between the governments of Turkmenistan and Azerbaijan on Joint Exploration and Development of Hydrocarbon Resources of the Dostluk Field in the Caspian Sea as reported in 'Meeting of the Presidents of Turkmenistan and Azerbaijan', 21 January 2021, mfa.gov.tm/en/news/2449.
[1009] Article F, Seabed boundary agreement between the Republic of Azerbaijan and the Republic of Kazakhstan and Protocol, Kazakhstan approval of Agreement and Protocol 2 July 2003; Azerbaijan approval of Agreement and Protocol 9 December 2003, Lathrop (n 2) 4048.
[1010] Statoil Azerbaijan Ashrafi Dan Ulduzu Aypara BV, SOCAR Oil Affiliate, Ashrafi-Dan Ulduzu-Aypara Area, PSA, 2018, resourcecontracts.org/contract/ocds-591adf-5535899866/view#/pdf.
[1011] Article 4(g), Agreement between the Commonwealth of the Bahamas and the Republic of Cuba for the Delimiting Line between their Maritime Zones, 9 March 2012, 2831 UNTS 2.
[1012] Article 26, Act to Provide for the Exploration and Production of Petroleum and for Matters Incidental Thereto, 1 March, 2016, environment.gov.bs/wp-content/uploads/2016/10/Petroleum-Act-2016.pdf.
[1013] An Act to Make Better Provision for the Exploration for, the Boring for and the Getting of Petroleum and for Matters Incidental thereto, 10 June 1971, laws.bahamas.gov.bs/cms/images/LEGISLATION/PRINCIPAL/1971/1971-0011/PetroleumAct_1.pdf.
[1014] Petroleum Regulations, 15 July 2016, laws.bahamas.gov.bs/cms/images/LEGISLATION/SUBORDINATE/2016/2016-0037/PetroleumRegulations2016_1.pdf.
[1015] Article 2, Agreement between the Kingdom of Saudi Arabia and the Government of Bahrain, 22 February 1958, 1733 UNTS 8.
[1016] Article 2, Agreement Concerning Delimitation of the Continental Shelf between Iran and Bahrain, 14 May 1972, 826 UNTS 234.
[1017] Article 44, Concession Contract of 15 December 1970 between Superior Oil (Bahrain) Inc, and the Ruler of Bahrain, *Barrows Basic Oil Laws and Concession Contracts Middle East*, Supplement No 32. Barrows Basic Oil Laws and Concession Contracts are published by region, namely, Asia and Australasia (hereinafter *Barrows* A&A), Central America and the Caribbean (hereinafter *Barrows* CAC), Europe (hereinafter *Barrows* Europe), the Middle East (hereinafter *Barrows* ME), and South and Central Africa (hereinafter *Barrows* SCA).

[1018] Bangladesh Petroleum Act, 1974 (Act No LXIX of 1974), extwprlegs1.fao.org/docs/texts/bgd66865.doc.
[1019] Article 33.5, Model Production Sharing Contract 2008, *Barrows* A&A, Supplement No 178.
[1020] Model Production Sharing Contract between PetroBengla and International Companies, 1993, *Barrows* A&A, Supplement No 129.
[1021] Articles 3 and 6, Treaty between the Republic of Guyana and the State of Barbados Concerning the Exercise of Jurisdiction in Their Exclusive Economic Zones in the Area of Bilateral Overlap within Each of Their Outer Limits and beyond the Outer Limits of the Exclusive Economic Zones of Other States, 5 May 2004, Lathrop (n 2) 3587.
[1022] Article 41(5) Chapter 282a Offshore Petroleum, 1 LRO 2007, barbadosparliament-laws.com/en/ShowPdf/282A.pdf.
[1023] Offshore Petroleum Regulations, 2013, energy.gov.bb/2015Licensing/documents/legal/26-offshore-petroleum-regulations-2013-2/file.
[1024] Belize declared a moratorium on offshore oil drilling. See Petroleum Operations (Maritime Zone Moratorium) Act, 2017, extwprlegs1.fao.org/docs/pdf/blz175462.pdf.
[1025] Petroleum Act Chapter 225, Revised Edition 2000, 5 July 1991, *Barrows* CAC, Supplement No 128.
[1026] Section 22.5, Belize Model Production Sharing Agreement, 2007, med.gov.bz/wp-content/uploads/2020/08/Belize-Model-Production-Sharing-Agreement.pdf.
[1027] Article 22.5, Agreement for Petroleum Exploration, Development and Production in Belize between the Government of Belize and RSM Production Corporation, 3 April 2000, *Barrows* CAC, Supplement No 117; Article 22.5, Production sharing agreement between the Government of Belize and Belize Natural Energy Ltd, 2 January 2003, *Barrows* CAC, Supplement 137; Article 22.5, Production sharing agreement between the Government of Belize and Northern Spirit Resources, Inc, 25 March 2010, resourcecontracts.org/contract/ocds-591adf-2346555490/view#/pdf; Article 22.5, Production sharing agreement between the Government of Belize and ZMT International, Inc, 25 March 2009, resourcecontracts.org/contract/ocds-591adf-8710976138/view#/pdf. These provisions preceded the 2007 model contract. They provide that the rules on sole-country unitisation shall be applied. These rules require the contractor to conclude an international unitisation agreement subject to approval of the petroleum agency.
[1028] Part 5.7, Petroleum Regulations, 9 August 1992, med.gov.bz/wp-content/uploads/2020/08/Belize-Petroleum-Regulations.pdf.
[1029] Petroleum Regulations, 2003, extwprlegs1.fao.org/docs/pdf/blz50061.pdf.
[1030] Article 6, Treaty on the Maritime Boundary Delimitation between the Federal Republic of Nigeria and the Republic of Benin, signed 4 August 2006, Lathrop (n 2) 4266.
[1031] Article 87, Loi N° 2019-06 du 15 Novembre 2019, sgg.gouv.bj/doc/loi-2019-06.
[1032] Loi No 2006-18 du 17 Octobre 2006, Code Petrolier en Republique Du Benin, *OGEL* Documents (copy with the author).
[1033] Article 13.4.1, 2020 Model Contract, Décret N° 2020-568 du 02 Décembre 2020, sgg.gouv.bj/doc/decret-2020-568.
[1034] Oil Exploration and Exploitation Contract Deep Offshore Block 4 between the Government of the Republic of Benin and the Addax Petroleum – Abacan Benin Consortium, 1 February 1997, resourcecontracts.org/contract/ocds-591adf-7143693099/download/word.
[1035] Ley No 1689 del 30 de Abril de 1996, biblioteca.unmsm.edu.pe/redlieds/Recursos/archivos/Legislacion/Bolivia/ley1689_hidrocarburos.pdf. Bolivia is landlocked.
[1036] Article 138, Ley de Hidrocarburos, 17 de Mayo de 2005, Gaceta Official No 2749, 19 May 2005.
[1037] Article 24, Unitization Regulation Annex, Regulation of Unitization (Hydrocarbons Area), Supreme Decree No 27124, 14 August 2003, gacetaoficialdebolivia.gob.bo/normas/descargarPdf/24679.
[1038] Total E&P Bolivie Sucursal Bolivia, Tecpetrol de Bolivia SA, Aquio, Service Contract, 2006, resourcecontracts.org/contract/ocds-591adf-5978990122/view#/pdf.
[1039] Agreement between the Government of Brazil and the Government of Uruguay Relating to the Maritime Delimitation between Brazil and Uruguay, 12 June 1975, Lathrop (n 2) 791.
[1040] Agreement between the Government of Brazil and the Government of France Relating to the Maritime Delimitation between Brazil and French Guiana, 30 January 1981, Lathrop (n 2) 782.
[1041] Article 27, Law No 9478, 6 August 1997, Official Federal Gazette of August 7, 1997, 1–4.
[1042] Articles 33-41, Law 12351, 22 December 2010. English text in National Agency of Petroleum, Natural Gas and Biofuels, Legislation for Exploration and Production of Oil and Natural Gas (Ministry of Mines and Energy, 2010), 69–71, 82–84.

[1043] CNPE Resolution No 8 of December 14, 2016 Procedures for Individualization of Production, pesquisa.in.gov.br/imprensa/jsp/visualiza/index.jsp?data=06/06/2017&jornal=1&pagina=22&totalArquivos=216.
[1044] Clause 12, ANP Concession Agreement for the Exploration, Development and Production of Oil and Natural Gas, 2004, www.brasil-rounds.gov.br/arquivos/Editais/Conc_agreement/Conc_agreement_R6_en.pdf.
[1045] Clause 12, ANP Concession Agreement for the Exploration, Development and Production of Oil and Natural Gas, 2008, www.eisourcebook.org/cms/Brazil,%20Model%20Concession%20Agreement,%20ANP%2010th%20Rnd,%202008.pdf.
[1046] Article 18, Round 2 of Tender for Production Sharing – Model of the Concession Agreement with the participation of Petrobras – 23 August 2017, *OGEL* Documents. See also 2017 Unitization Regulation, pesquisa.in.gov.br/imprensa/jsp/visualiza/index.jsp?data=08/09/2017&jornal=1&pagina=720&totalArquivos=752.
[1047] Statement of Tun Abdullah Ahmad Badawi on the Exchange of Letters between Malaysia and Brunei Darussalam, 16 March 2009, kln.gov.my/archive/content.php?t=7&articleId=735675.
[1048] Overseas Territories: The Sarawak (Definition of Boundaries) Order in Council No 1518 (1958), Lathrop (n 2) 924–28.
[1049] Oil Mining Enactment, 6 April 194, *Barrows* A&A, vol 1.
[1050] Article 36, Model Contract (Offshore), Petroleum Mining Enactment, 1963, *Barrows* A&A, Supplement No 3.
[1051] Petroleum Mining Act revised up to 15 September 2002, agc.gov.bn/AGC%20Images/LAWS/ACT_PDF/cap044.pdf.
[1052] Article 10.6, Model Petroleum Agreement of Brunei Darussalam between the Authority and Company A, and Company B, and Company C, 22 May 2002, *Barrows* A&A, Supplement No 151.
[1053] Article 11.8, Production Sharing Contract of 2003 between Brunei National Petroleum Corporation and Shell Deepwater Borneo Ltd, Diamond Energy Exploration & Production (Brunei Deepwater) BV and Conoco Philippes (UK), Ltd, Block K, *Barrows* A&A, Supplement No 174.
[1054] Article 11.5, Production Sharing Agreement for Block L Brunei Darussalam between BNPC and Loon Brunei Limited and Qaf Brunei Sendirian Berhad, 28 August 2006, resourcecontracts.org/contract/ocds-591adf-9845812582/view#/pdf.
[1055] Joint Statement on the 22nd Annual Leaders' Consultation between Malaysia and Brunei, 5 March 2019, mfa.gov.bn/Lists/Press%20Room/news.aspx?id=736&source=www.mfa.gov.bn/site/home.aspx.
[1056] Article 3, Agreement on Historic Waters of Vietnam and Kampuchea, 7 July 1982, Lathrop (n 2) 2364.
[1057] Articles 1-2, Memorandum of Understanding between the Royal Government of Cambodia and the Royal Thai Government Regarding the Area of their Overlapping Maritime Claims to the Continental Shelf, 18 June 2001, Lathrop (n 2) 3743.
[1058] Article 56, Petroleum Regulations, 28 September 1991, Petroleum Agreement dated 3 October, *OGEL* Documents.
[1059] Article 14, 1991 between the Government of Cambodia and Enterprise Oil Exploration Limited and Compagnie Europeenne des Petroles (Block II Offshore Cambodia), *Barrows* A&A, Supplement No 151; Chapter 14, Japex Petroleum Agreement dated 26 December 1991 between the Government of Cambodia and Japan Petroleum Exploration Co, Ltd (JAPEX) (Block III Offshore), *Barrows* A&A, Supplement No 139.
[1060] Article 33, Model Petroleum Agreement, 2004, resourcecontracts.org/contract/ocds-591adf-0311756882/view#/pdf.
[1061] Agreement between Cameroon and Nigeria, 1 June 1975, Lathrop (n 2) 846.
[1062] Article 80, Code pétrolier Loi n°99-013 du 22 décembre 1999, droit-afrique.com/upload/doc/cameroun/Cameroun-Code-petrolier-1999.pdf.
[1063] Article 114, Décret d'Application du Code Pétrolier droit-afrique.com/upload/doc/cameroun/Cameroun-Decret-2000-465-application-Code-petrolier.pdf. Article 114 authorises the petroleum minister to decide whether a shared resource should be developed as a single unit and to direct the licensee to act accordingly.
[1064] Model Production Sharing Contract of 2007, resourcecontracts.org/contract/ocds-591adf-1510528295/view#/pdf.
[1065] Article 5, Agreement between the Government of the Kingdom of Denmark and the Government of Canada Relating to the Delimitation of the Continental Shelf between Canada and Greenland, 13 March 1974, Lathrop (n 2) 380.

[1066] Agreement between the Government of Canada and the Government of the French Republic Relating to the Exploration and Exploitation of Transboundary Hydrocarbon, signed 15 May 2005, Lathrop (n 23) Report No 2-22.
[1067] Energy Safety and Security Act, SC 2015, c4, 26 February 2016, laws-lois.justice.gc.ca/PDF/2015_4.pdf; An Act respecting Canada's Offshore Oil and Gas Operations, enacting the Nuclear Liability and Compensation Act, publications.gc.ca/collections/collection_2015/lois-statutes/YX4-2015-4.pdf. These laws detail provisions on joint exploitation agreements and unitisation agreements of transboundary resources between the petroleum agency of Canada and the regulator of a provincial government.
[1068] Article 48, Canada Oil and Gas Operations Act (RSC, 1985, c O-7), as amended up to 2016, laws-lois.justice.gc.ca/PDF/O-7.pdf.
[1069] Article 57(2), Canada-Nova Scotia Offshore Petroleum Resources Accord Implementation Act (SC 1988, c 28).
[1070] Decree No 10-796 PR-PM-MPE, 30 September 2010, extwprlegs1.fao.org/docs/pdf/cha161463.pdf.
[1071] Loi relative aux hydrocarbures Loi n°07-006 du 2 mai 2007, droit-afrique.com/upload/doc/tchad/Tchad-Code-2007-hydrocarbures-MAJ-2010.pdf.
[1072] Article 13.4, EWAAH Investors Limited, PSA, 6 September 2019, resourcecontracts.org/contract/ocds-591adf-3143016856/view#/pdf; Article 13.4, ERHC Energy (BVI) Ltd, PSA,10 June 2011, resourcecontracts.org/contract/ocds-591adf-3056695267/view#/search/13.4.
[1073] Contrat de Partage de Production entre La Republique du Tchad et Le Consortium Mashak Petroleum LLC-Clogoil Systems, observatoire.td/upload/contrats/CPP1%20MASHAK.pdf.
[1074] Article 7, Agreement between the People's Republic of China and the Socialist Republic of Viet Nam on the Delimitation of the Territorial Seas, Exclusive Economic Zones and Continental Shelves of the Two Countries in Beibu Gulf/Bac Bo Gulf (with maps), 30 June 2004, 2336 UNTS 179.
[1075] Article 3, Memorandum of Understanding on Cooperation on Oil and Gas Development between the Government of the People's Republic of China and the Government of the Republic of the Philippines, 27 November 2018, fmprc.gov.cn/mfa_eng/wjdt_665385/2649_665393/t1616644.shtml.
[1076] President Order No 42, Law of the People's Republic of China on Exploration and Development of Resources in Deep Seabed Areas, 1 May 2016 (Chinese text), extwprlegs1.fao.org/docs/pdf/chn153328.pdf.
[1077] President Order No 36, Mineral Resources Law of the People's Republic of China, 19 March 1986, english.mofcom.gov.cn/aarticle/lawsdata/chineselaw/200211/20021100053795.html.
[1078] 'CNOOC and PetroVietnam Signed a Framework Agreement on Oil and Gas cooperation in the Beibu Gulf', 1 November 2005, gov-cn.translate.goog/jrzg/2005-11/01/content_88855.htm?_x_tr_sch=http&_x_tr_sl=zh-CN&_x_tr_tl=en&_x_tr_hl=fil&_x_tr_pto=op,sc.
[1079] 'Vietnam, China Issue Joint Statement', 21 June 2013, en.nhandan.vn/_mobile_politic/item/1813002-vietnam-china-issue-joint-statement.html.
[1080] Petroleum Regulations for Offshore Exploration and Exploitation dated 10 February 1982, *Barrows* A&A, Supplement No 74; Model Offshore Contract (incorporating corrections of 21 May 1982 by CNOOC), *Barrows* A&A, Supplement No 75; Offshore Contract dated 1 December 1983 between CNOOC and Pearl River Operating Co Getty Oil International (Orient), Inc, Japex, etc, *Barrows* A&A, Supplement No 98.
[1081] Section 11.7, March 1985 Offshore Model Contract for Second Round Bidding, *Barrows* A&A, Supplement No 88; Model Offshore Contract of October 1992 for the Fourth Round of Bidding, *Barrows* A&A, Supplement 120; Model Offshore Contract of September 1988 (Third Round), *Barrows* A&A, Supplement No 117.
[1082] ARCO Contract dated 3 May 1993 between China National Offshore Oil Corporation and ARCO China Inc (Contract Area 52/12, Qiong Dong Nana Basin, South China Sea), *Barrows* A&A, Supplement No 150.
[1083] Section 11.7, Petroleum Contract between China National Offshore Oil Corporation and Primeline Energy China Limited, Primeline Petroleum Corporation for Contract Area 25/34 in the East China Sea of the People's Republic of China, 24 March 2005, resourcecontracts.org/contract/ocds-591adf-0569891533/view#/pdf; s 11.7, Petroleum Contract between China National Offshore Oil Corporation and Primeline Energy China Limited, Primeline Petroleum Corporation for Contract Area 33/07 in the East China Sea of the People's Republic of China, 15 June 2012, resourcecontracts.org/contract/ocds-591adf-6266688800/download/word.

[1084] Article 3, Maritime Delimitation Treaty between Colombia and Honduras, 19 December 1999, un.org/Depts/los/LEGISLATIONANDTREATIES/PDFFILES/TREATIES/COL-HND1986MD.PDF.
[1085] Article 2, Maritime Delimitation Treaty between Jamaica and the Republic of Colombia, 14 March 1994, un.org/Depts/los/LEGISLATIONANDTREATIES/PDFFILES/TREATIES/JAM-COL1993MD.PDF.
[1086] Agreement Concerning Delimitation of Marine and Submarine Areas and Maritime Cooperation between the Republics of Colombia and Ecuador, 23 August 1975, un.org/Depts/los/LEGISLATIONANDTREATIES/PDFFILES/TREATIES/COL-ECU1975MC.PDF.
[1087] Treaty on the Delimitation of Marine and Submarine Areas and Related Matters between the Republic of Panama and the Republic of Colombia, 20 November 1976, un.org/Depts/los/LEGISLATIONANDTREATIES/PDFFILES/TREATIES/PAN-COL1976DM.PDF.
[1088] Treaty on Delimitation of Marine and Submarine Areas and Maritime Cooperation between the Republic of Colombia and the Republic of Costa Rica, signed 17 March 1977, un.org/Depts/los/LEGISLATIONANDTREATIES/PDFFILES/TREATIES/COL-CRI1977MC.PDF.
[1089] Agreement on Delimitation of Marine and Submarine Areas and Maritime Cooperation between the Republic of Colombia and the Dominican Republic, 13 January 1978, un.org/Depts/los/LEGISLATIONANDTREATIES/PDFFILES/TREATIES/COL-DOM1978MC.PDF.
[1090] Agreement on Delimitation of the Maritime Boundaries between the Republic of Colombia and the Republic of Haiti, 17 February 1978, un.org/Depts/los/LEGISLATIONANDTREATIES/PDFFILES/TREATIES/COL-HTI1978MB.PDF.
[1091] Legislacion Sobre Petroleas, Compilacion, 1999, servicios.minminas.gov.co/minminas/downloads/UserFiles/File/hidrocarburos/Codigo_Petroleos.zip.
[1092] Article 101, Ley 685 de 2001 (Agosto 15), Diario Oficial. Año Cxxxvii. No 44545, 15 August 2001, acnur.org/fileadmin/Documentos/BDL/2008/6513.pdf.
[1093] It is reported that Colombia and Jamaica have entered into a Cooperation Agreement on Oil Exploration within the Common Regime Area (ARC) of November 2008. Colombia reports that the agreement is currently in force; see cancilleria.gov.co/en/internacional/politica/regiones/america/jamaica. The text of the agreement is not in the public domain.
[1094] Clause 17, Model of Contract for Exploration and Exploitation, 2004, resourcecontracts.org/contract/ocds-591adf-1531285830/view#/pdf.
[1095] Article 30, Contrato de Exploracion y Produccion No 37, 31 March 2009, Agencia Nacional de Hidrocarburos y por la otro Morichal Petroleo y Gas CA, Valle Medio Magdalena Bloque Vmm-17, anh.gov.co/Asignacion-de-areas/Contratos%20EP%20y%20TEAS%20firmados/CTO%20EyP%20VMM%206%20%202009.pdf.
[1096] Contrato de Exploracion y Produccion de Hidrocarburos, Contratista: TELPICO LLC, Bloqué: VSM – 3, 10 March 2011, anh.gov.co/Asignacion-de-areas/CONTRATOS%20FIRMADOS%20EP%20y%20TEAS/CONTRATOS%20EyP%20TEAS%20%20%202011/CTO%20EyP%20VSM%203%202011.pdf.
[1097] Model Contract, Mining Concession, 2013, resourcecontracts.org/contract/ocds-591adf-7455827078/view#/pdf.
[1098] Shell Exploration and Production Colombia GmbH, COL-3, Concession, 2019, resourcecontracts.org/contract/ocds-591adf-8543458252/view#/pdf.
[1099] Article 4, Convention on the Delimitation of Maritime and Submarine Areas between the Republics of Costa Rica and Ecuador, signed 12 March 1985, Lathrop (n 2) 825.
[1100] Treaty Concerning Delimitation of Marine Areas and Maritime Cooperation between the Republic of Costa Rica and the Republic of Panama, 11 February 1982, Lathrop (n 2) 547.
[1101] Article 46 (h), Ley De Hidrocarburos No 7399, 3 May 1994, Gaceta No 95, 18 May 1994, bvs.sa.cr/ambiente/textos/leydehidrocarburos.pdf; Clause 18, Model Petroleum Contract 1999, *Barrows* CAC, Supplement No 114.
[1102] Reglamento Ley Hidrocarburos, Decreto No 24735-Mirenem, Gaceta No 230, 4 December 1995, sica.int/busqueda/busqueda_archivo.aspx?Archivo=leys_7009_1_27032006.pdf.
[1103] Clause 18, Model Petroleum Contract 1999, Barrows CAC, Supplement No 114.
[1104] Clause 16, Model Petroleum Contract 1989, *Barrows* CAC, Supplement No 75.
[1105] This type of entry refers to an instrument that has already been cited.
[1106] Agreement by Exchange of Notes between the Republic of Cuba and the United States of Mexico Concerning the Delimitation of Sea Space, 26 July 1976, Lathrop (n 2) 575.
[1107] Agreement between the Republic of Haiti and the Republic of Cuba Regarding the Delimitation of Maritime Boundaries between the Two States, 6 January 1978, Lathrop (n 2) 560.

[1108] Maritime Delimitation Treaty between the Republic of Honduras and the Republic of Cuba, 11 December 2013, Lathrop (n 2) 4741.
[1109] Agreement between the Government of Jamaica and the Government of the Republic of Cuba on the Delimitation of the Maritime Boundary between the two States, 18 July 1995, Lathrop (n 2) 2214.
[1110] Maritime Boundary Agreement between the United States of America and the Republic of Cuba (Provisional), Limits in the Sea No 110, 21 February 1990.
[1111] Article 16, Model Production Sharing Contract 1993, *Barrows* CAC, Supplement No 185.
[1112] Clause 16, Model Petroleum Contract 1999, *Barrows* CAC, Supplement No 112; Article 16, CubaPetrolea 1999 Model Hydrocarbons Production Sharing Contract, *Barrows* CAC, Supplement No 137.
[1113] Article 2, Agreement between the Republic of Cyprus and the Arab Republic of Egypt on the Delimitation of the Exclusive Economic Zone, 17 February 2003, Lathrop (n 2) 3924.
[1114] Framework Agreement between the Republic of Cyprus and the Arab Republic of Egypt Concerning the Development of Cross-Median Line Hydrocarbons Resources, signed 12 December 2013, Efimerida tis Dimokratias No 4196, 25 July 2014, 10703-10707, 58-63, mof.gov.cy/mof/gpo/gpo.nsf/All/A88D02909DC27F10C2257D20002C1DB5/$file/4196%2025%207%202014%20PARARTIMA%201o%20MEROS%20III%20.pdf.
[1115] Article 2, Agreement between the Government of the State of Israel and the Government of the Republic of Cyprus on the Delimitation of the Exclusive Economic Zone, 25 February 2011, 2740 UNTS 55.
[1116] Hydrocarbons (Prospection, Exploration and Exploitation) Law, 2007 (L4(I)/2007), 26 January 2007, extwprlegs1.fao.org/docs/pdf/cyp110631.pdf.
[1117] Article 21, Hydrocarbons (Prospection, Exploration and Exploitation) Regulations, 2007 and 2009, Official Gazette, Suppl III(I):26.1.2007 13 March 2009.
[1118] Section 5.7, Model Production Sharing Contract (February 2007), pwc.com.cy/en/energy-utilities-mining/assets/energy-model-production-sharing-contract.pdf.
[1119] Section 5.7, Model Exploration and Production Sharing Contract, 2 June 2016, meci.gov.cy/meci/hydrocarbon.nsf/All/1CB3AAD395B8100AC225847300303D03/$file/Model_EPSC%20(02%20June%202016).pdf.
[1120] Article 16, Agreement between Forest Cyprus Oil Corp and the Republic of Cyprus, 10 August 1962, *Barrows* Europe, Supplement No 2.
[1121] Article 7.4 (2), Model Production Sharing Contract, February 2012, resourcecontracts.org/contract/ocds-591adf-1348839751/view#/pdf.
[1122] Article 4, Agreement between Denmark and Norway Relating to the Delimitation of the Continental Shelf, 8 December 1965, 634 UNTS 71.
[1123] Article 2, Agreement between the Government of the Kingdom of the Netherlands and the Government of the Kingdom of Denmark Concerning the Delimitation of the Continental Shelf under the North Sea between the Two Countries, 1 August 1967, 604 UNTS 209.
[1124] Article 4, Agreement between the Government of the United Kingdom of Great Britain and Northern Ireland and the Government of the Kingdom of Denmark Relating to the Delimitation of the Continental Shelf between the Two Countries, 6 February 1967, 592 UNTS 209.
[1125] Article 2, Agreement between the Government of the Kingdom of Denmark Together with the Home Government of the Faroe Islands, on the One Hand, and the Government of the United Kingdom of Great Britain and Northern Ireland, on the Other Hand, Relating to the Maritime Delimitation in the Area between the Faroe Islands and the United Kingdom, 18 May 1999, un.org/depts/los/LEGISLATIONANDTREATIES/PDFFILES/TREATIES/DNK-GBR1999MD.PDF.
[1126] Article 2, Agreement between the Federal Republic of Germany and the Kingdom of Denmark Concerning the Delimitation of the Continental Shelf under the North Sea, 28 January 1971, Lathrop (n 2) 1809.
[1127] Article 3, Agreement between the Government of the Kingdom of Denmark, Together with the Government of the Faroes, on the One Hand, and the Government of Iceland, on the Other Hand, Relating to the Maritime Delimitation in the Area between the Faroe Islands and Iceland, 29 April 2008, Lathrop (n 2) 4561.
[1128] Article 11(2) and (3), Consolidated Act on the Use of the Danish Subsoil, as amended up to 1 May 2019, ens.dk/sites/ens.dk/files/OlieGas/consolidated_act_no._1190_of_21_september_2018_in_the_use_of_the_danish_subsoil.pdf.
[1129] Law No 181 Exploration and Utilization of Raw Materials in the Underground of the Kingdom of Denmark dated 8 May 1950, *Barrows* vol 1, no 1.

[1130] Section 2(3), Model License for Hydrocarbon Exploration and Production, 2018, ens.dk/sites/ens.dk/files/OlieGas/8th_round_model_licence.docx.
[1131] Order 372 respecting the monopoly of prospecting for and extraction of hydrocarbon, etc, in the Danish subsoil, 7 November 1963, *Barrows* Europe, Supplement No 4.
[1132] Agreement on the Delimitation of Marine and Submarine Areas and Maritime Cooperation between the Dominican Republic and the Republic of Colombia, 2 February 1979, Lathrop (n 2) 488.
[1133] Treaty on the Delimitation of Marine and Submarine Areas between the Dominican Republic and the Republic of Venezuela, 15 January 1982, Lathrop (n 2) 588.
[1134] Article 23, Law No 83-16, bndh.gob.do/wp-content/uploads/2016/04/Decree-establishing-the-Rules-of-Exploration-and-Production-of-.pdf.
[1135] Article 23, Hydrocarbon Exploration and Production Regulation, 29 February 2016, bndh.gob.do/wp-content/uploads/2016/04/Decree-establishing-the-Rules-of-Exploration-and-Production-of-.pdf.
[1136] Ordonnance-Loi No 81-013 du 2 Avril 1981 Portant Legislation Generale sur les Mines et les Hydrocarbures, droit-afrique.com/upload/doc/rdc/RDC-Code-1981-hydrocarbures-et-mines.pdf.
[1137] Article 9.5, Contrat de Partage de Production entre La Republique Democratique du Congo et L'Association Nessergy Ltd/Cohydro sur L'offshore Profond Gongolais (Couloir Maritime), October 2006, mines-rdc.cd/resourcecontracts/contract/ocds-591adf-0048769837/download/word.
[1138] Agreement between the Government of Peru and the Government of Ecuador Relating to the Maritime Boundary between Peru and Ecuador, 7 February 1975, and Agreement Relating to a Special Maritime Frontier Zone, 4 December 1994, Lathrop (n 2) 835–837.
[1139] Article 76, Reglamento de Operaciones Hidrocarburiferas Acuerdo Ministerial, 2 February 2018, controlhidrocarburos.gob.ec/wp-content/uploads/2018/03/Reglamento-de-operaciones-hidrocarburiferas.pdf.
[1140] Section 13.9, Service provision for the hydrocarbons (Crude Oil) exploration and exploitation contract, in the Block … of the Ecuadorian Amazon Region, *OGEL* Documents (copy with the author).
[1141] Section 14, Tecnipetrol, Inc, Bellweather International, Inc, Petroproduccion, Petroecuador, Charapa Marginal Field, PSA, 1999, resourcecontracts.org/contract/ocds-591adf-6116103360/view#/search/unifi.
[1142] Article 6, Treaty between the Federal Republic of Nigeria and the Republic of Equatorial Guinea Concerning Their Maritime Boundary, 29 June 2002, Lathrop (n 2) 2666; Article 2, Protocol in Implementation of Article 6.2 of the Treaty between the Federal Republic of Nigeria and the Republic of Equatorial Guinea Concerning Their Maritime Boundary, 29 June 2002, Lathrop (n 2) 3630.
[1143] Treaty on the Delimitation of the Maritime Frontier between the Republic of Cape Verde and the Republic of Senegal signed 17 February 1993, Lathrop (n 2) 2287.
[1144] Treaty Regarding the Delimitation of the Maritime Boundary between the Republic of Equatorial Guinea and the Democratic Republic of São Tomé and Príncipe, 26 June 1999, un.org/Depts/los/LEGISLATIONANDTREATIES/PDFFILES/TREATIES/GNQ-STP1999MB.PDF.
[1145] Article 56, Hydrocarbons Law No 8/2006, 3 November 2006, droit-afrique.com/upload/doc/guinee-equatoriale/GE-Code-hydrocarbures-2006-EN.pdf.
[1146] Code des hydrocarbures 1981 (abrogé) Loi n°1981-07 du 16 juin 1981, droit-afrique.com/upload/doc/guinee-equatoriale/GE-Code-hydrocarbures-1981-abroge-ESP.pdf
[1147] Section 12.4, Model Contract (English), Guinea Ecuatorial de Petroleos, PSA, 1982, resourcecontracts.org/contract/ocds-591adf-0907900772/view#/text.
[1148] Sections 12.4–12.5, Triton Equatorial Guinea, Inc, Block F, PSA, 1997, resourcecontracts.org/contract/ocds-591adf-7317531109/view#/pdf.
[1149] Article 118, Petroleum Regulations of the Republic of Equatorial Guinea, 20 June 2013, OGEL Documents (copy with the author).
[1150] Model Petroleum Production Sharing Contract of November 1998, *Barrows* SCA, Supplement No 140.
[1151] Article 22, Model production sharing contract of 2006 between the Republic of Equatorial Guinea and Guinea Ecuatorial de Petroleos and [The Company] for Block _, *Barrows* SCA, Supplement No 169.
[1152] Article 27, Legal Notice No 45/2000, the Revised Regulations on Petroleum Operations, extwprlegs1.fao.org/docs/pdf/eri203351.pdf.
[1153] Proclamation No 68/1995, Proclamation to Promote the Development of Mineral Resources, 20 March 1995, extwprlegs1.fao.org/docs/pdf/eri44710.pdf.

[1154] Section 9, Eritrea Model Production Sharing Contract 1997, resourcecontracts.org/contract/ocds-591adf-4406043787/download/pdf.
[1155] Proclamation No 295/1986, A Proclamation to Regulate Petroleum Operations, 26 March 1986, extwprlegs1.fao.org/docs/pdf/eth85045.pdf.
[1156] Article 9, Model Petroleum Agreement, 1986, *Barrows* SCA, Supplement No 85.
[1157] Article 9.1 (4), Model Production Sharing Agreement of 1994, *Barrows* Africa, Supplement 121, 26.
[1158] Article 9.1 (4), Model Petroleum Production Sharing Agreement, 2011, resourcecontracts.org/contract/ocds-591adf-9390285909/download/pdf.
[1159] Model Petroleum Agreement issued April 1973, *Barrows* SCA, Supplement No 37.
[1160] Article 3, Agreement between the Government of the French Republic and the Government of the Italian Republic Regarding the Delimitation of the Territorial Seas and Zones under National Jurisdiction between France and Italy, signed 21 March 2015, Lathrop (n 2) 11. Article 3 is a more detailed shared resource clause in that if 'a deposit located across the dividing line of the continental shelves are already being exploited, the Parties shall consult to determine the modalities of production of the said resources, after having consulted holders of production authorizations'.
[1161] Article 4, Convention between the Government of the French Republic and the Government of the Spanish State on the Delimitation of the Continental Shelves of the Two States in the Bay of Biscay, un.org/depts/los/LEGISLATIONANDTREATIES/PDFFILES/TREATIES/FRA-ESP1974CS.PDF.
[1162] Convention on Maritime Boundaries between the Government of the French Republic and the Government of the United Kingdom of Great Britain and Northern Ireland, 25 October 1983, un.org/depts/los/LEGISLATIONANDTREATIES/PDFFILES/TREATIES/FRA-GBR1983MB.PDF; Agreement between the Government of the French Republic and the Government of the United Kingdom of Great Britain and Northern Ireland Relating to the Completion of the Delimitation of the Continental Shelf in the Southern North Sea, 23 July 1991, un.org/depts/los/LEGISLATIONANDTREATIES/PDFFILES/TREATIES/FRA-GBR1991CS.PDF.
[1163] Agreement between the Government of the French Republic and the Government of the Republic of Seychelles Concerning Delimitation of the Maritime Boundary of the Exclusive Economic Zone and the Continental Shelf of France and of Seychelles, 19 February 2001, extwprlegs1.fao.org/docs/pdf/bi-32806.pdf.
[1164] Draft of Standard Prefectoral Decree Attached to Circular No 6951, 11 August 1947, *Barrows* Europe, vol 1, no 1; Executive Decree No 55-1349, 6 October 1955, *Barrows* Europe, vol 1, no 1.
[1165] Agreement on the Delimitation of the Maritime Border between the Gabonese Republic and the Democratic Republic of São Tomé and Príncipe, 26 April 2001, Lathrop (n 2) 3691.
[1166] Article 113, Loi No 011/2014 du 28 août 2014, droit-afrique.com/upload/doc/gabon/Gabon-Loi-2014-11-hydrocarbures.pdf.
[1167] Exploration and Production Sharing Contract between Republic of Gabon and Vaalco Gabon (Etame), Inc, 7 July 1995, sec.gov/Archives/edgar/data/894627/000089462718000013/egy-20171231xex10_1.htm.
[1168] Undated Model Production Sharing Contract between the Republic of Cameroon and the Holder, snh.cm/images/reglementation/EN/Model%20Production%20Sharing%20Contract.pdf.
[1169] Article 44, Exploration and Production Sharing Contract between the Gabonese Republic and Total Gabon, Diaba License (G4-223), 13 December 2006, sec.gov/Archives/edgar/data/1471261/000104746909009334/a2195051zex-10_5.htm.
[1170] Agreement between the Gambia and the Republic of Senegal, 27 August 1976, Lathrop (n 2) 854.
[1171] Petroleum (Exploration, Development and Production) Act, 2004, pura.gm/wp-content/uploads/2018/02/Petroleum-Act-2004-EDP-1-1.pdf.
[1172] Article 24.1, Petroleum License, 24 May 2012, between: the Republic of the Gambia and Camac Energy Block A5 (Gambia) Ltd, resourcecontracts.org/contract/ocds-591adf-5888157546/download/pdf; Article 24, Petroleum License, 24th May 2012, between: the Republic of the Gambia and Camac Energy Block A2 (Gambia) Ltd, resourcecontracts.org/contract/ocds-591adf-7711595368/view#/pdf.
[1173] Model Petroleum, Exploration, Development and Production License 2014, mop.gov.gm/sites/default/files/Model-Petroleum-EDP-Licence_Gambia-2014.pdf.
[1174] Article 27, Model Petroleum Exploration, Development and Production Licence 2022, mope.gm/download-file/559cb33c-8843-11ec-86ec-022a5fa1767e.
[1175] Treaty between the Kingdom of the Netherlands and the Federal Republic of Germany Concerning Arrangements for Co-operation in the Ems Estuary (Ems-Dollard Treaty), 8 April 1960, 509 TS 64 (1964). Article 48 provides that the spirit of good-neighbourliness shall govern the parties'

relations in regard 'to questions not expressly regulated in this Treaty which may arise in the Ems Estuary and which may affect common interests'.

[1176] Supplementary Agreement between the Federal Republic of Germany and the Netherlands to the Ems-Dollard Treaty, 14 May 1962, ibid 140.

[1177] Article 2, Treaty between the Kingdom of the Netherlands and the Federal Republic of Germany Concerning the Delimitation of the Continental Shelf under the North Sea, 7 December 1972, Lathrop (n 2) 1844.

[1178] Article 3, Agreement between the Kingdom of Sweden and the German Democratic Republic about the Delimitation of the Continental Shelf, 20 December 1978, Lathrop (n 2) 2036.

[1179] Federal Mining Act (BBergG) Federal Mining Act of 13 August 1980 (Federal Law Gazette I, 1310), last amended by Article 11 of the Act of 24 May 2016 (Federal Law Gazette I, 1217), gesetze-im-internet.de/englisch_bbergg/index.html.

[1180] Text of Prospecting Permit issued 7 June 1972 for Offshore Oil & Gas Operations, *Barrows* Europe, Supplement No 14.

[1181] Article 35, Petroleum (Exploration and Production) Act, 2016 Act 919, petrocom.gov.gh/wp-content/uploads/2018/12/Act-9190001.pdf.

[1182] Article 4(7), PNDC L84, Petroleum (Exploration and Production) Law, 1984, extwprlegs1.fao.org/docs/pdf/gha86268.pdf.

[1183] Model Petroleum Agreement of Ghana, 2000, resourcedata.org/dataset/rgi-ghana-model-petroleum-agreement/resource/3d164ee3-7b8f-4263-8dcd-23f84c70c2b3.

[1184] GNPC Model Petroleum Agreement, 2002, *OGEL* Documents (copy with the author).

[1185] Petroleum Agreement of 2005 between Ghana National Petroleum Corp. and Heliconia Energy Ghana Ltd, *OGEL* Documents (copy with the author).

[1186] Petroleum Agreement between Ghana National Petroleum Corporation and Vitol, 5 May 2008, *OGEL* Documents (copy with the author).

[1187] Clause 7.7, Petroleum Agreement among the Government of the Republic of Ghana, Ghana National Petroleum Corporation, Amerada Hess Ghana Limited in Respect of Deepwater Tano, 8 February 2006, resourcecontracts.org/contract/ocds-591adf-7847639074/view#/pdf; Article 8.20, Master Petroleum Agreement Deepwater Tano Block 2006, *OGEL* Documents.

[1188] Unitization and Unit Operating Agreement among Ghana National Petroleum Corporation, Tullow Ghana Limited, Kosmos Energy Ghana Hc, Anadarko Wctp Company, Sabre Oil & Gas Holdings Limited, Eo Group Limited covering the Jubilee Field Unit located offshore the Republic of Ghana, 13 July 2009, sec.gov/Archives/edgar/data/1509991/000104746911001716/a2201620zex-10_6.htm.

[1189] Erin Energy Ghana Limited, GNPC Exploration and Production Company Limited, Base Energy Limited, Ghana National Petroleum Corporation, Expanded Shallow Water Tano, Concession Agreement, 2015, resourcecontracts.org/contract/ocds-591adf-1707203194/view#/pdf; ENI Ghana Exploration & Production Limited, Vitol Upstream Tano Limited, Woodfields Upstream Limited, Ghana National Petroleum Corporation, Explorco, Cape Three Points Block 4, Concession Agreement, 2016, resourcecontracts.org/contract/ocds-591adf-2887938326/view#/pdf. Article 8.24-25 of these contracts adopts sole-country unitisation.

[1190] Article 2, Agreement between the Hellenic Republic and the Italian Republic on the Delimitation of the Zones of the Continental Shelf Belonging to Each of the Two States, 12 November 1980, Lathrop (n 2) 1598.

[1191] Articles 15 and 18, Law No 2289/95 Prospecting, Exploration and Exploitation of Hydrocarbons and Other Provisions, as amended up to 2011, *OGEL* Documents (copy with the author).

[1192] Article 11, Energean Oil & Gas SA, Trajan Oil & Gas Limited, Katakolo, PSA, 2014, resourcecontracts.org/contract/ocds-591adf-0131932458/view#/pdf.

[1193] Model Lease Agreement for the Block Area, 2014, *OGEL* Documents (copy with the author).

[1194] Total E&P Greece BV, Edison International SpA, Hellenic Petroleum SA, Company-State Contract, 2017, resourcecontracts.org/contract/ocds-591adf-4582727568/view#/pdf.

[1195] Article 7, Treaty between the Republic of Trinidad and Tobago and Grenada on the Delimitation of Marine and Submarine Areas, 27 April 2010, Lathrop (n 2) 4716.

[1196] Act No 22 of 1989 as amended by Act No 31 of 2007, laws.gov.gd/index.php?option=com_edocman&task=document.viewdoc&id=129&Itemid=203.

[1197] Agreement dated 4 July 1996 between the Government of Grenada and RSM Corporation, *Barrows* CAC, Supplement No 115.

[1198] Article 62, Decreto Ley Numero 109-83, Ley De Hidrocarburos, 15 September 1983 at sice.oas.org/Investment/NatLeg/GTM/Hidrocarburos_s.pdf.
[1199] Article 263, Reglamento General de la Ley de Hidrocarburos, 15 December 1983, mem.gob.gt/wp-content/uploads/2015/06/1_Ley_de_Hidrocarburos_y_su_Reglamento.pdf.
[1200] Articles 6 and 9, Reformas Al Acuerdo Gubernativo Número 1034-83, De Fecha 15 de Diciembre de 1983, Que Contiene el Reglamento General de la Ley de Hidrocarburos, mem.gob.gt/wp-content/uploads/2015/06/2._ACUERDO_GUBERNATIVO_NUMERO_165_2005.pdf.
[1201] Clause 13, Acuèrdase Aprobar el Modelo de Contrato de Administración y Producción Incremental en Operaciones Petroleras de Exploración y Explotación, Acuerdo Gubernativo Número 194-2005, 1 June 2005, mem.gob.gt/wp-content/uploads/2015/06/8._MODELO_DE_CONTRATO_DE_ADMINISTRACION_Y_PRODUCCION_INCREMENTAL.doc.
[1202] Clause 9 and 12, Contrato No 2-2009, Contrato de Operaciones Petroleras de Administracion y Ejecusion de los Convenios para la Conservacio y Produccion Eficiente de las Areas de Rubeisanto, Teirra Blanca, Caribe y Chinaja Ceste, mem.gob.gt/wp-content/uploads/2015/10/2-2009.pdf.
[1203] Model Contract of 1976 and Regulations to the Model Contract, *Barrows* CAR, Supplement No 20.
[1204] Exchange of letters, 26 April 1960, The Law of the Sea Maritime Boundary Agreements (1942–1969), 60; Territorial sea and continental shelf boundary between Senegal and Guinea-Bissau (exchange of letters between Portugal and France), 26 April 1960, Lathrop (n 2) 872.
[1205] Management and Cooperation Agreement between the Government of the Republic of Senegal and the Government of the Republic of Guinea-Bissau, Lathrop (n 2) 2257. Under art 1-2, they defined a zone for purposes of joint exploitation of fisheries and continental shelf resources. They agreed to establish a joint authority to regulate activities within the zone.
[1206] Law No 2/82 on liquid and gas hydrocarbons research and exploitation, extwprlegs1.fao.org/docs/pdf/gbs118431.pdf.
[1207] Decree-Law No 4/2006 on the Hydrocarbon Exploitation Policy within the Continental Shelf of the Republic of Guinea-Bissau, extwprlegs1.fao.org/docs/pdf/gbs120545.pdf.
[1208] Each concession is approved by law. See, for example, Decreto No 08/2011 de 1 de Fevereiro, Licenca Sucesso Bloco 4B, extwprlegs1.fao.org/docs/pdf/gbs118224.pdf.
[1209] Article 69, Petroleum (Exploration and Production) Act of Guyana, 14 April 1986, parliament.gov.gy/documents/acts/8170-act_no._3_of_1986_petroleum_(exploration_and_production)_act_1986.pdf.
[1210] Petroleum (Production) Act, Cap 65:05, Chapter 6, extwprlegs1.fao.org/docs/pdf/guy39225.pdf.
[1211] Article 31.1, Petroleum Prospecting License between the President of the Cooperative Republic of Guyana and Esso Exploration and Production Guyana Limited, 14 June 1999, resourcecontracts.org/contract/ocds-591adf-2947803650/view#/pdf.
[1212] Article 31.1, Ratio Energy Limited, Ratio Guyana Limited, Kaieteur Block, PSA, 2015, resourcecontracts.org/contract/ocds-591adf-2701587320/view#/pdf.
[1213] Tullow Guyana BV, Eco Oil and Gas Limited, Orinduik Block, PSA, 2016, resourcecontracts.org/contract/ocds-591adf-2603001790/view#/pdf.
[1214] Regulations made under Petroleum (Exploration and Production) Act 1986, 3 July 1986, ggmc.gov.gy/sites/default/files/law/petroleum_regulations_no_5_of_1986.pdf.
[1215] Article 3, Treaty between the Government of the Republic of Honduras and the Government of the United Mexican States on Maritime Delimitation, 30 November 2006, Lathrop (n 2) 4210.
[1216] Treaty between the Government of the United Kingdom of Great Britain and Northern Ireland and the Government of the Republic of Honduras Concerning the Delimitation of the Maritime Areas between the Cayman Islands and the Republic of Honduras, 1 March 2002, Lathrop (n 2) 3571.
[1217] Article 50, Decree 194-84, 31 October 1984, Containing the Hydrocarbon Law, *Barrows* CAC, Supplement No 56.
[1218] Ley General De Minería Decreto No 32-2013, 23 January 2013, poderjudicial.gob.hn/CEDIJ/Leyes/Documents/Ley%20General%20de%20Mineria%202013%20(14,6mb).pdf.
[1219] Reglamento de la Ley General de Minería, 2 August 2013, tsc.gob.hn/biblioteca/index.php/reglamentos.
[1220] Articles 5-6, Agreement on the Continental Shelf between Iceland and Jan Mayen, 2 June 1982, 2124 UNTS 261.

[1221] Agreed Minutes Concerning the Right of Participation Pursuant to art 5 and art 6 of the Agreement of 22 October 1981 between Iceland and Norway on the Continental Shelf in the Area between Iceland and Jan Mayen, 3 November 2008, 85 *Law of the Sea Bulletin* 27.
[1222] Agreement between Norway and Iceland Concerning Transboundary Hydrocarbon Deposits, 3 October 2011, 2888 UNTS 13.
[1223] Section 19, Act on Prospecting, Exploration and Production of Hydrocarbons No 13, 13 March 2001, as amended up to 2013, nea.is/media/olia/Act-No-13-2001-14102014.pdf.
[1224] Section 10, Licence for Exploration and Production of Hydrocarbons No 2013/01, 4 January 2013, nea.is/media/2013/Leyfi-a-ensku-Faraoe-Isl-Kolvetni-og-Petoro.pdf.
[1225] Section 10, Licence for Exploration and Production of Hydrocarbons No 2014/01, 22 January 2014, orkustofnun.is/gogn/Frettir/licence-2014-01-cnooc-eykon-petoro.pdf.
[1226] Rules on Prospecting, Exploration and Production of Hydrocarbons, 2009, nea.is/media/olia/Regulation_38_2009.pdf.
[1227] Article 4, Agreement between the Government of the Republic of India and the Government of the Kingdom of Thailand on the Delimitation of Seabed Boundary between the Two Countries in the Andaman Sea, 15 December 1978, Lathrop (n 2) 1440.
[1228] Article 3, Agreement between the Government of the Republic of India, the Government of the Republic of Indonesia and the Government of the Kingdom of Thailand Concerning the Determination of the Trijunction Point and the Delimitation of the Related Boundaries of the Three Countries in the Andaman Sea, 2 March 1979, Lathrop (n 2) 1386.
[1229] Article 5, Agreement between India and Maldives on Maritime Boundary in the Arabian Sea and Related Matters, 8 June 1978, Lathrop (n 2) 1397.
[1230] Article 6, Agreement between India and Sri Lanka on the Maritime Boundary between the Two Countries in the Gulf of Manaar and the Bay of Bengal and Related Matters, 10 May 1976, Lathrop (n 2) 1426.
[1231] 5.4, Directorate General of Hydrocarbon, Ministry of Petroleum, Good International Petroleum Industry Practices (GIPIP), 19 February 2016, dghindia.gov.in/assets/downloads/GIPIP.pdf. The directorate declares sole-country unitisation and cross-border unitisation as good international petroleum industry practices. It recognises that cross-border unitisation typically involves the licensees, but it should take place only after the host states have agreed to a maritime boundary.
[1232] Article 21, Production Sharing Contract between the Government of India and Gujarat State Petroleum Corporation Limited and Gail (India) Limited and Jubilant Capital Ptv Limited and Geoglobal Resources (Barbados) Inc with Respect to Contract Area Identified as Block Cb-Onn-2003/2, 23 September 2005, at resourcecontracts.org/contract/ocds-591adf-7119806732/view#/pdf; art 12, 2005 Model Production Sharing Contract between the Government of India and XYZ, petroleum.nic.in/sites/default/files/MPSC%20NELP-V.pdf.
[1233] Article 2, Agreement between the Government of the Republic of Indonesia and the Government of the Kingdom of Thailand Relating to the Delimitation of a Continental Shelf Boundary between the Two Countries in the Northern Part of the Strait of Malacca and in the Andaman Sea, 16 July 1973, Lathrop (n 2) 1462.
[1234] Article 2, Agreement between the Government of the Republic of Indonesia and the Government of the Kingdom of Thailand Relating to the Delimitation of a Continental Shelf Boundary between the Two Countries in the Northern Part of the Strait of Malacca and in the Andaman Sea, 16 July 1973 and Agreement between the Government of the Republic of Indonesia and the Government of the Kingdom of Thailand Relating to the Delimitation of the Seabed Boundary between the Two Countries in the Andaman Sea, 18 February 1978, Lathrop (n 2) 1642.
[1235] Article 3, Agreement between the Governments of the Republic of Indonesia, the Government of Malaysia and the Government of the Kingdom of Thailand Relating to the Delimitation of the Continental Shelf Boundaries in the Northern Part of the Strait of Malacca, 16 July 1973, Lathrop (n 2) 1452, 1471.
[1236] Article 6, Agreement between the Government of the Republic of Indonesia and the Government of Papua New Guinea Concerning the Maritime Boundary between the Republic of Indonesia and Papua New Guinea, 26 November 1974, 975 UNTS 3.
[1237] Article 4, Agreement between the Government of the Socialist Republic of Vietnam and the Republic of Indonesia Concerning the Delimitation of the Continental Shelf Boundary, 29 May 2007, Lathrop (n 2) 4313.
[1238] Law No 22/2001, 23 November 2001, Petroleum and Natural Gas, extwprlegs1.fao.org/docs/pdf/ins42692.pdf. Some parts were declared unconstitutional by the Indonesian Supreme Court.

[1239] Article 43, Regulation on Upstream Oil and Gas Business Activities No 35, 2004, *OGEL* Documents (copy with the author).
[1240] Contract of Work between PN Pertambangan Minjak Nasional (Permina) and PT Stanvac Indonesia, *OGEL* Documents.
[1241] Production Sharing Contract between Badan Pelaksana Kegiatan Usaha Hulu Minyak Dan Gas Bumi (Badan Pelaksana) and Contractor, 2013, eiti.ekon.go.id/en/draft-kontrak-psc/?aid=1083&sa=1.
[1242] Huffco/Total et al. Unitization Agreement, 1 January 1980 (n ilam Structure), *Barrows* A&A, Supplement No 162.
[1243] Model Production Sharing Contract of 2003 (Segaf Contract Area), *Barrows* A&A, Supplement No 157.
[1244] Agreement Concerning the Sovereignty over the Islands of Al-Arabiyah and Farsi and the Delimitation of the Boundary Line Separating the Submarine Areas between the Kingdom of Saudi Arabia and Iran, 29 January 1969, 696 UNTS 195.
[1245] Article 2, Agreement Concerning the Boundary Line Dividing the Continental Shelf between Iran And Qatar, 10 May 1970, Lathrop (n 2) 1516.
[1246] Offshore Boundary Agreement between Iran and (UAE) Dubai, signed 31 August 1974, Lathrop (n 2) 1538.
[1247] Agreement Concerning Delimitation of the Continental Shelf between Iran and Oman, 28 May 1975, 972 UNTS 265.
[1248] Article 4 and Article 5, Agreement on the Delimitation of the Maritime Boundary in the Sea of Oman between the Islamic Republic of Iran and the Sultanate of Oman (with Chart), 16 September 2016, Reg No 54173.
[1249] 'Iran, Iraq Strike Understanding for Development of Joint Oilfields', 7 April 2019, en.shana.ir/news/288279/Iran-Iraq-Strike-Understanding-for-Development-of-Joint-Oilfields.
[1250] Petroleum Act dated 6 August 1974, *Barrows* ME, Supplement No 44.
[1251] Petroleum Law, Iranian Islamic Parliament, 1987, *Barrows* ME, Supplement No 105. See also Act Amending 1987 Petroleum Act of Iran (2011), *OGEL* Documents (copy with the author).
[1252] Iran Petroleum Act, 2009, *OGEL* Documents (copy with the author).
[1253] Exploration and Production Contracting Agreement between NIOC and Continental Oil Company, 6 April 1969, *Barrows* ME, Supplement No 26.
[1254] Preamble and art 2, General Conditions, Structure and Model of the Upstream Oil and Gas Contracts, 2 August 2016, *OGEL* Documents.
[1255] Amiri Decree No 217 of 2017. See 'Kuwait Okays Oil Field Work with Iraq', *Oil & Gas Journal*, 11 September 2017, ogj.com/articles/2017/09/kuwait-okays-oil-field-work-with-iraq.html.
[1256] Final Report on the Demarcation of the International Boundary between the Republic of Iraq and the State of Kuwait by the United Nations Iraq-Kuwait Boundary Demarcation Commission, 21 May 1993, Lathrop (n 2) 2397.
[1257] Article 11, Iraq Oil and Gas Law 2007, *OGEL* Documents (copy with the author).
[1258] Article 36, Law No 229, Oil Wealth Preservation Regulation, 2 January 1971, *Barrows* ME, Supplement No 29.
[1259] Hydrocarbon Resource Reservation Law No (84) for 1985, oil.gov.iq/?page=323.
[1260] New Regulations for Ministry of Oil and Minerals, Law No 41 of 1969, *Barrows* ME, Supplement No 27.
[1261] Articles 2, 12 and 36, Oil Wealth Preservation Regulation, 2 January 1971, *Barrows* ME, Supplement No 29.
[1262] Article 3, Agreement between the Republic of Ireland and the United Kingdom of Great Britain and Northern Ireland Concerning the Delimitation of the Continental Shelf between the Two Countries, 11 January 1990, Lathrop (n 2) 1774; Agreement between the Government of Ireland and the Government of the United Kingdom of Great Britain and Northern Ireland Establishing a Single Maritime Boundary between the Exclusive Economic Zones of the Two Countries and Parts of Their Continental Shelves, 31 March 2014, Lathrop (n 2), 5151.
[1263] Petroleum and Other Minerals Development Act, 1960, irishstatutebook.ie/eli/1960/act/7/enacted/en/html.
[1264] Article 33, Licensing Terms for Offshore Oil and Gas Exploration, Development & Production 2007, gov.ie/pdf/75206/?page=null. http://www.dCACe.gov.ie/documents/LicensingTerms%202007.pdf.
[1265] Maritime Boundary Agreement between the Government of the State of Israel and the Government of the Hashemite Kingdom of Jordan, 17 February 1996, Lathrop (n 2) 2460.

[1266] Article 38, Petroleum Law 5712-1952 (1952), energy.gov.il/English/LegislationLibraryE1/Part2pl.doc.
[1267] Article 4.2.3, Petroleum Regulations (Principles for Offshore Petroleum Exploration and Production) 5777-2016, energy-sea.gov.il/English-Site/PublishingImages/Pages/Forms/EditForm/Petroleum%20Regulations%20%28Principles%20for%20Offshore%20Petroleum%20Exploration%20and%20Production%29%20%20%205777-2016.pdf (unofficial English translation).
[1268] Schedule 6, Model License (2016), in Ministry of National Infrastructure, Energy and Water Resources, Bid Round Documents, 1st Offshore Bidding Round (2016), 39, energy-sea.gov.il/English-Site/Pages/News%20And%20Media/Call_for_Bids_Israel%201st%20Offshore%20Bid%20Round%20-%20updated%20schedule%20June%2017.pdf (unofficial English translation).
[1269] Article 2, Agreement between Italy and Yugoslavia Concerning the Delimitation of the Continental Shelf between the Two Countries in the Adriatic Sea, 21 January 1970, Lathrop (n 2) 1634.
[1270] Article 4, Agreement between the Government of the Italian Republic and the Government of the Tunisian Republic Relating to the Delimitation of the Continental Shelf between the Two Countries, 6 December 1978, Lathrop (n 2) 1621.
[1271] Act No 613 Law for Exploration and Production of Liquid and Gaseous Hydrocarbons in the Territorial Sea and Continental Shelf, 21 July 1967, *Barrows* Europe, Supplement No 12; Article 38, the Oil Law, 5712-1952, as amended in 1989, nevo.co.il/law_html/law01/315_001.htm#Seif26.
[1272] Law No 6 Governing Exploration for and Production of Liquid and Gaseous Hydrocarbons, 11 January 1957, *Barrows* Europe, Supplement No 125.
[1273] Loi 70-489, Portant Code Petrolier, 3 August 1970, *Journal Officiel de la République de Côte d'Ivoire No 39*, 12 August 1970.
[1274] Article 56, Code Petrolier, 31 May 1996, *Barrows* SCA, Supplement No 133.
[1275] Loi N° 2014-138 du 24 Mars 2014, Portant Code Minier, extwprlegs1.fao.org/docs/pdf/ivc146577.pdf.
[1276] Article 12.4, 1990 Model Petroleum Production Sharing Contract, *Barrows* SCA, Supplement 113.
[1277] Article 12, BP Exploration, Kosmos Energy Cote d'Ivoire, Petroci Holding, Block CI-526, PSA, 2017, resourcecontracts.org/contract/ocds-591adf-6801345335/view.
[1278] Agreement between Japan and the Republic of Korea Concerning Joint Development of the Southern Part of the Continental Shelf Adjacent to the Two Countries, 22 June 1978, 1225 UNTS 1114.
[1279] Law of 14 June 1978 to Implement the Agreement Regarding Joint Development of the Southern Part of the Continental Shelf Adjacent to Japan and the Republic of Korea, *Barrows* A&A, Supplement No 60.
[1280] Article 2, Seabed Boundary Agreement between the Republic of Kazakhstan and the Russian Federation with Protocol, Kazakhstan approval 14 November 2002; Russian approval 7 April 2003, Lathrop (n 2) 4022.
[1281] Article F, Seabed boundary agreement between the Republic of Azerbaijan and the Republic of Kazakhstan and Protocol, Kazakhstan approval of Agreement and Protocol 2 July 2003; Azerbaijan approval of Agreement and Protocol 9 December 2003, Lathrop (n 2) 4048.
[1282] Article 89, Law of Subsoil and Subsoil Use, amended up to 24 June 2010, wto.org/english/thewto_e/acc_e/kaz_e/wtacckaz69_leg_3.pdf; art 14.4, Decree No 454, Statute on the Ministry of Oil and Gas of the Republic of Kazakhstan, 20 May 2010, *OGEL* Documents (copy with the author).
[1283] Marsel Petroleum LLP, Exploration License, Translated Contract, 2007, resourcecontracts.org/contract/ocds-591adf-2849121033/view#/pdf.
[1284] Agreement between the United Republic of Tanzania and the Republic of Kenya on the Delimitation of the Maritime Boundary of the Exclusive Economic Zone and the Continental Shelf, 23 June 2009, Lathrop (n 2) 4788.
[1285] Petroleum (Exploration and Production) Act, 16 November 1986, nationaloil.co.ke/pdf/petroleum_act_kenya.pdf.
[1286] Article 63, Petroleum (Exploration, Development and Production) Bill of 2015, Kenya Gazette Supplement No 128, 2313.
[1287] Article 21, Production Sharing Contract between the Government of the Republic of Kenya and Camac Energy Kenya Limited Relating to Block L16, 10 May 2012, sec.gov/Archives/edgar/data/1402281/000135448812003921/cak_ex105.htmavailable.

[1288] Article 30, Model Contract Attached to Petroleum (Exploration and Production) Regulations, 1984 [LN 193/1984], Kenya Gazette Supplement No 128, 2432.

[1289] Sea Bottom Mineral Resources Development Law, Law 2184, 1 January 1970, *Barrows* A&A, Supplement No 29; Enforcement Decree of the Sea-Bottom Mineral Resources Development Law, 30 May 1970, *Barrows* A&A, Supplement No 29.

[1290] Submarine Mineral Resources Development Law, the Enforcement Decree and the Enforcement Regulations, *Barrows* A&A, Supplement No 89.

[1291] Articles 2-3, Amendment of 24 September 1970 to Wendell Phillips Contract of 24 September 1970 (Concerns Possible Boundary Dispute), *Barrows* A&A, Supplement No 48.

[1292] Article 11.6, Agreement for Offshore Petroleum Exploration and Production between the Government of Korea and Korea Petroleum Development Corporation and Zapata Exploration Company, 1981, *Barrows* A&A, Supplement No 85.

[1293] Model Contract of Concession Agreement for Petroleum Exploration and Production between the Government of Korea, Korea Petroleum Development Corporation and International Companies, 1985, *Barrows* A&A, Supplement No 85.

[1294] Article 4, Kuwait-Saudi Arabia Agreement for the Partition of their Neutral Zone, 21 March 1961, (1965) 4 ILM 1134.

[1295] Annex I, Agreement between the Kingdom of Saudi Arabia and the State of Kuwait Concerning the Submerged Area Adjacent to the Divided Zone, 30 July 2001, 2141 UNTS 251. Annex 1 declares that the 'the natural resources in the submerged area adjacent to the divided zone shall be owned in common' by the parties.

[1296] Article 7, Law No 19 of the Year 1973 Concerning the Conservation of Petroleum Resources, resourcedata.org/dataset/rgi-law-no-19-of-the-year-1973-concerning-the-conservation-of-petroleum-resources/resource/acae0960-637f-4c18-871a-8f7368b5b4d6.

[1297] Article 4, Agreement dated 10 December 1957 between the Government of Saudi Arabia and Japan Petroleum Trading Company Ltd for Exploitation of the Saudi Arabian Offshore Portion of the Neutral Zone, *Barrows* ME, Supplement No 65.

[1298] Article 38 (1), Offshore Petroleum Resources Law, Law 132 24/8/2010, lpa.gov.lb/Library/Assets/Gallery/asdasdas/Laws/OPRL%20-%20English.pdf.

[1299] Article 21.5, Exploration and Production Agreement for Petroleum Activities in [Number of Block] between the Republic of Lebanon and [XXX] et al, databank.com.lb/docs/Exploration%20and%20production%20model.pdf.

[1300] Article 21.5, Total E&P Liban, Eni Lebanon, Novatek Lebanon, Production Agreement, Block 9, 2018, resourcecontracts.org/contract/ocds-591adf-1121032259/view#/pdf.

[1301] Petroleum Activities Regulations for Lebanon Implementing Law No 132 dated 24 August 2010 (Offshore Petroleum Resources), databank.com.lb/docs/Petroleum%20Activities%20Regulations%20for%20Lebanon-English.pdf.

[1302] Article 29.1, Act to Amend and Restate the New Petroleum Law of Liberia, 5 October 2016, lpra.gov.lr/images/Laws_and_Regulations/Petroleum_EP_Law_2016_Final_1.pdf.

[1303] Article 2.5.12, Act Adopting the New Petroleum Law of the Republic of Liberia, extwprlegs1.fao.org/docs/pdf/lbr143351.pdf.

[1304] Article 12.4, Act to Ratify PSC between Liberian National Oil Company and Oranto Petroleum Limited 2009, resourcecontracts.org/contract/ocds-591adf-4413175528/download/pdf.

[1305] ExxonMobil Exploration and Production Liberia Limited, Canadian Overseas Petroleum (Bermuda) Limited, National Oil Company of Liberia, Block 13, PSA, 8 March 2013, resourcecontracts.org/contract/ocds-591adf-6713867467/view#/pdf.

[1306] Article 12.4, Repsol Exploración SA, National Oil Company of Liberia, Block LB-16, PSA, 2015, resourcecontracts.org/contract/ocds-591adf-9922636059/view#/pdf.

[1307] Article 3, Agreement between the Republic of Malta and the Great Socialist People's Libyan Arab Jamahariya Implementing Article III of the Special Agreement and the Judgment of the International Court of Justice, 11 December 1987, Lathrop (n 2) 1661.

[1308] See Annual Report 2013 of the Ministry for Foreign Affairs of the Government of Malta, 9. It was reported that 'the two countries had agreed to opt for joint oil exploration'. See 'Libya and Malta Agree Oil Deal; Will Collaborate on Exploration', 2 September 2013, english.libyanembassy.org/?p=5827 (copy with the author).

[1309] Agreement between the Great Libyan Arab Socialist People's Jamahariya and the Republic of Tunisia to Implement the Judgment of the International Court of Justice in the Tunisia-Libya Continental Shelf Case, 11 April 1989, Lathrop (n 2) 1679.

[1310] Article 4, Memorandum of Understanding between the Government of the Republic of Turkey and the Government of National Accord-State of Libya on Delimitation of the Maritime Jurisdiction Areas in the Mediterranean, 8 December 2019, Registration No 56119.

[1311] Libyan Petroleum Law Amendment, 21 November 1965, (1966) 5 ILM 442.

[1312] Petroleum Regulation No 8 for the Conservation of Petroleum Resources (1972), *OGEL* Documents (copy with the author).

[1313] Petroleum Law (25/55) (as amended), 11 May 2012, security-legislation.ly/sites/default/files/lois/169-Law%20No.%20%2825%29%20of%201955_EN.pdf.

[1314] Section 32.12, 7 November Block Exploration and Production Sharing Agreement ('Petroleum Agreement') between Joint Exploration, Exploitation and Petroleum Services Company ('Joint Oil') and Canadian Superior Energy Inc, 27 August 2008, sec.gov/Archives/edgar/data/1177470/000134100412001088/soq_6k.htm.

[1315] Article 33, Petroleum Regulation No 8, for the Conservation of Petroleum Resources, 11 May 2012, *OGEL* Documents (copy with the author).

[1316] Memorandum of Understanding between the Kingdom of Thailand and Malaysia on the Delimitation of the Continental Shelf Boundary between the Two Countries in the Gulf of Thailand, 15 July 1982, Lathrop (n 2) 1105; Memorandum of Understanding between the Kingdom of Thailand and Malaysia on the Establishment of a Joint Authority for the Exploitation of the Resources of the Sea-Bed in a Defined Area of the Continental Shelf of the Two Countries in the Gulf of Thailand, 21 February 1979, Lathrop (n 2); Proclamation Establishing the Exclusive Economic Zone of the Kingdom of Thailand in the Gulf of Thailand Adjacent to the Exclusive Economic Zone of Malaysia, 16 February 1988, ibid; Agreement between the Government of Malaysia and the Government of the Kingdom of Thailand on the Constitution and Other Matters Relating to the Establishment of the Malaysia-Thailand Joint Authority, 30 May 1990, Lathrop (n 2).

[1317] Memorandum of Understanding between Malaysia and the Socialist Republic of Vietnam for the exploration and exploitation of petroleum in a defined area of the continental shelf involving the two countries, 4 June 1993, Lathrop (n 2) 2341. Under Article 3, the parties agreed to authorize their respective national petroleum corporations (namely, Petronas and Petrovietnam) 'to enter into a commercial arrangement … for the exploration and exploitation of petroleum' and that 'the terms and conditions of that arrangement shall be subject to the approval of the Government of Malaysia and the Government of the Socialist Republic of Vietnam'.

[1318] Joint Statement on the 22nd Annual Leaders' Consultation between Malaysia and Brunei, 5 March 2019, mfa.gov.bn/Lists/Press%20Room/news.aspx?id=736&source=http://www.mfa.gov.bn/site/home.aspx; Joint Statement on the 23rd Annual Leaders' Consultation between Brunei and Malaysia, 4–5 April 2021, mfa.gov.bn/Lists/Press%20Room/news.aspx?id=904&source=http://mfa.gov.bn/site/home.aspx.

[1319] Malaysia-Thailand Joint Authority Act 1990, 30 August 1990, mtja.org/assets/pdf/en/act440.pdf. The law designates the petroleum ministry to regulate the involvement of Malaysia in the joint authority, particularly relating to the conduct of petroleum operations and the adoption of standards regarding such operations (art 15).

[1320] Petroleum Development Act 1974 Act 144, 1 October 1974; the official version as of June 2013 is available at agc.gov.my/agcportal/uploads/files/Publications/LOM/EN/Act%20144%20-%20Petroleum%20Development%20Act%201974.pdf.

[1321] Article 9, Petroleum Mining Act 1966, with amendments up to 1 January 2006, *OGEL* Documents.

[1322] Article 19, Contract between Malaysia-Thailand Joint Authority and Petronas Carigali Sdn Bhd and Triton Oil Company of Thailand Relating to Exploration and Production of Petroleum for Malaysia-Thailand Joint Development Area Block A-18, 1994, sec.gov/Archives/edgar/data/99830/0000912057-94-001477.txt.

[1323] Malaysia- Thailand Joint Authority Procedures for Production Operations, 14 December 2009, mtja.org/pdf/MTJA_procedures_for_production_operations_rev1_14dec09_bw.pdf.

[1324] Article 46, Model Contract attached to Petroleum Mining Rules, 11 April 1968, *Barrows* A&A, Supplement No 21.

[1325] Article 43, Code des hydrocarbures, Loi No 2015-035 du 16 juillet 2015, extwprlegs1.fao.org/docs/pdf/mli153041.pdf.

[1326] Loi N°04-037, 2 August 2004, Portant Organisation de la Recherche, de L'exploitation, du Transport et du Raffinage des Hydrocarbures, extwprlegs1.fao.org/docs/pdf/mli96752.pdf.

[1327] Article 9.9, Convention type de Partage de Production, mines.gouv.ml/sites/default/files/2019-09/CPP%20TYPE.pdf.
[1328] Act No 4, Petroleum Production Act, 1958, *Barrows* Europe, Supplement No 19.
[1329] Article 23, Model Clauses attached to the Petroleum (Production) Regulations, 23 September 1969, *Barrows* Europe, Supplement No 16.
[1330] Memorandum of Understanding between Pétroles du Sénégal (Petrosen), Société Mauritanienne Des Hydrocarbures et de Patrimoine Minier (SMHPM) and Kosmos Energy, 2016, reported without the full text in Kosmos Energy, Greater Tortue, Kosmos Energy Annual Report 2016, 13, annualreports.com/HostedData/AnnualReports/PDF/NYSE_KOS_2016.pdf.
[1331] Interstate Cooperation Agreement on the Development and Exploitation of the Grand Tortue/Ahmeyim Field Reservoirs between the Islamic Republic of Mauritania and the Republic of Senegal, signed 9 February 2018 by the Minister of Petroleum and Energy of Senegal and the Minister of Petroleum, Energy and Mines of Mauritania, 63 *Official Journal of the Republic of Senegal* 7119, 58.
[1332] Treaty on the Delimitation of the Maritime Frontier between the Islamic Republic of Mauritania and the Republic of Cape Verde, 19 September 2003, Lathrop (n 2) 3702.
[1333] Law No 2019-12 and Law No 2019-014, 20 February 2019, *Official Journal of the Islamic Republic of Mauritania No 1433*, 15 March 2019, 162–64.
[1334] Loi règlementant les activités aval du secteur des hydrocarbures Ordonnance n°2002-005 du 28 mars 2002, droit-afrique.com/upload/doc/mauritanie/Mauritanie-Ordonnance-2002-05-petrole-aval.
[1335] Article 53, Law No 2010-33 dated 20 July 2010 Instituting Code of Crude Hydrocarbons, petrole.gov.mr/IMG/pdf/code_des_hydrocarbures_in_english.pdf.
[1336] Article 9.9, Contrat d'Exploration – Production (2011), petrole.gov.mr/IMG/pdf/cep_type_definitif_-_23_octobre_2011.pdf.
[1337] Article 9.9, Exploration and Production Contract between the Islamic Republic of Mauritania and Kosmos Energy Mauritania Bloc C8, 5 April 2012, sec.gov/Archives/edgar/data/1509991/000110465913080961/a13-19720_1ex10d17.htm; art 9.9, Exploration and Production Contract between the Islamic Republic of Mauritania and Kosmos Energy Mauritania Bloc C13, 5 April 2012, sec.gov/Archives/edgar/data/1509991/000110465913080961/a13-19720_1ex10d19.htm.
[1338] Treaty Concerning the Joint Management of the Continental Shelf in the Mascarene Plateau Region, 13 March 2012, 2847 UNTS 307; Treaty Concerning the Joint Exercise of Sovereign Rights over the Continental Shelf in the Mascarene Plateau Region, 12 March 2012, 2847 UNTS 277.
[1339] Petroleum Act, 16 April 1970, global-regulation.com/law/mauritius/8166225/petroleum-act.html.
[1340] Article 6, Agreement between the United States of America and the United Mexican States Concerning Transboundary Hydrocarbon Reservoirs in the Gulf of Mexico, 18 July 2014, TIAS No 14-718.
[1341] Treaty on Maritime Boundaries between the United Mexican States and the United States of America. Mexico City, 13 November 1997, 2143 UNTS 405.
[1342] Article 1, Ley de Hidrocarburos, 11 August 2014, dof.gob.mx/nota_detalle.php?codigo=5355989&fecha=11/08/2014.
[1343] Clause 9.1, 2012 PEMEX Model Contract, 15 September 2021 at rondasmexico.gob.mx/media/1094/eng_ci_17-dic-15_r01l01-2015.pdf.
[1344] Clause 9.1, 2018 Contract No. CNH-R02-L04-AP-CS-G10/2018 at rondasmexico.gob.mx/esp/contratos/cnh-r02-l04-ap-cs-g102018/?tab=02.
[1345] Article 7, Agreement on the Delimitation of the Maritime Boundary between the Republic of Mozambique and the United Republic of Tanzania signed 5 December 2011, Lathrop (n 2) 4800.
[1346] Article 38, Petroleum Law No 21/2014, 18 August 2014, inp-mz.com/core/uploads/Unoffical-Translation-Petroleum-Law.pdf.
[1347] Article 35, Decree No 34/2015 approving the Regulation of Petroleum Operations, 31 December 2015, extwprlegs1.fao.org/docs/pdf/moz152026.pdf.
[1348] Article 16.4, Model Contract, PSA, 2016, inp.gov.mz/index.php/en/content/download/1273/8607/file/EPCC.pdf.
[1349] Agreement between the Government of the Socialist Republic of the Union of Burma (Myanmar) and the Government of the Kingdom of Thailand on the Delimitation of the Maritime Boundary between the Countries in the Andaman Sea, 12 April 1982, Lathrop (n 2) 1351.
[1350] Service Contract for Offshore Petroleum Operations, 11 July 1974, between Myanma Oil Corporation and Esso Exploration and Production Burma Inc, *Barrows* A&A, Supplement No 70.

[1351] Production Sharing Contract between Myanma Oil and Gas Enterprise and Total Myanmar Exploration and Production, 9 July 1992, resourcecontracts.org/contract/ocds-591adf-6716589315/view#/pdf.
[1352] Agreement between the Government of the Kingdom of the Netherlands and the Government of the United Kingdom of Great Britain and Northern Ireland Relating to the Exploitation of Single Geological Structures Extending across the Dividing Line on the Continental Shelf under the North Sea, 23 December 1966, Treaty Series No 24 (1967). Under art 1, a shared resource shall be subject to an inter-state agreement based on the proposal of the licensees.
[1353] Agreement between the Kingdom of Belgium and the Kingdom of the Netherlands Relating to the Delimitation of the Territorial Sea and Agreement between the Kingdom of Belgium and the Kingdom of the Netherlands Relating to the Delimitation of the Continental Shelf, 1 January 1999, Lathrop (n 2) 2946.
[1354] Section 11, Continental Self Mining Law, 1965, *Barrows* Europe, Supplement No 8.
[1355] Mining Act of the Netherlands, 1 January 2003, nlog.nl/sites/default/files/2019-02/2019-01-01%20Translation%20Mijnbouwwet%20in%20English.pdf.
[1356] Mining Act of the Netherlands (Mijnbouwwet) as amended up to 2012, nlog.nl/cmis/browser?id=1c894b3c-2abe-493c-8e18-833d44da5160%3B1.0.
[1357] Article 47, Law No 286, Special Law on the Exploration and Exploitation of Hydrocarbon, 12 June 1998, *OGEL* Documents (copy with the author). The Spanish text is available at idbdocs.iadb.org/wsdocs/getdocument.aspx?docnum=38241553.
[1358] Article 28, Ley No 372, Ley Especial Sobre Exploración y Explotación de Petróleo, 26 November 1958, legislacion.asamblea.gob.ni/gacetas/1958/12/g278.pdf.
[1359] Article 24.3, Model Petroleum Concession Contract 2000, *Barrows* CAR, Supplement No 121.
[1360] Clause 25(3), Concession Agreement for the Exploration and Exploitation of Hydrocarbons, 'Perlas' Prospect, 5 March 2009, sec.gov/Archives/edgar/data/822746/000114420411029215/v222400_ex10-8.htm. This provides for inter-state agreement on shared resource with the technical assistance of the contractor. See also Clause 25(2), Concession Agreement for the Exploration and Exploitation of Hydrocarbons for the 'Tyra' Prospect, 5 March 2009, sec.gov/Arhives/edgar/data/822746/000114420411029215/v222400_ex10-9.htm.
[1361] Article 125-131, Decree No 43-98, Special Hydrocarbon Exploration and Exploitation Law Exploration and Exploitation Law Regulation, La Gaceta No 117 of 24 June 1998.
[1362] Treaty between the Federal Republic of Nigeria and the Democratic Republic of São Tomé and Príncipe on the Joint Development of Petroleum and Other Resources in Respect of Areas of the Exclusive Economic Zone of the Two States, 16 January 2003, Lathrop (n 2) 3649;
[1363] Nigeria-São Tomé and Príncipe Joint Development Authority Model PSC, grip.st/docs/27---DT%20-%2027%20_JDA.pdf.
[1364] Petroleum Act Chapter P10 (Chapter 350 LFN 1990) Laws of the Federation of Nigeria, resourcegovernance.org/sites/default/files/documents/nigeria-pertoleum-act.pdf.
[1365] Nigeria-São Tomé and Príncipe Joint Development Authority Petroleum Regulations 2003, *Barrows* SCA, Supplement 158.
[1366] Article 48, Petroleum (Drilling and Production) Regulations, 27 November 1969, extwprlegs1.fao.org/docs/pdf/nig120683.pdf.
[1367] Production Sharing Contract between Nigerian National Petroleum Corporation and 1. Gas Transmission and Power Limited; 2. Energy 905 Suntera Limited; 3. Ideal Oil and Gas Limited Covering Block 905 Anambra Basin, resourcecontracts.org/contract/ocds-591adf-0523462294/view#/pdf.
[1368] Allied Energy PLC, CAMAC International (Nigeria) Limited, Nigerian Agip Exploration Limited, CAMAC Petroleum LImited, Oyo Field, PSA, 2011, resourcecontracts.org/contract/ocds-591adf-1761043738/view#/pdf.
[1369] Article 4, Agreement between the Government of the United Kingdom of Great Britain and Northern Ireland and the Government of the Kingdom of Norway Relating to the Delimitation of the Continental Shelf between the Two Countries, 29 June 1965, Treaty Series No 71 (1965).
[1370] Framework Agreement between the Government of the United Kingdom of Great Britain and Northern Ireland and the Government of the Kingdom of Norway Concerning Cross-boundary Petroleum Co-operation, 10 July 2007, 2491 UNTS 3.
[1371] Article 5 and Annex II, Treaty between the Kingdom of Norway and the Russian Federation Concerning Maritime Delimitation and Cooperation in the Barents Sea and the Arctic Ocean, 7 July 2011, Lathrop (n 2) 5189.

[1372] Section 4-7, Act No 72, 29 November 1996, as amended by Act No 65, 19 June 2015, npd.no/en/Regulations/Acts/Petroleum-activities-act.
[1373] Article 32, Royal Decree of 8 December 1972 Relating to Exploration for and Exploitation of Petroleum in the Seabed and Sub-strata of the Norwegian Continental Shelf, *Barrows* Europe, Supplement No 25.
[1374] Section 31, Royal Decree of 9 April 1965 Relating to the Exploration and Exploitation of Petroleum in the Seabed and Subsoil on the Norwegian Continental Shelf, *Barrows* Europe, Supplement No 5.
[1375] Section 82, Regulations to Act Relating to Petroleum Activities, Royal Decree 27 June 1997, as amended up to 2012, npd.no/en/Regulations/Regulations/Petroleum-activities.
[1376] Sections 1.1, 1.2, 5.1 and 5.2, UK-Norway Trans-boundary Oil and Gas Fields Guidelines for Development of Trans-boundary Oil and Gas Fields, npd.no/globalassets/1-npd/regelverk/forskrifter/en/transboundary-fields-1016.pdf.
[1377] Agreement between A/S Adventdalens Kullfelt and A/S Akers Mek. Verksted, for Svalbard Exploration, 1969, *Barrows* Europe, Supplement No 19.
[1378] Petroleum Reconnaissance License Form and Petroleum Production License Form, *Barrows* Europe, Supplement No 20.
[1379] Agreement Relating to the Unitisation and Operation of the Unknown Field, 23 April 2007, regjeringen.no/globalassets/upload/oed/pdf_filer_2/og/standard_unitavtale.pdf.
[1380] Article 6, Muscat Agreement on the Delimitation of the Maritime Boundary between the Sultanate of Oman and the Islamic Republic of Pakistan, 21 November 2000, Lathrop (n 2) 2818.
[1381] Article 6, International Boundary Agreement between the Sultanate of Oman and the Republic of Yemen, 17 December 1992, 1709 UNTS 432.
[1382] Article 4, Agreement to Mark the Maritime Borders between the Republic of Yemen and the Sultanate of Oman, 10 April 2004, Lathrop (n 2) 3909.
[1383] Petroleum and Mineral Law, 1 January 1975, *Barrows* ME, Supplement No 58.
[1384] Articles 33–35, Royal Decree No 8/2011 issuing the Oil and Gas Law, pdo.co.om/hseforcontractors/LegalRequirements/8-2011%20Oil%20and%20Gas%20Law.pdf.
[1385] Exploration and Production Sharing Agreement (undated), *OGEL* documents (copy with the author).
[1386] Agreement between the Government of Chile and the Government of Peru Relating to the Maritime Boundary between Chile and Peru, 23 September 1954, Lathrop (n 2) 799.
[1387] Article 32, Law No 26221, Organic Law for Hydrocarbons, 13 August 1993, perupetro.com.pe/wps/wcm/connect/corporativo/4114be82-e203-4b22-a346-6d6f53eacfbf/2_Ley_Org%C3%A1nica_de_Hidrocarburos.pdf?MOD=AJPERES.
[1388] Article 5.9, License Agreement for the Exploration and Exploitation of Hydrocarbons in Lot Z-68 between Perupetro SA and Tullow Peru Limited, 17 July 2020, perupetro.com.pe/wps/wcm/connect/corporativo/17f82470-7193-4a76-aa00-dd0be51dea75/Testimonio+Z-68.pdf?MOD=AJPERES.
[1389] Agreement between the Government of the Republic of the Philippines and the Republic of Indonesia Concerning the Delimitation of the Exclusive Economic Zone Boundary, 1 August 2019, UN Registration No 55946.
[1390] Petroleum Act No 387 of 1949, 18 June 1949, extwprlegs1.fao.org/docs/texts/phi47547.doc.
[1391] Presidential Decree No 87, 31 December 1972, officialgazette.gov.ph/1972/12/31/presidential-decree-no-87-s-1972.
[1392] Presidential Decree No 1857, 1 January 1983, officialgazette.gov.ph/1983/01/01/presidential-decree-no-1857-s-1983.
[1393] CNOOC/ PETROVIETNAM/ PNOC, Joint Statement on the Signing of a Tripartite Agreement for Joint Marine Seismic Undertaking in the Agreement Area in the South China Sea (JMSU), 14 March 2005, Makati Shangri-la Hotel, ph.china-embassy.org/eng/sgdt/t187333.htm.
[1394] Model Service Contract (2019), doe.gov.ph/sites/default/files/pdf/energy_resources/pcecp_20190425-final_model_petroleum_service_contract.pdf.
[1395] Articles 6-7, Agreement for Settlement of the Offshore Boundary and Ownership of Islands between the Emirates of Qatar and Abu Dhabi, 20 March 1969, *Barrows* ME, Supplement No 28.
[1396] Agreement on the Delimitation of the Offshore and Land Boundaries between the Kingdom of Saudi Arabia and Qatar, 4 December 1965, 1733 UNTS 19.
[1397] Joint Minutes on the Land and Maritime Boundaries to the Agreement of 4 December 1965 between the State of Qatar and the Kingdom of Saudi Arabia on the Delimitation of the Offshore and Land Boundaries, 16 December 2008, Lathrop (n 2) 4423.

[1398] Qatar Law (3) of 2007 on the Exploitation of Natural Resources, almeezan.qa/LawView.aspx?opt&LawID=2600&language=en.
[1399] Article 34.7, Model Exploration and Production Sharing Agreement between the Government of Qatar and Contractor (1997), *Barrows* ME, Supplement No 150.
[1400] Model Development and Production Sharing Agreement between the Government of Qatar and Contractor (2002, North Field), *Barrows* ME, Supplement No 155. Model Development & Production Sharing Agreement of 2002 between the Government of Qatar and Contractor (North Field), *Barrows* ME, Supplement No 155. Article 37 provides that were the operations of a contractor 'will result in a dispute over a boundary line with a neighbouring state or states, the GOVERNMENT may set limits on the conduct of the Petroleum Operations within that specific area … provided that … [w]hen the reason for setting the restrictions on the operating area no longer exists, such limits shall be lifted by the GOVERNMENT … If the GOVERNMENT should set limits on the area of operations … the CONTRACTOR shall have full recourse to the provisions of Force Majeure'.
[1401] Protocol Approving Offshore Unitization Prospects 14K and A-IMI, signed 10 September 2001, Lathrop (n 2) 428.
[1402] Article 61, Hydrocarbons Code Law No 28-2016, 12 October 2016, droit-afrique.com/uploads/Congo-Code-2016-Hydrocarbures.pdf.
[1403] Article 38, Portant Code Petrolier De La Republique de Guinee, 8 August 2014, mines.gov.gn/assets/uploads/2016/03/Code-Petrolier.pdf.
[1404] Article 35, Law No L/95/036/CTRN, 30 June 1995, droit-afrique.com/images/textes/Guinee/Guinee%20-%20Code%20minier.pdf.
[1405] Article 7.8, Hydrocarbon Production Sharing Contract between the Republic of Guinea and SCS Corporation, 22 September 2006, resourcecontracts.org/contract/ocds-591adf-4957567520/download/pdf.
[1406] Operating Agreement between SCS Corporation and Dana Petroleum (E&P) Limited Based on the 2002 Model Form International Operating Agreement of AIPN, 28 January 2010, sec.gov/Archives/edgar/data/937136/000114420410004433/v172634_ex10-1.htm.
[1407] Agreement between the Government of the Kingdom of Sweden, the Government of the Polish People's Republic and the Government of the USSR Concerning the Common Delimitation Point of Their Maritime Boundaries in the Baltic Sea, un.org/depts/los/LEGISLATIONANDTREATIES/PDFFILES/TREATIES/SWE-POL-RUS1989MB.PDF.
[1408] Law of the Russian Federation No 2395-1 of February 21, 1992 about Subsoil, cis-legislation.com/document.fwx?rgn=1494.
[1409] Article 15, Exploration and Production-Sharing Contract for Hydrocarbons between Republic of Sacha (Yakut) and Russian Federation on the One Hand and the Sacha-Austrian Joint Venture TAKT on the Other, resourcecontracts.org/contract/ocds-591adf-3525416018/download/pdf.
[1410] Agreement on the Delimitation of the Maritime Border between the Gabonese Republic and the Democratic Republic of São Tomé and Príncipe, signed 26 April 2001, Lathrop (n 2) 3691.
[1411] Article 44, Fundamental Law on Petroleum Operations Law No 16/2009, 3 July 2009, stp-eez.com/DownLoads/LR_Docs_Eng/Schedule_1A_Petroleum_Operations_Law_16_2009_Eng.pdf.
[1412] Article 11, Petroleum Operations Regulations, 24 February 2010, stp-eez.com/DownLoads/LR_Docs_Eng/Shedule_2_Pet_Oper_24Feb10.pdf; Model Production Sharing Contract (2010), last accessed on 15 September 2021 at stp-eez.com/downloads/lr_docs_eng/eez_psc_eng.pdf.
[1413] Production Sharing Contract between the Democratic Republic of São Tomé and Príncipe represented by the Agência Nacional do Petróleo of São Tomé and Príncipe and Galp Energia São Tomé E Príncipe, Unipessoal, Lda for Block 6, 12 January 2016, sec.gov/Archives/edgar/data/1509991/000155837016005628/kos-20160331ex100600740.htm.
[1414] Agreement between the Democratic Republic of Sudan and the Kingdom of Saudi Arabia Relating to the Natural Resources of the Sea-Bed and Sub-soil of the Red Sea in the Common Zone, 26 August 1974, *Barrows* ME, Supplement No 154.
[1415] Section 3, Royal Decree No M-27, 7 September 1968, extwprlegs1.fao.org/docs/pdf/sau159314.pdf.
[1416] Concession Contract of 21 December 1967 between General Petroleum and Minerals Organization (PETROMIN) and AGIP Saudi Arabia including text of Petromin Concession dated 21 December 1967 as Annex A, *Barrows* ME, Supplement No 21.
[1417] Treaty on the Delimitation of the Maritime Frontier between the Republic of Cape Verde and the Republic of Senegal, signed 17 February 1993, Lathrop (n 2) 2287.

[1418] Article 60, Sénégal Code Pétrolier 2019 Loi n°2019-03 du 1er février 2019, droit-afrique.com/uploads/Senegal-Code-2019-petrolier.pdf.

[1419] Articles 9.6-9.9, Convention-Type de Recherche Et D'exploitation des Hydrocarbures 1998, agc-sngb.org/en/wp-content/uploads/2014/10/ResearchContract.pdf.

[1420] Article 9.6, Contract between the Republic of Senegal (Minister of State, Minister of International Cooperation, Air Transport, Infrastructure and Energy) and PetroTim Limited and Société des Pétroles du Sénégal, (PETROSEN), Saint Louis Offshore Profond, 17 January 2012, Sec.gov/Archives/edgar/data/1509991/000110465914075847/a14-19714_1ex10d1.htm.

[1421] Agreement between the Union of the Comoros and the Republic of Seychelles on the Delimitation of the Maritime Boundary of the Exclusive Economic Zone and the Continental Shelf in the Indian Ocean, signed 17 February 2012, Lathrop (n 2) 5046. Article 4 contains a broad resource cooperation clause.

[1422] Agreement between the Government of the Republic of Seychelles, the Government of the Union of the Comoros and the Government of the United Republic of Tanzania on the Delimitation of the Maritime Boundary of the Tripoint of the Exclusive Economic Zone and the Continental Shelf in the Indian Ocean, signed 17 February 2012, Lathrop (n 2) 5056.

[1423] Agreement between the Government of the United Republic of Tanzania and the Government of the Republic of Seychelles on the Delimitation of the Maritime Boundary of the Exclusive Economic Zone and the Continental Shelf, 23 January 2002, Lathrop (n 2) 3802.

[1424] Petroleum Mining Act, 26 July 1976, petroseychelles.com/images/pdfs/Seychelles%20Petroleum%20Mining%20Act.pdf.

[1425] Petroleum Mining Act 2012, seylii.org/sc/legislation/consolidated-act/167.

[1426] Article 24, Republic of Seychelles Model Petroleum (2013), petroseychelles.com/images/pdfs/Model%20Petroleum%20Agreement%202013.pdf.

[1427] Article 62, Oil/Gas-Petroleum Exploration and Production Act, 25 July 2011, sierra-leone.org/Laws/2011-07.pdf.

[1428] Article 16, Petroleum Exploration and Production Act, 16 August 2001, extwprlegs1.fao.org/docs/pdf/sie60993.pdf.

[1429] Model Petroleum License No 000-000-2012, undated, nma.gov.sl/resourcecontracts/contract/ocds-591adf-8902140898/download/pdf.

[1430] Article 87, Act No 28 Mineral and Petroleum Resources Development Act, 3 October 2002, Government Gazette of Republic of South Africa No 448, 5.

[1431] Mineral and Petroleum Resources Development Regulations, 10 October 2002, as amended up to 2011, cer.org.za/wp-content/uploads/2014/02/Regualtions.pdf.

[1432] Article 34, OK Energy Limited, Exploration License, 2019, resourcecontracts.org/contract/ocds-591adf-7096109034/view#/pdf.

[1433] Spanish Petroleum Law, 15 December 1958, *Barrows* Europe, vol II, No 2.

[1434] Lei 34/1998, do 7 de Octubre, do Sector de Hidrocarburos, 8 October 1998, as amended up to 2011, boe.es/buscar/pdf/1998/BOE-A-1998-23284-consolidado.pdf.

[1435] Articles 67-68, Regulations Implementing the 1958 Spanish Petroleum Law, *Barrows* Europe, vol II, no 2.

[1436] Article 18, Petroleum Resources Act No 26, 9 September 2003, prds-srilanka.com/pdfs/petResources.pdf.

[1437] Article 12, Petroleum Resources Agreement for the Exploration and Production of Oil and Natural Gas in the Mannar Basin, Block No Sl 2007-01-001, between the Government of Sri Lanka and Cairn Lanka (Pvt) Ltd, 7 July 2008, prds-srilanka.com/pdfs/PRA-1.pdf.

[1438] Article 30, Sri Lanka Model Petroleum Resources Agreement (2013), prds-srilanka.com/pdfs/MPRA-20170420.pdf.

[1439] Decree of 8 May 1986 (Mining Decree), Official Gazette 1986 no 28, staatsolie.com/media/0vwhuuv3/mining-decree-1986.pdf.

[1440] Article 24, Petroleum Law 1990 of Suriname, Official Gazette of the Republic of Suriname (1991 no 7); Law of 2 October 2001, Amending the Petroleum Law, 1990, Official Gazette of Republic of Suriname (2001 no 58).

[1441] Article 9.9, Production Sharing Contract for Petroleum Exploration, Development and Production Relating to Block 45 Offshore Suriname between STAATSOLIE MAATSCHAPPIJ SURINAME NV (hereinafter referred to as 'Staatsolie') and Kosmos Energy Surinam, 13 December 2011, sec.gov/Archives/edgar/data/1509991/000110465913080961/a13-19720_1ex10d21.htm.

[1442] Model Contract, PSA, 2015, resourcecontracts.org/contract/ocds-591adf-2983786244/view#/pdf.
[1443] Agreement between the Republic of Finland and the Kingdom of Sweden on the Delimitation of the Boundary between the Continental Shelf and Fishery Zone of Finland and the Economic Zone of Sweden in the Aland Sea and the Northern Baltic Sea, 30 July 1995, ecolex.org/server2neu.php/libcat/docs/TRE/Full/Other/TRE-152664.pdf.
[1444] Agreement between the Government of the Republic of Estonia and the Government of the Kingdom of Sweden on the Delimitation of the Maritime Zones in the Baltic Sea, 26 July 2000, Lathrop (n 2) 3105.
[1445] Law Relating to the Continental Shelf, 3 June 1966, *Barrows* Europe, Supplement No 10.
[1446] Minerals Act, 1 July 1992 and Minerals Ordinance, 1 July 1992, as amended up to 2007, sgu.se/en/mining-inspectorate/legislation/mineral-act-199145.
[1447] Agreement on the Delimitation of the Maritime Boundary between the United Republic of Tanzania and the Union of the Comoros, signed 5 December 2011, Lathrop (n 2) 5066. The parties agree to cooperate in 'the exploration and exploitation of resources found along the common boundary' (art 4).
[1448] Article 78(5), Petroleum Act, 18 September 2015, tpdc.co.tz/wp-content/uploads/2016/02/SHERIA-PETROLEUM-ACT-2015-Updated-version-15-6.pdf.
[1449] Articles 46-47, Petroleum (Exploration and Production) Act No 27 of 1980, tpdc.co.tz/wp-content/uploads/2015/04/psaandact1980.pdf.
[1450] Article 32, Model Production Sharing Agreement between the Government of the United Republic of Tanzania and Tanzania Petroleum Development Corporation and ABC Ltd for Any Area (2013), tpdc.co.tz/pdfstuff/Model%20Production%20Sharing%20Agreement%20(2013).pdf.
[1451] Article 4, Agreement between the Government of the Kingdom of Thailand and the Government of the Socialist Republic of Vietnam on the Delimitation of the Maritime Boundary between the Two Countries in the Gulf of Thailand, 27 December 1997, Lathrop (n 2) 2692.
[1452] Minerals Act of Thailand and Ministerial Regulations (1967), extwprlegs1.fao.org/docs/pdf/tha155180.pdf.
[1453] Section 72, Petroleum Act B E 2514, as amended by Minerals Act, B E 2560 (2017), extwprlegs1.fao.org/docs/pdf/tha181040.pdf.
[1454] Petroleum Mining Code for the Joint Petroleum Development Area (2005), web01.anpm.tl/webs/anptlweb.nsf/vwAll/Resource-Petroleum%20Mining%20Code/$File/PMCtoCoM0602.pdf?openelement.
[1455] Article 19, Law No 13 /2005 on Petroleum Activities, timor-leste.gov.tl/wp-content/uploads/2010/03/Law_2005_13_petroleum_activities_.pdf.
[1456] Model Production Sharing Contract for the Offshore of Timor-Leste (2020), licensinground.anpm.tl/wp-content/uploads/2020/02/Offshore-PSC-Model.pdf.
[1457] Agreement between the Government of Trinidad and Tobago and the Government of the Republic of Venezuela on the Delimitation of Marine and Submarine Areas, 23 July 1991, Lathrop (n 2) 670; Letter of Intent and Memorandum of Understanding dated 12 August 2003 Concerning the Procedure for Unitization of Hydrocarbon Reservoirs that Extend Across the Delimitation Line between the Republic of Trinidad and Tobago and the Bolivarian Republic of Venezuela, 12 August 2002, Barrows CAC, Supplement No 129; Framework Treaty Relating to the Unitisation of Hydrocarbon Reservoirs that Extend across the Delimitation Line between the Republic of Trinidad and Tobago and the Bolivarian Republic of Venezuela, 16 August 2010, 2876 UNTS 3; Unitisation Agreement for the Exploitation and Development of Hydrocarbon Reservoirs of the Loran-Manatee Field that Extends across the Delimitation Line between the Republic of Trinidad and Tobago and the Bolivarian Republic of Venezuela (with annexes), 16 August 2010, ibid, 55.
[1458] Article 10.13, Petroleum Regulations attached to Petroleum Act No 49, 30 December 1969, *Barrows* CAC, Supplement No 126.
[1459] Continental Shelf Act, Chapter 1:52, Act 43 of 1969, amended in 1986.
[1460] Article 43(t), Petroleum Regulations attached to Act No 46, An Act to Consolidate and Amend the Law Relating to Petroleum so as to Make Better Provision for the Exploration for, and the Development and Production of, Petroleum, and for Matters Consequential or Incidental, 30 December 1969, as amended up to 2010, energy.gov.tt/wp-content/uploads/2013/11/Petroleum_Act.pdf.
[1461] Hydrocarbons Code, Law No 99-93, 17 August 1999, as amended up to 2003, etap.com.tn/uploads/telechargement/code_hydrocarbures.pdf. Articles 10.3, 26.3 and 45 merely provide that a

contract area shall adhere to an existing international boundary. Article 16 states that if a deposit straddles a perimeter, then the perimeter shall be adjusted. Thus, the law does not subscribe to the notion of unitised production.

[1462] Section 4, Regulations for Administration of the Petroleum Law of the Republic of Turkey, 28 July 1955, OG 9102, 1 September 1955, *Barrows* ME, Vol II /Page B-1.

[1463] ETAP, YNG, Concession Permis Araifa – Tunisia, 2013, resourcecontracts.org/contract/ocds-591adf-0624472233/view#/pdf.

[1464] Agreement between the Republic of Turkey and the Republic of Bulgaria on the Determination of the Boundary in the Mouth Area of the Mutluderel Rezovska River and Delimitation of the Maritime Areas between the Two States in the Black Sea, 4 November 1998, Lathrop (n 2) 2879.

[1465] Articles 70-73, Petroleum Law (Law No 6326), as amended up to 5 April 1973, *Barrows* ME, Supplement No 42.

[1466] Article 10(6), Turkish Petroleum Law No 6491, 30 May 2013, shb.gen.tr/uploads/mevzuat/TURKISH_PETROLEUM_LAW_.pdf.

[1467] The various emirates issue their respective petroleum laws and contracts. See Akin Gump Strauss Hauer & Feld LLP, *Business Laws of the United Arab Emirates* (Toronto, Thomson Reuters, 2011) 3032.

[1468] Offshore Boundary Agreement between Abu Dhabi and Dubai, 18 February 1968, Lathrop (n 2) 1480.

[1469] Article 4, Agreement between Petroleum Concession Limited and the Shaikh of Dubai, 22 May 1937 in Coll 30/139 'Oil: Debai Commercial Concession and Exchange of Notes', British Library: India Office Records and Private Papers, IOR/L/PS/12/3873, 14, in Qatar Digital Library qdl.qa/archive/81055/vdc_100000000648.0x0001b9.

[1470] Article 4, Agreement between His Excellency Shaikhk Ahmad Bin Rashid, Ruler of Umm-al-Qaiwain Arabia and Petroleum Concessions Limited, 20 March 1945, in Confdl 86/47 Umm-al-Qawain Oil' [6r] (11/44), 14-15, British Library: India Office Records and Private Papers, IOR/R/15/1/701, qdl.qa/archive/81055/vdc_100025702415.0x00000.

[1471] Article 43, Offshore Concession Agreement and Operating Agreement between Government of Abu Dhabi and Maruzen Oil Co, Ltd, etc, 6 December 1967, *Barrows* ME, Supplement No 24; Article 42, Agreement dated 31 January 1970 between Abu Dhabi Government and Middle East Oil Co, Ltd, *Barrows* ME, Supplement No 46; Article 42, 1973 Model Agreement, *Barrows* ME, Supplement No 36.

[1472] Article 20, sch 4, Petroleum (Production) Regulations 1966, *Barrows* Europe, Supplement No 10.

[1473] Petroleum (Production) Act, 1918, 8 & 9 Geo 5 c 52.

[1474] Petroleum (Production) Act, 1934, 24 & 25 Geo 5 c 36.

[1475] Continental Shelf Act, 12 April 1964, legislation.gov.uk/ukpga/1964/29/pdfs/ukpga_19640029_en.pdf.

[1476] Article 27, Schedule 5, Model Clauses for Production Licenses in Seaward Areas, Petroleum (Production) Regulations, 20 August 1976, SI 1976/1129; art 28, Schedule, Model Clauses for Seaward Area Production Licenses, Petroleum Licensing (Production) (Seaward Areas) Regulations, 6 April 2008, legislation.gov.uk/uksi/2008/225/pdfs/uksi_20080225_en.pdf.

[1477] Part A, License No 293 between the Secretary of State for Energy and the British National Oil Corporation, 27 April 1979, dataogauthority.blob.core.windows.net/external/Redacted_Licence_Docs/P293_LICENCE_Redacted.pdf.

[1478] Article 4.2, Guidance on the Content of Offshore Oil and Gas Field Development Plans (2013), assets.publishing.service.gov.uk/government/uploads/system/uploads/attachment_data/file/265842/FDP_guidance_notes_November_2013_web.pdf. However, see Guidance on the Content of Offshore Oil and Gas Field Development Plans (2021), ogauthority.co.uk/media/7804/guidance-on-the-content-of-offshore-oil-and-gas-field-development-plans.pdf.

[1479] Article 28, License No P2343, Seaward Production License between the Oil and Gas Authority and Statoil UK Limited, 18 October 2017, dataogauthority.blob.core.windows.net/external/Redacted_Licence_Docs/P2343_LICENCE_Redacted.pdf.

[1480] Transboundary Hydrocarbon Agreements, 43 US Code § 1356b.

[1481] 'Formulation of United States Policy on the Resources of the Continental Shelf and on Coastal Fisheries', in United States Department of State (USDOS), Foreign Relations of the United States (FRUS), 1945, vol II, 1502.

[1482] Outer Continental Shelf Lands Act, 7 August 1953, 67 Stat 462 §1337.

[1483] Final Notice of Sale Package Central Gulf of Mexico Planning Area (CPA) Outer Continental Shelf (OCS) Oil and Gas Lease Sale 241, 23 March 2016, boem.gov/Final-Notice-of-Sale-Package-for-Sale-241.
[1484] Article 6 and Article 7, Delimitation Treaty between the Kingdom of the Netherlands and the Republic of Venezuela, 15 December 1978, Lathrop (n 2) 631.
[1485] Maritime Boundary Treaty between the United States of America and the Republic of Venezuela, 24 November 1980, Lathrop (n 2) 701.
[1486] Delimitation Treaty between the Government of the Republic of Venezuela and the Government of the French Republic, 28 January 1983, Lathrop (n 2) 613.
[1487] Article 21, Decreto No 310, Decreto Con Rango y Fuerza de Ley Orgánica de Hidrocarburos Gaseosos, Gaceta Oficial de la Republica de Venezuela No 36793, 23 September 1999, pdvsa.com/images/pdf/marcolegal/LEY_ORGANICA_DE_HIDROCARBUROS_GASEOSOS.pdf.
[1488] Article 21, Decree No 1510, Hydrocarbons Organic Law, 2 November 2001, Official Gazette No 37323.
[1489] Article 43, Ley Orgánica de Hidrocarburos, 24 May 2006, pdvsa.com/images/pdf/marcolegal/LEY_ORGANICA_DE_HIDROCARBUROS.pdf.
[1490] Article 19, Reglamento sobre la Conservación de los Recursos de Hidrocarburos Gaceta Oficial No 28.851 de fecha 13 de Febrero de 1969, minpet.gob.ve/images/biblioteca/leyes/reglamento_conservacion_recursos_hidrocarburos.pdf.
[1491] Articles 67(5) and 68, Law No 95/2015/ND-CP, Decree detailing some article of the Petroleum Law, 16 October 2015, thukyluat.vn/vb/decree-no-95-2015-nd-cp-detailing-some-articles-of-the-petroleum-law-47ded.html#TaiVe.
[1492] Article9, Decree No 18-L/CTN, Hanoi, 6 July 1993, Law on Petroleum, last accessed on 15 September 2021, at vietnamembassy-usa.org/news/2002/10/law-petroleum-6-jul-93-amended-9-jun-2000.
[1493] Law No 19/2000/QH10 Petroleum Law, 9 June 2000, vbpl.vn/TW/Pages/vbpqen-toanvan.aspx?ItemID=388.
[1494] Article 33.2, Petroleum Contract dated 15 September 1978 for Blocks 01 and 02 TLD between La Societe du Petrole et du Gaz du Viet Nam & the Bow Valley Canadian, *Barrows* A&A, Supplement No 76.
[1495] Article 18.2.2, Decree No 33/2013/ND-CP dated 22 April 2013 of the Government issuing the contract model for the Contract for Oil and Gas Products Division, thuvienphapluat.vn/van-ban/Doanh-nghiep/Nghi-dinh-33-2013-ND-CP-Hop-dong-mau-Chia-san-pham-dau-khi-183124.aspx.
[1496] Law No (22) of 21 November 2010 Concerning Mines & Quarries, extwprlegs1.fao.org/docs/pdf/yem185121E.pdf.
[1497] Occidental of Yemen (Block 75), LLC, TG Holdings Yemen Inc, Yemen General Corporation for Oil and Gas, Block 75, PSA, 2007, resourcecontracts.org/contract/ocds-591adf-0281884724/view#/pdf.

Bibliography

BOOKS

ALVAREZ J, *International Organizations as Law-Makers* (Oxford, Oxford University Press, 2006)

AMERICAN PETROLEUM INSTITUTE, *Model Form of Unit Operating Agreement* (Washington DC, American Petroleum Institute, 1957)

ANDERSON D, *Modern Law of the Sea Selected Essays* (Leiden, Nijhoff, 2008)

AREND A, *Legal Rules and International Society* (Oxford, Oxford University Press, 1999)

AUST A, *Modern Treaty Law and Practice* (Cambridge, Cambridge University Press, 2007)

AUSTIN J, *The Province of Jurisprudence Determined* (London, John Murray, 1832)

BARNES R, *Property Rights and Natural Resources* (Oxford, Hart Publishing, 2009)

BARRETT J and BURKE N, *Report on the Obligations of States under* Articles *74(3) and 83(3) of UNCLOS in Respect of Undelimited Maritime Areas* (London, British Institute of International and Comparative Law, 2016)

BARROWS G, *Worldwide Concession Contracts and Petroleum Legislation* (Tulsa, OK, PennWell Books, 1983)

BARTON B, LUCAS A, BARRERA-HERNÁNDEZ L and RØNNE A, *Regulating Energy and Natural Resources* (Oxford, Oxford University Press, 2006)

BECKER-WEINBERG V, *Joint Development of Hydrocarbon Deposits in the Law of the Sea* (New York, Springer, 2014)

BENVENISTI E, *Sharing Transboundary Resources International Law and Optimal Resource Use* (Cambridge, Cambridge University Press, 2002)

BERMAN P, *Global Legal Pluralism: A Jurisprudence of Law beyond Borders* (Cambridge, Cambridge University Press, 2012)

BLAKE G, HILDESLEY W, PRATT M, RIDLEY R and SCHOFIELD C (eds), *The Peaceful Management of Transboundary Resources* (Leiden, Nijhoff, 1995)

BLAKE G, PRATT M, SCHOFIELD C and BROWN J (eds), *Boundaries and Energy: Problems and Prospects* (New York, Kluwer, 1998)

BOYLE A and CHINKIN C, *The Making of International Law* (Oxford, Oxford University Press, 2007)

BROLMANN C and RADI Y (eds), *Research Handbook on the Theory and Practice of International Law-Making* (Cheltenham, Edward Elgar, 2016)

BRÖLMANN C, *Institutional Veil in Public International Law: The International Organizations and the Law of Treaties* (Oxford, Hart Publishing, 2007)

BRUNET-JAILLY E (ed), *Border Disputes: A Global Encyclopedia, Vol 1, Territorial Disputes* (California, ABC-CLIO, 2015)

BUNTER M, *The Promotion and Licensing of Petroleum Prospective Acreage* (New York, Kluwer, 2002)

CAMERON P and STANLEY M, *Oil, Gas, and Mining: A Sourcebook for Understanding the Extractive Industries* (Washington DC, World Bank, 2017)

CAMERON P, *International Energy Investment Law: The Pursuit of Stability* (Cambridge, Cambridge University Press, 2012)

CASSESE S, CAROTTI B, CASINI L, CAVALIERI E and MacDONALD E (eds), *Global Administrative Law: The Casebook* (New York, Institute for International Law and Justice, 2012)

CHARNEY J, COLSON D, ALEXANDER L and SMITH R (eds), *International Maritime Boundaries*, vol 5 (Leiden, Nijhoff, 2005)

COMMITTEE OF LEGAL ADVISERS ON PUBLIC INTERNATIONAL LAW (CAHDI), *Expression of Consent by States to Be Bound by a Treaty: Analytical Report and Country Reports* (Strasbourg, Council of Europe, 2001)

CONGRESSIONAL RESEARCH SERVICE, *Treaties and other International Agreements: The Role of the United States Senate: A Study Prepared for the Committee on Foreign Relations* (Washington DC, US General Printing Office, 2001)

COTTIER T, *Equitable Principles of Maritime Boundary Delimitation: The Quest for Distributive Justice in International Law* (Cambridge, Cambridge University Press, 2015)

CULVER K and GIUDICE M, *Legality's Borders: An Essay in General Jurisprudence* (Oxford, Oxford University Press, 2010)

D'ASPREMONT J, *Formalism and the Sources of International Law* (Oxford, Oxford University Press, 2011)

——. *Epistemic Forces in International Law: Foundational Doctrines and Techniques of International Legal Argumentation* (Cheltenham, Edward Elgar, 2015)

——. (ed), *Participants in the International Legal System: Multiple Perspectives on Non-state Actors in International Law* (New York, Routledge, 2011)

DAINTITH T, *Finders Keepers? How the Law of Capture Shaped the World Oil Industry* (New York, Routledge, 2010)

DUNOFF J, RATNER S and WIPPMAN D, *International Law: Norms, Actors, Process* (New York, Kluwer, 2015)

DUVAL C, LE LEUCH H, PERTUZIO A and WEAVER J, *International Petroleum Exploration and Exploitation Agreements: Legal, Economic and Policy Aspects* (New York, Barrows, 2009)

ELFERINK A, *The Delimitation of the Continental Shelf between Denmark, Germany and the Netherlands: Arguing Law, Practicing Politics?* (Cambridge, Cambridge University Press, 2013)

FOX H (ed), *Joint Development of Offshore Oil and Gas: A Model Agreement for States for Joint Development with Explanatory Commentary*, vols 1 and 2 (London, British Institute of International and Comparative Law, 1989)

FRIEDMANN W, HENKIN L and LISSITZYN O (eds), *Transnational Law in a Changing Society: Essays in Honor of Philip C Jessup* (New York, Columbia University Press, 1972)

FRIEDMANN W, *The Changing Structure of International Law* (New York, Columbia University Press, 1964)

HAKIM A, *The Middle Eastern States and the Law of the Sea* (Manchester, Manchester University Press, 1979)

HART HLA, *The Concept of Law* (Oxford, Clarendon, 1961)

——. *Essays in Jurisprudence and Philosophy* (Oxford, Clarendon, 1983)

HENCKAERTS J and DOSWALD-BECK L, *International Humanitarian Law: Volume 1, Rules* (Cambridge, Cambridge University Press, 2006)

HIGGINS R, *Problems and Process: International Law and How We Use it* (Oxford, Clarendon, 1994)

HOLLAND T, *The Elements of Jurisprudence* (Oxford, Clarendon, 1916)

HUNTER T (ed), *Regulation of the Upstream Petroleum Sector: A Comparative Study of Licensing and Concession Systems* (Cheltenham Edward Elgar, 2015)

HYDE C, *International Law Chiefly as Interpreted and Applied by the United States* (Boston, Little, Brown and Company, 1922)

JENNINGS A, *Oil and Gas Exploration Contracts* (London, Sweet & Maxwell, 2002)

KAMMERHOFER J and D'ASPREMONT J (eds), *International Legal Positivism in a Postmodern World* (Cambridge, Cambridge University Press, 2014)

KELSEN H, *Introduction to the Problems of Legal Theory* (PAULSON B and PAULSON B trans) (Oxford, Oxford University Press, 1934)

——. *General Theory of Law and State* (WEDBERG A trans) (Cambridge, MA, Harvard University Press, 1949)

——. *The Law of the United Nations: A Critical Analysis of its Fundamental Problems* (Westport, CT, Praeger, 1954)

——. *What is Justice? Justice, Law and Politics in the Mirror of Science: Collected Essays* (Berkeley, University of California Press, 1960)
KEMP A, *The Official History of North Sea Oil and Gas Vol 1: The Growing Dominance of the State, Whitehall Histories: Government Official History Series* (New York, Routledge, 2012)
——. *The Official History of North Sea Oil and Gas Vol 2: Moderating the State's Role, Whitehall Histories: Government Official History Series* (New York, Routledge, 2012)
KIM SP, *Maritime Delimitation and Interim Arrangements in Northeast Asia* (Leiden, Nijhoff, 2004)
KISS A and SHELTON D, *Guide to International Environmental Law* (Leiden, Brill, 2007)
KLABBERS J, *The Concept of Treaty in International Law* (Leiden, Brill, 1996)
——. *Introduction to Institutional International Law* (Cambridge, Cambridge University Press, 2002)
KOLB R, *Theory of International Law* (Oxford, Hart Publishing, 2016)
LAGONI R and VIGNES D (eds), *Maritime Delimitation* (The Hague, Martinus Nijhoff, 2006)
LATHROP C (ed), *International Maritime Boundaries* (Leiden, Brill, 2011)
LAUTERPACHT H, *The Function of Law in the Community* (Oxford, Clarendon, 1933)
——. *International Law* (Cambridge, Cambridge University Press, 1977)
LE LEUCH H, *Good Practice Note on (Upstream) Natural Gas: A Guidance Note to Complement the Extractive Industry Sourcebook: Good-Fit Practice Activities in the International Oil, Gas & Mining Industries* (Washington DC, World Bank, 2012)
LEAL-ARCAS R, *Energy Transit Activities: Collection of Intergovernmental Agreements on Oil and Gas Transit Pipelines and Commentary* (Brussels, Energy Charter Secretariat, 2015)
LINDBLOM A, *Non-governmental Organizations in International Law* (Cambridge, Cambridge University Press, 2005)
MALANCZUK P, *Akehurst's Modern Introduction to International Law* (Oxfordshire, Routledge, 2002)
McBETH B, *British Oil Policy* (London, Frank Cass, 1919–39)
McDOWELL E (ed), *Digest of US Practice in International Law* (Washington DC, US Government Printing Office, 1977)
McHARG A, BARTON B, BRADBROOK A and GODDEN L (eds), *Property and the Law in Energy and Natural Resources* (Oxford, Oxford University Press, 2010)
MIYOSHI M, *The Joint Development of Offshore Oil and Gas in Relation to the Maritime Boundary Delimitations* (Durham, International Boundaries Research Unit, 1999)
MOUTON M, *The Continental Shelf* (Leiden, Nijhoff, 1952)
MURPHY B (ed), *Conservation of Oil and Gas: A Legal History* (New York, American Bar Association, 1948)
NORDQUIST M, MOORE J, CHIRCOP A and LONG R (eds), *The Regulation of Continental Shelf Development: Rethinking International Standards* (Leiden, Nijhoff, 2013)
NOORTMANN M, REINISCH A and RYNGAERT C (eds), *Non-state Actors in International Law* (Oxford, Hart Publishing, 2015)
NOORTMANN M and RYNGAERT C (eds), *Non-state Actor Dynamics in International Law: From Law Taking to Law Making?* (Farnham, Ashgate, 2016)
NORTHCUTT E, *The Oil and Gas Conservation Statutes* (Washington DC, Government Printing Office, 1933)
ONORATO W, *Legislative Frameworks Used to Foster Petroleum Development Policy Research Working Paper No 1420* (Washington DC, World Bank, 1995)
OPPENHEIM L, *International Law. A Treatise* (London, Longmans, Green and Co, 1912)
ORFORD A and HOFFMANN F (eds), *The Oxford Handbook of the Theory of International Law* (Oxford, Oxford University Press, 2016)
PARRY C, *The Sources and Evidences of International Law* (Manchester, Manchester University Press, 1965)
PAUWELYN J, WESSEL R and WOUTERS J (eds), *Informal International Lawmaking* (Oxford, Oxford University Press, 2012)

PETERS A, KOECHLIN L and FÖRSTER T, *Non-state Actors as Standard Setters* (Cambridge, Cambridge University Press, 2009)
POSTEMA G, *A Treatise of Legal Philosophy and General Jurisprudence Vol 2* (New York Springer, 2011)
PRIBRAN A, *The Secret Treaties of Austria-Hungary, 1879–1914* (Cambridge, MA, Harvard University Press, 1920)
RAZ J, *The Authority of Law: Essays on Law and Morality* (Oxford, Clarendon, 1979)
REINALDA B (ed), *The Ashgate Research Companion to Non-state Actors* (Farnham, Ashgate, 2011)
ROBERTS P, *Joint Operating Agreements: A Practical Guide* (London, Global Business Publishing, 2015)
ROGGENKAMP M (ed), *Energy Law in Europe: National, EU and International Law and Institutions* (Oxford, Oxford University Press, 2001)
SALMOND J, *Jurisprudence* (London, Sweet & Maxwell, 1924)
SCHACTER O, *International Law in Theory and Practice* (Leiden, Nijhoff, 1991)
SCHMITT M, *Tallinn Manual 2.0 on the International Law Applicable to Cyber Operations* (Cambridge, Cambridge University Press, 2017)
SCHOENBAUM T, *Peace in Northeast Asia: Resolving Japan's Territorial and Maritime Disputes with China, Korea and the Russian Federation* (Cheltenham, Edward Elgar, 2008)
SCOTT A, *The Evolution of Resource Property Rights* (Oxford, Oxford University Press, 2008)
SEARLE J, *The Construction of Social Reality* (New York, Free Press, 1995)
SHELTON D (ed), *Commitment and Compliance: The Role of Non-binding Norms in the International System* (Oxford, Oxford University Press, 2000)
SLAUGHTER A, *A New World Order* (Princeton, Princeton University Press, 2004)
SMITH E, DZIENKOWSKI J, ANDERSON O, CONINE G and LOWE J (eds), *Materials on International Petroleum Transactions* (Colorado, Rocky Mountain Mineral Law Foundation, 1993)
SPECIAL UNIT FOR SOUTH-SOUTH COOPERATION UNITED NATIONS DEVELOPMENT PROGRAMME, *Effective Hydrocarbon Management: Lessons from the South* (New York, United Nations Development Program, 2009)
SUÁREZ F (WILLIAMS G et al, trans), *Selections from Three Works: A Treatise on Laws and God the Lawgiver, a Defence of the Catholic and Apostolic Faith, a Work on the Three Theological Virtues: Faith, Hope, and Charity* (Lancaster, Carnegie, 1944)
TALUS K (ed), *Research Handbook on International Energy Law* (Cheltenham, Edward Elgar, 2014)
TAMADA D and ZOU K, *Implementation of the United Nations Convention on the Law of the Sea: State Practice of China and Japan* (Basingstoke, Springer Nature, 2021)
TAMANAHA B, *A General Jurisprudence of Law and Society* (Oxford, Oxford University Press, 2001)
——. *A Realist Theory of Law* (Cambridge, Cambridge University Press, 2017)
THIRLWAY H, *The Sources of International Law* (Oxford, Oxford University Press, 2014)
TIAN H, JI C and JIANG L (ed), *Collection of Documents on Sino-Japanese Post-war Relations: 1945–1970* (Beijing, China Social Science Publisher, 1996)
TORDO S, *Fiscal Systems for Hydrocarbons Design Issues* (Washington DC, World Bank, 2007)
——. *National Oil Companies and Value Creation*, vol 1 (Washington DC, World Bank, 2011)
TRINDADE A, *International Law for Humankind: Towards a New Jus Gentium* (Leiden, Nijhoff, 2006)
TULLY S, *Corporations and International Law-Making* (Leiden, Nijhoff, 2007)
TUSON P, QUICK E and BURDETT A (eds), *Records of Bahrain Primary Documents (1820–1960)*, vol VII (Slough, Slough Archive Edition, 1993)
TWINING W, *General Jurisprudence: Understanding Law from a Global Perspective* (Cambridge, Cambridge University Press, 2009)
UNITED STATES DEPARTMENT OF STATE, *Digest of United States Practice in International Law* (Oxford, Oxford University Press, 2006)

WITTGENSTEIN L, *Philosophical Investigations* (New Jersey, Blackwell, 2001)

WOLFRUM R and RÖBEN V (eds), *Developments of International Law in Treaty Making* (New York, Springer, 2005)

WORLD BANK, *Vietnam's Petroleum Sector: Technical Assistance for the Revision of the Existing Legal and Regulatory Framework* (Washington DC, World Bank, December 2003)

ZILLMAN D, MCHARG A, BARRERA-HERNANDEZ LILA and BRADBROOK A (eds), *The Law of Energy Underground* (Oxford, Oxford University Press, 2014)

BOOK CHAPTERS

BERMAN P, 'Non-state Lawmaking through the Lens of Global Legal Pluralism' in HELFAND M (ed), *Negotiating State and Non-state Law: The Challenge of Global and Local Legal Pluralism* (Cambridge, Cambridge University Press, 2015) 15–40

BIANCHI A, 'Reflexive Butterfly Catching: Insights from a Situated Catcher' in PAUWELYN J, WESSEL R, and WOUTERS J (eds), *Informal International Lawmaking* (Oxford, Oxford University Press, 2012), 200–18

BONNICI J and MESTDAGH K, 'Balancing Norms in Cyberspace: State and Non-state Actor Normativity in Cyberspace' in DEKKER I and WOUTER W (eds), *Governance and International Legal Theory* (New York, Springer, 2004) 355–79

BUNDY R, 'Natural Resource Development (Oil and Gas) and Boundary Disputes' in BLAKE G, HILDESLEY W, PRATT M, RIDLEY R and SCHOFIELD C (eds), *The Peaceful Management of Transboundary Resources* (Leiden, Nijhoff, 1995) 23–40

CADDELL R, 'Treaties, Secret' in WOLFRUM R (ed), *Max Planck Encyclopedia of Public International Law* (Oxford, Oxford University Press, 2008)

CAMERON P and NOWINSKI R, 'Joint Development Agreements: Legal Structure and Key Issues' in BECKMAN R, TOWNSEND-GAULT I, SCHOFIELD C, DAVENPORT T and BERNARD L (eds), *Beyond Territorial Disputes in the South China Sea Legal Frameworks for the Joint Development of Hydrocarbon Resources* (Cheltenham, Edward Elgar, 2013) 152–78

CHINKIN C, 'Normative Development in the International Legal System' in SHELTON D (ed), *Commitment and Compliance: The Role of Non-binding Norms in the International System* (Oxford, Oxford University Press, 2000) 21–42

CHOW-BING N, 'Prospects for Sino–Malaysian Joint Development in the South China Sea: Lessons from Malaysia's Experiences' in QI H and XUE S (eds), *Cooperative Development in the South China Sea: Policies, Obstacles, and Prospects* (New York, Routledge, 2020) 58–76

COSTELLOE D and FITZMAURICE M, 'Lawmaking by Treaty: Conclusion of Treaties and Evolution of Treaty Regimes in Practice' in BROLMANN C and RADI Y (eds), *Research Handbook on the Theory and Practice of International Law-Making* (Cheltenham, Edward Elgar, 2016) 111–32

D'AMATO A, 'Non-state Actors from the Perspective of the Policy-Oriented School: Power, Law, Actors and the View from New Haven' in D'ASPREMONT J (ed), *Participants in the International Legal System Multiple Perspectives on Non-state Actors in International Law* (Abingdon, Routledge, 2011) 64–75

D'ASPREMONT J, 'Non-state Actors from the Perspective of Legal Positivism: The Communitarian Semantics for the Secondary Rules of International Law' in D'ASPREMONT J (ed), *Participants in the International Legal System Multiple Perspectives on Non-state Actors in International Law* (Abingdon, Routledge, 2011) 23–40

——. 'From a Pluralization of International Norm-Making Processes to a Pluralization of the Concept of International Law' in PAUWELYN J, WESSEL R and WOUTERS J (eds), *Informal International Lawmaking* (Oxford, Oxford University Press, 2012), 185–99

——. 'Herbert Hart in Today's International Legal Scholarship' in KAMMERHOFER J and D'ASPREMONT J (eds), *International Legal Positivism in a Postmodern World* (Cambridge, Cambridge University Press, 2014) 114–50

——. 'Non-state Actors and The Social Practice of International Law' in NOORTMANN M, REINISCH A and RYNGAERT C (eds), *Non-state Actors in International Law* (Oxford, Hart Publishing, 2015) 11–32

——. 'International Law-Making by Non-state Actors: Changing the Model or Putting the Phenomenon into Perspective?' in NOORTMANN M and RYNGAERT C (eds), *Non-state Actor Dynamics in International Law: From Law Taking to Law Making?* (Farnham, Ashgate, 2016) 171–94

——. 'Subjects and Actors in International Lawmaking: The Paradigmatic Divide in the Cognition of International Norm-Generating Processes' in BROLMANN C and RADI Y (eds), *Research Handbook on the Theory and Practice of International Law-Making* (Cheltenham, Edward Elgar, 2016) 32–55

——. 'Toward a New Theory of Sources in International Law' in ORFORD A and HOFFMANN F (eds), *The Oxford Handbook of the Theory of International Law* (Oxford, Oxford University Press, 2016) 546–66

DESHMAN A, 'International Organizations and Horizontal Review: The World Health Organization, the Parliamentary Council of Europe, and the H1N1 Pandemic' in CASSESE S, CAROTTI B, CASINI L, CAVALIERI E and MacDONALD E (eds), *Global Administrative Law: The Casebook* (New York, Institute for International Law and Justice, 2012) 324–32

FITZMAURICE G, *Some Problems Regarding the Formal Sources of International Law* in *Symbolae Verzjil* (Leiden, Nijhoff, 1958)

FOX H, 'Summary of Conference Discussions and the Research Team's Response' in FOX H (ed), *Joint Development of Offshore Oil and Gas: A Model Agreement for States for Joint Development with Explanatory Commentary*, vol 2 (London, British Institute of International and Comparative Law, 1989) 25–51

GAULT I, 'Petroleum Development Offshore: Legal and Contractual Issues' in BEREDJICK N, WÄLDE T and GAULT I (eds), *Petroleum Investment Policies in Developing Countries* (New York, Kluwer, 1988) 101–64

HAMMER U, 'Models for State Ownership on the Norwegian Continental Shelf' in McHARG A, BARTON B, BRADBROOK A and GODDEN L (eds), *Property and the Law in Energy and Natural Resources* (Oxford, Oxford University Press, 2010) 159–66

HWANG Y and FRETTINGHAM E, 'Sovereignty and Identity: Taiwan's Claims in the South China Sea' in HWANG Y and FRETTINGHAM E, *Maritime and Territorial Disputes in the South China Sea Faces of Power and Law in the Age of China's Rise* (New York, Routledge, 2021) 69–90

HELFER L, 'Flexibility in International Agreements' in DUNOFF J and POLLACK M (eds), *Interdisciplinary Perspectives on International Law and International Relations* (Cambridge, Cambridge University Press, 2013) 175–96

JENKS C, 'Multinational Entities in the Law of Nations' in FRIEDMANN W, HENKIN L and LISSITZYN O (eds), *Transnational Law in a Changing Society: Essays in Honor of Philip C Jessup* (New York, Columbia University Press, 1972) 70–83

KAMMERHOFER J, 'Non-state Actors from the Perspective of the Pure Theory of Law' in D'ASPREMONT J (ed), *Participants in the International Legal System Multiple Perspectives on Non-state Actors in International Law* (Abingdon, Routledge, 2011) 54–63

KAMMINGA M, 'The Evolving Status of NGOs under International Law: A Threat to the Inter-state System?' in KREIJEN G, BRUS M, DUURSMA J, DE VOS E and DUGARD J (eds), *State, Sovereignty, and International Governance* (Oxford, Oxford University Press, 2004) 387–406

KLABBERS J and TOUKO P, 'Normative Pluralism: An Exploration' in KLABBERS J and PIIPARINEN T (eds), *Normative Pluralism: Exploring Global Governance* (Cambridge, Cambridge University Press 2013) 13–34

KLEINLEIN T, 'Non-state Actors from an International Constitutionalist Perspective: Participation Matters!' in D'ASPREMONT J (ed), *Participants in the International Legal System Multiple Perspectives on Non-state Actors in International Law* (Abingdon, Routledge, 2011) 41–53

LINDBLOM A, 'Non-governmental Organizations and Non-state Actors in International Law' in REINALDA B (ed), *The Ashgate Research Companion to Non-state Actors* (Farnham, Ashgate, 2011) 147–60

MALANCZUK P, 'Multinational Enterprises and Treaty-Making' in GOWLLAND-DEBBAS V, HADJ-SAHRAOUI H and HAYASHI N (eds), *Multilateral Treaty-Making: The Current Status of Challenges to and Reforms Needed in the International Legislative Process* (Leiden, Nijhoff, 2000) 45–72

MARTIN T, 'Energy and International Boundaries' in TALUS K (ed), *Research Handbook on International Energy Law* (Cheltenham, Edward Elgar, 2014) 181–87

MBENGUE M, 'Non-state Actors in International Environmental Law: A Rousseauist Perspective' in D'ASPREMONT J (ed), *Participants in the International Legal System: Multiple Perspectives on Non-state Actors in International Law* (New York, Routledge, 2011) 372–89

MENSAH T, 'Joint Development Zones as an Alternative Dispute Settlement Approach in Maritime' in LAGONI R and VIGNES D (eds), *Maritime Delimitation* (Hague, Nijhoff, 2006) 151–60

MUCHLINSKI P, 'Multinational Enterprises as Actors in International Law: Creating "Soft Law" Obligations and "Hard Law" Rights' in NOORTMANN M and RYNGAERT C (eds), *Non-state Actor Dynamics in International Law: From Law Taking to Law Making?* (Farnham, Ashgate, 2016) 9–40

NIJMAN J, 'Non-state Actors and the International Rule of Law: Revisiting the "Realist Theory" of International Legal Personality' in NOORTMANN M and RYNGAERT C (eds), *Non-state Actor Dynamics in International Law: From Law Taking to Law Making?* (Farnham, Ashgate, 2016) 91–124

OKOWA P, 'Interpreting Constitutive Instruments of International Criminal Tribunals: Reflections on the Special Court for Sierra Leone' in FITZMAURICE M, ELIAS O and MERKOURIS P (eds), *Treaty Interpretation and the Vienna Convention on the Law of Treaties: 30 Years on* (Hague, Martinus Nijhoff, 2010) 333–55

ONG D, 'South-East Asian State Practice on the Joint Development of Offshore Oil and Gas Deposits' in BLAKE G, HILDESLEY W, PRATT M, RIDLEY R and SCHOFIELD C (eds), *The Peaceful Management of Transboundary Resources* (Leiden, Nijhoff, 1995) 77–96

OUTHIT P, 'Unitisation as Between Companies – of Fields between States (International)' in COMMITTEE ON ENERGY and NATURAL RESOURCES, SECTION ON BUSINESS LAW, *Proceedings of the Petroleum Law Seminar*, vol 2 (London, International Bar Association, 1978) 26.1–26.24

PAUWELYN J, 'Is it International Law or Not, and Does it Even Matter?' in PAUWELYN J, WESSEL R, and WOUTERS J (eds), *Informal International Law-Making* (Oxford, Oxford University Press, 2012) 125–61

PETERS A, KOECHLIN L and FÖRSTER T, 'Towards Non-state Actors as Effective, Legitimate, and Accountable Standard Setters' in PETERS A, KOECHLIN L and FÖRSTER T, *Non-state Actors as Standard Setters* (Cambridge, Cambridge University Press, 2009) 492–562

PETERS A, KOECHLIN L, FÖRSTER T and ZINKERNAGEL G, 'Non-state Actors as Standard Setters: Framing the Issue in an Interdisciplinary Fashion' in PETERS A, KOECHLIN L and FÖRSTER T (eds), *Non-state Actors as Standard Setters* (Cambridge, Cambridge University Press, 2009) 1–32

PETMAN J, 'De-formalization of International Organizations Law' in KLABBERS J and WALLENDAHL A (eds), *Research Handbook on the Law of International Organizations* (Cheltenham, Edward Elgar, 2011) 398–430

POLLACK M and SHAFFER G, 'The Interaction of Formal and Informal International Lawmaking' in PAUWELYN J, WESSEL R, and WOUTERS J (eds), *Informal International Lawmaking* (Oxford, Oxford University Press, 2012) 241–70

REDGWELL C, 'International Soft Law and Globalization' in BARTON B, LUCAS A, BARRERA-HERNÁNDEZ L and RØNNE A, *Regulating Energy and Natural Resources* (Oxford, Oxford University Press, 2006) 89–109

REDGWELL C and RAJAMANI L, 'Energy Underground: What's International Law Got to Do with it?' in ZILLMAN D, MCHARG A, BARRERA-HERNANDEZ L and BRADBROOK A (eds), *The Law of Energy Underground* (Oxford, Oxford University Press, 2014) 101–22

REISMAN W, 'The Democratization of Contemporary International Law-Making Processes and the Differentiation of Their Application' in WOLFRUM R and RÖBEN V (eds), *Developments of International Law in Treaty Making* (New York, Springer, 2005) 15–38

RONNE A, 'Energy Law in Denmark' in ROGGENKAMP M (ed), *Energy Law in Europe: National, EU and International Law and Institutions* (Oxford, Oxford University Press, 2001) 323–428

SCHACTER O, 'Towards a Theory of International Obligation' in KOSKENNIEMI M (ed), *Sources of International Law* (New York, Routledge, 2017) 3–26

SIMMONS B, 'International Law and International Relations' in WHITTINGTON K, KELEMEN D and CALDEIRA G (eds), *The Oxford Handbook of Law and Politics* (Oxford, Oxford University Press, 2008) 188–208

SOMEK A, 'Beyond Kelsen and Hart' in KAMMERHOFER J and D'ASPREMONT J (eds), *International Legal Positivism in a Postmodern World* (Cambridge, Cambridge University Press, 2014) 151–81

TALUS K, 'Internationalization of Energy Law' in TALUS K (ed), *Research Handbook on International Energy Law* (Cheltenham, Edward Elgar, 2014) 3–17

——. 'Oil and Gas: International Petroleum Regulations' in MORGERA E and KULOVESI K (eds), *Research Handbook on International Law and Natural Resources* (Cheltenham, Edward Elgar, 2016) 243–60

TELMAN DA, 'International Legal Positivism and Legal Realism' in KAMMERHOFER J and D'ASPREMONT J (eds), *International Legal Positivism in a Postmodern World* (Cambridge, Cambridge University Press, 2014) 241–63

TEUBNER G, 'Global Bukowina: Legal Pluralism in the World Society' in TEUBNER G (ed), *Global Law without a State* (Pennsylvania, Brookfield, 1997) 3–28

TOWNSEND-GAULT I and STORMONT W, 'Offshore Petroleum Joint Development Arrangements: Functional Instrument? Compromise? Obligation?' in BLAKE G, HILDESLEY W, PRATT M, RIDLEY R and SCHOFIELD C (eds), *The Peaceful Management of Transboundary Resources* (Leiden, Nijhoff, 1995) 51–76

TYLER T, LOFTIS J, HAWKER E, VIZCARRA H and KHAN I, 'Developing Arctic Hydrocarbon Resources: Delineating and Delimiting Boundaries for Field Development in the Arctic' in NORDQUIST M, MOORE J, CHIRCOP A and LONG R (eds), *The Regulation of Continental Shelf Development: Rethinking International Standards* (Leiden, Nijhoff, 2013) 319–51

VENZKE I, 'Postmodern Perspectives on Orthodox Positivism' in KAMMERHOFER J and D'ASPREMONT J (eds), *International Legal Positivism in a Postmodern World* (Cambridge, Cambridge University Press, 2014) 182–210

VINOGRADOV S, 'The Legal Status of the Caspian Sea and its Hydrocarbon Resources' in BLAKE G, PRATT M, SCHOFIELD M and BROWN J (eds), *Boundaries and Energy: Problems and Prospects* (Kluwer, 1998) 137–56

VON BOGDANDY A, DANN P and GOLDMANN M, 'Developing the Publicness of Public International Law: Towards a Legal Framework for Global Governance Activities,' in BOGDANDY A, WOLFRUM R, BERNSTORFF J, DANN P and GOLDMANN M (eds), *The Exercise of Public Authority by International Institutions: Advancing International Institutional Law* (Springer, 2010) 3–32

WAWRYK A, 'Petroleum Regulation in an International Context: The Universality of Petroleum Regulation and the Concept of Lex Petrolea' in HUNTER T (ed), *Regulation of the Upstream Petroleum Sector: A Comparative Study of Licensing and Concession Systems* (Cheltenham Edward Elgar, 2015) 3–35

WOLFRUM R, 'Legal Pluralism from the Perspective of International Law' in KÖTTER M, RÖDER T, SCHUPPERT G and WOLFRUM R (eds), *Non-state Justice Institutions and the Law Decision-Making at the Interface of Tradition, Religion and the State* (London, Palgrave Macmillan, 2015) 216–33

WOUTERS J and HAMID L, 'Custom and Informal International Lawmaking' in BRADLEY C (ed), *Custom's Future International Law in a Changing World* (Cambridge, Cambridge University Press, 2016) 332–59

JOURNAL ARTICLES

ABBOTT K, KEOHANE R, MORAVCSIK A, SLAUGHTER A and SNIDAL D, 'The Concept of Legalization' (2000) 54 *International Organization* 401–19

ADAMS M, CHARLES J, ROBERT K, LAPOINTE A and MEURER R, 'Mineral Resource Management of the Outer Continental Shelf' (1975) *Geological Survey Circular* 1–32

ALLOTT P, 'Language, Method and the Nature of International Law' (1971) 45 *British Yearbook of International Law* 79–135

ANDRASSY J, 'Le Droit International de Voisinage' (1951) 79 *Collected Courses of The Hague Academy of International Law* 86–97

ASHWARYA S, 'Post-2003 Iran–Iraq Cooperation in the Oil and Gas Sector: Initiatives, Challenges, and Future Scenarios National Iranian Oil Company' (2017) 4 *Contemporary Review of the Middle East* 84–118

AUST A, 'The Theory and Practice of Informal International Instruments' (1986) 35 *International and Comparative Law Quarterly* 787–812

BALL M, 'Petroleum Withdrawals and Restorations Affecting the Public Domain' (1916) *United States Geological Survey Bulletin No 623*

BASTIDA A, OKOYE A, MAHMUD S, ROSS J and WÄLDE T, 'Cross-border Unitization and Joint Development Agreements: An International Law Perspective' (2006) 28 *Houston Journal of International Law* 355–422

BAXTER R, 'International Law in 'Her Infinite Variety' (1980) 29 *International Comparative Law Quarterly* 549–66

BECKETT J, 'Behind Relative Normativity: Rules and Process as Prerequisites of Law' (2001) 12 *European Journal of International Law* 627–50

BERMAN P, 'A Pluralist Approach to International Law' (2007) 32 *Yale Journal of International Law* 301–330

BESSON S and MARTÍ J, 'Legitimate Actors of International Law-Making: Towards a Theory of International Democratic Representation' (2018) *Jurisprudence* 1–37

BLAKE G and TOPALOVIC D, 'The Maritime Boundaries of the Adriatic Sea' (1996) 1(8) *Maritime Briefing* 1–67

BLYSCHAK P, 'Offshore Oil and Gas Projects amid Maritime Border Disputes: Applicable Law' (2013) 6 *Journal of World Energy Law and Business* 210–33

BODANSKY D, 'Customary (and Not So Customary) International Environmental Law' (1995) 3 *Indiana Journal of Global Legal Studies* 105–19

BROUDE T, HAFTEL Y and THOMPSON A, 'The Trans-Pacific Partnership and Regulatory Space: A Comparison of Treaty Texts' (2017) 20 *Journal of International Economic Law* 391–417

BROWNLIE I, 'Legal Status of Natural Resources in International Law (Some Aspects)' (1979) 162 *Collected Courses of The Hague Academy of International Law*

BURN G, TYLER T, ZADKOVICH J and LOFTIS J, 'Legal Issues in Cross-border Resource Development' (2015) 8 *Journal of World Energy Law & Business* 154–172

CAMERON P, 'The Rules of Engagement: Developing Cross-border Petroleum Deposits in the North Sea and the Caribbean' (2006) 55 *International Comparative Law Quarterly* 559–86
CAMERON P, 'Cross-border Unitisation in the North Sea' (2007) 5 *Oil, Gas & Energy Law* 1–12
CAPPS P and COLLINS R, 'Doing Law beyond the State: Methodological Questions in International and Transnational Legal Theory' (2015) 6 *Transnational Legal Theory* 561–64
CARTY A, 'Critical International Law: Recent Trends in the Theory of International Law' (1991) 2 *European Journal of International Law* 66–96
CHINKIN C, 'The Challenge of Soft Law: Development and Change in International Law' (1989) 38 *International Comparative Law Quarterly* 850–66
CORBETT P, 'The Consent of States and the Sources of the Law of Nations' (1925) 6 *British Yearbook of International Law* 20–30
D'ASPREMONT J, 'Softness in International Law: A Self-Serving Quest for New Legal Materials' (2008) 19 *European Journal of International Law* 1075–94
——. 'Wording in International Law' (2012) 25 *Leiden Journal of International Law* 575–602
——. 'The Idea of "Rules" in the Sources of International Law' (2014) 84 *British Yearbook of International Law* 103–30
——. 'The International Court of Justice, the Whales, and the Blurring of the Lines between Sources and Interpretation' (2017) 27 *European Journal of International Law* 1027–41
DAINTITH T, 'Regulation by Contract: The New Prerogative' (1979) 32 *Current Legal Problems* 41–64
——. 'Against *Lex Petrolea*' (2017) 10 *Journal of World Energy Law & Business* 1–13
ELLIS J, 'Shades of Grey: Soft Law and the Validity of Public International Law' (2012) 25 *Leiden Journal of International Law* 313–34
FALK R and STRAUSS A, 'On the Creation of a Global Peoples Assembly: Legitimacy and the Power of Popular Sovereignty' (2000) 36 *Stanford Journal of International Law* 191–220
FASTERNATH U, 'Relative Normativity in International Law' (1993) 4 *European Journal of International Law* 305–40
FENWICK C, 'The Sources of International Law' (1918) 16 *Michigan Law Review* 393–401
GARCIA-CASTRILLON C, 'Reflections on the Law Applicable to International Oil Contracts' (2013) 6 *Journal of World Energy Law and Business* 129–62
GOLDMANN M, 'Inside Relative Normativity: From Sources to Standard Instruments for the Exercise of International Public Authority' (2008) 9 *German Law Journal* 1865–908
GOLDMANN M, 'We Need to Cut off the Head of the King: Past, Present and Future Approaches to International Soft Law' (2012) 25 *Leiden Journal of International Law* 335–68
GRISEL F, 'Treaty-Making between Public Authority and Private Interests: The Genealogy of the Convention on the Recognition and Enforcement of Foreign Arbitral Awards' (2017) 28 *European Journal of International Law* 73–88
GRISON N, 'NATO's Energy Security Policy Put to the Caspian Test' (2003) 12 *Connections: The Quarterly Journal* 83–95
HARDWICKE R, 'The Rule of Capture and its Implications as Applied to Oil and Gas' (1935) 13 *Texas Law Review* 391–422
HENKIN L, 'International Law: Politics, Values and Functions General Course on Public International Law' (1989) 216 *Collected Courses of The Hague Academy of International Law* 9–416
HEWITT T, 'An Asian Perspective on Model Oil and Gas Services Contracts' (2010) 28 *Journal of Energy and Natural Resources Law* 331–74
HIGGINS R, 'Policy Considerations and the International Judicial Process' (1968) 17 *International Comparative Law Quarterly* 58–84
——. 'The Taking of Property by the State: Recent Developments in International Law' (1982) 176 *Collected Courses of The Hague Academy of International Laws* 263–392
HUDSON M, 'The Registration and Publication of Treaties' (1925) 19 *American Journal of International Law* 273–92

KAMMERHOFER J, 'Uncertainty in the Formal Sources of International Law: Customary International Law and Some of Its Problems' (2004) 15 *European Journal of International Law* 523–53

——. 'Kelsen – Which Kelsen? A Reapplication of the Pure Theory to International Law' (2009) 22 *Leiden Journal of International Law* 225–249

KEITH H, 'Conflict Avoidance through Prior Agreement: Offshore Delimitation Agreements, Offshore/Onshore Unitization and/or Joint Development Agreements' (1996) 11 *ICSID Review-Foreign Investment Law Journal* 286–98

KINGSBURY B, 'The Concept of Law in Global Administrative Law' (2009) 20 *European Journal of International Law* 23–57

KINGSBURY B, KRISCH N and STEWART R, 'The Emergence of Global Administrative Law' (2005) 68 *Law and Contemporary Problems* 15–61

KLABBERS J, 'The Redundancy of Soft Law' (1996) 65 *Nordic Journal of International Law* 167–82

——. 'The Undesirability of Soft Law' (1998) 67 *Nordic Journal of International Law* 381–91

KOH H, 'Transnational Legal Process' (1996) 75 *Nebraska Law Review* 181–208

KOSKENNIEMI M, 'The Politics of International Law' (1990) 1 *European Journal of International Law* 4–32

——. 'Global Governance and Public International Law' (2004) 37 *Kritische Justiz* 241–54

——. 'International Law and Hegemony: A Reconfiguration' (2004) 17 *Cambridge Review of International Affairs* 197–218

——. 'Constitutionalism as Mindset: Reflections on Kantian Themes about International Law and Globalization' (2007) 8 *Theoretical Inquiries in Law* 9–36

KRISCH N and KINGSBURY B, 'Introduction: Global Governance and Global Administrative Law in the International Legal Order' (2006) 17 *European Journal of International Law* 1–13

LAGONI R, 'Oil and Gas Deposits across National Frontiers' (1979) 73 *American Journal of International Law* 215–243

LAUTERPACHT H, 'Sovereignty over Submarine Areas' (1950) 27 *British Yearbook of International Law* 376–433

LIANG Y, 'The Progressive Development of International Law and its Codification under the United Nations' (1947) 41 *American Society of International Law Proceedings* 24–39

——. 'Roscoe Pound and the Science of International Law' (1947-48) 22 *Tulane Law Review* 369–83

——. 'Methods for the Encouragement of the Progressive Development of International Law and its Codification' (1948) 111 *Yearbook of World Affairs* 24–29

——. 'The General Assembly and the Progressive Development and Codification of International Law' (1948) 42 *American Journal of International Law* 66–97

——. 'The Preparatory Work for the International Law Commission' (1950-51) 13 *Heidelberg Journal of International Law* 249–65

LIPSON C, 'Why are Some International Agreements Informal?' (1991) 45 *International Organizations* 495–538

LOJA M, 'Is the Rule of Capture Countenanced in the South China Sea? The Policy and Practice of China, the Philippines and Vietnam' (2014) 32 *Journal of Energy of Natural Resources Law* 483–508

——. 'Who Owns the Oil that Traverses a Boundary on the Continental Shelf in an Enclosed Sea? Seeking Answers in Natural Law through Grotius and Selden' (2014) 27 *Leiden Journal of International Law* 893–911

MANIRUZZAMAN AFM, 'The New Generation of Energy and Natural Resource Development Agreements: Some Reflections' (1993) 11 *Journal of Energy and Natural Resources Law* 207–47

MARTIN T, 'Dispute Resolution in the International Energy Sector: An Overview' (2011) 4 *Journal of World Energy Law and Business* 332–68

MIYOSHI M, 'The Basic Concept of Joint Development of Hydrocarbon Resources on the Continental Shelf' (1988) 3 *International Journal of Estuarine and Coastal Law* 1–18

——. 'The Joint Development of Offshore Oil and Gas in Relation to Maritime Boundary Delimitation' (1999) 2 *Maritime Briefing* 1–47

MOORE S, 'Law and Social Change: The Semi-autonomous Social Field as an Appropriate Subject of Study' (1973) 7 *Law & Society Review* 719–46

MORAVCSIK A, 'Taking Preferences Seriously: A Liberal Theory of International Politics' (1997) 51 *International Organization* 513–53

MORRIS J, 'The North Sea Continental Shelf: Oil and Gas Legal Problems' (1967-68) 2 *International Law* 191–214

MULLIGAN A, 'Framing Deformalisation in Public International Law' (2015) 6 *Transnational Legal Theory* 635–60

NYE J and KEOHANE R, 'Transnational Relations and World Politics: An Introduction' (1971) 25 *International Organization* 329–49

OKOYE A, WEAVER J, ASMUS D, BASTIDA E, ROSS J, MAHMUD S and WÄLDE T, 'International Unitization of Oil and Gas Fields: The Legal Framework of International Law, National Laws, and Private Contracts – AIPN' (2007) 5 *Oil, Gas & Energy Law* 1–138

ONG D, 'Joint Development of Common Offshore Oil and Gas Deposits: Mere State Practice or Customary International Law' (1999) 93 *American Journal of International Law* 771–804

ONORATO W, 'Apportionment of an International Common Petroleum Deposit' (1968) 17 *International Comparative Law Quarterly* 324–37

——. 'Joint Development of Hydrocarbon Resources: An Overview of Precedents in the North Sea' (1981) 6 *Energy* 1311–24

——. 'A Case Study on Joint Development: The Saudi Arabia/Kuwait Partitioned Neutral Zone' (1985) 10 *Energy* 539–44

PAPPA M, 'Private Oil Companies Operating in Contested Waters and International Law of the Sea: A Peculiar Relationship' (2018) 16 *Oil, Gas & Energy Law* 1–26

PARRY C, 'The Practice of States' (1958) 44 *Transactions of the Grotius Society* 145–86

PERRY A, 'Oil and Gas Deposits at International Boundaries: New Ways for Governments and Oil and Gas Companies to Handle an Increasingly Urgent Problem' (2007) 2 *Oil, Gas & Energy Law*, ogel.org/article.asp?key=2412

POSNER R, 'Legal Formalism, Legal Realism, and the Interpretation of Statutes and the Constitution' (1986-87) 37 *Case Western Reserve Law Review* 179–217

QI H, 'Joint Development in the South China Sea: China's Incentives and Policy Choices' (2019) 8 *Journal of Contemporary East Asia Studies* 220–39

RATNER S, 'Drawing a Better Line: UTI Possidetis and the Borders of New States' (1996) 90 *American Journal of International Law* 590–624

RAUSTIALA K, 'Form and Substance in International Agreements' (2005) 99 *American Journal of International Law* 581–614

REDGWELL C, 'Mind the Gap in the GAIRS: The Role of Other Instruments in LOSC Regime Implementation in the Offshore Energy Sector' (2014) 29 *International Journal of Marine and Coastal Law* 600–21

REISMAN W, 'Eritrea-Yemen Arbitration (Award, Phase II: Maritime Delimitation)' (2000) 94 *American Journal of International Law* 721–36

ROBERTS A and SIVAKUMARAN S, 'Lawmaking by Non-state Actors: Engaging Armed Groups in the Creation of International Humanitarian Law' (2012) 37 *Yale Journal of International Law* 107–51

ROUGHTON D, 'Rights (and Wrongs) of Capture: International Law and the Implications of the *Guyana v Suriname* Arbitration' (2008) 26 *Journal of Energy and Natural Resources Law* 374–401

RUGGIE J, 'Reconstituting the Global Public Domain' (2004) 10 *European Journal of International Relations* 499–531

RYNGAERT C, 'Non-state Actors: Carving out a Space in a State-Centred International Legal System' (2016) 63 *The Netherlands International Law Review* 183–95

SANCHEZ G and MCLAUGHLIN R, 'The 2012 Agreement on the Exploitation of Transboundary Hydrocarbon Resources in the Gulf of Mexico: Confirmation of the Rule or Emergence of a New Practice?' (2015) 37 *Houston Journal of International Law* 681–792

SCHACHTER O, 'International Law in Theory and Practice: General Course in Public International Law' (1982) 178 *Collected Courses of The Hague Academy of International Law* 13–395

——. 'The Decline of the Nation-State and its Implications for International Law' (1997) 36 *Columbia Journal of Transnational Law* 7–22

SCHREUER C, 'The Waning of the Sovereign State: Towards a New Paradigm for International Law?' (1993) 4 *European Journals of International Law* 447–471

SHAFFER G and GINSBURG T, 'The Empirical Turn in International Legal Scholarship' (2012) 106 *American Journal of International Law* 1–46

SHAFFER G and POLLACK M, 'Hard vs Soft Law: Alternatives, Complements, and Antagonists in International Governance' (2010) 94 *Minnesota Law Review* 706–99

SHIHATA I and ONORATO W, 'The Joint Development of International Petroleum Resources in Undefined and Disputed Areas' (1996) 11 *ICSID Review* 299–317

SIMMA B, 'NATO, the UN and the Use of Force: Legal Aspects' (1999) 10 *European Journal of International Law* 1–22

SIMMA B and PAULUS A, 'The International Community: Facing the Challenge of Globalization' (1998) 9 *European Journal of International Law* 266–77

SINGH S, 'Narrative and Theory: Formalism's Recurrent Return' (2014) 84 *British Yearbook of International Law* 304–343

SLAUGHTER A, 'International Law in a World of Liberal States' (1995) 6 *European Journal of International Law* 503–38

SONG Y, 'Peaceful Proposals and Maritime Cooperation between Mainland China, Japan, and Taiwan in the East China Sea: Progress Made and Challenges Ahead' (2016) 22 *Asian Yearbook of International Law* 20–49.

STONE SWEET A, 'Constitutionalism, Legal Pluralism and International Regimes' (2009) 16 *Indiana Journal of Global Legal Studies* 621–45

TALUS K, LOOPER S and OTILLAR S, '*Lex Petrolea* and the Internationalization of Petroleum Agreements: Focus on Host Government Contracts' (2012) 5 *Journal of World Energy Law and Business* 181–93

TAMANAHA B, 'Understanding Legal Pluralism: Past to Present, Local to Global' (2008) 30 *Sydney Law Review* 375–411

TASIOULAS J, 'In Defence of Relative Normativity: Communitarian Values and the *Nicaragua* Case' (1996) 16 *Oxford Journal of Legal Studies* 85–128

TREVISANUT S, 'The Role of Private Actors in Offshore Energy: Shifting Models of Participation' (2014) 29 *International Journal of Marine and Coastal Law* 645–65

TUNKIN G, 'International Law in the International System' (1975) 147 *Collected Courses of The Hague Academy of International Law* 9–216

UTTON A, 'Institutional Arrangements for Developing North Sea Oil and Gas' (1968-69) 9 *Virginia Journal of International Law* 66–81

VALENCIA M and MIYOSHI M, 'Southeast Asian Seas: Joint Development of Hydrocarbons in Overlapping Claim Areas?' (1986) 16 *Ocean Development and International Law* 211–54

VAN DER BURG W, 'Two Models of Law and Morality' (1999) 3 *Associations* 61–82

WALDOCK H, 'The Legal Basis of Claims to the Continental Shelf' (1950) 36 *Transactions of the Grotius Society* 115–48

WEAVER J and ASMUS D, 'Unitizing Oil and Gas Fields around the World: A Comparative Analysis of National Laws and Private Contracts' (2006) 28 *Houston Journal of International Law* 3–103

WEIL P, 'Towards Relative Normativity in International Law' (1983) 77 *American Journal of International Law* 413–42

WEIL P, 'The Court Cannot Conclude Definitively … *Non Liquet* Revisited' (1998) 36 *Columbian Journal of Transnational Law* 109–19

YOUNG R, 'Equitable Solutions for Offshore Boundaries: The 1968 Saudi Arabia-Iran Agreement' (1970) 64 *American Journal of International Law* 152–57

ZIMNITSKAYA H and VON GELDERN J, 'Is the Caspian Sea a Sea and Why Does it Matter?' (2011) 2 *Journal of Eurasian Studies* 1–14

List of Cases, Reports and UN Documents

CASES

Aegean Sea Continental Shelf, Interim Protection, Order of 11 September [1976] ICJ Rep 3

Anglo-Iranian Oil Co case (jurisdiction), Judgment of July 22nd, 1952: ICJ Reports 1952, p 93

Arbitral Award Rendered on October 23, 1909, in the Matter of the Delimitation of a Certain Part of the Maritime Boundary between Norway and Sweden (Grisbadarna Arbitration) 11 Reports of International Arbitral Awards 155

Award in the Arbitration Regarding the Delimitation of the Maritime Boundary between Guyana and Suriname, 17 September 2007, Reports of International Arbitral Awards, vol 30

Award of the Arbitral Tribunal in the Second Stage of the Proceedings between Eritrea and Yemen (Maritime Delimitation), Decision of 17 December 1999

Case Concerning the Land and Maritime Boundary between Cameroon and Nigeria (Cameroon v Nigeria; Equatorial Guinea Intervening), Judgment of 10 October 2002

Conciliation Commission on the Continental Shelf Area between Iceland and Jan Mayen: Report and Recommendations to the governments of Iceland and Norway, Decision of June 1981, 20 International Legal Materials

Continental Shelf (Libyan Arab Jamahiriya/Malta), Judgment [1985] ICJ Rep

Continental Shelf (Tunisia/Libyan Arab Jamahiriya), Judgment [1982] ICJ Rep

Delimitation of the Maritime Boundary in the Gulf of Maine Area, Judgment [1984] ICJ Rep

Dispute Concerning Delimitation of the Maritime Boundary between Ghana and Côte d'Ivoire in the Atlantic Ocean (Ghana v Côte d'Ivoire), Judgment, 23 September 2017

Government of the State of Kuwait v American Independent Oil Company (1982) 21 International Law Material 976

Jennison v Kirk, 98 US 453

Kelly v Ohio Oil Co, 39 LRA 765 (1897)

Military and Paramilitary Activities in and Against Nicaragua (Nicaragua v United States of America), Merits, Judgment [1986] ICJ Rep 14

North Sea Continental Shelf Cases Judgment of 20 February 1969 (Federal Republic of Germany v Denmark; Federal Republic of Germany v The Netherlands) [1969] ICJ Rep 3

Oil Platforms (Islamic Republic of Iran v United States of America), Judgment [2003] ICJ Rep 61

PCA Case N° 2013–19 In the Matter of the South China Sea Arbitration, 12 July 2016

Reparations for Injuries Suffered in the Service of the United Nations [1949] ICJ Rep 174

Republic v Provincial Government of Palawan, GR Nos 170867 and 185941 (Resolution), 21 January 2020

RSM Production Corporation v Grenada, ICSID Case No ARB/05/14

North Sea Continental Shelf Cases (Federal Republic of Germany/The Netherlands) [1969] ICJ Rep 3

South West Africa, Second Phase, Judgment [1966] ICJ Rep

SS Lotus Case (France v Turkey), 1927 PCIJ (Ser A) No 10

Territorial and Maritime Dispute (Nicaragua v Colombia) [2012] ICJ Rep 624

Westmoreland Natural Gas Company v DeWitt, 130 Pa 235, 18 Atl 724, 5 LRA 731 (1889)

Wood County Petroleum Co v West Virginia Transportation Co (1886) 28 W Va 10

REPORTS FROM GOVERNMENTS AND INTERNATIONAL ORGANISATIONS

1988 Report of the ILA Sixty-Third Conference Poland

2010 Report of the ILA Seventy-Fourth Conference Hague

2016 Report of ILA Seventy-Seventh Conference Johannesburg

Federal Oil Conservation Board Complete Record of Public Hearings (1927), 10 and 11 February 1926 (Washington DC, Government Printing Office, 1926)

Address by Henry l. Doherty in Federal Oil Conservation Board, Complete Record of Public Hearings, 10 and 11 February, 1926

Address by ML Requa, Vice-President of the Sinclair Consolidated Oil Corporation, *American Petroleum Institute Bulletin No 132*, 10 December 1920

Committee of Legal Advisers on Public International Law (CAHDI) Expression of Consent by States to Be Bound by a Treaty Analytical Report and Country Reports, CAHDI (2000) 13 FINAL, 23 January 2001

Committee on the Peaceful Uses of the Sea-Bed and the Ocean Floor beyond the Limits of National Jurisdiction (General Assembly Resolution No 2467 A (XXIII), 21 December 1968)

Comptroller General of the United States, *Report to the Congress: The United Kingdom's Development of its North Sea Oil and Gas Reserves* (Washington DC, US General Accounting Office, 1977)

Department of the Interior, Report II–IV of the Federal Oil Conservation Board to the President of the United States, January 1928 (Washington DC, Government Printing Office, 1928)

Director of the Geological Survey to the Secretary of the Interior regarding wastage resulting from competitive drilling and Letter of the Secretary of

Interior to the President, 17 September 1909, regarding wastage arising from competitive drilling, *United States Geological Survey Bulletin No 623*

Fisheries Management Regional Report 2002/01 (Fisheries and Oceans Canada Maritimes Region, 2002)

Letter of the Secretary of Interior to the President, 17 September 1909, *United States Geological Survey Bulletin No* 623

Memorandum from Monroe Leigh, Legal Adviser, Department of State, to all key Department personnel, of 12 March 1976, US Department of State, *Digest of United States Practice in International Law*, 1976

Norwegian Petroleum Directorate (NPD), The Norwegian Petroleum Directorate's Resource Classification System 2016

World Bank, Supporting Gas Project Negotiations and Enhancing Institutional Capacities Report No PIDISDSA21346, 6 April 2017

UN DOCUMENTS

UN Doc A/CN4/23, 14 April 1950, Report on the Law of Treaties by Special Rapporteur James Brierly

Statement of His Excellency, Brigadier David Granger, President of the Cooperative Republic of Guyana to the 70th session of the United Nations General Assembly, September 29, 2015

UN Doc A/55/10, Report of the International Law Commission, 1 May–9 June and 10 July–18 August 2000

UN Doc A/56/10, Report of the International Law Commission on the work of its fifty-Third session, 23 April–1 June and 2 July–10 August 2001

UN Doc A/58/817, 11 June 2004, Report of the Panel of Eminent Persons on United Nations-Civil Society Relations (Cardozo Report)

UN Doc A/62/10, Report of the International Law Commission on the work of its fifty-ninth session (7 May–5 June and 9 July–10 August 2007)

UN Doc A/65/10, 2010, Report of the International Law Commission, May–August 2010

UN Doc A/2456, Draft Articles on the Continental Shelf in Report of the International Law Commission covering the work of its Fifth Session, 1 June–14 August 1953

UN Doc A/2934, Report of the International Law Commission covering the work of its Seventh Session, 2 May–8 July 1955

UN Doc A/3159, Report of the International Law Commission covering the work of its Eighth Session, 23 April–4 July 1956

UN Doc A/C.6/62/SR.22, 4 December 2007, Official Records of the Sixty-Second Session, Sixth Committee, 22nd meeting

UN Doc A/C.6/62/SR.23, 6 December 2007, Official Records of the Sixty-Second Session, Sixth Committee, 23rd meeting

UN Doc A/C.6/62/SR.24, 13 December 2007, Official Records of the Sixty-Second Session, Sixth Committee, 24th meeting

UN Doc A/C.6/62/SR.25, 10 December 2007, Official Records of the Sixty-Second Session, Sixth Committee, 24th meeting

UN Doc A/C.6/62/SR.26, 13 December 2007, Official Records of the Sixty-Second Session, Sixth Committee, 26th meeting

UN Doc A/C.6/63/SR.16, 10 November 2008, Official Records of the Sixty-Third Session, Sixth Committee, 16th meeting

UN Doc A/C.6/64/SR.17, 11 November 2008, Official Records of the Sixty-Third Session, Sixth Committee, 17th meeting

UN Doc A/C.6/64/SR.18, 9 December 2009; Official Records of the Sixty-Fourth Session, Sixth Committee, 18th meeting

UN Doc A/C.6/64/SR.20, 17 December 2009, Official Records of the Sixty-Fourth Session, Sixth Committee, 20th meeting

UN Doc A/C.6/64/SR.21, 22 December 2009, Official Records of the Sixty-Fourth Session, Sixth Committee, 21st meeting

UN Doc A/C.6/64/SR.22, 8 February 2010, Official Records of the Sixty-Fourth Session, Sixth Committee, 22nd meeting

UN Doc A/C.6/64/SR.23, 18 December 2009, Official Records of the Sixty-Fourth Session, Sixth Committee, 23rd meeting

UN Doc A/CN.4/19, 23 March 1950, Replies from Governments to Questionnaires of the International Law Commission

UN Doc A/CN.4/23, 14 April 1950, Report on the Law of Treaties by Special Rapporteur, James Brierly

UN Doc A/CN.4/32, 14 July 1950, Memorandum on the Regime of the High Seas of the Secretariat of the International Law Commission

UN Doc A/CN.4/42, 10 April 1951, Second report of the Special Rapporteur, Mr JPA François

UN Doc A/CN.4/60, 19 February 1953, Fourth report of the Special Rapporteur, Mr JPA François

UN Doc A/CN.4/79, 1 March 1954, Sixth report of the Special Rapporteur, Mr JPA François

UN Doc A/CN.4/97, Corr 1 and Add 1–3, Regime of the High Seas and Regime of the Territorial Sea, Report by JPA Francois, Special Rapporteur, 27 January 1956

UN Doc A/CN.4/533 and Add 1, First Report on Shared Natural Resources, Special Rapporteur, 30 April and 30 June 2003

UN Doc A/CN.4/580, Fourth Report on Shared Natural Resources, Special Rapporteur Chusei Yamada, 6 March 2007

UN Doc A/CN.4/49, Draft Articles on the Continental Shelf and Related Subjects Prepared by the International Law Commission, 30 July 1951

UN Doc A/CN.4/595, International Law Commission, 26 March 2008

UN Doc A/CN.4/607 and Add 1, Comments and observations received from Governments, 29 January and 17 June 2009

UN Doc A/CN.4/621, 9 March 2010, Shared Natural Resources: feasibility of future work on oil and gas: Paper prepared by Shinya Murase

UN Doc A/CN.4/638, 19 January 2011, Topical summary of the discussion held in the Sixth Committee of the General Assembly during its Sixty-Fifth Session, prepared by the Secretariat

Un Doc. A/CN.4/659, 14 March 2013, Formation and evidence of customary international law, Memorandum by the Secretariat

UN Doc A/CN.4/710, 12 January 2018, Memorandum by the Secretariat (Identification of customary international law Ways and means for making the evidence of customary international law more readily available

UN Doc A/CN.4/L.717, 17 July 2007, Shared Natural Resources Report of the Working Group

UN Doc A/CN.4/L.883/Add.1, 20 June 2016, Draft report of the International Law Commission: Identification of customary international law

UN Doc A/CONF.13/25, 3 January 1958, Recent developments in the technology of exploiting the mineral resources of the continental shelf, by Martinus Mouton

UN Doc A/CONF.13/C.3/SR.26–30, 24 February to 27 April 1958, Summary Records of the 26th to 30th Meetings of the Third Committee

UN Doc A/CONF.62/C.2/SR.17, 26 July 1974, Summary records of meetings of the Second Committee 17th meeting

UN Doc A/CONF.62/L.47, 24 March 1980, Report of the Chairman of negotiating group 7

UN Doc A/CONF.62/122, 7 October 1982, United Nations Convention on the Law of the Sea

UN Doc A/RES/65/19, 10 January 2011, Responsibility of States for internationally wrongful acts

UN Doc NG7/45, 22 August 1979, Report of the Chairman of negotiating group

UN Doc S/22515, 22 April 1991, Letter dated 21 April 1991 from the Permanent Representative of Iraq to the United Nations addressed to the Secretary General

UN Doc S/PV.2977 23 February 1991,

UN Doc A/73/10, 30 April–1 June and 2 July–10 August 2018, International Law Commission (ILC) Draft Conclusions on Identification of Customary International Law,

United Nations, Report of the Committee on the Progressive Development of International Law and its Codification on the Methods for Encouraging the Progressive Development of International Law and its Eventual Codification' 41 *American Journal of International Law Supplement* 18 (1947) 18–26

UN Doc A/CN4/42, 10 April 1951, Second Report on the Regime of the High Seas by Special Rapporteur J P A François

UN Doc A/CN4/60, 19 February 1953, Fourth Report on the Regime of the High Seas – The Continental Shelf and Related Subjects, by Special Rapporteur JPA François

UN Doc A/CN4/79, 1 March 1954, Sixth report of the Special Rapporteur JPA François

UN Doc A/CN4/97, Corr 1 and Add 1–3, 27 January 1956, Regime of the High Seas and Regime of the Territorial Sea, Special Rapporteur JPA François
UN Doc A/CN4/49, Draft Articles on the Continental Shelf and Related Subjects Prepared by the International Law Commission, 30 July 1951
UN Doc A/2934, Report of the International Law Commission covering the work of its Seventh Session, 2 May–8 July 1955
UN Doc A/CN4/104, Report of the International Law Commission on the Work of its Eighth Session, 4 July 1956, Official Records of the General Assembly, Eleventh Session, Supplement No 9
UN Doc A/CONF13/C3/SR26–30, 24 February to 27 April 1958, Summary Records of the 26th to 30th Meetings of the Third Committee
UN Doc A/CONF13/C4/SR31–35, Summary Records of the 31st to 35th Meetings of the Fourth Committee
UN Doc A/CONF13/25, 3 January 1958, Recent developments in the technology of exploiting the mineral resources of the continental shelf
UN Doc A/CONF62/C2/SR17, 26 July 1974, Summary records of meetings of the Second Committee, 17th meeting
UN Doc A/CONF62/L47, 24 March 1980, Report of the Chairman of Negotiating Group 7
UN Doc A/CN4/23, 14 April 1950, Report on the Law of Treaties by Special Rapporteur James Brierly
UN Doc A/CN4/607 and Add 1, 607 and Add 1, 29 January and 17 June 2009, ILC Shared Natural Resources: Comments and Observations Received from Governments
UN Doc A/CN4/533 and Add 1, 30 April and 30 June 2003, First Report on Shared Natural Resources, Special Rapporteur
UN Doc A/C6/64/SR17, 8 February 201o, Report of the International Law Commission on the work of its Sixty-First Session
UN Doc A/CN4/L717, 17 July 2007, Fifth report on identification of customary international law by the Special Rapporteur
UN Doc A/C6/62/SR22, 4 December 2007, Report of the International Law Commission on the work of its Fifty-Ninth Session
UN Doc A/C6/62/SR25, 10 December 2007, Summary record of the 25th meeting of the Sixth Committee
UN Doc A/C.6/62/SR.24, 13 December 2007, Summary record of the 2th meeting of the Sixth Committee
UN Doc A/C6/63/SR16, 10 November 2008, Summary record of the 16th meeting of the Sixth Committee
UN Doc A/C6/65/SR17, 2 December 2010, Summary record of the 17th meeting of the Sixth Committee
UN Doc A/C6/64/SR18, 9 December 2009, Summary record of the 18th meeting of the Sixth Committee
UN Doc A/C6/64/SR20, 17 December 2009, Summary record of the 20th meeting of the Sixth Committee

UN Doc A/C6/64/SR21, 22 December 2009, Summary record of the 21st meeting of the Sixth Committee

UN Doc A/C6/64/SR22, 8 February 2010, Summary record of the 22nd meeting of the Sixth Committee

UN Doc A/CN4/621, 9 March 2010, Shared natural resources: feasibility of future work on oil and gas – paper prepared by Shinya Murase

UN Doc A/CN4/638, 19 January 2011, Topical summary of the discussion held in the Sixth Committee of the General Assembly during its Sixty-Fifth Session, prepared by the Secretariat

UN Doc A/65/10, May–August 2010, Report of the International Law Commission, Sixty-Second Session

Index

Note: Alphabetical arrangement is word-by-word, where a group of letters followed by a space is filed before the same group of letters followed by a letter, eg 'legal norms' will appear before 'legality'. In determining alphabetical arrangement, initial articles and prepositions are ignored.